T0342177

SORTING OUT THE MIXED ECONOMY

HISTORIES OF ECONOMIC LIFE

Jeremy Adelman, Sunil Amrith, and Emma Rothschild,
Series Editors

Sorting Out the Mixed Economy

THE RISE AND FALL OF WELFARE AND DEVELOPMENTAL STATES IN THE AMERICAS

AMY C. OFFNER

PRINCETON UNIVERSITY PRESS

PRINCETON & OXFORD

Published by Princeton University Press
41 William Street, Princeton, New Jersey 08540
6 Oxford Street, Woodstock, Oxfordshire OX20 1TR

press.princeton.edu

Library of Congress Control Number 2019940870
ISBN 978-0-691-19093-8

British Library Cataloging-in-Publication Data is available

Editorial: Eric Crahan and Thalia Leaf
Production Editorial: Leslie Grundfest
Jacket Design: Layla Mac Rory
Production: Merli Guerra
Publicity: Alyssa Sanford and Julia Hall
Copyeditor: Dawn Hall

Jacket image: Leopoldo Richter (1896–1984), Untitled. Gouache & ink on paper.
Private collection. Photo © Christie's Images / Bridgeman Images

This book has been composed in Arno

Printed on acid-free paper. ∞

Printed in the United States of America

10 9 8 7 6 5 4 3 2

For my father and in memory of my mother

CONTENTS

ILLUSTRATIONS

Maps

Figures

ACKNOWLEDGMENTS

MY FIRST THANKS go to Eric Foner. Very few people would respond positively to a student's idea to change her region of study halfway through a doctoral program and drop out of school to remediate herself in another country. He did. His level-headed management of bizarre circumstances, wide-ranging interests, elegant writing, and unshakable commitment to his students are models to me. John Coatsworth and Anders Stephanson changed my path as a historian, leading me into the study of Latin America, US foreign policy, and economic thought. At every stage along the way, Elizabeth Blackmar has been a peerless model of intellectual creativity and a guiding intellectual influence, helping me relate my curiosities and commitments to worthwhile questions about capitalist development, ideology, and the social production of space. This book's genesis owed, finally, to imaginative questions and criticism I received from Matthew Connelly, Timothy Mitchell, Sanjay Reddy, Herb Sloan, and the late Fritz Stern.

I am grateful to many colleagues who read and commented on the manuscript. David Engerman, Ann Farnsworth-Alvear, Sarah Barringer Gordon, Marco Palacios, and Kathy Peiss read the entire book or very nearly all of it, in some cases more than once. Many others critiqued individual chapters, commented on conference papers, and discussed the book's animating ideas with me. I thank Michele Alacevich, Andrés Álvarez, Leandro Benmergui, Chris Capozzola, Ben Coates, Chris Dietrich, Kate Epstein, Ansley Erickson, Arturo Escobar, Yvonne Fabella, Karen Ferguson, Andrew Friedman, Alyosha Goldstein, Adam Goodman, Richard Harris, Mark Healey, Rebecca Herman, Jimena Hurtado, Louis Hyman, Richard Immerman, Daniel Immerwahr, Rob Karl, Jennifer Klein, Paul Kramer, Nancy Kwak, Catherine LeGrand, Ricardo López, Casey Lurtz, Stephen Macekura, Andrew Needham, Alice O'Connor, Tore Olsson, Julia Ott, Kim Phillips-Fein, Mariano Plotkin, Daniel Rodgers, Mary Roldán, Susana Romero Sánchez, Eduardo Sáenz Rovner, Roger Sandilands, Andrew Sandoval-Strausz, Brad Simpson, the late Judith Stein, David Suisman, Rebecca Tally, Julia Adeney Thomas, Lorrin Thomas, Christy Thornton, Alejandro Velasco, Bob Vitalis, Barbara Weinstein, Alden Young, the late Marilyn Young, and Andrew Zimmerman.

Two intellectual communities deserve special mention. First, a remarkable number of my colleagues at the University of Pennsylvania, past and present, discussed this work with me, and everyone offered moral and practical support along the way. In addition to those mentioned above, I particularly thank Eiichiro Azuma, Mia Bay, Lee Cassanelli, Brent Cebul, Alex Chase-Levenson, Antonio Feros, Steve Hahn, Peter Holquist, the late Michael Katz, Ada Kuskowski, Sophia Lee, Walter Licht, Stephanie McCurry, Ben Nathans, Marcy Norton, Vanessa Ogle, Dan Raff, Sophie Rosenfeld, Tom Sugrue, Melissa Teixeira, Heidi Voskuhl, Tamara Walker, and Beth Wenger. Beyond my own university, I owe a debt of gratitude to colleagues at the Charles Warren Center for American History, where I drafted a significant portion of this book. Kirsten Weld and Brandon Terry led a brilliant workshop, and I learned much from my fellow fellows: Megan Black, Nick Bromell, Chris Clements, Kendra Field, Jeff Gonda, Jeff Gould, Forrest Hylton, Destin Jenkins, Carlota McAllister, Stuart Schrader, Nina Silber, and Shatema Threadcraft.

At Princeton University Press, I have been lucky to work with wonderful people. Jeremy Adelman took an interest in this book when it was still taking shape. He helped me think through questions large and small, saved me from bad writing, and communicated a genuine enthusiasm for new work that I will not forget. Eric Crahan, Thalia Leaf, and Amanda Peery guided me through the publication process with enormous professionalism and patience. Bob Bettendorf, Leslie Grundfest, Dawn Hall, Chris Lapinski, Layla Mac Rory, and Pamela Weidman kept me on schedule, caught errors in the manuscript, wrote jacket text, and designed the cover. Shane Kelley created the book's maps.

A portion of chapter 3, in an earlier version, appeared in *Making Cities Global: The Transnational Turn in Urban History*, ed. A. K. Sandoval-Strausz and Nancy H. Kwak (Philadelphia: University of Pennsylvania Press, 2018). I am grateful to Bob Lockhart and Peter Agree of Penn Press for their work on that volume, as well as the support and generosity they have shown me during my time at Penn.

This project depended on the work of many archivists, librarians, and university and public officials who helped me access historical documents. I thank Donald Davis of the American Friends Service Committee; Mauricio Tovar, Fabio Castro, and the staff of the Archivo General de la Nación; Rodrigo Torres of the Corporación Autónoma Regional del Valle del Cauca; Valoise Armstrong of the Eisenhower Library; Lucas Clawson, Roger Horowitz, and Lynsey Sczechowicz of the Hagley Library; Stephen Plotkin of the Kennedy Library; Daniel Linke of Princeton University's Mudd Library; Bethany Antos and Thomas E. Rosenbaum of the Rockefeller Archive Center; Emilsen Quimbayo of the Universidad de los Andes; José Alberto Giraldo López and the archival staff of the Universidad del Valle; Gabriel Escalante Guzmán of the

Universidad Nacional de Colombia; David Null, Beverly Phillips, and Kurt Brown of the University of Wisconsin; Bertha Wilson and Marlene Justsen of the World Bank; and the staffs of the Archivo de Bogotá, Baker Library, Bancroft Library, Biblioteca Luis Angel Arango, California State Archives, Carter Library, Columbia University Rare Book and Manuscript Library, Rubenstein Library at Duke University, Hoover Institution, National Archives in College Park and Washington, DC, Tamiment Library, Tufts University Archives, Archivo Institucional of the Universidad de los Andes, and Instituto Colombiano de Desarrollo Rural. I thank Adriana Rivera Páez and Fanny de Rivera for granting access to the papers of Jorge Enrique Rivera Farfán and Jorge Alberto Rivera Páez, and Stephen Wyckoff for granting access to the Florence Richardson Wyckoff papers.

Peter Carey opened the office records of Self-Help Enterprises to me and helped arrange my oral history interviews in California. Luis Jaime Grau Peña of the Asociación de Juntas de Acción Comunal in Ciudad Kennedy helped me find original residents of the housing project. I thank both of them, as well as all those who agreed to be interviewed. Lina Medina and Trishula Patel transcribed the interviews, and Geoffrey Durham, Luis Ferré Sadurní, Morteza Mobasheri, Abeer Saha, Daniela Samur, Sandra Yellowhorse, and David Zeledon provided superb research assistance in other areas.

Historical research creates a great deal of administrative work for other people. I thank Taylor Baciocco, Octavia Carr, Susan Cerrone, Yvonne Fabella, Milena Gómez Kopp, Ana Grigera, Travis Hensley, Zuzanna Kobrzynski, Monnikue McCall, Sharee Nash, Arthur Patton-Hock, Mauricio Pérez, Joan Plonski, Bekah Rosenberg, and Michael Stratmoen for helping me navigate Columbia, the Universidad Externado, NYU, Penn, Harvard, and the Library of Congress.

For grants and fellowships, I thank the Anti-Discrimination Center, the Center for the United States and the Cold War at NYU, the Charles Warren Center for American History at Harvard, the Columbia University Department of History and Institute for Latin American Studies, the Duke University Center for the History of Political Economy, the Eisenhower Library, the Hagley Library, the Hoover Institution Workshop in Political Economy, the Inter-American Foundation, the Kluge Center at the Library of Congress, Princeton University Libraries, the Lyndon B. Johnson Presidential Library, the Penn Undergraduate Research Mentoring Program, the Penn University Research Foundation, the Rockefeller Archive Center, the Mellon Foundation/ ACLS Dissertation Completion Fellowship, the Richard Shryock Memorial Fund at the University of Pennsylvania, the Social Science Research Council International Dissertation Research Fellowship, and the Society for Historians of American Foreign Relations.

As I visited archives throughout the United States and Colombia, I took advantage of the couches, kitchens, and all-around generosity of just about everyone I knew. When I made it back to New York, Bogotá, or Philadelphia, I was lucky to have people who made me feel at home. And in all these places, I had the good fortune to meet fellow researchers who helped me in a thousand ways. Thanks to Jenna Feltey Alden, Melissa Borja, Sarah Bridger, Armando Castillo, Lina del Castillo, Rodrigo Castro, Allieth Colmenares, James Connolly, Angélica Escudero, Jhon Florián, Mitch Fraas, Courtney Fullilove, Sergio González, Daniel Gutiérrez, Andrew Greenberg, Yesid Hurtado, Greta Marchesi, Ted McCormick, Ben McKean and Dana Howard, Molly McOwen and Craig Cook, Lina Medina, Caela O'Connell and Julianna Parks, Roona Ray, Fabio Sánchez, Justin Steil and Ana Muñoz, and Sean Yuan. Heartfelt thanks to the Willdorfs, Neimans, Carstensens, Schneiders, and Milders who housed, fed, and talked with me during my travels.

This project would have been unthinkable without a few people. Constanza Castro introduced me to Bogotá, taught me more than I can say about Colombia, and was a true friend. Theresa Ventura and Jim Kane, I'll simply say that I have no idea what I would have done without you.

It would take another book and a different author to account for my family's role in all of this. My parents, Carl and Susan Offner, were irrepressibly proud, loving supporters. My mother died while I was writing this book; she was an intellectually ambitious feminist, a gifted teacher, and a lifelong activist who prepared me to deal with much bullshit in life. My father introduced me to US foreign policy in Latin America in the 1980s, and with it the possibilities of social mobilization. My research is partly but unmistakably an exploration of his long-ago comment to me that political organizing depends on recognizing the contradictory ideas that exist within the mind of every person. For conversations, books, and the examples of their own lives, I thank my parents and my late grandparents, Beatrice and Lawrence Neiman and Abe and Lillian Offner. I send loving thanks to my brother David Offner, sister-in-law Tessa Warren, and magnificent nieces Esme and Noa Offner for sharing life at the end of the family line with me.

A NOTE ON LANGUAGE

"AMERICA" IS the most contested concept in the Americas, claimed by residents of the United States as a label for their country and by Latin Americans as a label for the entire hemisphere. When writing about multiple states and groups of people within the Americas, it turns out that the Latin American vocabulary provides the only clear, precise way to name and distinguish among them. This book uses the terms *America* and *Americans* to refer to the Western Hemisphere and its inhabitants. It uses the terms *United States* and *North Americans* to refer to that country and its residents. It uses the terms *Latin America* and *Latin Americans* in ways that all of us do. Readers in the United States might find this language strange, but the odd experience of seeing the United States as part of a continent can turn out to be instructive. And we have all been called worse.

In the US context, this book refers to Native American reservations and Puerto Rico as imperial sites. It refers to Latin American countries as foreign sites in relation to the United States. This is not to contest research that interprets the United States as a global empire but rather to clarify the distinctive roles that Indian country and unincorporated territories played as points of connection between the mainland United States and the Third World.

Colombia's political jurisdictions do not map precisely onto English-language terms, but departments are roughly the equivalent of US states, *municipios* are counties or county seats, and *corregimientos* and *veredas* are administrative units with fewer political powers, the equivalent of towns and villages. *Resguardos* are indigenous territories governed by *cabildos*.

Introduction

IN 1976, DAVID LILIENTHAL announced the end of an era. "The old slogans—Square Deal, New Deal, Great Society—no longer fit; they are irrelevant to our present imperatives," he wrote in *Smithsonian* magazine.[1] Lilienthal spoke with some authority. As chairman of the Tennessee Valley Authority (TVA) during the 1940s, he had been a face of the New Deal state. In the ensuing decades, he had advised development programs throughout the Third World, and during the 1960s, he had wound his way home to participate in the Great Society. Now seventy-seven years old, Lilienthal articulated the wisdom of a new age. The heyday of midcentury statecraft was over, and he did not mourn its passing.

Lilienthal wrote amid a shattering political-economic transformation that historians are still struggling to name and understand. The final decades of the twentieth century saw the dismantling of welfare and developmental states across the First and Third Worlds. New calls for fiscal austerity, privatization, deregulation, and the decentralization of state functions rolled back some of the most ambitious achievements of midcentury public policy, dealt a blow to labor movements worldwide, and brought economic inequality to heights not seen since the 1920s. The world at the turn of the twenty-first century seemed radically new, and in crucial ways, it was.

Yet new orders always grow in some way from old ones. Lilienthal witnessed the death of the midcentury order with equanimity because, ironically enough, he had authored some of the ideas that dismantled it. He had never set out to do so, but by the 1970s it was clear that some of the practices that had built welfare and developmental states could also take them apart. In the capitalist economies of the First and Third Worlds, midcentury governments had often fulfilled responsibilities by delegating them to regional and private intermediaries. They had stretched miserly budgets by mobilizing volunteer labor, loosening regulations, and pushing costs onto the recipients of social services. Those strategies of state restructuring and belt tightening had passed hand to hand over decades, traversing world regions and histori-cal epochs to construct successive political-economic orders that seemed utterly antagonistic in retrospect, even to their creators. When Lilienthal declared the New Deal irrelevant, he was in fact noting that one of his most prized ideas—the notion of state decentralization—had come to serve such novel purposes that he himself could no longer regard it as an instrument of New Deal statecraft.

This book journeys across the postwar Americas to uncover the midcentury world to which Lilienthal belonged and the unseen possibilities that lay within it. It starts from the idea that the fate of the US welfare state and Latin American developmental states cannot be understood in isolation from one another. Lilienthal belonged to a generation of North Americans who threw their energies into the Third World after 1945, and their work overseas did more than remake foreign lands; it shaped the possibilities of policy making at home. Within the Western Hemisphere, long exchanges between US and Latin American societies endowed their political economies with some of the same internal contradictions. When the crises of the 1970s and 1980s came, the divergent promises that they harbored became vividly apparent. The mo-bilization of the right and the explosive conflicts of those decades did not simply substitute one set of ideas for another, obliterating all that came before. Instead, they sorted out the elements of midcentury mixed economies, de-stroying some practices, redeploying others, and retrospectively redefining them all as emblems of two different eras.

———

Seeing this history requires looking at the United States as many of its early architects did, and as many Latin Americans still do: as part of a hemisphere. American societies, with all their evident distinctions and inequalities, are products of a shared history; they grew from the same roots and entwined with one another as they aged. Colonized contemporaneously, nearly all at-tained independence together in the Age of Revolutions, and during the nine-teenth century, they became competitors in a shared struggle to define revolu-tion, sovereignty, republic, empire, liberalism, and America itself. Yet the same period produced striking differences within the hemisphere. Latin American societies, which as colonies had boasted incomparably grander cities and greater reserves of wealth, suffered extraordinary destruction during indepen-dence and recovered by reinvesting themselves in primary commodity pro-duction, the historic specialization of New World colonies. Meanwhile, the United States transformed itself into the world's leading industrial power. By the early twentieth century, the United States had become an aspiring global empire and Latin America its major site of intervention: a place where US Marines, economic advisors, and private investors jockeyed for position with Europeans and built the capacities of the US state.[2]

The ties that bound the regions made the Depression a shared catastrophe. From the 1870s on, foreign investment and markets constituted the twin pillars of export-led growth in Latin America, and as they collapsed in the 1930s, the whole continent came to varying degrees of crisis. Searching for a new pattern of economic activity, Latin Americans invented import substitution industrialization (ISI), and with it a new structuralist school of economic thought that identified primary commodity production and economic liberalism as the sources of the region's poverty. Across the hemisphere—from the New Deal to Brazil's Estado Novo, Colombia's Revolución en Marcha, Argentine Peronism, and the reinvigoration of the Mexican Revolution—governments established new public financial institutions and social welfare agencies, land reform laws and agricultural stabilization schemes, price regulations and consumer protections, labor codes and tax reforms. They imagined alternative international economic systems, the US government seeking to stabilize national income and access to foreign markets while Latin Americans aimed to raise primary commodity prices and protect infant industries. War emboldened all those aspirations. The destruction that swept Europe, Asia, and Africa made the entire Western Hemisphere a booming "arsenal of democracy" in which Latin America churned out supplies of rubber, tin, copper, and petroleum while US factories transformed them into airplanes and Liberty Ships. As the war neared its end, Americans of every kind converged at Bretton Woods, heirs to a shared history and authors of competing postwar visions. They set out to build a new world.[3]

All of these events left two striking legacies in the Americas. First, by an unexpected route, Latin America had acquired a remarkable place in world history: it was the only region to attain independence in the Age of Revolutions and wind up part of the Third World. Born as the United States' rivalrous twin, it never abdicated that role. But as a new process of decolonization unfolded after 1945, Latin America acquired a second family as the elder sibling to postcolonial Africa and Asia. Latin American economists led the new United Nations Economic Commission for Latin America (CEPAL) and made ISI and economic structuralism into beacons for the Third World. At the birth of the Cold War, the United States and the Soviet Union declared themselves the only conceivable models of political-economic order, but Latin American structuralists offered an alternative. They became the first of many to disrupt the binary logic of the Cold War, joined in time by Algerian nationalists, Cuban and Chinese communists, Eastern European market socialists, the Asian Tigers, and many more.[4]

Second, and just as important, American societies emerged from the war with a doubled, internally contradictory notion of poverty. When the crisis of the 1930s began, Americans saw before them two separate problems. First and foremost was the poverty of nations, measured in macroeconomic terms and visible in new national income accounts that governments assembled all over the globe after the 1920s. Second was an extraordinary proliferation of poor people who had always existed within nations, now visible in a continent's worth of urban shantytowns, land conflicts, work stoppages, and lines snaking out the doors of churches and charities. The proliferation of poor people inspired panic and demanded remedy, but what gave the Great Depression its magnificent name was the sense that something deeper had gone wrong—that the growing ranks of the poor might not signify ordinary hard times on a large scale, but instead a historic or structural cataclysm. No one agreed on the cause of the Great Depression, but nearly everyone thought it exposed a profound flaw in the national or international economic order. Examining the United States, Harvard economists Alvin Hansen and Lauchlin Currie perceived the awful destiny of "mature" industrial capitalist economies: this one had reached a terminal state of stagnation and could grow no more. Latin American structuralists decried the folly of primary commodity production. Using the best data available, they argued that prices of primary goods fell over time in relation to those of manufactures, that the falling terms of trade had condemned Latin America to poverty, and that industrialization offered the only way out. Across the hemisphere, economists fought over the relative efficacy of fiscal and monetary policy, businessmen looked to cartelization and price controls, and newly formed unions and regulatory agencies constrained the power of private capital to make all sorts of economic decisions unilaterally. In all of these ways, the Great Depression focused attention on the structure of national economies and the procedures by which they generated and allocated resources. The poverty of nations struck Americans as a systemic consequence of political-economic order, and economists defining the macroeconomy as their object attained unprecedented influence in government, promising to diagnose and treat the problem.[5]

Yet the shared bounty of war—and its new susceptibility to measurement and international comparison—led Americans to divergent conclusions about poverty and the nation. In Latin America, the interwar drive to industrialize and invent a new national pattern of economic activity gained legitimacy through the experience of wartime growth. The region's progress was plain for all to see in national accounts, as was Europe's destitution and the astonishing ascent of the United States. What had begun in Latin America as an improvisational experiment in macroeconomic reform became a formal postwar project to eradicate the poverty of nations through continued structural reinvention—a project called development centered on macroeconomic transformation, surrounded by social reform.

In the United States, the events of the 1940s taught most New Dealers the opposite lesson. They emerged with narrowed sights by 1950, comforted by the return of growth and concerned mainly with sustaining it, not with achieving profound structural change. At the war's conclusion, wider ambitions to regulate private capital, redistribute income and wealth, and reassign responsibilities among public and private institutions did survive among industrial unions, civil rights activists, consumer advocates, communists, and the left flank of the Democratic Party. Those groups had spent the war years pushing the Roosevelt administration to ensure full employment, desegregate workplaces, enforce price controls, and create industrial boards with labor, management, and government representation to direct production. In 1945, they hoped to create a lasting form of social democracy and demolish the color line that ran through US economic life. But these were not most Democrats, and their demands fell victim to a postwar offensive by businessmen, Republicans, and Dixiecrats buoyed by a rising tide of anticommunism. The Employment Act of 1946 signaled the triumph of a restrictive version of Keynesianism in the United States; the federal government took responsibility for sustaining economic growth with fiscal and monetary policy but divested itself of broader obligations to regulate private capital.[6]

The United States was thus a country that never published a postwar development plan. The very idea of it seemed absurd. The dynamism of the war economy and the restoration of welfare capitalism restored an embattled faith that the country represented a historical endpoint toward which others might progress. Over the course of the late 1940s and early 1950s, that conviction politically resignified domestic programs that had recently gone under the name *development*. During the Depression, the Roosevelt administration had seen in the South and West common problems of rural societies and had channeled public investment there to construct hydraulic works, generate electricity, improve soils, stabilize prices, and raise agricultural productivity. Some of those initiatives lived on in the postwar era, reconceived as elements of a military Keynesian program that ringed US cities with suburbs and turned the South and West into the Sunbelt, the fastest-growing region of the United States.[7] Federal spending transformed the nation, but by the 1950s, North Americans ceased to think of their state as a developmental one at all—that is, a state charged with turning a poor country into a rich one. In their minds, it became something different: a welfare state that guarded against insecurity in a land of abundance.

During the postwar era, poverty in the United States thus came to appear once more as an aberrant feature of an otherwise sound economic order. By statistical measures, the poverty *of* the nation was no more. And as suburban-ization and the rise of the Sunbelt became great engines of growth during the 1950s, it seemed gone for good. US macroeconomic performance became the envy of the earth for a time, and officials in Washington could scarcely ac-knowledge the ways that their chosen pattern of growth generated poverty and inequality. When the country's leading social scientists and policy makers looked at urban cores and rural communities impoverished by the growth of suburbs, or African Americans suffering soaring unemployment rates in the booming Sunbelt, they saw poverty amid plenty, or the problem of poor peo-ple themselves. What had once been a perceived symptom of the Great Depression—the existence of some number of poor people—became the purported essence of the problem of poverty after 1950.[8]

Postwar order in the Americas grew from the myth that Latin American nations had to face macroeconomic disorder that made them poor countries, but the United States confronted only marginal pockets of poverty within a healthy political economy. Those incommensurate notions of poverty facili-tated an enormous circulation of people, policies, and ideas within the hemi-sphere. During the late 1940s, a generation of New Dealers and veterans of the Marshall Plan fanned out across Latin America, promising to adapt what they considered the lessons of capitalist recovery to what they understood as the problem of capitalist development. Within the region, no country inspired more ambitious dreams, scrupulous study, or relentless intervention than Co-lombia. Among the large states of Latin America, Colombia is today the least studied, and it chiefly attracts students of political violence, drugs, and security policy. But at midcentury, the US government, international lenders, and de-velopment theorists all believed that Colombia could become a model of capi-talist development and liberal democratic reform. Colombia became the site of the World Bank's first comprehensive country survey in 1949, the world's leading per-capita recipient of World Bank loans from 1950 to 1974, and a "showcase" of the Alliance for Progress, an inter-American development pro-gram launched in 1961. The economist Albert O. Hirschman spent the mid-1950s working as an advisor in Colombia and used his experience to write one of the foundational books in development economics, *The Strategy of Eco-nomic Development.* Lauchlin Currie, an influential New Deal economist, led the 1949 World Bank mission, assumed Colombian citizenship during the 1950s, and spent the rest of his life there. David Lilienthal remade himself as an international development consultant in the 1950s and found his first job in Colombia. The country's privileged position in the minds and careers of foreign advisors made it a crossroads for global intellectual currents and gave its development programs outsized significance. For many North Americans, Colombia was the first place where they directly confronted a piece of the mythic Third World, struggled to adapt their knowledge and experience to it, and fashioned lessons that they carried to projects worldwide.[9]

The North Americans who traveled to Colombia invested enormous hope in it, and they hoped for more than capitalist development. As Hirschman recalled decades later, midcentury development theorists believed that "all good things go together"; growth would generate democracy and social justice. By the close of the twentieth century, Colombia's ceaseless civil war and intractable economic inequality stood as harsh rebukes to that idea. Nonetheless, Colombian history is hardly a case of foreign experts fumbling and failing in the Third World. More disturbingly, Colombia revealed what success could look like. The country never became a model of social justice, and by 1991 its democracy appeared so broken that Colombians tore up their century-old constitution and set out to reinvent the state from scratch. Through all those decades of crisis, Colombia met international growth goals, barred communists from national politics, and maintained close ties with the US government. It approximated US officials', economic advisors', and international lenders' dreams for Latin America during the Cold War. As Hirschman acknowledged, the course of Latin American history exposed the madness of development theorists' foundational assumptions and aims.[10]

For decades, Colombian housing complexes, river valleys, planning agencies, and universities became international laboratories for new thinking about political economy. The broad conception of Latin America's problems demanded every sort of person for every conceivable task: economists to write national plans, architects to design new cities, sociologists to fashion community development programs, and consulting firms to furnish technical advice and international social connections. North Americans collaborated and struggled with Latin Americans of all sorts, and together they transformed the country. The pages that follow explore landmark projects: the birth of Colombia's first regional development corporation, the fate of its land reform program, and the making of the largest housing project built in the hemisphere under the Alliance for Progress. They are equally concerned with the transformation of knowledge that attended the life and death of development. The postwar project of forming an economy went hand in hand with the invention of economics as an independent discipline in Latin America, a region where political economy had long existed within schools of law and administration. Until 1945, economic policy makers in Colombia had been brilliant polymaths trained as lawyers, businessmen, and engineers. In the succeeding decades, Colombian universities aggressively recruited foreign funders and professors to train a new kind of economist: a credentialed specialist who could bring a new rationality to statecraft. The reconstruction of the national economy thus involved a reordering of the system of professions, a conceptual recategorization of worldly problems, and a redefinition of the imagined boundary between the economic and the noneconomic. Latin American development became an essential part of one of the profound transformations of the twentieth century: the rise of economists as policy makers and public intellectuals, and the making of economics as a distinct, authoritative, globally recognizable form of knowledge.[11]

Development programs simultaneously became social crossroads. Under their auspices, government officials, social scientists, businessmen, and community development workers hailing from the North and South Atlantic toiled and fought with one another, and with a great variety of Colombians whom they considered objects of reform. As it turned out, rural wage workers and campesinos, urban squatters, college students, and purportedly reactionary latifundistas all became agents of reform in their own right. The project of crafting an economy and inventing a new economics profession became something much broader and less determinate as Colombians nested their own aspirations within national policies and bent ascendant forms of economic reasoning to their own ends. Rural migrants who populated urban housing projects used their homes to sustain household economies within the national economy. Wealthy cattle ranchers and urban capitalists confronted hostile public policies by appropriating and redeploying forms of economic argument that the state would hear. Refashioning the ideas of economists and development agencies, they crafted vernacular economic explanations of their place in the nation, the relationship between their interests and the national interest, and the purported public value of concentrated wealth and inequality.

In these moments, it became clear that the developmental state incubated quite unexpected processes of intellectual transformation. Housing programs and land reform touched the lives of millions of people and became powerful instruments of ideological change among Colombians who had to deal with the state, and who could best defend their interests by appealing to its most cherished principles. That pressure to argue in legible ways never produced consensus around any policy but instead encouraged the popularization of economic reasoning as a mode of political contestation. Indeed, development made economics more than an authoritative form of expertise; it became a popular language of legitimation that pointed to many possible ends. Within the history and sociology of economic thought, the simultaneous construction of a global profession and the reproduction of nationally distinctive variants has become a rich area of research. But the popularization of economic reasoning is little understood and hardly even conceived as a constitutive part of the globalization and differentiation of knowledge. The finest place to study that process is in the realm of public policy, a social crossroads par excellence and an inescapably transnational one in the developmentalist era. In teaching noneconomists to argue in economic terms, land reform and housing policy extended economists' influence while undermining their ability to control the use and meaning of their knowledge.[12]

As Americans developed wide-ranging visions of economic order and reason, they exposed the multiple possibilities that Depression-era policies harbored. In Colombia, veterans of the Roosevelt administration argued among themselves about the true lessons of the New Deal and adapted it in ways that can seem utterly counterintuitive. New Dealers redeployed US public housing law to cultivate private homeownership in Latin America. They crafted markedly austere forms of social welfare provision, mobilizing unpaid labor to limit the need for public spending. Men remembered as architects of a powerful central state at home became evangelists for state decentralization abroad. Those apparent contradictions stemmed partly from the simple fact that New Dealers were collaborating with Colombians whose own Depression-era policies had focused on formalizing private property ownership in the countryside, whose central state was notoriously weak, and who lived in a country marked by deep regional divisions and a little-noted tradition of administrative decentralization.[13] But the peculiar fate of the New Deal abroad stemmed just as much from contradictions within it. The Roosevelt administration had presented innumerable remedies for the Depression and relied on local governments and agencies to implement them. The concrete manifestations of New Deal policies had already proliferated across the national territory by the late 1940s, and foreign aid programs became greenhouses incubating possibilities only half seen at home.

Colombia thus serves several purposes in this story. It is a place worth understanding in its own right. It is an illustrative site of US foreign policy experimentation that shaped the fate of the New Deal. And it is a vantage point from which to see the United States anew. Looking north from Latin America, our eyes settle on midcentury policies that have largely escaped the gaze of US historians—initiatives of the 1940s, 1950s, and 1960s that occasioned little comment at the time but turned out to be consequential to US history.

Within Colombia, Americans spun out the inchoate promises of the 1930s under extraordinary new circumstances. During the late 1940s and 1950s, the central preoccupation of Colombian life was political violence, which briefly brought an end to democracy itself in 1953, temporarily toppled the country's party system, and left Colombians deeply skeptical about politics, partisan mobilization, and the legitimacy of the national state.[14] Over the course of the 1950s, those fears combined with Cold War anticommunism and the power of Colombian business associations to constrain the forms that state-building could take.[15] So, too, did the fiscal strangulation of a government that struggled to raise tax revenues. During the first half of the twentieth century,

Colombia's state expenditures hovered between 4 and 6 percent of GDP; not until the 1970s did they regularly reach 10 percent annually.[16] US and World Bank loans compounded those pressures. Both institutions maintained that accelerating growth required concentrated public investments in industrial production and closely related infrastructure; for the time being, social welfare programs had to function on a shoestring. When Lauchlin Currie delivered his 1950 country survey to the World Bank, Vice President Robert Garner was incensed that it even discussed social policy. "Damn it Lauch," he cursed. "We can't go messing around with education and health. We're a *bank!*"[17] Laboring under all those pressures, Colombian elites and US advisors came to believe that Bogotá could best fulfill its widening obligations by acting through autonomous agencies, regional authorities, private intermediaries, and volunteer community action organizations. Those ideas resonated powerfully with New Dealers raised on federalism and familiar with the growing administrative state at home.[18] Adapting and melding national policy traditions under novel constraints, Americans of all kinds turned to new forms of state decentralization, private delegation, and austere systems of social welfare provision. These innovations built the Colombian state, expanded its responsibilities, and became hallmarks of midcentury developmentalism.

The practices of devolving responsibility and squeezing social spending flourished within national plans that are often remembered as great symbols of state centralism and munificence. During the early postwar decades, CEPAL and most Latin American officials believed that development required powerful central planning agencies that could model the national economy and chart its course. Those plans in turn required national powers to set tariffs, taxes, and exchange rates in the interest of industrialization. But despite the common association of development with centralized power, the fulfillment of plans fell to a great variety of institutions both public and private, many of them strapped for cash. Some parts of the public sector, such as local governments, were not even routinely included in national planning and budgeting procedures. According to CEPAL's own statistics, Latin American states became far more complex than many economists acknowledged during the late 1950s and 1960s, as decentralized agencies and autonomous public enterprises grew more rapidly than the public sector overall.[19]

Latin American experiments in state-building became objects of fascination in the United States during the 1960s. The Alliance for Progress, launched in 1961, funneled unprecedented levels of US aid to anticommunist development projects across the continent. As it began, John F. Kennedy declared the 1960s the "development decade," and a stint overseas became as common for US researchers, government functionaries, and college graduates as a trip through the colonies had once been for their British counterparts in the age of empire. Yet as capital, military equipment, social scientists, and volunteers flowed south, their attempts to remake foreign societies became bound up in affairs back home. When the Alliance began, North Americans were already embroiled in conflicts that defied US policy makers' sense of their own society as a model to others. Native Americans battled the federal government in defense of their own sovereignty. A rising tide of social movements denounced US corporations as engines of racial inequality, class exploitation, ecological depredation, and imperialist war. North Americans fought over the same questions that development projects raised overseas: what were the proper roles of state action and voluntarism, of for-profit and nonprofit activity, and of national and local initiative in the provision of social welfare and the generation of prosperity? Conflicts that predated the 1960s became acute during that decade, and North Americans came to invoke foreign experience in struggles at home.

A hallmark of US political argument in the 1960s was in fact its insistent reference to Latin America, Africa, and Asia. North Americans who agreed on nothing else concurred that those world regions offered lessons for the United States, and they mobilized stylized depictions of "underdeveloped" societies to advance every domestic program imaginable. Their capacity to reason across region depended on a general insistence that at the national level, the United States was nothing like Colombia, but that it contained little Colombias within it. "US ghettoes are underdeveloped countries right next door to rich, powerful, mature economic regions which tend to dominate them," David Lilienthal declared in 1968.[20] Stokely Carmichael and Charles V. Hamilton agreed at least on that point. Their 1967 blockbuster *Black Power* declared that "black people in this country form a colony, and it is not in the interest of the colonial power to liberate them."[21] As these remarks suggested, the equation of poor communities at home with poor countries abroad taught no single lesson; it was a language of politics that served contradictory purposes for a generation of activists, intellectuals, and government officials. The Black Panther Party, Young Lords, National Congress of American Indians, and American Indian Movement stood at the forefront of social movements that described their own communities as colonial or postcolonial societies in order to critique economic and political relationships within the United States. They indicted US officials as imperialists siphoning resources from reservations and hollowed-out cities, and they looked to the Third World as a source of strategy and solidarity. For many policy makers, the very same comparison between the First and Third Worlds allowed them to treat impoverished communities at home not as products of exploitation but as nations unto themselves—aberrant, internally pathological features of an otherwise sound political economy. When rising social movements and explosive political violence forced them to confront the injustices of the affluent society, they turned not to suburbs or Sunbelt metropolises to understand the roots of their problems, but instead cast their sights on the Third World, insisting that knowledge of poverty lay there. Many anthropologists, political scientists, sociologists, and urban planners followed their lead, transposing concepts that they had recently developed abroad. They analyzed US cities as urban villages, and some deployed the homogenizing, stigmatizing categories of modernization theory to compare the mentalities and social structures of poor people across the globe. Cumulatively, these voices formed a discordant choir announcing the news from the Third World. Their comparisons between home and away generated as many practical experiments and stylized pieces of wisdom as there were political traditions in the United States.[22]

US businessmen and Native American nations built some of the first practical bridges between First and Third World policy. These groups had always functioned across the fictive divide separating foreign from domestic, and during the Kennedy years, they made novel use of the federal government's interest in foreign aid. Since the 1950s, Native tribes battling for their own survival had demanded that Washington treat them as developing nations, and during the 1960s, they convinced the federal government to adapt foreign assistance programs on reservations. Meanwhile, businessmen active in both foreign and Indian affairs forged interlocking networks across the hemisphere to shape public policy. These incipient connections multiplied after 1963, when Lyndon Johnson became president. Johnson cared nothing for Latin America and came into office like a wrecking ball, gutting the Alliance for Progress and recalling foreign aid officials to conduct the War on Poverty. Over the next five years, an unruly assembly of North Americans filed home, all promising to repatriate the lessons of the Third World. Inserting themselves into domestic conflicts, they began a new process of international translation that recalled their experiences in Latin America: they struggled to adapt their knowledge to new circumstances and became subject to processes of social mediation that determined the final meaning of their work. By the late 1960s, domestic and foreign policies bore striking new resemblances, and North Americans found that they could move in countless directions across the First and Third Worlds.

Within the United States, however, they could not go just anywhere. The prevailing definition of poverty channeled federal funding and veterans of the Third World to a single corner of the government: the welfare state. North Americans had crafted lessons for every aspect of Colombian policy making from as many features of US society, but during the 1960s, the Kennedy and Johnson administrations were not looking for a comprehensive macroeconomic plan or another TVA. All the divergent possibilities that existed within developmental statecraft became transmuted into lessons on just one subject at home: the treatment of the poor and the provision of social welfare. Historians have tended to notice the direct connection that grew between community development abroad and community action at home. Sargent Shriver, the head of the Peace Corps, became director of the Office of Economic Opportunity (OEO), the main organ of the War on Poverty. Under his leadership, the OEO's community action program tapped a generation of social scientists who had spent years implementing community development programs overseas. Volunteers in Service to America (VISTA), a signal program of the Great Society, began as a glimmer in the Kennedy administration's eye, originally known as the "Domestic Peace Corps."[23] But community action turned out to be just one idea carried home from the Third World. The northward shift in federal spending after 1963 brought with it people of every social experience, professional qualification, and political persuasion. Few had any programmatic experience that could serve a domestic antipoverty program; they were not teachers, social workers, or welfare administrators. But they did have experience building state institutions and articulating them with all sorts of private activity. When the War on Poverty began, many veterans of the Third World viewed it as more than a set of services and entitlements to the poor; they took it as an occasion to restructure the welfare state.

The history of international development contributed to two epochal transformations in US social welfare policy. First, when the War on Poverty began, businessmen who had insinuated themselves into Latin American statecraft, university reform, and development policy writ large turned homeward declaring themselves public servants fit to administer the War on Poverty—by contract, and at a profit. The US government had long relied on for-profit contracting to carry out foreign aid, military, and public works programs, but never the areas of social welfare that the Johnson administration now targeted. Following the enticements of federal budget appropriations, US aid contractors joined with military contractors and corporations active on Indian reservations to remake the welfare state in the image of foreign and imperial policy. Industrial corporations ultimately ran the majority of the War on Poverty's training and education programs in US cities and Indian country. Turning manpower programs into for-profit ventures, they imbued them with doubled purposes and irresolvable contradictions. Light manufacturers that used capital flight as a business strategy now treated job-training contracts as subsidies that helped them shift employment around the country, evade the Fair Labor Standards Act, and undermine unionization. Executives capitalized on left-wing critiques of public education to present corporate management, the profit motive, deprofessionalization, and deunionization as paths to progress in teaching. In all these ways, businessmen fit the War on Poverty into their long-standing battles against organized labor, government regulation, and the left. Before the 1960s, they had fought those battles by resisting the welfare state or trying to shape it from without, but their experience inside the developmental state gave them a new perspective: they now entered the welfare state and conducted its work. In the process, businessmen who faced a crisis of legitimacy during the 1960s arrived at a novel public defense of themselves and their firms. Addressing North Americans who had come to doubt the virtues of the US pattern of growth, and who condemned corporations' core productive activities as sources of the country's crises, businessmen presented a new response: the corporation was not mainly an instrument to build cars, but rather a for-profit social problem solver that could fix the very problems social movements identified. In 1966, David Lilienthal invented the phrase "social entrepreneurship" to convey the idea that corporate managers might continually shift the line between public and private goods, redefine the realms of for-profit and nonprofit activity, and thus solve the full range of society's problems. Generally mistaken as an artifact of the late twentieth century, the term originated in the social combat of the 1960s and in the mind of an old New Dealer turned for-profit development consultant.[24]

Businessmen never ran most of the War on Poverty, and the second lesson that came home from the Third World harbored a more ambiguous promise. The 1960s seemed a moment of triumph for a generation of social democrats, civil rights organizers, radical pacifists, and Native American tribal leaders who had long struggled to channel federal housing funds to tenant farmers, sharecroppers, migrant farmworkers, and Indians living on reservations. For decades, all of those groups had taken inspiration from build-your-own-home programs overseas and in US territories. In rural communities especially, they imagined the owner-built home as a source of autonomy for farmworkers, a challenge to employers' power, and a foundation of political citizenship. From the 1930s to the 1950s, the federal government had promoted those programs in foreign and imperial contexts but generally discouraged their growth on the mainland, forcing activists to launch small-scale, private experiments of their own. Those private initiatives became nationwide public policy during the War on Poverty. The transformation of rural self-help housing from a struggling private activity to a federal government mission illuminated multiple ways that influence could operate internationally. In training and education, US officials at the highest levels of government chose deliberately to remake the welfare state in the image of foreign and imperial policy. When it came to housing, grassroots activists and officials in the Bureau of Indian Affairs spoke explicitly of foreign models, but other rural housing officials generally did not. Their sense of the possible had simply changed through decades when austere homeownership programs proliferated abroad as celebrated instruments of US aid. During the 1960s, officials began to authorize proposals they had once rejected, and in doing so, they opened new pathways to international housing advisors, architects, and community workers who had cut their teeth abroad. The result was a transformation of rural housing provision that pointed toward multiple futures. Here was a policy that dramatically expanded the reach of the state, building homes in places and for people that conventional public housing had never reached. Here, too, was a policy that receded from the model of public housing, offering much smaller subsidies to the poor and sidelining public construction and ownership as foundations of shared economic security.

By the late 1960s, Colombia's developmental state and the US welfare state had come to generate novel forms of state decentralization, private and for-profit delegation, and austere social welfare provision. Those techniques originated as ways for deeply compromised, internally embattled governments to fulfill extraordinary promises under punishing ideological, material, and political constraints. Welfare and developmental states contained profound contradictions, and in ways unforeseen, incubated practices susceptible to appropriation and redeployment for very different purposes during the 1970s and 1980s.

The economies and states that came to crisis after 1970 had grown up together, interpreting and borrowing from one another's experiments. Their historical interrelationship recasts central problems in twentieth-century political economy. It suggests that one way of tracing the route from the New Deal to the Great Society is by traveling through Latin America. One way of understanding the history of economic development is by studying its relation to First World programs for economic recovery and reform. And one way of explaining the making and unmaking of welfare and developmental states as concurrent, transnational processes is by analyzing their shared, mutually constituted internal contradictions, the varied possibilities they contained, and the mounting pressures and crises that foreclosed some of their most egalitarian promises and turned some of their most ambiguous practices to deeply inegalitarian ends. Contradictions within midcentury political economy have long fascinated historians and are in principle evident from any perspective. But their accumulation along the path from the First World to the Third World and back is stunning to witness.

This history forces us to rethink accounts of the midcentury state's destruction that center on the mobilization of the right and the southward projection of power by US and multilateral institutions. For good reason, a great deal of writing on the unraveling of welfare and developmentalist projects has pointed to half a century of conflict between right and left, and capital and labor, culminating in a political and intellectual coup from the right during the successive crises of 1973 to 1991—the oil shocks and stagflation, the debt crisis, and the collapse of the Soviet Union. These stories' protagonists are rightfully known to us all today: neoclassical and Austrian economists; right-wing business and religious networks; military dictators; the Carter, Reagan, and Clinton administrations; the World Bank and International Monetary Fund (IMF); and an army of US foundations and think tanks.[25] Yet these accounts leave us with confounding puzzles. Many purportedly novel practices of the late twentieth century—including the ones in this book—had earlier lives as developmentalist phenomena. Some of the leading policy makers within the World Bank and IMF were Latin Americans who believed they were carrying forward the lessons of midcentury statecraft. Radical liberalization programs rarely relied on coups or massive purges but drew strength from existing institutions and officials with long careers inside the state.[26] For all the influence and intellectual production of the right, for all the power of lenders to demand structural adjustment, much of the raw material they had to work with during the 1970s and 1980s came from the repertoire of midcentury state-building itself. Writing about the socialist economies of Eastern Europe, sociologist Johanna Bockman argues that "neoliberal capitalism was a parasitic growth on the very socialist alternatives it attacked." The process of historical change differed within the capitalist economies of the United States and Colombia, but Bockman is right that the midcentury order contained within it seeds of many others.[27]

Writing a history across region and time demands analytic concepts that travel well and say what they mean. The story that unfolds in the following pages strains national vocabularies, and it strains the imagination of historians who live in a world no one could foresee in 1950. This book ultimately forsakes some of the standard keywords that historians use to interpret twentieth-century political economy. It is not a book about liberalism and its unraveling; the term that runs through US history bears meanings so different in the rest of the world that it fails as an analytic category. Neither is this a book about neoliberalism, at least until the very end. Virtually no one in the story had any intention of building the political-economic order that bears that label today; in their own moment, their ideas and policies were developmentalist and welfarist, which is not to say that they were benign or that anyone should regard them with nostalgia. This is a book about the competing possibilities that lay within midcentury capitalism and midcentury state-building. It requires a vocabulary that captures those contradictions, not one that reads future political-economic orders back on them.

Fortunately, the midcentury period provides valuable keywords of its own. In the United States, Colombia, and much of the First and Third Worlds, policy makers and intellectuals commonly invoked the notion of the mixed economy to describe capitalist orders. An evocative term of its time, the mixed economy is also a powerful category for historical analysis. In its time, it was an imagined path between laissez-faire and socialism, or between the stylized ideals of pure private competition and complete state ownership. In that wide expanse grew a remarkable variety of lived practices and ideals, including the ones in this book. States grew by local and private devolution, tax-starved governments supplemented public spending with private volunteer labor, and businessmen jockeyed with economists as stewards of the state. By design and as a point of pride, every project of purported "state-led" development was in equal measure a private initiative; every national economic plan intersected with a business plan; and policy makers routinely debated just which government agency, for-profit corporation, or nonprofit community organization could best carry out a given task under very immediate circumstances. Mixed economies relied on the imagined dichotomy between public and private while systematically conjoining the two, producing manifold articulations of state and capital and multiple accounts of the relationship between public and private interest.

When capitalist economies came to crisis in the 1970s and 1980s, North Americans and Latin Americans did not merely reach for new ideas; they reordered their political-economic systems using the tools already at hand. They sorted out the mixed economy, selectively redeploying its practices of decentralization, private delegation, and austere social welfare provision, setting each in a new political-economic order that altered its meaning and purpose. Policies born together at midcentury came to appear in hindsight as expressions of two opposing impulses. Some became remembered as iconic features of Keynesianism and developmentalism, while others became known as hallmarks of neoliberal capitalism. Comprehending midcentury political economy requires recognizing that our own moment has changed the meanings of words and practices in ways that make our world legible while obscuring the past.

All this is to say that if we want to understand the cataclysm of the late twentieth century, we should study it as we do the Age of Revolutions, the era of slave emancipation, the crisis of the Great Depression, and the postwar process of decolonization. All of those upheavals remade societies not by inverting their every feature but by extinguishing a few of their defining elements and breathing new life into others. All were multisited, transnational processes in which influence moved in many directions across lines of imperial, national, and social division. And all of them involved a great deal of narration in the moment and commemoration afterward that produced memories of colonialism, slavery, and economic liberalism convenient to the projects that succeeded them. Our own world is the product of just such an epochal transformation, and we should recognize stories of total rupture and inversion as a form of memory that makes contemporary political conflict possible.

———

This book begins in Colombia, where Latin Americans laboring to transform their society enlisted US allies and helped to transform the advisors themselves. Part I explores the construction of a developmental state that was, in the eyes of its architects, a decentralized one that grew through regional and private delegation. The distinctive structure of the Colombian state made it possible to carry out the iconic tasks of midcentury developmentalism, from land reform to mass housing construction. Those projects in turn became environments in which Latin American landowners and capitalists learned to argue in economic terms, popularizing the modern notion of the economy and bending it to their own purposes. Part II explores the contradictions of Colombia's attempt to conjure a new generation of professional economists to serve as stewards of the state. In a country where the decentralized state and the notion of the public were so intricately bound to private action, interest, and institutions, the establishment of economics faculties in universities unexpectedly produced two rival disciplines and professions. Economists and managers emerged from the same university reform project during the 1960s, each group offering its own account of the relationship between public and private interest, and each presenting its practitioners as the rightful stewards of the state. Part III looks out from midcentury Colombia. It follows the trails of businessmen, government officials, community development workers, and architects into the War on Poverty's training, education, and housing programs. It traces the careers of Colombian economists who wound up in the Bretton Woods institutions in the era of structural adjustment. And it crosses the divides of the 1970s, 1980s, and 1990s in both Colombia and the United States, showing how Americans met the crises of those decades by reinventing the characteristic practices of the mixed economy.

PART I

Building the Decentralized State

1

Decentralization in One Valley

AS THE SECOND WORLD WAR entered its final year, David Lilienthal neared the end of his time as chairman of the Tennessee Valley Authority (TVA). He wanted Americans to understand one thing. Writing in the *New York Times*, he explained that the New Deal agency had not only brought electricity to one of the poorest regions of the United States. It had proven that "there is an alternative to . . . cumbersome, top-heavy, over-centralized government." The TVA, he insisted, was "the first major exception in more than fifty years to the trend toward centralized administration of Federal functions."[1]

Lilienthal thought he had challenged half a century of centralization, but Colombian economist Eduardo Wiesner did him one better. Wiesner wrote nearly sixty years after Lilienthal, when midcentury welfare and developmental states had come undone. He took some credit for their dismantling. During the 1980s, Wiesner had served as the Western Hemisphere director for the International Monetary Fund (IMF), pushing through structural adjustment programs throughout the region. By the 1990s, he was an advisor to the World Bank and an international authority on state decentralization. The decentralizing reforms of the late twentieth century, he maintained, bucked traditions so old as to defy historical accounting. "The centralist tradition in Latin America goes back at least as far as Castile, Spain in the 16th century, and perhaps even to pre-Columbian times," he explained in 2003.[2]

How did midcentury welfare and developmental states come into being, and how did they come apart? Curiously, both processes depended on forms of state decentralization that their champions hailed as historically unprecedented. Decentralization was in fact an enduring and characteristic form of government in the Americas by the time of the Great Depression. It was reimagined and redeployed twice during the subsequent years, first as a developmentalist prescription to expand the responsibilities of weak states, and later as an instrument to break down established state functions. When Wiesner arrived at the World Bank, he picked up a tool that Lilienthal had sharpened for him.

The line connecting Lilienthal to Wiesner runs through Colombia's Cauca Valley, Lilienthal's "second favorite Valley" and the place where he began his career as an international consultant.[3] The Cauca Valley Corporation (CVC), founded in 1954 and modeled in part on the TVA, was an iconic regional development project of the midcentury era. It was, in Lilienthal's view, "a pioneering demonstration of regional and decentralized development of natural resources and economic activities."[4] The CVC embodied one time-bound ideal of decentralization that had two dimensions. First, creating the corporation required devolving national power to a regional body. Second, it blurred the line between public and private authority, as the state vested powers in private businessmen and remade public enterprise in the image of the for-profit, private-sector corporation. During the 1950s, the CVC's conception of decentralization held enormous appeal for international funders and capitalists in both the United States and Colombia. Mobilizing extraordinary political and economic power, they inscribed it in the Colombian state.

———

At the age of fifty, David Lilienthal reflected on his nineteen years of public service and concluded that the work was not very lucrative. In early 1950, the former TVA chairman decided to become a businessman.

Lilienthal's turn to private enterprise was his second major career change. After graduating from Harvard Law School in 1923, he had spent eight years litigating labor, railroad, and public utility cases. He left private legal practice in 1931 to work in government, first as a public utility regulator with the Wisconsin Public Service Commission and in 1933 as a member of the Roosevelt administration. For the next eight years, he sat on the board of the TVA, and from 1941 to 1946 he served as the agency's director and chairman. The TVA transformed Lilienthal into a national authority on energy policy, and in 1946 he accepted the chairmanship of the new Atomic Energy Commission (AEC), a federal agency that oversaw military and civilian uses of nuclear power in peacetime.[5]

By 1950, he was hunting for a better-paying job and decided to parlay his TVA experience into an international consultancy. "It could be spade-work," he explained to his friend Edward R. Murrow, "for a policy and program for world economic development that might . . . avoid a repetition of China in Southeast Asia." Eager to redeploy the TVA idea in service of the Cold War, Lilienthal looked for a flush, politically like-minded patron. The Institute for World Government offered him money, but he considered the group too closely associated with world federalism.[6] World Bank president Eugene R. Black suggested that Lilienthal lead a mission to Guatemala. It was a novel job; the World Bank, created in 1944 to finance postwar reconstruction in Europe, had only recently broadened its sights to address Third World development. Black offered to pay up to $5,000 per month, but Lilienthal declined: "I told him this was not adequate compensation."[7]

Lilienthal finally found his match on Wall Street. In 1950, the advertising executive Albert Lasker introduced him to André Meyer, senior partner at the investment bank Lazard Frères.[8] Meyer and the other Lazard partners immediately impressed Lilienthal. "But," he acknowledged, "whether I can actually contribute something that will fill their needs, or whether their interests will help me move toward an eventual capital gain only some time will tell."[9] Meyer had no such concerns. Throughout his career, he enlisted high government officials as partners in the firm, paid them extravagantly, and frankly acknowledged that they might know nothing about banking, but they had useful connections and could learn. Meyer put Lilienthal in charge of a small company that Lazard had acquired, Minerals Separation North America, and the old New Dealer spent the next several years shepherding the company through a series of profitable mergers, acquisitions, and public stock offerings.[10]

Lilienthal used his time at Lazard to establish a reputation among businessmen and bankers in the United States. His 1953 book, *Big Business*, vindicated the modern corporation as an instrument of social and economic progress. Massive corporations could serve the public interest, he argued, so long as they assumed decentralized forms. The book celebrated the sprawling conglomerate firms that took shape during the mid-twentieth century. Industrial corporations that had once specialized in defined areas of production—steel, chemicals, or automobiles—had begun entering entirely new sectors and dividing themselves into vast systems of subsidiaries. What could appear a shocking form of corporate consolidation became, in Lilienthal's telling, a new form of competition that the public should welcome. According to Lilienthal, nineteenth-century antitrust legislation relied on an outdated notion of competition—an image of many small firms competing to offer the lowest prices. In the present day, he maintained, the total number of firms in an industry might decline, but each industrial behemoth could enter new areas of production traditionally dominated by any other. Prices might become uniform, but massive corporations now competed in research and advertising. Lilienthal's book was breezy and at times deliberately evasive. He refused, for instance, to offer any "precise definition of what is 'big,'" and instead packed the book with anecdotal examples of DuPont, General Motors, and other firms improving and diversifying their products. On that basis, he argued that "Big Business" could provide for economic prosperity, growing consumer choice, "a stronger democracy and an even greater people."[11]

Lilienthal's book read to corporate executives as a valuable retort to organized labor, consumer advocates, and the waning regulatory impulse of the New Deal state. Indeed, where New Dealers Adolf Berle and Gardiner Means had argued that the modern corporation had dangerously concentrated economic power, Lilienthal insisted that the "New Competition" among conglomerates prevented "Big Business" from abusing its power, as he claimed "Big Government" could. The state, after all, was a true monopoly with no legal competitor.[12] Corporate executives from Wall Street to Detroit appreciated that message, and forty-two wrote to Lilienthal congratulating him on the book. General Motors distributed a condensed version of *Big Business* to over 100,000 employees.[13]

Lilienthal, however, regarded his activities with Lazard as entirely consistent with his earlier work in government. In *Big Business*, he insisted on the importance of decentralization within large corporations, and here he drew on his experience as a public servant. Lilienthal had long prized decentralization in government; since his time as TVA chairman, he had maintained that functional autonomy from Washington facilitated effective decision-making, undergirding the institution's success. Moreover, he had argued that decentralization was the proper form of public administration for a democratic society, as it permitted grassroots participation and local control. For Lilienthal, decentralization solved the problem that led Friedrich Hayek to argue in the 1940s that private competition should be the organizing principle of all social activity. Hayek took the example of Nazi Germany to indicate that planning simply could not occur in contemporary society without descent into anti-democratic means; social interests conflicted too deeply for national democratic processes to resolve them.[14] Lilienthal, however, maintained that the New Deal's alphabet soup of agencies and autonomous corporations reconciled planning with democracy. Autonomous public agencies were effective instruments of planning and reform, he argued, and more democratic than Congress or other centralized political bodies, which he derided as "Big Government."[15]

As he left public employment, Lilienthal adapted the idea of administrative decentralization to reason about capital. He melded his experience in the TVA with the example of General Electric and the ideas of its president, Ralph Cordiner. In writing *Big Business*, Lilienthal read GE publications that highlighted the company's subcontracting relationships with tens of thousands of suppliers. "Through G-E subcontracts," the company explained, "small businesses get into defense production, [and] small communities stay economically healthy."[16] Cordiner, a radical opponent of unions and taxation, argued for

FIGURE 1.1. In 1952, General Motors published an abridged edition of Lilienthal's book *Big Business* and distributed it to 100,000 employees. (General Motors Media Archive)

decentralization in broad ethical and political terms. He insisted that corporations should foster individual responsibility among their employees: managers should have no assistants, and individuals, not committees, should make all decisions within the company. Moreover, corporations should reject central planning. As president, Cordiner broke GE into dozens of departments and divisions that produced their own plans and budgets, and he called each division a "family of businesses."

Cordiner's vision of individuals and departments relating through contract and competition fused a traditional managerial opposition to workers' collective action with a Cold War concept of individual freedom. He invoked the specters of Soviet planning and British "Socialist-Labor planners" to claim that central planning and command were rigid, ineffective, and destructive to individuals. "Decentralization, on the other hand, implies freedom for individu als everywhere in the organization to act on the basis of their knowledge," he contended. Not only was such a system ethically superior, but it also generated better information and elicited higher productivity. Lilienthal echoed Cordiner's arguments in *Big Business*, maintaining that organizational decentralization nurtured individual responsibility, spread economic benefits, and made giant corporations fit for democracy. His defense of big business and his career in government were of a piece; he defended "bigness" in both sectors, arguing that large organizations simply needed to assume decentralized forms.[17]

Lilienthal had set out to work overseas in 1950 but had gravitated toward lucrative banking and publishing contracts that enmeshed him in domestic private enterprise. In 1953, having attained recognition among bankers and businessmen, he found a chance to go abroad.[18] The opportunity came through Milo Perkins, a friend from New Deal days. Perkins had been a successful burlap bag manufacturer and jute speculator in Texas until Franklin D. Roosevelt appointed him assistant secretary of agriculture in 1935. Working under Henry Wallace, he designed the national food stamp program and helped create the school lunch program, enabling poor people to buy agricultural surpluses that would otherwise have rotted on the market. Perkins and Wallace went on to lead the federal Board of Economic Warfare from 1941 to 1943, diverting economic resources from the Axis powers and planning a postwar economic order.

Halfway through the war, however, Perkins found himself unemployed; he and Wallace lost their jobs in 1943 for publicly maligning the secretary of commerce. Perkins decided to return to private business, this time as an international economic and management consultant. In 1944, he began advising US corporations on investment in Latin America and Europe.[19] Traveling through the Andean region in 1951 on behalf of Standard Oil, Perkins stopped for a few days in the city of Cali, Colombia. There he met José Castro Borrero, the former mayor and the regional head of the Asociación Nacional de Industriales (ANDI), the Colombian equivalent of the National Association of Manufacturers. Castro guided Perkins around Cali, introducing him to the area's leading businessmen, farmers, cattle ranchers, and politicians. The city lay in the center of the Valle del Cauca, a long river valley formed by the Cauca River, and the physical setting reminded Perkins of the Tennessee Valley. He and Castro discussed the TVA during the visit, and after two years of correspondence, Perkins approached Lilienthal to ask if he would conduct a study of the Cauca Valley. Lilienthal agreed on the condition that he receive a formal invitation from the Colombian head of state, which Castro quickly arranged. In 1954, Lilienthal and his wife, Helen, sailed into the port of Buenaventura, and Lilienthal began a new career as an advisor peddling lessons from the TVA.[20]

Lilienthal and the businessmen of the Cauca Valley found that they were enormously like-minded, and they formed an alliance in 1954 with lasting consequences for Colombia and the United States. Together they helped to reorder the landscape, economy, and class relations of the Cauca Valley. They facilitated the rise of economics and management education in Colombia. Most importantly, they modified the practice of governance in Colombia, promoting a distinctive vision of state decentralization. The CVC quickly became a favorite project of the World Bank, the US government, Colombian officials, and Lilienthal himself. Its success, in their terms, gave them the confidence and notoriety to take its lessons abroad.

———

Colombia is a country of regions. Nearly all the population lives in the Andean and Caribbean sections of the country, which are themselves divided by three segments of the Andes: the western, central, and eastern cordilleras. The Cauca Valley lies between the western and central cordilleras, extending from the department of Cauca in the south, northward through the department of Valle del Cauca and finally into the department of Caldas. Cali, one of Colombia's four major cities and the capital of the department of Valle, sits in the middle (maps 1.1 and 1.2). During the colonial period, this area was a center of Colombian slavery, and over the second half of the nineteenth century, sugar production became the area's leading economic activity. Although the Cauca Valley produced important political families before the twentieth century, the grueling task of crossing the Andes left it relatively isolated from Colombia's other population centers in the central and eastern cordilleras and the Atlantic coast. The opening of the Panama Canal and the growth of land and air transportation during the twentieth century transformed the Cauca Valley into a national industrial center, producing for new domestic markets and exporting goods through the Pacific port of Buenaventura.[21]

While Valle businessmen took great interest in the TVA, they sold Lilienthal on the Cauca Valley precisely because it was not much like the Tennessee Valley. New Dealers had gone to the Tennessee Valley because it was one of the poorest parts of the United States. The Cauca Valley resembled the

MAP 1.1. Major Mountains and Rivers of Colombia

Tennessee Valley in that it possessed a river, and it harbored considerable class and regional inequality within the departments. But the central department of Valle, which quickly became the primary area of CVC activity, was one of the richest departments in Colombia. The valley was in fact one of just three regions in the world that could produce sugarcane year-round, and by the time Lilienthal arrived, it was home to tremendous agricultural wealth. Both Lilienthal and Castro Borrero argued that the Cauca Valley was the perfect site for a regional development corporation precisely because it was so likely to produce a success story that other regions and countries would want to emulate.[22]

In Lilienthal's view, one of the Cauca Valley's great advantages was its capitalist class. The area's leading businessmen identified powerfully with the Valle region and related to the government in Bogotá as provincial advocates. At the same time, they were cosmopolitan in their education, business activities, and social relationships. Harold Eder, who accompanied Lilienthal throughout his 1954 visit, was general manager of the sugar company Manuelita and heir to one of the country's largest agro-industrial fortunes. His grandfather, James M. "Santiago" Eder, had immigrated to Colombia during the early 1860s, having already been an immigrant once in his life. Born to a family of German Jewish descent in present-day Latvia, Santiago Eder had moved with his family to the United States in 1851 at the age of twelve. He became a US citizen and after graduating from Harvard Law School, he traveled to Colombia to pursue a career in business. Settling in Valle, he bought the Manuelita estate from the family of novelist Jorge Isaacs, imported machinery from Europe, and created the country's first capital-intensive sugar operation. Buying up adjacent properties, Eder became one of Colombia's largest sugar manufacturers. He introduced new methods of cultivating coffee, tobacco, and indigo, and he formed business partnerships in coffee exporting, transportation, print media, and banking. His grandson, Harold Eder, spent his teenage years in the United States, where much of the extended family still lived, and earned a BA in electrical engineering from MIT. After pursuing graduate studies at the London School of Economics, he returned to Valle, and in 1930 took over Manuelita.[23]

Eder and José Castro Borrero were two of the regional leaders of ANDI who impressed Lilienthal. Bernardo Garcés Córdoba, the "genius of the Cauca Valley" in Lilienthal's estimation, was an economist educated in Canada, the United States, Great Britain, and France.[24] Valle governor Diego Garcés Giraldo was the grandson of Julio Giraldo, a transplanted Antioquian businessman whose children had married into Cali's richest families. Educated abroad, he had commercial interests in agriculture, real estate, banking, drug manufacturing and distribution, sugar and alcohol production, and trade in imported goods.[25] Manuel Carvajal had completed high school in Brussels and served as minister of mines under President Laureano Gómez. He was manager and co-owner of Carvajal & Cía., a printing, publishing, and office supply firm that became Colombia's first multinational corporation.[26]

Lilienthal's hosts were products of nineteenth-century alliances forged between the Cauca Valley's wealthiest mining and agricultural families, on the one hand, and immigrant merchants and businessmen from the departments of Antioquia and Caldas, the United States, and Europe, on the other. Their families had grown intertwined through a century of marital and business partnerships; the names Borrero, Caicedo, Carvajal, Eder, Garcés, Giraldo, and Lloreda formed complex family trees and appeared everywhere in government and civic spheres. Valle's largest companies were family enterprises wholly owned by these men, their relatives, and their business partners.[27]

Among the landowners and businessmen in the Cauca Valley, the leaders of ANDI took unusual interest in raising regional productivity. Their peers were, of course, hardly seignorial lords. Since the mid-nineteenth century, public property in the Cauca Valley had been cleared and improved by small settlers or *colonos*, who in turn suffered usurpation by wealthy land entrepreneurs. Whether working the land themselves or appropriating the fruits of others' labor, both eagerly produced for markets near and far and understood the essential value of improving the land. At the highest level, moreover, Colombian officials beginning in the 1880s embraced the positivist tradition that promised "order and progress" through the purportedly scientific application of technical knowledge.[28]

Nonetheless, during the first half of the twentieth century, there was no general agreement on what progress entailed in the Cauca Valley or the specific investments needed to attain it. The leaders of ANDI advocated a massive program of public investment to raise regional productivity. They took up the mission from an earlier generation and ultimately fit themselves into one of the great global drives of the twentieth century. Beginning in the 1920s, a small minority of Valle capitalists had developed hopes of using scientific research to expand and diversify agricultural production. Departmental officials including Secretary of Industry Ciro Molina Garcés attracted agricultural missions from Britain and Puerto Rico during the late 1920s, and Molina created an agricultural experiment station in the city of Palmira in 1928. In 1934, the departmental secretary of agriculture, Demetrio García Vásquez, championed the creation of the Escuela Superior de Agricultura Tropical in Cali; a decade later, the school moved to nearby Palmira and became the National University's Faculty of Agronomy.[29] A 1936 drought inspired headier ambitions to control the region's water supply. Hydraulic engineering promised to raise agricultural productivity and simultaneously generate electric power for industrial expansion. From 1943 to 1952, Valle became the site of seven studies by US and Colombian engineering firms. They proposed a set of regional development policies that, within a few short decades, became worldwide symbols of dystopic master planning: damming the Cauca River and its tributaries to generate electricity, channeling the waters to irrigate dry lands, draining flooded properties, and erecting flood protection along the banks. By the 1950s, ANDI emerged as the principal advocate of these plans. The 1952 ANDI General Assembly in Cali called on the departmental government to create an "Autonomous Planning Board" with broad powers to direct the region's economic development. Composed of capitalists from Valle's principal economic sectors, the board would research natural resources, design projects for their exploitation, raise domestic and foreign capital to establish new businesses, and construct electricity, irrigation, and drainage systems.[30]

This was the moment when Perkins passed through the Cauca Valley. His 1951 conversation with José Castro Borrero was in fact part of a broad lobbying effort through which ANDI enlisted US support. By 1953, Castro had secured the interest of John C. Cady, director of the US foreign aid program Point IV in Colombia. Cady met with ANDI representatives, engineers, and local and national officials and concluded that "Valle has one of the greatest development potentials in this country if not in all of Latin America." Echoing ANDI, he lamented that the region suffered from "an atrociously low rate of productivity," inadequate power supply, and lack of drainage and irrigation. The region, he concluded, needed a long-term, planned investment program and a new "'authority' mechanism" to carry it out.[31]

When Lilienthal arrived in Cali, he found an organized, influential group of businessmen espousing his own beliefs with incipient backing from the US government. Advising in such circumstances was an easy job.

———

Lilienthal's principal contributions to the CVC were his name and connections. Indeed, Cali's capitalists needed political leverage more than ideas. The obstacle they faced was the national government's reluctance to devolve funds and state powers to an already prosperous region and to provincial businessmen with no strong political ties to the capital. The very forms of decentralization that the CVC embodied turned out to be the most controversial element of the program. For capitalists struggling to wrest power from Bogotá, a foreign advisor was a political weapon, and Lilienthal played his role well.

During his visit, Lilienthal met with the head of state, General Gustavo Rojas Pinilla, and insisted on the importance of administrative decentralization within the country's development program. Colombia's 1886 Constitution had transformed a federal republic into a politically centralized state;

the president appointed departmental governors, who in turn appointed mayors. The national government had jurisdiction over mines and public lands that republican states had once controlled, and the president had the right to declare national states of siege. By the turn of the twentieth century, Bogotá financed and administered schools, prisons, the army, and the judicial system. The centralism of the Colombian government derived not only from the constitution but also from the nature of Rojas's regime. His government was a military dictatorship that had come to power through a 1953 coup, temporarily ending a century of national political domination by Colombia's Liberal and Conservative Parties. During the late 1940s, those parties had lost legitimacy as they became vehicles for La Violencia, the extraordinary wave of political violence that lasted into the mid-1960s and killed 200,000 Colombians. When Rojas seized power, he did so with widespread popular consent, promising to end La Violencia and inaugurate a new era of peace and prosperity. To achieve those ends, he built a robust central government. He eliminated elected town councils and departmental assemblies, and he set out to pacify the countryside with a nationally directed program of infrastructure development.[32]

The idea of an autonomous regional development corporation did not simply defy the formal political centralism of the Colombian state. It challenged one of the primary forms of decentralization that did exist. Colombia's 1886 Constitution had paired political centralization with administrative decentralization. Departmental governments thus continued to administer monopolies controlling liquor, tobacco, tolls, and an assortment of local products. But ANDI did not want to vest new powers in the established political jurisdiction of the department. It imagined a new jurisdiction: the region defined by a river valley. That was a jurisdiction for which no governing authority existed, and Cali's industrialists proposed to conjure one from the landowners, manufacturers, and bankers invested in the region.[33]

While visiting Colombia, Lilienthal nonetheless learned of practices that resembled his own notion of decentralization. Just as the Roosevelt administration had used autonomous public agencies to build the New Deal state, the Colombian government had met the crisis of the Great Depression by forming new public financial institutions under autonomous or private administration. The Caja Agraria, a state bank providing credit to farmers, and the Instituto de Crédito Territorial, a national housing lender, were autonomous public agencies. The Fondo Cafetero was a public financial institution administered by the Coffee Growers' Federation, a private business association or *gremio*. Lilienthal met with representatives of the Caja Agraria and the Fondo Cafetero in 1954 and noted approvingly that "each is set up and operating almost entirely as a private corporation would be."[34] Extending the example of the Fondo Cafetero was simple enough to imagine. Lilienthal's partners, after all, represented one of Colombia's most powerful *gremios*, ANDI. Moreover, they were local leaders from a historically isolated region. Despite the national government's formal powers, the Colombian state had never been powerful in Cali, and Valle's businessmen identified foremost as regional boosters. Colombians assimilated Lilienthal's message of administrative decentralization through regional resentments and a distinctive set of national policy traditions.

While preparing his recommendation, Lilienthal lined up powerful allies abroad, most important among them Robert Garner, the vice president of the World Bank. Writing to Milo Perkins, Lilienthal relayed Garner's support for a "privately financed and manned development corporation" that could be a "demonstration project for Latin America." By this time, Perkins was living in Arizona, melding New Deal agricultural reform with home lawn care by developing and marketing "miracle grass" that could grow in harsh environments. Over the summer of 1954, the two men corresponded about Lilienthal's yard in Connecticut and their guarded hope for the decentralization of the Colombian state. While warning of "the tendency of all the South American countries to go a route of excessive statism," Perkins observed that "Colombia has done a better job [than others] of not going berserk on this front." By the end of the summer, they learned that Rojas had decided to publicize Lilienthal's report. "The recognition of President Rojas Pinilla," Perkins wrote, "now convinces me that he is a very discerning individual!"[35]

Lilienthal's 1954 report to Rojas fashioned lessons for Colombian development by amplifying technocratic elements of the New Deal. Recapitulating ANDI's program, he endorsed hydraulic engineering, electric power production, and technical reforms to soil and land use practices. He called on Rojas to establish an autonomous regional development authority to design and implement the measures in all three departments of the Cauca Valley. Invoking the TVA as a model, he explained that the new public authority required the full support of the national government as well as complete freedom from political control; it should operate independently of Bogotá and function like a private-sector corporation. The region's businessmen, he noted, demonstrated an admirable interest in mechanized production and intensive use of natural resources, making Valle fit for independent action.[36]

On October 22, 1954, Rojas delighted the old New Dealers by adopting Lilienthal's recommendations and creating the Corporación Autónoma Regional del Cauca (known in English as the Cauca Valley Corporation and in both languages as the CVC). Heeding Lilienthal's advice, Rojas granted the public body a special legal status: the CVC became Colombia's first autonomous corporation. Creating the CVC required changing the Colombian constitution to allow such agencies to exist and perform functions previously reserved for the central government. The constitutional reform took place in 1954 under the guidance of Diego Tobón Arbeláez, the vice-president of ANDI and a Medellín lawyer who had written his doctoral thesis in 1939 on administrative law in Europe and the United States.[37] Rojas appointed Bernardo Garcés Córdoba as the CVC's executive director, and Diego Garcés Giraldo became chairman of the board.[38]

Until the CVC's charter was approved, however, the corporation's specific powers remained unclear. In the interim, Lilienthal used his relationship with the World Bank to lean on the government. When Rojas received the board's proposed charter, Lilienthal met with him and the Council of Ministers to urge its adoption, and informed Rojas that so much as modifying its terms could incite international retribution. Threatening the head of state, Lilienthal explained that if the government rejected the principle of decentralization and subjected the CVC to "small-gauge and petty political pressures," the decision could "dilute if not destroy the World Bank's interest in the enterprise."[39]

The resulting charter was a remarkable document. Drafted by the board and issued as a presidential decree in 1955, it devolved sweeping powers to the corporation. The members of the board could sign international loan contracts, take land through eminent domain, adjudicate the use of water and public lands, charge rates for water and electricity, buy property, and manage assets. The corporation acquired equally wide-ranging responsibilities for land reclamation, electric power production and distribution, conservation, forestry, and the development of agriculture, livestock, mining, communications, transportation, and industry. The capitalists who made up the board were to operate with little national oversight and run the corporation as they would a private-sector company. Indeed, the charter established the CVC as a public enterprise formally committed to capital accumulation in order to finance its own expansion.

The charter's provisions revealed a tension at the heart of the mixed economy. On the one hand, the CVC expanded public responsibilities in the Cauca Valley. Before 1954, Bogotá had no regional development program and could scarcely have implemented one in any case. The state assumed those responsibilities by re-creating itself in the image of private enterprise, decentralizing public functions, and vesting public powers in the leaders of a private business association. Furthermore, the charter limited the CVC to providing infrastructure to support private entrepreneurship, demarcating industrial and agricultural investment as the province of private capital. Counterintuitively, the CVC charter enshrined the principles that the national government should not itself guide economic development, and that no public body should undertake most forms of productive activity. Lilienthal endorsed that division of labor. As he noted, the New Deal had never demonstrated the independent value of state action but had shown the necessity of properly combining public and private initiative.[40]

The production of the charter made clear Lilienthal's role as a source of prestige and political leverage. His ideas were so similar to those of the board that he simply urged them on as they sent him drafts of the document in 1955.[41] Nonetheless, Colombian newspapers, politicians, and CVC leaders routinely referred to the Cauca Valley program as "Plan Lilienthal," and the CVC's consultant on Wall Street quickly became a national symbol of economic development in Colombia.[42] In 1956, Palmira's Antonio Ricaurte School, named for a military hero of Colombian independence, sought to rechristen itself the Lilienthal Institute of Commerce, stopping only when Lilienthal personally declined the honor.[43]

The former TVA chairman not only lent the CVC his name, but he also provided a direct line to Wall Street and the World Bank. Just after the charter was approved, Lilienthal created his own consulting firm, the Development & Resources Corporation (D&R), with financial backing from Lazard Frères. The CVC contracted with D&R for engineering work as well as the less tangible service of opening doors to funders in the North Atlantic.[44] D&R taught Bernardo Garcés Córdoba and the board to secure financing from the World Bank, Point IV, and the Export-Import Bank. Garcés Córdoba coached his colleagues on how to deal successfully with Lazard's bankers.[45] And Lilienthal intervened directly with the World Bank, helping plan a 1955 mission to advise the CVC.[46] By early 1956, the World Bank had designated the CVC as the top priority within its national plan for Colombia, identifying the corporation as a model of rational planning and apolitical stability.[47]

———

Aside from his name and rolodex, Lilienthal chiefly offered the CVC his advice on management and administration. As he explained to Robert Garner:

> The economics and the engineering, the agricultural education and extension, and all the rest of the components of the program are vital; they are the flesh and blood setting. But the vital spark, the thing that can make it something of lasting and widespread meaning, that goes beyond the matter of dams and drainage and demand curves, etc., is on another level. It deals with an art of organization and management that encourages action at the grass roots, and stimulates individual initiative, and risk-taking, and individual responsibility.[48]

Lilienthal valued management as an activity with social and ethical significance. All of his work since the 1930s had stemmed from the conviction that

FIGURE 1.2. "The Cauca Valley Bible": A 1954 cartoon from *El País* in Cali shows a child telling his father, "Daddy, I bet you're still reading the Lilienthal Plan." Although Colombian capitalists designed the CVC, they found it convenient to present the corporation as the brainchild of a foreign advisor. Lilienthal quickly became the public face of the corporation. (*El País*)

people and nature required skilled handling to generate what he saw as progress: a world in which individuals responsibly channeled their energies, and
natural resources, including the atom itself, were harnessed and controlled to
meet human needs. He prized technical work but was never himself a techni-
cian; within the TVA, he was not an engineer, and in the AEC he was not a
physicist. He had been a manager for most of his career and in his most celebrated public positions.

All participants in economic programs required noneconomic explanations
of the value of their work—ideas "on another level" from material considerations. For Lilienthal, the Cold War provided one meaningful legitimation of
regional development. The realization of human and natural potential through
management provided another.

Lilienthal in fact proposed that management replace economics as the
guiding force in development programming. He contrasted decentralized
management with what he imagined as "careful, orderly, national economic
planning." The latter, he feared, was "too theoretical" to meet challenges that
were "essentially practical." Furthermore, he associated economic theory with
state centralism. National economic planning, he wrote, failed to "inculcate
and encourage individual initiative" and produced the "blighting effect of
overcentralization." He quoted Latin American historian Frank Tannenbaum,
a one-time Industrial Workers of the World organizer who had advised Mexican president Lázaro Cárdenas and helped design the US Farm Security Administration. Tannenbaum maligned national planning as "congenial even to
the most conservative Latin Americans, for to them the notion is old and inevitable. The government must do everything, for no one else will." He pre-
dicted that national planners would soon "discover that they have strengthened the central political machine at the expense of the localities and increased
the barriers to representative government and political stability."[49] Lilienthal
and Tannenbaum captured a common belief among US anticommunists,
whether McCarthyites, liberals, or former anarchists. Albert Waterston, the
World Bank's loan officer for Colombia during the 1950s, observed that during
the Marshall Plan years, no one at the World Bank believed in national planning. "[Economic] planning was a dirty word," he recalled, a tool of communists and fascists.[50] Lilienthal trumped Waterston, adding that it was unnecessary. Managers in regional organizations could design development programs,
relying on information from engineers and applied scientists.

Former TVA managers led D&R. Lilienthal himself served as chairman and
CEO, and he recruited Gordon R. Clapp as president. Clapp had been the
TVA's personnel director and general manager during the 1930s and had succeeded Lilienthal as chairman in 1946. He prided himself on directing the TVA
according to technocratic principles, arguing that "the authority of *knowledge*

in a program of this kind is the basis for its success." The job of a manager, he believed, was to insulate engineers and scientists from public pressure. In 1942, Clapp pushed through the construction of the Douglas Dam in Tennessee against local and congressional protest. Opponents warned that the dam would flood farmland; Clapp replied that those farms were the best site for a dam. Members of Congress balked, but after Pearl Harbor, with war production creating tremendous demand for electric power, they gave in and approved the project, displacing 201 landowners and 324 tenant farmers. Clapp considered the dam a triumph of technical knowledge over politics.[51]

Lilienthal and Clapp arrived in Colombia as evangelists for technocratic, decentralized management. Lilienthal, of course, had already tried to popularize his ideas in the United States, arguing that decentralization fostered grassroots democracy. But by the late 1940s, he and the TVA had come under attack at home for failing to live up to their promises. Writing in 1949, Philip Selznick captured what had become mounting criticism of the TVA, arguing that the agency's commitment to master planning and monumental works undermined its pursuit of democracy and environmental conservation. Lilienthal himself complained in 1953 that the TVA had spawned no imitators in the United States; he blamed the "Washington bureaucracy" for scuttling his idea.[52] Lilienthal had reached a dead end as a management propagandist within his own government.

Working in Colombia gave Lilienthal a new opportunity, this time using the CVC to popularize his ideas. As Hirschman later remarked, advisors rarely go abroad to reproduce what they have created at home. More often, they seek to fulfill dreams that they could not realize domestically.[53] For Lilienthal, however, the Colombian context altered the substance of his arguments. In the United States, he had championed not only decentralization and technical mastery but also grassroots participation, however false the promise. In Colombia, that commitment vanished. No one with any knowledge of the CVC's leadership could possibly believe that the corporation was a grassroots affair. When addressing Robert Garner or US audiences, Lilienthal called the CVC a locally controlled organization simply because its leaders were Colombian. But in Colombia itself, legitimations of the CVC and its administrative model necessarily took other forms.

Bernardo Garcés Córdoba, the CVC's executive director, defended decentralization on grounds that it made state action effective and facilitated technocratic decision-making. Writing in 1955 to the executive director of Rojas's National Planning Committee, Garcés addressed suspicions that decentralization would sap Bogotá's power. Latin American countries, he wrote, faced the challenges of internal diversity, poor communications, and weak central states, which together prevented national governments from competently addressing public problems. Lacking the familiarity and resources to develop sound plans for far-flung regions, central states tended to undertake projects such as single-purpose dams that controlled water flows but neglected or exacerbated other difficulties. By decentralizing their operations, national governments could in fact become more potent authorities, able to design and administer well-conceived, integrated regional plans.[54]

According to Garcés, decentralized public enterprise had the added benefit of evading civil service regulations. He depicted the civil service as a patronage system that undermined efficiency and quality, and publicly announced the CVC's intention to adopt private-sector systems of personnel management. The CVC, he explained in 1955, "must have full freedom to choose its personnel without subjection to external pressures; [and] to pay them according to their ability and efficacy, without regard to official [public-sector] pay scales."[55]

Decentralization, in Garcés's formulation, did not imply democratic decision-making or grassroots control. Experts should make policy, he believed, and regionally situated experts were simply the best qualified to do so. They directly experienced problems, observed public opinion, and therefore had the information necessary to divine and serve the public interest. Garcés's vision of policy making extended from the nineteenth-century positivist ethos, which assigned *técnicos* the responsibility of ensuring "order and progress." He never considered that the public should participate in designing or administering policy, nor did he recognize competing interests within a single region. Instead, Garcés conceived of a region as a natural unit defined geographically and believed that its physical attributes gave rise to shared human problems and a general public interest. Technical experts, regionally identified but professionally autonomous, became modern-day republican elites in his eyes, ideally equipped to intuit and serve that interest.

Garcés invoked the TVA as evidence that decentralization and technocracy could ameliorate the problems of a region. The New Deal was an ideal teaching tool; Colombians regarded it with respect but knew little about its functioning, allowing Garcés to portray it as he wished. In speaking to the National University's Faculty of Agronomy in Palmira, he depicted the Tennessee Valley as an idyllic region free of social conflict and ecological stress thanks to the skill and social sensitivity of the TVA's technical staff:

> The labor of the TVA has been to reestablish the community between man, earth, water, and forests. Its activity has essentially consisted in promoting a harmonious, rational exploitation of resources that accords with the interests of the entire population.... The principal merit of the TVA has been putting *técnicos* in intimate contact with the problems they must study and resolve, working near to the people and the land.[56]

In Garcés's depiction, local technocrats were ideal public authorities, and decentralization a tool to empower them.

José Castro Borrero, the regional head of ANDI, laid out a sweeping argument for the CVC in a July 1955 speech at Cali's Biblioteca Departamental. Castro argued for the transcendental value of imposing order on the natural world. Natural resources, he explained, "were put on earth by God" to serve human beings, who needed to overcome "deficiencies of a moral, spiritual, and intellectual order." Amalgamating Catholic and humanist understandings of human suffering, Castro held that hydraulic engineering and intensified capitalist production were means to alleviate profound human afflictions. "Monumental as it might be," he told the audience, "a dam taken alone is infinitely inferior to a man's ignorance and pain." Quoting a CVC engineering report, he charged that the nation had "not only an economic but a social and Christian duty" to promote economic development in the Cauca Valley.

Castro linked the goal of "moral, spiritual, and intellectual" improvement to an economic program of export-oriented industrialization. Export-led growth flew in the face of Latin American import substitution strategies during the 1950s, but support for industrialization was common enough. Castro described a chain of problems that he believed had obstructed Colombia's industrial development. First, the prices of national manufactures were too high to compete in international markets. The excessive cost of commodities came from the limited scale of production; manufacturing needed to expand in order to lower unit prices. In turn, he argued that the principal factor limiting industrial expansion was a lack of investment, which he attributed to the country's high cost of living. The Colombian middle class spent the great majority of its income on food and housing, he explained, leaving little to invest in production. Industrialization, then, depended on freeing up some of the national income for capital investment. Castro proposed to do this by raising productivity in the agricultural and livestock sectors, lowering the price of food. Through hydraulic works and efficient exploitation of natural resources, the Cauca Valley could become a breadbasket for the country, reduce the proportion of national income going to food, and thus foment industrial expansion. The CVC's overriding mission, in this scheme, was to raise rural productivity. Castro proudly noted that the region had already produced one model of efficient production and price stability: the sugar industry, which had adopted methods of "technification and industrial exploitation."[57]

While Lilienthal assailed national planning and economic theory, Castro recognized that the TVA was in fact a model of technocratic master planning, albeit on a regional scale. He praised the example and called for comprehensive regional planning in the Cauca Valley, incorporating economics, engineering, chemistry, architecture, and agronomy. Calling for the creation of new university programs in economics and public administration, he suggested that the CVC could provide research and training opportunities for Colombian students and professors.

Having initially justified the program in transcendental terms, Castro finally added that it would serve political and social ends specific to Colombia during the 1950s. Political violence had been the central preoccupation of Colombian life for the better part of a decade, and Castro argued that economic development could provide a new public purpose to displace the "political hatreds" of La Violencia. At the same time, it could stave off "revolutionary and anarchic" social conflict. According to Castro, popular revolt was rooted in a lack of education and the experience of economic devastation from flooding. Workers and campesinos could become revolutionaries or businessmen depending on the ideological direction they received and the adequacy of regional hydraulic systems. The CVC, on this logic, offered economic security and incentives for class collaboration to the poor. In dampening social conflict, it would also protect the rich.[58]

Castro's arguments for the CVC emphasized a few concerns irrelevant to Lilienthal, notably spiritual enlightenment and the problem of political violence. Castro embraced economics as a part of planning and sought to build up the discipline in Colombia. And while he agreed with Lilienthal that development could prevent revolution, he thought of social conflict in purely local terms: the rich in the Cauca Valley needed protection from the poor. International communism figured nowhere in his talk. Castro and Lilienthal set out a common agenda for the CVC, aiming to raise regional productivity using hydroelectric works, land reclamation, and new methods of production. Where they differed, particularly on the value of economics, the CVC's Colombian leadership held sway. Lilienthal, after all, was simply writing letters from Manhattan.

———

As Castro described a new era of national peace to his audience, he went so far as to imagine a bipartisan political order not much different from the National Front, the coalition government that ruled Colombia from 1958 to 1974. He envisioned a system in which the Liberal and Conservative Parties, restored to power, would choose their candidates from rosters drawn up by the opposing party. Politicians, motivated by self-interest, would moderate their views in order to secure nominations, effectively eliminating the far right and left from national politics. Invoking Lilienthal's old slogan from TVA days, as well as Colombia's Revolución en Marcha of the 1930s, Castro declared that a new political order would revive the spirit of "democracy on the march."[59]

In July 1955, with a military dictatorship ruling Colombia and some of the country's leading political figures living in exile, few could imagine that Liberals and Conservatives would soon enter into a sixteen-year power-sharing agreement, divide all national positions between them, and bar all other parties from office. Castro's vision of the coming political order presaged the powerful identification that the CVC developed with the National Front, and indeed the role that the corporation's leaders played in establishing the new government. Although Rojas had created the CVC and approved its charter, his relationship with the organization disintegrated as he refused to honor the commitments he had made. To realize the expansive powers that the CVC possessed on paper, the corporation's leaders turned to pressuring Rojas and ultimately committed themselves to toppling the government. The birth of the National Front secured the CVC's power in the Cauca Valley and made the autonomous corporation a model for national initiatives during the 1960s.

In retrospect, the CVC's advocates considered it odd that Rojas had agreed to create the corporation at all. Ideologically he shared little with ANDI and brazenly opposed its national leadership in disputes over fiscal, monetary, and trade policies.[60] Executive director Bernardo Garcés Córdoba suspected that the president "never intended to go beyond a propaganda gesture or, more likely . . . once he realized what the Corporation implied in the way of delegating authority he profoundly disliked the whole idea." Hirschman, who served on Rojas's National Planning Council and later consulted for the CVC, thought the administration sabotaged the organization because its leaders were "known to be out of sympathy" with his government, and because he "favored the poorer Eastern provinces of the country."[61] Indeed, when Lilienthal first visited Colombia in 1954, Rojas had sent him to the eastern plains, urging him to focus his efforts there.[62] Lilienthal's own machinations suggest another reason for the conflicts that followed the CVC's birth: Rojas had only approved the corporation's charter under duress, facing a credible threat of retaliation from the World Bank.

From late 1955 through Rojas's fall in May 1957, the CVC weathered merciless attacks from the national government. Rojas removed Diego Garcés Giraldo as governor of Valle in October 1955, several months after Garcés refused to contribute departmental funds to the president's political party, the Movimiento de Acción Popular.[63] More importantly, Rojas simply refused to appropriate national funds that he promised to the CVC. As the corporation struggled to survive financial strangulation, it found steadfast support in the US embassy. The new Point IV director, Walter Howe, made the CVC his regional partner, jointly administering all US assistance programs in the three departments of the Cauca Valley. In 1955, the US government signed contracts directly with the CVC, rather than the national or departmental governments, to develop education and agricultural extension initiatives. To make those contracts possible, Point IV, US Ambassador Philip W. Bonsal, and the CVC persuaded the departmental governments and the national Ministry of Agriculture to turn over all regional extension programs to the corporation.[64]

The CVC's leaders wanted to direct more than agricultural extension, however. The real source of authority in the Cauca Valley, they believed, was control of electric power. William Hayes, a CVC consultant and former assistant general manager of the TVA, explained the necessity of monopolizing the electric power supply, arguing that control of energy had been the basis of the TVA's influence in the Tennessee Valley.[65] Based on that advice, the CVC spent its early years fighting the Rojas administration for two reforms. First, it demanded that the national government surrender its shares in Valle's main power company, the Central Hidroeléctrica del Río Anchicayá (CHIDRAL). CHIDRAL was a public enterprise jointly owned by the national government, the departmental government of Valle, and the municipal government of Cali.[66] The controlling interest rested with Bogotá, and the CVC demanded those shares for itself. Second, the CVC called on the national government to support construction of the Calima Dam, a new hydroelectric installation that the corporation had designed and hoped to administer.

Over the course of nearly two years, Rojas obstructed both of these demands.[67] The conflict dealt in technicalities, but its length and intensity arose from the underlying dispute: both Rojas and the CVC were fighting to define the powers and structure of the state.[68] Rojas refused to give up the CHIDRAL shares and in fact proposed to expand CHIDRAL under national control instead of building Calima under CVC authority. He denied that there was any need for Calima, accusing the CVC of inflating its projections of the demand for electricity. The CVC responded by hiring Albert Hirschman and his consulting partner, George Kalmanoff, to conduct a new study of electricity demand, which confirmed the corporation's figures.[69]

Rojas, however, refused to concede. He repeatedly blocked national funding to the CVC, and by July 1956, the corporation could not pay its employees.[70] The entire board resigned in protest, and the CVC spent the next year organizing a domestic and international assault on the regime.[71] Bernardo Garcés Córdoba began by summoning Lilienthal to Colombia. The CVC's advisor met with Rojas on July 11, and the next day he staged a public scene, threatening to cut D&R's contract because of the government's intransigence. In October, D&R briefly allowed its contract to expire. In response, forty-nine Colombian organizations and officials representing banks, businesses, newspapers, radio stations, universities, civic organizations, and exclusive social clubs issued a letter promising to press Rojas to fund the CVC.[72]

While Bogotá withheld national funds, the CVC looked for alternative sources of income. The US aid program Point IV secured money through Public Law 480, and a local bank manager authorized overdrafts out of political sympathy.[73] The corporation's most important income stream was also the most improbable: the CVC began collecting taxes. It administered a gasoline tax and created a new property tax at the rate of 4/1,000. The board came up with the idea of taxing property in the department of Valle in 1955, and Rojas approved the measure in July 1956. Both Hirschman and Garcés Córdoba believed that Rojas expected the tax to incite local resistance and kill the CVC.[74] Indeed, many businessmen and cattle ranchers outside ANDI's circles protested furiously, arguing that the tax would destroy local enterprise. Wielding invented figures, they accused the CVC of bleeding taxpayers to overpay an army of foreign engineers. But however much they complained, the corporation had acquired the power to tax. It stayed alive on the revenues and permanently retained this form of state power.[75]

Meanwhile, the CVC's foreign backers turned the corporation's grievances into international liabilities for Rojas. D&R, Lazard Frères, and the World Bank developed a unified position that the Colombian government needed to fund Calima and service its backlog of commercial trade debts. The World Bank's director of operations for the Western Hemisphere warned the Colombian ambassador that Rojas's treatment of the CVC and D&R would have consequences for US-Colombian relations. The Bank discouraged Lazard from investing in Colombia and simultaneously declared its own moratorium on new loans until the government paid down its debt.[76] In January 1957, the acting director of Point IV recommended that the US government stop automatically renewing aid contracts with Colombia, listing among his concerns the "very precarious situation" of the CVC.[77] For its part, D&R allowed its contract to expire in March 1957.[78] Throughout 1956 and 1957, Garcés Córdoba bombarded the Rojas administration with letters relaying threats from Lilienthal and the World Bank. He fed national newspapers information on international interest in the CVC, and when *Time* magazine inquired about Lilienthal's status as an advisor, he cannily referred the reporter to Rojas's National Planning Committee for comment.[79] As pressure mounted in late 1956, Luis Morales Gómez, the Treasury minister, tried to secure money for the CVC, and in January 1957 he visited New York in hopes of settling the trade debt. According to Garcés Córdoba, the minister harbored no deep commitment to the CVC but recognized the need "to retrieve the international position of Colombia."[80]

Morales Gómez failed to change national policy. On April 15, 1957, the national government told the CVC that the corporation would have no role in the production and distribution of electric power, and two days later, Garcés Córdoba resigned as executive director. The members of the board—themselves replacements for the first board that had resigned a year earlier—prevented Rojas from appointing the head of CHIDRAL as executive director by announcing that they, too, would resign, leaving the CVC with no board to receive Garcés's resignation.[81]

The public revolt of Valle's leading businessmen, following the rebukes by Lilienthal, D&R, the World Bank, and Point IV, contributed to a massive wave of protest against the government. Rojas had repressed communists and student movements from the start, and by April 1957 he had also alienated the country's major business associations, church leaders, anticommunist trade unionists, and Liberal and Conservative leaders who had tried to work within the regime. The first week of May saw massive student protests and a national capital strike, with banks, stores, and industries shutting their doors. Less than a month after Garcés Córdoba submitted his resignation, Rojas himself resigned the presidency.[82]

The CVC had hardly acted alone in toppling Rojas, but the notoriety of its leaders as opponents of the dictatorship earned them respect in the National Front. By November 1957, the transitional government had begun transferring its CHIDRAL shares to the CVC, and in 1958, Bogotá devolved to the CVC the portion of the national liquor tax destined for electrification in the Cauca Valley.[83] Harold Eder, who had never held public office in his life, became Colombia's minister of development in December 1957. Bernardo Garcés Córdoba, back at work as the CVC's executive director, expected Eder to be frustrated by "the inefficiency of public servants" but nonetheless rejoiced at new political order.[84]

Looking beyond Bogotá, Garcés Córdoba rapidly reestablished ties with the World Bank and D&R. Writing to Lilienthal, Clapp, and Waterston, he insisted that the CVC needed a token Bank loan to produce results before the public grew impatient. Moreover, the national government needed the symbolism of international financing to legitimate itself during the political transition. The future of Latin American democracy, he wrote, depended on the success of the National Front.[85] The World Bank immediately resumed activity in Colombia, financing the expansion of CVC-controlled CHIDRAL in 1958 and extending the first of two loans for Calima in 1960.[86] D&R quickly renewed its contract with the CVC, and Lilienthal congratulated his client on the "enormous increase in the prestige of Colombia."[87]

The CVC had endured two years of political strife and risked its own destruction, but through that process, backed by the US government, the World Bank, Lilienthal, and D&R, it won control of electric power in Valle and

FIGURE 1.3. CVC executive director Bernardo Garcés Córdoba (*second from right*) stands with CVC engineers at the site of the Calima Dam, circa 1960. (*Génesis y desarrollo de una visión de progreso* [Cali: CVC, 2004], 133)

secured its autonomy from Bogotá. In achieving those goals, the CVC made its version of decentralization an established practice of governance in Colombia.

———

In the Cauca Valley during the 1950s, decentralization represented a way of building a developmental state within the constraints of a discredited political order, a usurping capitalist class, a government with no effective reach beyond the capital, and an anticommunist fear of central planning. The corporation's birth illuminated a distinguishing characteristic of midcentury development programs. In areas from agrarian reform to housing policy to economics education, the Colombian government assumed broad new responsibilities by ceding authority to local, regional, and private institutions. It seemed the only strategy possible.

The CVC's version of decentralization was one among several that emerged across the twentieth century. Conceived by men who spent their lives moving between government and private enterprise, it reflected a vision of the two realms as not just compatible but comparable; Lilienthal considered the state and the corporation to be structural analogues and regarded managers as legitimate stewards of the state. Cali's capitalists had a jaundiced view of the national government, but they remade the state on a regional scale in the image of for-profit, private enterprise. Within Colombia, the mobilization of private enterprise as a model or instrument of government was already embedded in Depression-era economic policy, which had placed a major public financial institution in the hands of the Coffee Growers' Federation. But the CVC differed from the Fondo Cafetero. Not only did the corporation seize an unprecedented range of public powers, but it also invented a fundamentally new jurisdiction in Colombian governance: the region, purportedly defined by nature itself, and endowed by nature with unique challenges that no existing level of government could resolve. By the late 1950s, the CVC's twin impulses toward regional devolution and privatization constituted one distinctive, influential notion of decentralization.

The CVC not only established a new practice of decentralization, but the circumstances of its birth also gave the idea new legitimacy. The assaults on the CVC by an increasingly unpopular dictator lent credence to the idea that national political power was corrupting and destabilizing, and that economic development programs should operate independently of the government. When Rojas removed Diego Garcés Giraldo as governor of Valle, Point IV director Walter Howe feared that the decision would hurt the CVC. Bernardo Garcés Córdoba immediately reassured him. "[The] CVC," he explained, "was instituted precisely in order to free development plans from the uncertainties arising from political and similar influences."[88] Garcés's narrow conception of politics masked the fact that the corporation owed its very existence to extraordinary mobilizations of political power. Valle's capitalists and their international allies showed themselves willing to threaten and harm the Colombian government during the 1950s, and in doing so, they saved the corporation from imminent destruction. Yet they persistently denied the political nature of their work, rhetorically equating politics only with dictatorship, venal partisanship, and overreaching central power. By that definition, regional autonomy and private initiative became appealing safeguards against politics.

The CVC's notion of apolitical autonomy became embedded in new, equally time-bound definitions of democracy. In the United States, Lilienthal had argued that decentralization reconciled planning with democratic governance; in Colombia, the CVC's founders tied the corporation's fortunes to the birth of the National Front. The transit from the Tennessee Valley to the Cauca Valley emptied the concept of democracy of any association with "the grass roots." Democracy in the CVC's terms involved the ascent of autonomous regional technocracies and a highly constrained system of electoral competition between two parties. For Cali's industrialists, that arrangement seemed a democratic path between authoritarianism and uncontrolled partisan violence. The deeply compromised political system emerging in Colombia represented a democratic innovation of its time, forged in the crucibles of the Great Depression, the Second World War, La Violencia, and the early Cold War. In its systematic exclusions, it bore the marks of its moment and makers, and in time, it came to symbolize antidemocratic rot to critics who reimagined the practices of regional autonomy, private delegation, and democracy itself.

For the time being, however, the National Front promised great things. In 1958, Colombia's new government took shape and ushered in a period of economic and social reform that gave the CVC national significance. The corporation became a model for regional development corporations across Colombia, and the national government celebrated it as a vehicle of planned progress. In the Cauca Valley, the powers that the CVC secured in the 1950s made it the face of the developmental state. By the 1970s, the power and example of the decentralized corporation had reordered the political economy of the region and the very terms in which political economy was discussed.

2

Land Reform in Local Hands and Local Minds

WHAT COULD A decentralized state do? In the Cauca Valley, the CVC performed the iconic functions of the developmental state, giving the national government unprecedented reach and power. The autonomous corporation was in fact the public authority that administered Colombia's 1961 land reform law in one of Latin America's richest agricultural regions. No policy more powerfully symbolized the promise of midcentury developmentalism, and none depended more systematically on local intermediaries whose skills and relationships undergirded every property negotiation, cadastral survey, and forcible eviction. The CVC translated the letter of the law into facts on the ground.

The CVC also interpreted the law and sealed its fate in the Cauca Valley. Crafted in the wake of the Cuban revolution, Colombia's agrarian reform aimed to show Latin Americans that capitalist development could deliver economic redistribution and social justice. It was a model anticommunist initiative that made Colombia a showcase of the Alliance for Progress, and when it eventually failed to redistribute much of anything, it became one of the great fiascos of the Alliance. In history and popular memory, the law fell victim to landowner resistance and competing government commitments during the 1960s, and met its death a decade later, when the national state turned on the law and gutted its implementation.[1] But in the Cauca Valley, something very different happened. Land reform failed to redistribute property not because landowners obstructed it, but because they captured it and used it for entirely different ends. The CVC and its international allies insinuated themselves into the Alliance for Progress and scrupulously applied the law along the Cauca River, employing it as an instrument to raise productivity at the expense of equality. Land reform provided the financing, legal authority, and ideological legitimacy to displace campesinos and expand agribusiness. From the perspective of its administrators, it was a success.[2]

The CVC simultaneously turned land reform into a powerful instrument of ideological transformation. During the corporation's first decade, it faced ferocious resistance from cattlemen and campesinos who considered the CVC's program a threat to their very existence. Land reform touched all of their lives, and the CVC used it to reform large landowners' minds and political vernacular along with their property. By the end of the decade, the experience of land reform had taught large landowners to express their interests using simple forms of economic argument, defending concentrated wealth by identifying it with the drive for productivity. This revolution in reasoning in a corner of Latin America formed one part of a profound shift in the modern world, where increasing numbers of people came to speak in economic terms, and economics itself ascended as an internationally recognizable form of knowledge. That process involved more than the professionalization of economists; it depended on the popularization of economic thought and the growth of rather distinct professional and vernacular versions of economic argument. In the Cauca Valley, landowners never studied economics. The law and the regional corporation were their teachers, introducing them by force to a distinctive economic vocabulary and making it an essential language of legitimation.

———

Bernardo Garcés Córdoba led a worldly life. From his office in Cali, the CVC's executive director kept up with acquaintances from his student days at McGill and the Fletcher School of Diplomacy, trading letters with foreign ambassadors and economists. He had a fluent command of English and French, traveled widely in Europe and the United States, and read and responded to international journalists and intellectuals.[3] Garcés understood the United States, Canada, and Europe more intimately than David Lilienthal understood Colombia; he acted as an indispensable intermediary who offered outsiders comprehensible interpretations of Colombian society and integrated foreigners into local networks of power. He was "brilliant," according to World Bank economist John Conger, and "one of the best salesmen in the world." The Rockefeller Foundation's director for social sciences, Kenneth W. Thompson, confided to a colleague that Garcés was "one of the most impressive Latin Americans" he had ever met.[4]

Garcés was also a local. Born in 1919 in Cali, he owned an agricultural supply store in the city, selling farm products to Valle landowners. Farther north near Tuluá, he owned a 128-hectare plantation where workers cultivated sugarcane and manufactured *panela* (map 2.1). Garcés raised dairy cows in the slopes of the Andes and had business interests in local fisheries and

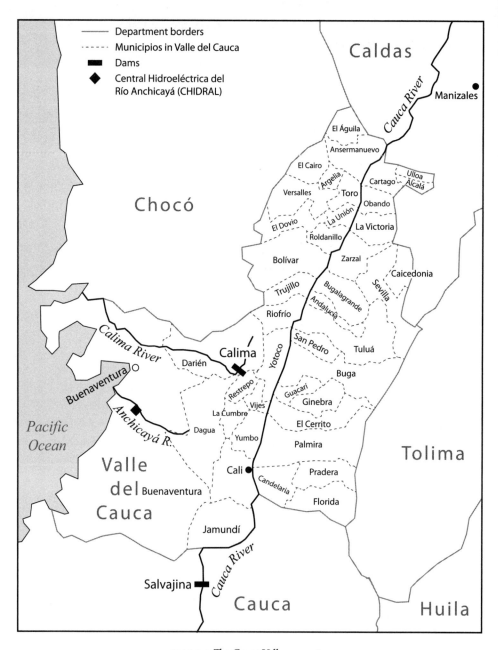

MAP 2.1. The Cauca Valley, ca. 1985

agricultural marketing. His economic activities had made him into a modest agricultural innovator in the Cauca Valley. Garcés's store in Cali sold such novelties as calcium and phosphorous supplements for livestock, and by the mid-1950s he was experimenting with grass silage systems to stabilize the feed supply over the course of the year.[5]

During the late 1950s, 4 percent of *vallecaucanos* owned 60 percent of the department's land. Garcés was part of that minority, and he knew the other members of the group: sugar magnates and agriculturalists in the south and cattle ranchers farther north. These men had come to monopolize the fertile flatlands between the cordilleras during the early twentieth century, forcing smallholders to supplement production on their own shrunken plots with wage labor on plantations. Campesinos still predominated in the mountains, where they grew coffee and food crops on land too poor to attract much competition from the wealthy. The flat zone between the mountains was the prize in Valle—the most fertile ground in Colombia, and some of the best in the world.[6]

Garcés was not happy with this state of affairs. The problem, in his view, was not economic concentration but the foolishness of using any of Colombia's best agricultural land for cow pasture and small-scale *minifundia* production. Garcés proposed to move livestock into the mountains, echoing a prescription in Lauchlin Currie's 1950 World Bank report. The flatlands could then support intensive commercial agriculture, facilitated by vast drainage and irrigation works, mechanized production, reformed tilling and rotation practices, and new seeds and crop varieties. Garcés imagined a diversified landscape of fruit, vegetables, soybeans, rice, and cotton grown for domestic and international markets. Sugar plantations with nine-month crop cycles could add cacao and African oil palm to their annual schedules, raising year-round productivity. Cattle ranches, banished to the hills, could improve breeds and intensively feed animals with nutritional supplements and soil-conserving grasses. Coffee farms could introduce cattle and poultry operations to counterbalance lulls in crop cycle.

Throughout the CVC's long fight with the Rojas regime, Garcés maintained a parallel correspondence on agriculture with the corporation's backers. Seeking funding and technical assistance, he wrote regularly to the World Bank, the United Nations, Point IV, the National Planning Council in Bogotá, and economists and agronomists beyond Colombia. The Cauca Valley, he explained, needed a comprehensive program of land reclamation—drainage, irrigation, and flood control—as well as farm relocation and intensive production of new crops. That program in turn required a corps of agricultural extension agents and researchers to conduct soil studies, run experiment stations, and study food marketing. Cali's private cannery needed loans to bring new fruit and vegetable harvests to world markets. And the entire department needed an efficient marketing system: a new slaughterhouse, a better transportation system, and a national price policy to guarantee adequate returns to farmers and affordable food to consumers.

To Garcés, the wisdom of this plan was self-evident. Economic productivity was, in his view, intimately related to the well-being of all Colombians; cattle ranchers and *minifundistas* in the valley obstructed cultivation that could feed people at lower cost, create jobs, boost exports, reduce food imports, and generate foreign exchange to finance industrialization. Seen from this perspective, the pursuit of productivity became an ethical obligation; a person using a valuable resource to achieve any other end was either selfish or ignorant. Garcés took a dim view of many of Valle's landowners, workers, and campesinos, complaining that they had "no training, no initiative, no sense of responsibility." Transforming agricultural production, he believed, would require transforming the people of the Cauca Valley. Through education and incentives, he and the CVC aimed to make vallecaucanos embrace productivity as a goal.[7]

Garcés spoke for a vanguard of rural capitalists in Valle who aimed above all to forge a new consensus among members of their own class. A cattleman himself, he bristled at the stereotype of ranchers as feudal lords attached to property only for reasons of status and power. As he knew, many cattlemen had gone to considerable lengths to raise productivity since the 1850s. They had cleared territory, imported grasses for pasture, developed new breeds, fenced their properties with barbed wire, and carefully managed herds. Ironically, the drive for improvement had generated the very pattern of land use that the CVC now criticized; only since the late nineteenth century had vallecaucanos begun to drain the river valley and move cattle ranches out of the mountains. In the present day, the CVC's opponents were a vocal segment of ranchers. Some took little interest in productivity, and others responded more or less rationally to national tax policy, which had exempted cattle ranches from most levies until the CVC began collecting a land tax in 1956. For these landowners, the corporation's birth had been an onerous burden, and they resented the pressure that taxation created to extract more income from their farms. The CVC argued that those sacrifices would eventually redound to their benefit, but during the late 1950s and early 1960s, that argument was a hard sell.[8]

Nevertheless, Garcés was no voice in the wilderness. During the CVC's early years, a few like-minded landowners scattered across the department began approaching the corporation for assistance with drainage, flood control, land management, and productivity initiatives. The CVC received a particularly enticing invitation in late 1956 from landowners in the northern municipios of Roldanillo, La Unión, and Toro.[9] These counties between the western

TABLE 1. Number and Area of Properties in Roldanillo, La Unión, and Toro, 1959

Property size (Hectares*)	Properties		Area		Average size (Hectares)
	#	%	Hectares	%	
>1	535	35.3	285	1.7	0.53
1–less than 5	606	39.9	1,408	8.4	2.32
5–less than 10	177	11.6	1,166	7.0	6.58
10–less than 50	138	9.2	3,048	18.2	22.08
50–less than 100	26	1.7	1,772	10.6	68.15
100–less than 200	18	1.2	2,520	15.1	140.00
200–less than 500	15	0.8	3,869	23.2	322.41
500 and over	4	0.3	2,644	15.8	661.00
TOTAL	1,516	100.0	16,712	100.0	11.03

*1 hectare = 2.471 acres

Source: Informe CVC C-04267 Rev. 1, "Proyecto Roldanillo-La Unión-Toro: Estado y Progreso," January 1965, 148, INAT. These data contain minor errors. For instance, the number of properties listed totals 1,519, not 1,516, and some of the percentage calculations are slightly off. It is impossible to determine which figures are inaccurate, and the errors are of a small order. I have therefore reproduced the table as it appears in the original.

   In 1972, INCORA held that these figures erroneously counted some landless farmworkers as small landowners because of the local custom of referring to the person who worked the land as the owner. Nonetheless, this is the best data available, and INCORA continued to publish it despite any reservations. Instituto Colombiano de la Reforma Agraria, *Estudio de evaluación de los proyectos de adecuación de tierras, primera fase: Estado actual de los proyectos*, vol. 3, December 1972, P-21, INAT.

cordillera and the Cauca River had excellent soils, but residents struggled with flooding, droughts, and salinity. Backed by the departmental government, they asked the CVC to undertake a major program of drainage and flood protection, and the corporation swiftly agreed, approving a pilot land reclamation project in January 1957.[10]

When the CVC began work in Roldanillo, La Unión, and Toro, 87 percent of the area's population lived on plots smaller than 10 hectares (table 1). Together, these families owned just 17 percent of the area's land. They used their properties to grow food crops as well as coffee and cacao, perennials that generated income over many years and appealed to minifundistas, who preferred economic security to the pursuit of spectacular returns. At the other end of the social spectrum, the richest 2.5 percent of landowners controlled over half of the area's land. They maintained properties exceeding 100 hectares and devoted their holdings to extensive cattle raising. During the late 1950s, there was no industry whatsoever in the three municipios. The closest sugar refinery lay across the river in Zarzal, the nearest dried milk plant farther south in

Bugalagrande, and the local cotton gin more than eighty kilometers down the river in Buga. Wholesalers had to send products all the way to Cali for canning.[11]

To Garcés and the CVC board, these municipios exemplified the misuse and the promise of the Cauca Valley. The CVC's pilot project, known as Rolda-nillo-La Unión-Toro (RUT), became the corporation's first attempt to enlist landowners in the pursuit of increased agricultural productivity. In 1957 and early 1958, the corporation planned a land reclamation program to support the cultivation of fruit, vegetables, and other annual crops for domestic and inter-national markets. These were to be the first in a series of drainage, irrigation, and flood control projects that would culminate in massive dam construction along the Cauca River, making the entire valley fit for intensive agriculture. The corporation's engineers began by designing canals and pumping stations for drainage and irrigation, and in May 1959 contractors began construction. In less than three years, they completed 40 percent of the works, and the CVC began plans to make RUT the country's first irrigation district. Point IV took interest in the project, sending irrigation specialists from the United States and Peru to advise on its technical, financial, and administrative requirements.[12]

The CVC acknowledged that building hydraulic works meant displacing people, damaging property, and disrupting existing patterns of access to land and water. Dislocation, in the board's view, was not an insoluble problem; it simply required monetary compensation. Before beginning construction in 1959, the corporation purchased the tracts of land that lay in the path of the works.[13] Shortly afterward, it agreed to pay residents who lost access to the river where they watered their livestock.[14] And in early 1961, the board took up the problem of displacement. At first, construction had chiefly affected large landowners, and they had agreed to sell small portions of their proper-ties. But the works soon encroached on minifundistas' lands. In August 1961, the board resolved to "relocate some small landowners whose plots and houses will be destroyed for the construction of the works."[15]

At the very moment when the CVC prepared to expel and resettle mini-fundistas, however, it ran out of money. The corporation had financed RUT with its tax revenues and PL 480 funds that the US government had supplied during the Rojas years. By 1961, with the works far from complete and no ir-rigation yet available, the project was in dire financial straits. The World Bank invited a loan application, and closer to home, the CVC detected a funding opportunity in a bill that the Colombian Congress was debating. Law 135 of 1961 was the latest version of a land reform proposal that President Alberto Lleras Camargo's administration had advanced as a banner initiative of the National Front. On taking office in 1958, the president had established both tax reform and land reform as leading government priorities, promising to deliver progressive redistribution, higher productivity, and a better financed state all at once. The CVC board decided to capture some of the funds.[16]

———

During the early 1960s, the CVC worked fastidiously to shape Colombia's land reform, blunting its redistributive promises. Throughout its negotiations with the national government, the corporation's decentralized status mattered. The corporation was a trusted regional ally that the central state needed, and its efficacy made it a model on which the government began to refashion public administration. In the heyday of land reform, the CVC mediated the meaning of the law in the Cauca Valley and cast its imprint on the state at large.

The corporation had begun weighing in with national officials in 1959, arguing that the National Front's proposed land reform law should prioritize productivity, not equality. Writing to Gustavo Balcázar Monzón in the House of Representatives, Bernardo Garcés Córdoba maintained that the country needed "a better utilization of agricultural land. Therein lies true agrarian reform. Nothing is gained by making small plots out of lands that, for economical production, must often be used in large units." The proper end of reform, in this formulation, was not redistribution but increased production. Appropriating the resonant language of past land reform laws and constitutions across Latin America, Garcés asserted that land had a "social function"; it existed to be productive. The earth should produce for the good of all, "even when that does not suit the individual owner." The social function of property was an idea with a long lineage in Latin America, borrowed from French jurisprudence during the 1920s and inflected by Catholic social thought, Mexican revolutionary politics, and populist programs of the Depression and war years. In Colombia, the concept had earned pride of place in the constitutional reform of 1936, which in turn informed the country's first thwarted land reform, Law 200 of 1936.[17]

As Garcés appealed to the familiar idea of property's social function, he subtly altered the term's meaning. Across the late nineteenth and early twentieth centuries, the principle of awarding land to cultivators had fired the imaginations of Colombian *colonos*. These peasants had settled the country's frontier regions in hopes that breaking the land would confer ownership. But they soon found themselves fending off wealthy land entrepreneurs looking to usurp and consolidate property. For nearly a century, the two groups battled over land rights, and each developed distinctive legal arguments in its defense. Colonos claimed strands of Colombian law that promised ownership to cultivators on untitled lands. Land entrepreneurs, meanwhile, prevailed on local political authorities to award them titles, and waving their papers in the air, decried colonos as illegal squatters. The 1936 agrarian reform law promised finally to define property rights in the countryside, and its promises were deeply ambiguous. On the one hand, the law formalized titles for peasants who had invaded untitled lands during the late 1920s and early 1930s, legalizing facts it could not reverse. Based on the idea of property's social function, it further promised that squatters who cultivated idle private property for five years would receive title to it. Yet the law's most consequential provision supported large landowners. It held that in all future land invasions on untitled property, land entrepreneurs need only demonstrate their extended residence, not a title or any particular use of the land. As Colombian politics lurched rightward after the 1930s, the national government never enforced the principle of cultivators' rights. Instead, the law gave lasting comfort to large landowners, who learned from Colombia's first agrarian reform that possession was indeed nine-tenths of the law.[18]

In embracing the social function of property, Garcés wrested the concept from colonos and transformed its political-economic implications. Peasant leagues of the early twentieth century and the 1936 agrarian reform had cast progressive redistribution as productivity's necessary complement, or even its precondition. Garcés disagreed. In his view, the drive for productivity should undermine the claims of minifundistas as well as extensive cattle ranchers. Aligning intensive agricultural production with the interest of society at large, he characterized large-scale sugar, fruit, and vegetable plantations as authentic servants of the general good.

As debate over land reform intensified in Colombia, Garcés relayed the news to D&R, sharing his conviction that the legislation should conform to the CVC's existing program. "Land reform is in the air throughout Latin America," he wrote to Lilienthal in 1960. "I am quite convinced of its necessity, but I am afraid that the issue is being obscured by demagogy and sentimentalism. The idea of giving every peasant family a plot of land as the prime motive may easily lead to creating a mass of rural paupers." Only large and medium farms could afford to adopt machinery, and as a result, it would be economically disastrous to break up estates in "regions like the flat area of the Cauca Valley, suitable for mechanized agriculture." The government should establish lower, not upper bounds on farm size, eliminating small properties rather than dividing large ones.

The problem remained, of course, that many large landowners did not use their properties productively. They had learned from the 1936 law that occupying land was enough to keep it, and Garcés set out to change their minds. Indeed, the mind struck him as an essential object of reform because the state's coercive capacities were so limited and direct methods of discipline so few. As he told Lilienthal, the Colombian government suffered "a great dearth of managerial talent" and was not "capable of supervising and enforcing complicated compulsory production programs." Garcés began to imagine incentive systems that would refashion individual commitments. Taxing land, he argued, would impel landowners to raise production; letting property sit idle would become an expensive proposition, prodding landowners to bring new land into cultivation. He held up the CVC's land tax as a model, recasting the measure as more than a revenue strategy. It was a tool that could elicit new behavior from cattlemen who might be complacent, but who perished the thought of losing money.[19]

Garcés described taxation in several forms as the key to enlisting landowners in a drive for productivity. In 1958, the CVC had decided to finance RUT not only through its land tax but also through a new valorization tax, a common fiscal tool in Colombia. Valorization taxes had originated in the country in 1921 to build flood protection and irrigation works. Unable to finance construction and recognizing that the works would raise local property values, the national government required local landowners to reimburse part of the cost of the project once they began receiving its benefits. The tax was low enough to ensure that landowners made money from the works, but it still recouped part of the public expense. By the 1950s, valorization taxes financed urban and rural infrastructure projects throughout Colombia, and the CVC enthusiastically embraced them.[20] According to the corporation, the taxes promised to make landowners see themselves as beneficiaries and defenders of development projects. Writing about road construction in 1956, Garcés explained to the governor of Valle that valorization taxes could transform the commitments of landowners. "Assuming that we are dealing with rational people, if the charge represents a fraction of an effective and evident benefit, there is no reason to foresee resistance by the contributors," he wrote. "It is conceivable that property owners would *compete* to secure the construction of infrastructure through this system."[21] In the context of fierce debates over land reform, this argument mattered. The CVC presented land reclamation, mechanization, and other technical interventions as land reform, and it offered a financing mechanism that promised to make large landowners into advocates rather than adversaries.[22]

Garcés never targeted the minds of minifundistas, but he insisted that simple economic reasoning showed how much they had to gain from the CVC's program. The spread of intensive agriculture and liquidation of small properties would allow them to escape the material hardship of small family farming and become wage workers in expanding agribusiness operations. Writing to Point IV and the National Planning Department, Garcés maintained that nothing would raise rural incomes like pushing marginal landowners into capitalist employment relationships. Valle's sugar workers earned "the highest wage in Colombia: over $20 [pesos] per day including social benefits," he noted. Their working conditions and economic security far surpassed those of smallholders cultivating 5 or 6 hectares of optimal land. Garcés scoffed at Liberal and Conservative proposals for land redistribution and the colonization of peripheral territory, accusing their authors of making policy "on emotional grounds." "We would be working against the economic facts and reason if we were to embark upon a wholesale carving up of the land," he explained to Charles Fossum of Point IV.[23]

Garcés appealed to "economic facts" to legitimate productivity measures, and he derided those who supported redistribution as irrational, demagogic, subversive, and criminal. In an extended 1961 letter to Carlos Lleras Restrepo, the bill's principal author, Garcés attacked a draft provision allowing for expropriation of "adequately exploited lands." That promise, Garcés wrote, created "serious dangers of an extreme interpretation with demagogic ends." He warned that small landowners in Valle might break up agribusiness holdings, and he tied that prospect to officials' greatest fears in 1961: the waning terror of La Violencia and the emergence of rural guerrilla organizations inspired by the Cuban revolution. "Valle," he gravely reminded Lleras, "has been subject to action by agitators who have made a veritable industry out of appropriating private property by more or less violent means."[24]

Lleras Restrepo sympathized with the CVC's points, and by the time the law passed in December 1961, Garcés declared himself satisfied with it. The law created a new national agency, the Instituto Colombiano de la Reforma Agraria (INCORA). Within the boundaries of land reclamation projects, INCORA could buy land to build infrastructure, something that the CVC desperately needed. It could also pare any property down to 100 hectares through negotiated purchase or compensated expropriation. However, it could not reduce holdings any further, and it reserved the right to exempt properties from the 100-hectare property cap if the owners paid valorization taxes for land reclamation. The CVC had explained to the minister of agriculture that reclamation works required long-term investments by landowners; they paid taxes for public infrastructure and had to install secondary irrigation equipment on their own farms. Property owners would never assume those burdens, Garcés reasoned, if they knew that the state might seize their land before the investments yielded returns. The law's offer of long-term exemptions from expropriation to willing taxpayers allowed the CVC to approach landowners in RUT with an attractive offer: if they covered part of the cost of land reclamation by paying a valorization tax, they could count on profits from the works and protect themselves from redistribution.[25]

The CVC did have to reconcile itself to the 100-hectare property cap and hope that INCORA would grant exemptions to landowners who paid valorization taxes. It conceded that much to gain support for the rest of its program. One hundred hectares was hardly a punishing restriction; it was ten times what the corporation believed a landowner in Valle's irrigable flatlands needed in order to employ machinery.[26] Garcés understood from speaking with US officials that they would only fund projects that included some land redistribution, and while the CVC would have preferred to make no such gesture, it considered US expectations minimal enough to meet. In 1961, the corporation agreed to apply the 100-hectare limit within RUT and thereby obtained the promise of national and international financing. President Lleras offered to fund land purchases necessary for reclamation works, and he authorized the CVC to report the decision in its US loan applications. Three weeks before the land reform bill became law, Garcés candidly assured Barend deVries of the World Bank that the measure was "reasonable," and a modest property cap was a tolerable price to pay—not only for funding but also for the credibility to direct the law's implementation. "The best prospect of a sound, non-demagogic application of the reform lies in an organization like CVC having charge of it in the Valley," he explained.[27]

The funding requirements of the Alliance for Progress forced the CVC to embrace a small measure of redistribution, but in general, US government priorities closely resembled those of the CVC. In the wake of the Cuban revolution, State Department officials had rushed to back anticommunist land reform laws in Latin America, and by land reform they chiefly meant measures to increase productivity. Speaking among themselves and at OAS meetings, US policy makers maintained that expanding output would raise rural living standards without requiring extensive redistribution of private property. They championed the colonization of peripheral public lands, technical efforts to survey and classify territory, formalization of titles, and technical reforms to intensify production. Where governments lacked untitled public land to distribute, they could divide private holdings that they deemed inadequately exploited, but breaking up productive private property figured only as a last resort.[28]

US officials and the CVC differed only in their assessment of the political risks associated with widespread land hunger. The CVC asserted that wage labor could support economic prosperity and implied that higher incomes would deliver political stability. State Department officials, on the other hand, believed that only landownership could turn peasants away from revolutionary activity. They recognized Colombians' urgent desire for property, and President Lleras encouraged them to believe that the population was inclined toward communist insurrection if the government did not address their concerns. There was no time to teach budding revolutionaries about the economic advantages of intensive capitalist farming, they concluded. When Point IV

director Charles Fossum arrived in Colombia in early 1960, he already believed
that countering the appeal of Cuba might mean accepting redistributive measures that he considered economically unwise. His colleague Wymberley
Coerr made the case to US ambassador Dempster McIntosh in Bogotá: "Faced
with the time pressure of [Cuban] competition, we may in our program have
to concentrate at least as much on effective propaganda as on sound economics."[29] The CVC's combination of productivity measures and grudging concessions to redistribution perfectly met US requirements.

The CVC made the negotiations of 1960 and 1961 a platform to discuss
more than redistribution and productivity; the corporation also called on Colombian officials to honor the principle of decentralization. With the fall of
Rojas, the CVC had secured control of hydraulic programs in the Cauca Valley,
but Lleras Restrepo's bill initially assigned those responsibilities to INCORA.
Working with a legal advisor from Point IV, the CVC contended that the bill
would create administrative chaos in its jurisdiction and demanded that IN-
CORA devolve all powers contained in the corporation's charter.[30] Bogotá
agreed and went even further. While Lleras Restrepo steered the law through
Congress in 1961, the national government created two other decentralized
regional corporations fashioned after the CVC. The Corporación Autónoma
Regional de la Sabana de Bogotá y de los Valles de Ubaté y Chiquinquirá
(CAR) carried out the same functions in the plateau surrounding Bogotá.
Farther north, the Corporación Autónoma Regional de los Valles del Magdalena y del Sinú (CVM) oversaw development projects on the Atlantic coast
(see map 1.2). The CVC advised in the creation of both entities and in short
order helped CAR secure a consulting contract with D&R.[31]

Colombia's proliferating regional development corporations became pipe-
lines to national office during the National Front, ultimately producing key
officials with whom the CVC negotiated the terms of its projects.[32] INCORA's
first director, Enrique Peñalosa, was a young economist who came to the land
reform agency directly from his position as the first executive director of CAR.
He knew the CVC's leaders well; he had received their counsel during CAR's
creation, and at the CVC's behest, he had worked with the 1955 World Bank
mission that advised the corporation. Peñalosa likewise knew the owners of
Valle's agribusiness operations. In 1961, the year he began working for CAR,
he coauthored a report on the sugar industry for Asocaña, the national association of sugar producers. Founded and headquartered in Cali, the gremio's
leadership overlapped with the CVC board.[33]

Peñalosa offered the CVC a cooperative partner in Bogotá and helped Lilienthal and D&R secure a privileged place within the Alliance for Progress.
For Lilienthal, the aid program presented an enticing opportunity to general-
ize the CVC's model of decentralization and multiply D&R's private

contracts.[34] Peñalosa himself had hired D&R as a consultant to CAR, and he quickly made the company an advisor to INCORA. The latter contract was a prized achievement for the old New Dealer. Since the 1960 US presidential campaign, Lilienthal and Garcés had encouraged John F. Kennedy and other US officials to launch a new foreign aid program. They had presented the CVC as a model project and emphasized the importance of channeling funds through regional, semipublic, and private intermediaries.[35] Kennedy responded enthusiastically, and in 1961 he offered Lilienthal the post of assistant secretary of state for Latin America. But Lilienthal declined the position. As he explained to Garcés, he considered private business activity superior to actual officeholding as a method of directing public policy. "What I am doing in Development & Resources is in fact public service, and can be more effective than any formal post however exalted, in getting things done," he wrote. "I am resolved to continue to function through the medium of this nongovernmental development agency." Lilienthal did accept the vice chairmanship of the National Advisory Council of the Peace Corps in 1961, but he mainly focused his efforts on winning contracts and recognition for D&R, the CVC, and CAR within the Alliance for Progress. "I felt certain [in 1954] that the time would come when CVC would prove to be a beacon-light to the whole of Latin America," he wrote to Garcés in 1961, "and I feel that time has come."[36]

Like D&R, the CVC set about capturing the flood of international development assistance that became available during the early 1960s. The corporation recognized that the US government, Inter-American Development Bank, and World Bank needed to find overseas initiatives that met peculiar criteria. For political reasons, projects had to be shovel ready; anticommunist funders wanted rapid demonstrations of success to counter Cuba's example. Programs had to generate revenue to repay international loans. And they needed local administrators who knew how to navigate complex application processes and employ planning, accounting, and managerial procedures recognizable to foreign officials. The businessmen who led the CVC possessed obvious advantages in all of these areas, and they brilliantly exploited them.[37] During 1960 and 1961, the CVC attracted international missions dealing with community development, agricultural production, land reform, public works, and agricultural education.[38] The UN Special Fund sent a multiyear mission to develop production initiatives with the CVC and the Universidad del Valle in Cali. In 1961, the CVC became one of the first organizations in the world to receive Peace Corps volunteers.[39]

By the end of 1961, the CVC and its supporters had won favored positions within the Alliance for Progress, and they believed that Colombia's land reform law could accommodate their existing program. As 1962 began, the corporation entered formal negotiations with INCORA to secure funding for RUT. These negotiations mattered as much as the actual drafting of the law, since the statute contained provisions encouraging both redistribution and productivity. Over 1962 and 1963, the CVC shaped the national government's interpretation of the law to ensure that INCORA redistributed as little land as legally permissible.

The RUT negotiations revolved around an apparently simple question: how much redistribution could INCORA require in return for financing irrigation works? The law demanded that nationally funded projects apply the 100-hectare property cap within their geographic limits. In 1959, thirty-seven landowners had owned farms larger than 100 hectares in RUT, collectively controlling 54 percent of the land. But those landowners saw land reform coming, and they found ways to make themselves legally untouchable. The land reclamation works that the CVC had begun building in 1959 had raised property values in RUT, which accelerated private land purchases and sales during the late 1950s and early 1960s. Large landowners participated in the active real estate market, shuffling their holdings and selling off portions of their farms to family members. By the time INCORA arrived in Valle in 1962, there had been no real change in the distribution of economic power within RUT, but only nineteen farms exceeded 100 hectares. Cutting those properties down to 100 hectares each would free up only 688 hectares of land. The land reform agency therefore proposed lowering the property cap within RUT to 50 hectares, which would break up twenty-two more farms and redistribute an additional 1,578 hectares, more than tripling the amount of land redistributed.[40]

The CVC heatedly rejected INCORA's proposed 50-hectare property cap, arguing that it would alienate the very landowners the corporation was struggling to convert. Land reclamation would allow farmers to exploit those 1,578 hectares "technically," Garcés wrote to INCORA director Enrique Peñalosa. They "should have the opportunity to demonstrate that they can do it. All of them have enthusiastically and decidedly cooperated with us in our efforts to recuperate those lands, precisely in the hope to be able to work them adequately one day."[41] For the CVC, RUT existed to turn landowners into advocates for productivity, and INCORA needed to support that goal.

The conflict between the CVC and INCORA continued as planning began for a second project across the river from RUT in an area that stretched between the municipios of Bugalagrande and Cartago. Garcés conceded that from a technical perspective, 50 hectares was "a logical unit" in the region. The quality of the soil meant that even very small plots could generate high annual incomes if the owners grew lucrative cash crops and employed machinery. But maintaining good relations with landowners mattered more to him than achieving ideal farm sizes. If projects taught rich farmers that land reclamation meant losing their property, they would never support another productivity initiative, nor would they continue to make capital investments in their own holdings. Realizing that INCORA might simply withdraw from CVC's projects, Garcés proposed that the agency think of Valle as the site of a scientific experiment, collecting data on landowners of varying abilities who worked farms ranging from 10 to 100 hectares, endowed with drainage, irrigation, and other technical improvements. The agency could use the results to establish sound property sizes for its future projects.[42]

INCORA ultimately embraced the CVC's reasoning and agreed to keep the property cap at 100 hectares in both projects. As Peñalosa explained to the INCORA board in July 1962, "it did not appear prudent to create additional resistance, nor to create enemies for the CVC." The corporation was desperate to win the support of landowners, and INCORA considered the corporation an indispensable local ally against them; the perverse result was that INCORA became landowners' best defender. In June 1963, INCORA signed a contract with the CVC to finance the completion of RUT. The contract provided funds from INCORA while delegating project administration to the CVC. Minister of Agriculture Virgilio Barco announced that the new land reclamation works would "considerably augment production." Peñalosa declared his hope that RUT, the first irrigation district in Colombia, might become "the 'showcase' of the country," itself the showcase of the Alliance for Progress.[43]

Beyond RUT, the CVC convinced INCORA to make extraordinary concessions to landowners who invested in production. When planning the project between Bugalagrande and Cartago, the corporation grew concerned that much of the land belonged to Hernando Caicedo, owner of the Riopaila sugar mill. Caicedo had privately contracted with the CVC to build land reclamation works on Riopaila property in 1959, and in 1963 asked the corporation to exclude his holdings from the new project so that he could evade INCORA's property caps. The corporation frankly explained to Enrique Peñalosa that Caicedo's infrastructure had technical deficiencies, but that he used the land productively and should therefore be exempt from the project. "Even when privately constructed works do not resolve problems in the most complete or economic way, as the proposed works would do, it is evident that the Caicedos have been able to put all the lands under their control into cultivation, and they will likely be able to maintain their property in reasonably satisfactory conditions," Garcés explained. INCORA agreed, and the two agencies redrew the borders of the project to exclude the municipios of Bugalagrande and Zarzal, leaving only those between La Victoria and Cartago.[44]

By the end of 1963, the CVC and INCORA had agreed on plans for both RUT and La Victoria–Cartago, and the corporation resumed construction

FIGURE 2.1. In its 1966 annual report, Colombia's agrarian reform agency, INCORA, showcased new irrigation works in La Unión, Valle del Cauca. INCORA noted that the works allowed landowners to cultivate a new crop: pineapple imported from Martinique. It made no mention of the hundreds of campesinos displaced by the works. (INCORA, *Five Years of Agrarian Reform: Report of Activities, 1966* [Bogotá: INCORA, 1967], 26)

with national funding. The lengthy negotiations between the two agencies had given RUT's large landowners years to prepare for INCORA's arrival, and almost to a person, they escaped redistribution. When the CVC began purchasing land from farmers who owned more than 100 hectares, only three of them remained in RUT. INCORA and the CVC bought 105 hectares from them in all.[45]

With large landowners protected from expropriation, the people who lost their land in RUT were almost exclusively the poorest people who lived there: farmers with virtually no land at all. Land reform became a massive displacement program designed to eliminate what the CVC called "anti-economic" minifundia.[46] INCORA and the CVC held that midsized farms were more productive than either very large or very small ones, and they set out to eradicate properties smaller than 3 hectares. Because they refused to break up large properties, there was not enough available land to resettle all dispossessed minifundistas. And in any event, INCORA and the CVC had no intention of relocating most of the displaced. They argued that new intensive agriculture would support a larger wage labor force and implied that through dispossession, land reform would provide such an agrarian working class. Displacement, a chronic problem with many roots in twentieth- and twenty-first-century Colombia, was in this context an affirmative state project to transform Colombia's rural class structure. Depriving poor people of land and making them into displaced persons was a deliberate policy that gave former minifundistas no option but to depend entirely on wage labor. Garcés promoted Bugalagrande-Cartago to the US embassy in 1962 by noting that the project would provide some land to resettle selected minifundistas, but that "a great deal of weight should be given to the large amount of employment at favourable wage rates that will be created through the establishment of intensive agriculture."[47]

The CVC presented displacement as a form of development in quite a few contexts during the same period. In 1962, while planning what became a vast land reclamation project in northern Cauca, Garcés wrote to the minister of public works that "the current towns of Timba (Cauca) and Timba (Valle) will disappear." He argued that their obliteration by the Timba Dam would benefit the inhabitants, who would leave behind settlements entirely lacking in "geographic, economic, or historic interest" to find new lives in "model towns established according to modern urban planning norms."[48] Two years later, while planning a new system of supermarkets to overhaul food marketing in Cali, Garcés forthrightly proposed to push most shopkeepers out of business. He considered it necessary to keep "*some* of them in business and on the side of the new enterprise," but did not concern himself with "what to do with displaced shopkeepers."[49] Garcés understood that capitalist development destroyed the means by which some groups of people survived, separating them from their property and altering their class relationships. Displacement was one way to describe those changes in class and economic structure, and he defended it without apology.

In RUT, the CVC and INCORA finally justified displacement by characterizing minifundistas as unfit stewards of the land. They argued that some lived on properties too small to cultivate and were not agriculturalists at all; they used their properties exclusively for housing while working for large landowners or in nearby cities. This reality reflected decades of encroachment by agribusiness on campesino lands, but the CVC and INCORA presented it as evidence that the small landowners lacked any desire to work the land and should surrender it to those who did.[50] As for those who did grow crops, Garcés described most as utterly incapable of efficient production. The CVC claimed the right to evaluate their capacities and dictate their futures. In the process, it explicitly discriminated against women, the elderly, and the sick. "For reasons of age, health, sex, inclination, etc., it may be established that it is preferable for some of the present owners to shift to other (urban) occupations and quarters," the corporation maintained in 1962.[51] The CVC eventually added widows to the list of people unqualified to own rural property. Based on those criteria, the corporation carried out an "on-the-spot analysis of each individual farm" in RUT and made a "careful selection" of vallecaucanos fit for landownership.[52]

In 1964, INCORA and the CVC took the farms of 401 minifundistas through purchase or compensated expropriation. The plots were so small that together they covered just 694 hectares, and the payments were too low for the owners to buy farms elsewhere. The agencies promised nothing more than to relocate a fraction of the displaced families—"roughly fifty, the best"—on whatever land it might eventually acquire in the project areas. Ultimately, those minifundistas' lands turned out to be the majority of the property taken by the land reform authorities. Three years after the 1964 dispossessions, INCORA had resettled eighty minifundistas. By 1972, when land reform was in full retreat, INCORA had redistributed just 430 hectares from large farms.[53]

———

Three decades later in Tierrablanca, a rural community in Roldanillo, residents remembered the day that the CVC had arrived in their vereda. As they told the story, a representative of the corporation had traveled to Tierrablanca on March 4, 1962, and announced that residents living in the path of construction had two weeks to sell their property at prices set by the Instituto Geográfico Agustín Codazzi in Bogotá. Those who refused to sell were evicted by police and expropriated. Without land, work, or housing, most sought refuge with relatives and friends before moving to urban areas. Residents recounted the experience in terms both concrete and mythic. The son of Guillermina Franco remembered that the CVC had razed the trees that his mother had tended in her yard. As a ten-year-old, he said, he had stood before the bulldozer until the driver knocked him aside. The consequences were swift and life-altering. His mother suffered a nervous breakdown and passed away soon after; every year during the month of March, neighbors described sensing her spirit on the site. During the 1990s, people in Tierrablanca condemned the CVC as the cause of their poverty. The corporation's irrigation and drainage canals had destroyed food crops and small landholdings, and those who remained resented paying taxes to maintain the infrastructure. Canal workers claimed that residents physically assaulted them.[54]

Residents of Tierrablanca had begun protesting as soon as the CVC began work in 1962. Initially, they complained about property damage from canal construction, to which the CVC simply replied that it provided financial compensation. Property damage in one vereda, the corporation added, was the price of progress for the river valley. "We want to convey once more," the CVC's secretary general wrote to a local official, "our deepest hope to have your cooperation and understanding to fix in a friendly manner the damages that you might suffer for . . . the future development of such a fertile and important region."[55]

That argument fell on deaf ears, and the CVC soon found itself engulfed by protest. Smallholders in Tierrablanca and nearby communities made wide-ranging demands of the corporation, beginning with calls for compensation that met their own standards of justice. In some cases, they believed that the CVC might offer them nothing at all. Residents of the veredas of Guayabal and El Palmar in Roldanillo repeatedly sought assurances of payment in 1962,[56] and as construction proceeded the next year in Tierrablanca, smallholders set out to secure as much benefit as they could from the project. The CVC's works had already disrupted local acqueduct lines, leaving residents without potable water for part of the year. Decrying the damage, they also demanded that the CVC provide electricity to the vereda. The corporation responded on that count, rapidly connecting Tierrablanca to the regional distribution system.[57] The CVC understood rural electrification as a tool to pacify the countryside, and it needed such an instrument in RUT. "As the mayor of Caicedonia once very graphically put it to me, electric light is worth more to him than 200 policemen," Garcés had explained to Point IV's Charles Fossum in 1962.[58] Quickly, however, the terms of electric service became a new source of contention. In 1965, residents of Tierrablanca refused to pay what they deemed exorbitant rates, and the CVC responded by cutting off the community's electricity. Residents appealed to the governor, who finally forced the agency to concede, reducing electricity rates and reconnecting the service.[59]

These demands for payment and public services were the sorts of complaints that the CVC's leaders believed they could manage, as they had a policy of compensating landowners. That policy constituted a potent form of power. It allowed CVC officials to quell some forms of protest, and more generally, it put them in a position to judge popular claims and dismiss quite a few of them. In 1963, citizens in La Unión demanded that the CVC build a bridge over the interception canal that had destroyed one of their roads. The corporation refused, telling the residents to change their transportation patterns and use bridges that it had constructed farther down the canal.[60] In late 1964, campesinos in RUT protested that canal construction had left them without water service; the CVC responded that they should expect to remain without water until early 1966.[61] Simultaneously, the corporation received an alarming report of the destruction of a small farm in Roldanillo belonging to Petrona Rayo Ayala. Most of her minifundio had been seized, and a CVC engineer had pressured her to allow heavy machinery on the portion she retained. Under duress, Rayo Ayala agreed, and soon saw her cistern and fences ruined. The CVC went on to dynamite her property to construct a canal. "Her house was left semi-destroyed," the report read, and Rayo Ayala found herself "at the mercy of her neighbors' charity." Garcés skeptically proposed to investigate the report, warning that "most of the time, things are not as they appear."[62]

While these residents petitioned the CVC, others obstructed its work. In 1963, small landowners held up the construction of RUT's marginal canal by refusing to sell their properties. They denied CVC staff access and information they needed to map the properties and arrange for compensated expropriation. Work on the drainage canal, meanwhile, stalled when a single landowner, Otoniel Londoño, refused to cooperate. By the end of 1963, both canals were at a standstill and the eastern irrigation canal had run into trouble. The infrastructure had to pass in front of a cemetery, and when the engineers arrived, they found "armed people prepared to impede the excavations."[63]

These widening protests exposed the varied demands of smallholders. Some contested the terms of compensation, but many others condemned displacement itself as a loss beyond compensation. The CVC had ready responses to the first group, but not the second; it could not manage conflict with people who declined to sell at any price and refused to consider another vocation. In 1964, minifundistas protested the marginal canal in Roldanillo, and Garcés lamented that "although favorable prices are paid, individuals are being evicted who are and want to continue to be farmers." For over a year, minifundistas in the vereda of Higuerón had alleged "that the project is for the rich, and that it seeks to eliminate small farmers." During 1964 and 1965, the CVC found itself answering to a national commission that the House of Representatives appointed to investigate the claims of minifundistas in RUT. The proceedings confirmed that for many smallholders, the level of compensation was a secondary concern. If they could not stay on their land, they wanted guaranteed resettlement, electric power, and the restoration of public services they had once enjoyed, most importantly water. In the face of those complaints, the CVC could only restate its position that intensive agriculture would produce "an increase in the employment opportunities for those small campesinos, selling their labor."[64]

By 1965, some smallholders resorted to desperate measures. The CVC began building the project's headquarters in La Unión that year and received an anonymous letter making "grave threats" if it did not remove a guard stationed at the construction site. According to one employee, "a group of bandits" planned to attack the camp where the CVC staff lived. The corporation requested protection from the departmental government and a permanent police detail for the site.[65] A year later, the conflict raged on as twenty-five landowners in RUT threatened the CVC staff.[66]

The CVC had reason to fear physical violence. Valle had experienced gruesome bloodshed during La Violencia and was one of the areas of Colombia that suffered the final stages of that conflict, Violencia Tardía, after the rise of the National Front. The end of La Violencia overlapped with the birth of a new armed conflict in Colombia, marked by the 1964 founding of the Fuerzas Armadas Revolucionarias de Colombia (FARC) in the mountains between the departments of Valle and Tolima. RUT itself was hardly the most dangerous portion of Valle, but violence was a real part of the society in which the CVC operated throughout its existence.[67] The CVC regularly obtained handguns from the Third Brigade of the Colombian Armed Forces for its engineers to carry while conducting land surveys and other routine work outside Cali.[68] From 1960 to 1966, it secured police and military protection for the construction of the Calima hydroelectric plant to guard dynamite, equipment, and staff members. During a 1962 strike at Calima, the corporation brought in the army against workers.[69] The following year, it requested police and army protection for its electric substations in Buga, Tuluá, Zarzal, and Cartago, after local residents shot holes in the connection lines.[70] And in 1965, CVC board member Harold Eder became one of the first people purportedly kidnapped and assassinated by the FARC. The perpetrators were never identified, and it may be that an older group of bandits did the deed. But in the Cauca Valley, the assassination of Harold Eder became a mythologized event symbolizing the birth of a new internal enemy.[71]

The CVC had one last reason to fear armed resistance. Threatening violence had been a key strategy of the CVC's earliest opponents and first targets of expropriation: large cattlemen. In 1958, shortly after creating the pilot project in RUT, the CVC had launched a second land reclamation initiative in

Aguablanca, then a rural area on the outskirts of Cali.[72] Unlike RUT, this project sought to reclaim land for urban and industrial development, allowing the city of Cali to expand. When the project was complete, Aguablanca become a haven for displaced rural migrants and a notorious symbol of urban poverty. But before it acquired that reputation, Aguablanca was a site of conflict among capitalists. In 1957, local cattlemen, including Ciro Velasco and Alberto Córdoba Firmat, blocked CVC engineers from entering their properties, and Bernardo Garcés Córdoba had to send police details to accompany the engineers.[73] Over the next two years, at least six ranchers refused to sell their properties, and the CVC launched its first expropriation proceedings.[74] Knowing its opponents, the corporation prepared for violence; when seizing Ciro Velasco's property in the early hours of July 17, 1958, the CVC brought along soldiers from the Third Brigade.[75]

In these early conflicts with minifundistas and cattlemen, the CVC's power grew out of the barrel of a gun. The corporation rarely brandished the weapon, and to be sure, the general story of political violence in Colombia was never one of engineers with revolvers. But the CVC's ability to expropriate land ultimately relied on its status as a government institution backed by the Colombian army. The threat of force was nevertheless a blunt instrument. It could throw Ciro Velasco off his property, but it could never quell dissent or convince cattlemen to plant fruit trees. And in any case, the CVC had no interest in fighting an armed conflict. The CVC wanted to change minds.

———

In the context of smallholder resistance and the CVC's past conflicts with cattlemen, the opposition it faced from large landowners during the 1960s was remarkable. The power and example of the CVC taught old landowner organizations to defend their interests in dramatically new ways. Forsaking threats of violence and established modes of argument, they embraced the drive for productivity and adopted simple forms of economic reasoning.

The major landowner organizations in Valle, the Sociedad de Agricultores del Valle and the Confederación de Ganaderos del Valle, had led the opposition to the CVC during the 1950s. Their members included Ciro Velasco, the Aguablanca landowner evicted from his home by the armed forces. During the 1950s, the Agricultores and Ganaderos had launched a national campaign against the corporation's land tax.[76] At the time, they had argued in stark political terms, claiming that the corporation had illegitimately appropriated powers over the people of the Cauca Valley. After the fall of Rojas in 1957, they dug in, depicting the CVC as a vestige of dictatorship and "a product of the most iron centralism." They claimed that the corporation tyrannically oppressed

FIGURE 2.2. A CVC staff newsletter from 1958 depicts the mobilization of local cattle ranchers who opposed the CVC's land tax of 4/1,000. (Lugi, idea de Casa, "A Que Te Cojo Ratón," *Ecos del Plan*, febrero de 1958, D&R Box 231, Folder 11)

Colombians with tax levies and wasteful expenditures, diverted public funds to enrich politically connected officials and industrialists, and violated "Colombian democratic postulates."[77] The landowners' attacks sparked a national debate over the constitutionality of the CVC's land tax, which had been established through a decree from Rojas rather than legislation. The CVC had to reestablish the tax in a law that Carlos Lleras Restrepo drafted and Congress passed in 1959.[78]

Bernardo Garcés Córdoba, himself a cattle rancher, spent a great deal of time meeting with cattlemen during the 1950s and countering their claims to politicians and the press. In his view, the CVC's critics objected to the land tax not so much for its financial cost, but "because it would imply a change in their work habits."[79] The land tax was a spur to productivity, and ranchers wealthy enough to sit on unused lands found it irritating for just that reason.

Garcés fervently wanted them to understand that producing more—which implied land reclamation, which implied taxation—was a price they had to pay to preserve their own concentrated wealth. He explained his view to a member of the Eder family in 1957. Discussing a book by the US geographer Raymond Crist, Garcés worried that it encapsulated a misconception that concentrated landownership obstructed productivity in Valle:

> I thought he was jumping to conclusions. A major part of the land not now under cultivation in the Valley cannot be planted to crops on account of floods and drainage problems. . . . [A]gricultural development is not possible under existing limitations.
>
> If, however, the landowners were to refuse to pay a small tax towards removing the physical limitations on the use of their land, they would be proving Crist and all similar critics right in their contention that poor land utilization is due primarily to landlords who own too much land and therefore derive sufficient income from it even under primitive management methods.
>
> I think that these landlords have to be led to produce more by information, persuasion and taxation.[80]

According to Garcés, Valle's richest families needed to legitimate concentrated wealth as a credible basis for economic production or face redistribution that would destroy their economic power. Paying taxes for land reclamation and putting land to productive use were the only ways to keep their property.

Garcés's defense of large landholdings was genuinely novel. At the national level, the Sociedad de Agricultores de Colombia had promoted agricultural improvements for decades, but it had not depicted the pursuit of productivity as the foundation of property rights. In 1936, the organization had battled Colombia's first land reform law by branding supporters as communists and criminals. Its mode of reasoning about land distribution and land claims was expressly political.[81]

After Congress reauthorized the CVC's land tax in 1959, the Ganaderos and Agricultores stopped campaigning against it, but they continued to oppose the CVC's agrarian program. "The hue and cry of the landowners gets louder and louder," CVC economist Antonio Posada wrote to Albert Hirschman in 1963. "Here in Valle they organized themselves into a pressure group and collected about $300,000 pesos to fight land reform."[82] As in the 1950s, the Ganaderos and Agricultores launched a national propaganda campaign, demanding that INCORA limit its activities in RUT and La Victoria–Cartago to land reclamation and irrigation, pursuing no redistribution whatsoever. The mobilization became such a problem that INCORA considered suspending the Valle projects in 1963. "There are many regions of the country that are demanding land reform," Carlos Lleras Restrepo fumed, "while in Valle almost everyone is a declared enemy of the plan."[83]

All the while, the CVC was laboring to protect landowners from redistribution. In 1962, Bernardo Garcés Córdoba had insisted that INCORA exempt RUT landowners from confiscation if they agreed to pay valorization taxes. Amid the landowner campaign of 1963, he took pains to reassure the Sociedad de Agricultores that the CVC and INCORA had no intention of breaking up large farms.[84] Enrique Peñalosa, too, declared that INCORA was less interested in subdividing properties than in increasing production and supporting commercialization. He justified the program as a way to meet macroeconomic goals; land reform should generate food, industrial inputs, and new exports to bring in foreign exchange. All of that activity would facilitate industrialization, providing jobs for people who had no future as farmers.[85]

Landowners in Valle were not blind to the opportunity that the CVC and INCORA gave them to evade redistribution. In 1963, while publicly attacking RUT and La Victoria–Cartago, these same landowner associations began a parallel campaign to exploit the land reform law's protection of intensively used land. The Ganaderos and Agricultores joined with Asocaña, the sugar gremio, to promote what they called the Plan Azucarero or Sugar Plan. They proposed to put 350,000 hectares into new sugarcane cultivation and build four new sugar mills to process it. The plan promised to expand employment in Valle's sugar industry from 20,000 to 140,000 jobs and spur the creation of 300,000 additional jobs in transportation, food processing, and related industries. Presenting the plan to INCORA, representatives of the Agricultores, Ganaderos, and Asocaña boasted that it would give Colombia an export crop that could succeed without trade protection and bring in a flood of foreign exchange. The speed with which they replaced talk of dictatorship and political illegitimacy with talk of macroeconomic policy suggested the power of the state to transform modes of reasoning. The landowners' form of economic argument had been available in public life for decades. But the land reform law of 1936 had never required them to use it, and during the 1950s, the specter of dictatorship had given talk of tyranny extraordinary power. Landowners turned to economic arguments when they became the only ones the state would hear.

The landowner groups hoped that the Plan Azucarero might convince INCORA to cancel the CVC's land reclamation projects, or at least implement them without applying the mandated property-size caps. Redistribution would fatally undermine the plan, they argued, since sugar required large land-holdings to achieve economies of scale. Furthermore, they intended to finance the plan with foreign capital, and the threat of land reform would drive away investors.[86] The CVC found itself in the delicate position of supporting the content of the Plan Azucarero while angling to secure contracts with INCORA to finance its land reclamation programs. The corporation's board decided to cast itself as a purely technical advisor on land use with no views on the ap-propriate size or distribution of property. When meeting with landowners and INCORA, CVC staff maintained that from a technical standpoint, their pro-grams were compatible: land reclamation could support expanded sugar pro-duction. In fact, they posited that the Plan Azucarero perfectly complemented INCORA's projects, since it guaranteed that new irrigation works would go to use. The implication that the CVC had no views on land distribution was, of course, disingenuous. The corporation was simultaneously bargaining with INCORA to prevent the imposition of a 50-hectare property cap.[87]

INCORA ultimately rebuffed the landowners' call to cancel the CVC's projects or fund them without applying the law's property caps. But it made the greatest concession it could within the law by agreeing that, wherever tech-nically feasible, it would put the land that it acquired into sugar production, fitting RUT and La Victoria–Cartago into the Plan Azucarero.[88] The plan proved significant not only for the ground ceded by INCORA but also for the novel way that large landowners defended their hold on property. Rather than threaten violence or challenge the political legitimacy of their opponent, they defended their property claims by binding them to the government's own goals of raising productivity and accelerating growth.

This form of argument gained strength over the course of the 1960s as land-owners became habituated to the terms of the land reform law. The terms themselves became even more explicit with time, as the national government modified the law to offer clearer protections to landowners who paid taxes and invested in production. Beginning in 1967, the CVC brokered deals that ex-empted landowners throughout the Cauca Valley from the land reform law so long as they paid for land reclamation works.[89] In 1968, the government of Carlos Lleras Restrepo—by now Colombia's president—amended the law to exempt landowners who made investments at least as great as the value of their properties.[90]

This peculiar interpretation of Colombia's land reform law transformed the reasoning that landowners used to defend their interests. By the end of the decade, the Sociedad de Agricultores, Asocaña, and individual landowners independently produced literature that criticized redistribution through ap-peals to productivity. The most intense conflict occurred in 1970, when INCORA announced its intention to break up large landholdings in the

OTRAS PRUEBAS GRAFICAS EN DONDE

SALTA A LA VISTA EL

ATROPELLO

y la ZARPA del "INCORA"

HACIENDA "CASITAS"   Máquina cosechadora en plena acción en un sembrado de soya.

HACIENDA "CASITAS"
En plena producción. Aspecto de uno de los lotes sembrados de sorgo (millo).

HACIENDA "CASITAS"   Un camión recibe soya para transportar a los centros de consumo.

FIGURE 2.3. "More graphic proof of INCORA's attacks and trickery." In 1970,
Valle landowners protested INCORA's plan to redistribute property in the municipio
of Jamundí by arguing that the current owners used it productively. This novel defense of
concentrated landholding represented a departure from the political arguments they had
used in recent decades. (Alejandro Martínez Caicedo, *El Zarpazo: Andanzas del INCORA
en el Valle del Cauca* [Bogotá?, 1970])

municipio of Jamundí. The Agricultores and Asocaña both held that redistribution would threaten agricultural productivity, and members put out a pamphlet featuring photographs of intensive farms in Jamundí dotted with trucks and tractors. The idea of cultivators' rights, once the province of colonos, had become the best defense of large rural capitalists.[91]

The CVC had thus developed a formula to tame land reform in the Cauca Valley, turning it into a productivity strategy and brokering a modus vivendi between large landowners and the state. Taxation and private investment in production, both guaranteeing sizeable profits for landowners, became the routine costs of maintaining large holdings. Expropriation had little real application, instead functioning as a threat that drove landowners to invest productively and identify their activities with national macroeconomic goals.[92] In that sense, the drive for reform did not equalize the distribution of property, but it did accomplish something. It created consensus around the pursuit of productivity among large landowners who had violently disagreed on the subject during the 1950s. The 1961 law transformed Valle's landowner organizations, teaching them to defend inequality using relatively simple economic arguments that the government recognized. Land reform was a social process through which landowners came to reason about social and ethical issues using economic claims.

The era of agrarian reform was a period of momentous change not only in the river valley and the minds of landowners but also in the lives of those displaced. Rosa Emilia Valencia was thirty-one years old when she lost her land in Tierrablanca. Leaving her home, she moved to the county seat of Roldanillo and became a domestic worker, washing clothes to support her six children.[93] Her experience was typical. Colombia's failure to redistribute land, coupled with the pervasive danger of political violence in rural areas, provoked a mass exodus from the countryside during the postwar years. Colombia had been an overwhelmingly rural country in 1938, with just over a quarter of the population living in urban areas. By 1960, nearly half of all Colombians made their homes in cities. Cali became the country's fastest-growing urban center, its sprawling shantytowns and vibrant informal economy testaments to the crises and resourcefulness of the rural poor. But in sheer size, nothing compared to Bogotá. Halfway across the country from the CVC—past the central cordillera and up into the eastern range of the Andes—the capital city swelled and buzzed with life.[94] The seat of government had become a haven for migrants in search of a home, and for the great majority, the ideal home was a house of one's own. For Colombians who had lost property rights in the countryside, the city became a place to reclaim them.

3

Private Homes and
Economic Orders

THE LARGEST HOUSING project built in Latin America under the Alliance for Progress was a private homeownership venture. Ciudad Kennedy, or Kennedy City, grew up on the outskirts of Bogotá during the early 1960s, a sprawling complex of private homes and apartments designed to house 84,000 people.[1] The promise of private property ownership fascinated everyone involved in the undertaking. Nearly four decades later, an original resident of Superblock 7 explained the origins of his neighborhood by digging up a newspaper ad from 1962. The faded scrap of paper showed a dapper man standing in front of a two-story home, and it issued a call to readers: "Become Mr. Property Owner."[2]

Ciudad Kennedy became an international exemplar of "aided self-help housing," a characteristic policy of midcentury developmentalism. Deployed in mixed economies worldwide, the program assigned governments the tasks of titling land, extending mortgage loans, supplying materials, and supervising construction while recipients built the housing and became property owners. Aided self-help allowed cash-strapped governments to fulfill their mandates by transferring to homeowners those burdens they could not bear themselves. In Colombia, it illuminated the essential hybridity of the developmental state. One of the country's most prominent decentralized agencies financed the homes, private initiative erected them, and the final product was a homeowning middle class that idealized private property and demanded that the government deliver it.

Ciudad Kennedy revealed the decentralized and semiprivate structure of the state, and simultaneously exposed the indeterminate ends that Depression-era policies harbored. In Colombia, self-help housing grew directly, if unexpectedly, from US public housing law and Colombia's agrarian reform of the 1930s. As North Americans and Latin Americans adapted those measures under postwar constraints, they found themselves generating practices that

FIGURE 3.1. "Conviértase en Don Propetario" ("Become Mr. Property Owner"). This advertisement by the ICT contractor COVICA promoted housing in Ciudad Kennedy. The three-bedroom featured here cost 33,600 pesos and offered a ten-year mortgage with a down payment of 11,200 pesos. (Momacu, *El Barrio Verde*, unpublished manuscript, Colección General, Biblioteca Luis Angel Arango, Bogotá, Colombia)

became characteristic of capitalism after the 1970s. Ciudad Kennedy helped create a state that was both developmentalist and austere. It strengthened residents' regard for both government and private capital as guarantors of social welfare. It expanded the welfare state while cultivating a middle-class consciousness among residents, narrowing their social solidarities and setting them against Colombians poorer than themselves. For residents, planners, funders, and critics alike, the homes in Kennedy symbolized wildly divergent visions of political-economic order and pointed toward multiple futures. Its contradictions remind us that mixed economies fused commitments that were only redefined as irreconcilable decades later.

Ciudad Kennedy's association with such varied ideals illuminates a striking feature of twentieth-century housing policy in Colombia: the private home held almost singular status as the intended product of government action and the imagined foundation of social peace. Here, as in many tax-poor regions of the Third World, the rise and fall of midcentury states did not chiefly involve the making and unmaking of state-owned residential property but rather the transformation of private homeownership. Understanding developmentalism's life and death means understanding the historical reinvention of the private home, whose mutable economic and social character made it a constitutive element of successive forms of capitalism.

The private home was both a changing institution and a site of ideological transformation. Like land reform, mass housing projects of the 1960s shaped the lives of millions of Colombians, and housing debates became vehicles expanding the use of economic reasoning in public life. For a new generation of Colombian economists, the arguments surrounding Ciudad Kennedy became an arena in which they jockeyed for influence and made themselves into preeminent state planners. Lauchlin Currie, arguably Colombia's most influential economist and a protagonist in the field's professionalization, emerged as a leading critic of self-help housing. He spent the 1960s and 1970s crafting an iconoclastic urban development plan that required large-scale public property ownership; unlike nearly all his compatriots, he imagined the private home as a complement to state-owned rental property. Just as controversially, he insisted that economists and economic planning agencies should take charge of urban planning. As Currie inserted himself into housing debates, he and his colleagues transformed public conceptions of what an economic question was and redefined the realms of life in which economists could exercise authority. Under their influence, businessmen and public officials began to treat housing as an instrument of macroeconomic policy, fundamentally altering the logic of social policy making. Yet economists' ascent as public intellectuals never gave them control over the application of their knowledge. The popularization and social mediation of their ideas—a process that seemed to demonstrate growing power—ultimately produced proliferating forms of private home-ownership, some of which Currie abhorred. The public that economists sought to transform was a protagonist in its own right, bending expertise to its ends and making economic reasoning a political language of legitimation. By the 1980s, Ciudad Kennedy was ancient history to Bogotano businessmen and politicians, who discussed the private home in new terms and assigned it economic purposes few had imagined in the 1960s.

———

Ciudad Kennedy was a spectacle of austere government at the heart of mid-century developmentalism. In the name of national development, social peace, anticommunist democracy, and community action, the Colombian state raised an army of unpaid laborers to erect what officials believed might be the world's largest experiment in self-help construction. The sheer scale of the project was a point of pride and an urgent necessity. The government designed Kennedy during the late 1950s to manage the mass exodus from the country-side that had begun in the 1940s and the crisis of governance that accompanied it. Between 1938 and 1964, Bogotá's population more than quintupled, rising from 330,312 to almost 1.7 million (table 2). Municipal and national officials found themselves facing a chronic housing shortage and a growing archipelago of illegal settlements. Some of the city's homeless found shelter through land invasions, building shantytowns on undeveloped property or seizing empty buildings. More commonly, they relied on "pirate urbanization," a system in which landowners legally sold plots to developers who turned them into illegal subdivisions, violating zoning laws or illicitly appropriating public services. For decades, these methods offered the most common paths to housing for low- and middle-income renters who, lacking any alternative, set themselves against government authorities. All of this activity elicited two swift responses from public officials. The first was simple repression: throughout the postwar years, the city sent police to clear invasions, sparking pitched battles with resi-dents but failing to stop the seizures. Simultaneously, the municipal and na-tional governments turned to legalization, formalization of titles, and large-scale housing construction to reclaim control of urban space. Ciudad Kennedy be-came a showcase of the second strategy.[3]

The question was how to build the housing, and on one count, there was no debate: the paramount goal was private homeownership. During the 1940s and 1950s, nearly every domestic official and foreign advisor involved in Co-lombian policy making agreed that planned communities of private homes could transform an unruly population, endowing the poor with new social and political loyalties that would restore order to the country. Colombian officials

TABLE 2. Population Growth in Bogotá

Year	Population
1912	121,257
1918	143,994
1928	235,421
1938	330,312
1951	715,250
1964	1,697,311
1973	2,571,548
1985	3,974,813
1993	4,945,448

Sources: Departamento Administrativo
Nacional de Estadística, *Anuario estadístico de
Bogotá, D.E., 1982* and Departamento
Administrativo Nacional de Estadística, *Censo
nacional* (1938, 1964, 1973, 1985, 1993).

embraced homeownership in part because the country's low-income housing authority had never pursued anything else. The Instituto de Crédito Territorial (ICT) did not directly build, own, or manage property but instead offered credit and public contracts to expand private homeownership. The agency was a product of an earlier era of reform, established in 1939 as a complement to the Liberal administration's agrarian reform law of 1936. Its original task had been to finance campesino housing within the country's new landscape of titled rural properties, and long after the agrarian reform waned, the ICT continued to operate on the notion that national progress and social peace depended on the formalization of small property ownership. The ICT was also one of the iconic autonomous public agencies of the 1930s, created alongside the Caja Agraria and Fondo Cafetero during a decade when the national government chartered new financial institutions to cope with the Great Depression. All three agencies operated relatively independently of Congress and focused intently on the countryside, aiming to quell peasant protest, put an end to land disputes, stabilize agricultural production, and raise rural incomes. When migrants began moving to Colombian cities during the 1940s, the ICT and its policies followed them. The institute gained responsibility for financing urban housing in 1942, and its original mission and capacities came to inform the possibilities of urban life.[4]

During the ICT's first two decades, the agency had prided itself on adhering to professional building standards; the idea of deputizing citizens to build their own shell homes was virtually unthinkable. The ICT employed architects and engineers to draw up plans and enjoyed the support of Colombian capitalists who did a thriving business supplying lumber, tile, bricks, cement, and skilled labor. At times, the agency turned to nonstandard materials to contain costs, notably experimenting with bricks made of soil and cement during the 1940s.[5] But experiments with materials were understood as new deployments of expert knowledge, never as gateways to the deprofessionalization of home-building. Indeed, officials took a paternalistic view of poor people, criticizing their "primitive" construction techniques and blaming them for their own ill health. According to a 1955 ICT report, Colombians living in cramped, unsanitary conditions were "literally underdeveloped groups" too ignorant to want anything better. As such, it became the ICT's task to remake the poor. Owning houses in conventionally built, planned communities would transform them into responsible citizens, teach them to save money, wean them from alcohol, and connect them to priests, teachers, social workers, and state inspectors who would educate and evaluate them. Supervised homeownership, the ICT promised, would "forge citizens" and create "a new civilization."[6]

Aided self-help housing was thus a foreign import in 1950s Colombia, carried south by veterans of US public housing policy. Counterintuitively, they, too, idealized the private home, and simply disagreed on the way to build it. In the United States, self-help housing had begun in the Puerto Rican city of Ponce during the 1930s under the terms of the US Housing Act of 1937. That New Deal law, the foundation of the country's twentieth-century public housing program, made federal money available to local housing authorities, which could use it to buy land and develop low-income housing. While officials in the continental United States used the funds to build subsidized public apartment buildings, Puerto Rican policy makers decided to turn the poor into homeowners. The idea was to reduce the cost of houses to an absolute minimum. The state provided a site, public services, mortgage loans, construction plans, and supervision. But recipients themselves built the houses and paid most of the costs associated with their construction.[7]

In Bogotá during the 1950s, aided self-help became the cherished ideal of advisors associated with Point IV and the Inter-American Housing and Planning Center (Centro Interamericano de Vivienda y Planeamiento or CINVA). Created in 1951 and based in the Colombian capital, CINVA was a technical agency of the Organization of American States (OAS), and it trained housing officials throughout the Americas. Its founding and original vision owed much to Jacob L. Crane, a veteran of the US Public Housing Administration who had participated in the Puerto Rican projects of the 1940s and coined the term "aided self-help housing." In 1947, he had joined the international office of the US Housing and Home Finance Agency (HHFA), the organizational predecessor to the Department of Housing and Urban Development. Working with State Department officials, Crane collected information on projects worldwide that resembled Puerto Rico's self-help initiatives, publicized them through government newsletters and manuals, and convinced Point IV to promote self-help housing policies abroad. By 1954, Point IV formally embraced aided self-help as "the most promising modern approach to housing problems in underdeveloped areas."[8] The US aid program had begun sending housing advisors to work inside the ICT a year earlier, and they became steadfast allies to CINVA.[9]

The path of self-help housing from Puerto Rico to Bogotá revealed distinctive circuits connecting the Western Hemisphere. Of all the countries that might have encouraged self-help in Colombia, the United States might seem one of the least likely. Among governments in the North Atlantic, it was in fact one of the most hostile to owner-building, at least on the mainland. State-sponsored self-help housing dated at least to the turn of the twentieth century in much of Europe and Canada, where it was often deployed as an emergency measure. During the interwar years and the post-1945 housing shortage, Finland, Greece, Germany, Austria, Spain, Canada, and the cities of Stockholm and Vienna had all turned to self-help housing to stretch meager budgets. South Africa sponsored a self-help housing program during the late 1940s, and by the 1950s, its example had influenced British colonial policy in Kenya, the Gold Coast, and the Indian subcontinent. Even the Soviet Union sponsored owner-building under the New Economic Policy of the early 1920s. But the United States had largely stood apart. The Roosevelt administration had dismissed amateur construction as a diversion from the task of resuscitating the construction sector during the Depression, and until the 1960s, federal loan and insurance programs generally constrained the practice on the US mainland. A few exceptions proved the rule. During the Depression years, unbeknownst to officials in Washington and against their wishes, some aspiring homeowners patched together loans from the Federal Housing Administration to build their own houses. Later, for a few months in 1947, the federal Veterans' Emergency Housing Program allowed owner-building under its auspices. And under the 1949 Housing Act, the Farmers Home Administration (FmHA), a division of the Department of Agriculture, began offering Section 502 loans to build or improve farm housing. The loans were limited in scope, available only to rural property owners and not to farmworkers. Many recipients used the funds to hire conventional building contractors, but the government did allow borrowers to act as their own general contractors, purchasing materials and performing some construction work themselves. Self-help thus became a small component of a little-noted rural program. FmHA collected no statistics on owner-building, suggesting the government's marginal interest in the practice, and it appears that unpaid labor played a modest role in the program. In 1952, FmHA reported that the average cost of homebuilding under Section 502 was $6,377, a "relatively low" figure because homeowners contributed an average of $650 in unpaid labor or salvaged materials. During the 1950s, then, state-sponsored self-help was quite restricted on the US mainland, and existed mainly as an imperial policy.[10] Its transmission to Colombia revealed the outsized significance of Puerto Rico in the minds of US foreign advisors, who imagined the island as a laboratory and gateway to the Third World. The role of the OAS in Colombia further revealed the distinctive institutional networks that tied the hemisphere together. Europe, Canada, and the British colonies might have had wider experience with state-sponsored self-help, but they exercised much less power in postwar Latin America.

In Bogotá during the 1950s, the advocates of aided self-help presented unpaid labor and cheap materials as necessities in a tax-starved, low-income country. T. Wilson Longmore, a rural sociologist sent to Bogotá by Point IV, began making the case in 1953. He arrived in Colombia just as Rojas seized power and announced a new housing policy: the military government would return migrants to the countryside and expand both rural and urban home building.[11] "The problem for the resettled person," Longmore argued, "is how to get the most house for the limited amount of money that is available to him."[12] Campesinos were cash poor, he recognized, but their labor power represented an underutilized resource for the ICT to mobilize.[13]

The very idea that unpaid labor might compensate for a lack of public investment and individual purchasing power suggested the profound ways in which the New Deal could be transformed in Puerto Rico and the Third World. During the pit of the Great Depression, the Roosevelt administration had directed public works spending into formal-sector construction to create paid jobs and boost consumer demand.[14] Housing planners in Colombia drew on entirely different strands of Depression-era policy, looking to Puerto Rico rather than the mainland, and they fortified the imperial tradition of self-help with new engineering and architectural research. Advisors from CINVA and Point IV spent the 1950s studying building materials and methods, convinced that cutting the cost of construction was the only way to house the poor. CINVA left its lasting mark on international home building in 1957 when engineer Raúl Ramírez invented the CINVA-RAM, a hand-operated press that made bricks from stabilized earth.[15] The center's research in the Third World also gathered strength from the explosion of do-it-yourself construction in the United States. Beginning in 1945, the postwar housing shortage inspired North Americans to buy unprecedented numbers of home-building kits, shell houses, and unfinished cores that they completed and maintained on their own.[16] The technical innovations that turned these North Americans into suburban homeowners found doubled use in Latin American cities, carried there by streams of US and Pan-American aid. In 1955, Point IV sent five architects and engineers from the University of Illinois Small Homes Council (SHC) to work with the ICT. The SHC, founded in 1944, had originally aimed to lower the cost of single-family homes in US suburbs. By the time the mission arrived in Colombia, its members had applied their tools in varied contexts from Oregon to Florida as well as the US Virgin Islands, Brazil, Paraguay, Guatemala, and El Salvador.[17]

Advisors from CINVA and Point IV depicted "auto-construction" as more than an economic necessity; it was a social good that encouraged community development. Longmore had begun his career in the US Department of Agriculture in 1936, a moment when the agency sponsored pioneering community development initiatives among farmers. Nearly two decades later in Colombia, he argued that "houses can be built by cooperative (social) action," a process "important to sound family development and hence to the wellbeing of the Republic."[18] Point IV praised community action "for stimulating organized self-help undertakings through the democratic process." Community development and self-help quickly became linked terms that suggested a natural relationship between two ostensibly distinct issues: on the one hand, mutual aid and democratic decision-making among neighbors, and on the other, the mobilization of resources by poor communities to reduce the financial obligations of national and international sponsors.[19]

Indeed, from the perspective of US aid administrators, self-help usefully pushed costs onto groups with fewer resources to cover them: foreign governments and ultimately poor people themselves. "Demonstration projects should have the maximum financial support of the host government and . . . make maximum use of family or group labor," explained Point IV officials in 1955. "The money cost of the projects should be kept at a level sufficiently low to make it possible for the owner to repay all or most of this over a reasonable period of years."[20] The US media celebrated self-help as a foreign aid strategy that asked very little of US taxpayers. According to the *New York Daily News*, the CINVA-RAM "might be called the Miraculous Building Block Machine": "It's a simple, hand-operated dingus. It costs about $30, can be put together by anyone from easily obtainable materials. . . . It promises to revolutionize low-cost housing construction in rural Latin America. It will cost the US taxpayer peanuts. . . . Know any billion-dollar giveaway project that's done anything a tenth as useful?"[21] US officials' insistence on austerity precluded any discussion of public ownership or formal-sector construction. With those options off the table, cutting the unit cost of housing through technical innovation became the basic challenge of policy making.

Self-help housing was slow to find advocates in Colombia, thanks to the ICT's self-proclaimed civilizing mission.[22] But the fall of the Rojas dictatorship in 1957 transformed housing policy, just as it changed the fate of the CVC. Incoming leaders of the National Front rushed to restore Colombia's alliance with the United States, and they simultaneously sought to consolidate popular support for the new government. On both counts, self-help housing held new appeal. Here was a policy that enlisted citizens and foreign funders alike in the work of the state. Here, too, was a program that promised to stretch the national budget to reach Colombians whom the ICT had never served: those too poor to buy a finished, conventionally built home. In 1957, the newly reconstituted ICT took up the counsel of the Small Homes Council, and by 1958, Colombia supplied a full 40 percent of all government officials enrolled in CINVA courses. A year later, the ICT announced that it would bring homeownership to the "lower-middle and lower classes" by offering new types of private property: "lots with communal public services, lots with complete public services, and different grades of incomplete houses." The Lleras administration simultaneously abandoned the Rojas regime's goal of returning displaced persons to the countryside and made urban self-help housing the cornerstone of Colombian policy.[23]

Under the National Front, self-help ascended together with community action as prized instruments of governance. In 1958, the Lleras Camargo administration established Acción Comunal, a national agency that incorporated local communities into the national state. The government created popularly elected Juntas de Acción Comunal (Community Action Boards, or JACs) in every urban neighborhood and rural subdivision in the country and funded them through the national budget. JACs provided a formal avenue through which Colombians could request government assistance and receive guidance to build their own schools, health clinics, roads, and water and sewer lines. From the start, these programs served competing purposes. On the one hand, they expressed Lleras Camargo's conviction that economic development and local civic participation could pacify the country. They simultaneously reduced the idea of democracy to mere participation; the Liberal and Conservative Parties relied on community action to legitimate their return to power and their exclusion of competing political organizations. Interestingly, Acción Comunal appealed just as powerfully to left-wing intellectuals involved in CINVA, including sociologist Orlando Fals Borda and historian Caroline Ware. Ware, a noted New Dealer, civil rights activist, and consumer advocate, taught classes at CINVA in 1953 and returned in 1959 as an OAS advisor to the community action program. She declared it a "pioneering" demonstration, "not only for the country but for the continent and even the world." The divergent promises of community action bound these leftists to the National Front and aligned all of them with an austere system of social welfare provision.[24]

The showpiece of the government's new housing policy was a massive project on the outskirts of Bogotá that ultimately became Ciudad Kennedy. The ICT drew up a plan in 1959, a year before most Colombians had even heard of John F. Kennedy, and initially called the development Ciudad Techo, a pun pitched at a very local audience. Techotiba was the name of an indigenous cacique who had once lived on the building site, and in Spanish, *techo* means roof or housing. Two years later, when the Alliance for Progress was born, Ciudad Techo was a shovel-ready project sponsored by an anticommunist government—an ideal object of Cold War aid. The US government quickly approved a loan for construction, and Kennedy himself visited Colombia in 1961 to lay the first brick at the housing project that eventually bore his name. Colombians, who rarely see a US president in the flesh, warmly remembered Kennedy's tour, and in the wake of his assassination, the city renamed the development for him.[25]

Ciudad Kennedy arose on a swampy patch of land southwest of Bogotá distinguished mainly as the site of an airport and a brewery. Construction began in 1962, and by 1965, it had grown to 10,233 homes, 80,000 residents, and 1,000 acres of urbanized land. More than 80 percent of the homes were single-family houses; the remainder were apartments in four-story buildings. The ICT arranged the properties in superblocks of 500 to 1,500 units connected internally by pedestrian walkways, and while home building was the first priority, the agency promised to equip superblocks with schools, shopping centers, parks, and a full range of public services as resources allowed. If Kennedy had been an independent city in 1965, it would have ranked as one of the twenty largest in Colombia. By 2005, it was the most populous of Bogotá's twenty localities, with a population of nearly one million people.[26]

In a functional sense, Ciudad Kennedy was the equivalent of public housing in the United States; both represented the most heavily subsidized state-sponsored units in the country, designed to serve people too poor to qualify for other publicly backed mortgage programs.[27] Yet CINVA, US housing advisors, and the Lleras administration had made certain that the project was, by mainland US standards, hardly public at all. Among the ICT's several systems of financing and construction, the most common was auto-construction: aspiring homeowners received mortgages with no down payments, an urbanized lot, and plans and materials that they used to erect a minimal shell house. Higher-income recipients could qualify for the ICT's "progressive development" program, which gave them a completed shell house to finish on their own. These two systems accounted for 70 percent of homes in Kennedy in

FIGURE 3.2. Ciudad Techo on December 17, 1961, when John F. Kennedy visited for a cornerstone-laying ceremony. (Cecil Stoughton [Harold Sellers], White House Photographs, JFK Library)

1965. Roughly 700 high-end units, meanwhile, came as fully constructed houses with ten-year mortgages and down payments totaling one-third of the price of the house. In those cases, private contractors built and advertised the units, symbolically obscuring the role of the state.[28] One such developer, COVICA, placed the 1962 ad inviting Colombians to "Become Mr. Property Owner." Although the resident who saved the clipping paid his mortgage to the ICT, he described himself and his neighbors as "COVICA recipients," casting the state's contractor as the guarantor of his well-being.[29]

The planning of Ciudad Kennedy brought into relief the competing political-economic possibilities latent within Depression-era policies. The very law that expanded public construction and ownership of low-income housing in the continental United States nurtured private homeownership in Puerto Rico and Colombia. The US government's characteristic method of implementing social policy through local government produced divergent systems of social welfare provision, and veterans of New Deal housing programs in Puerto Rico forged easy alliances with Colombians, whose own Depression-era institutions existed to foster small private property ownership in the countryside. If US historians have come to regard New Deal homeownership programs as incubators of right-wing, racist political mobilization that undermined public housing, then the unfolding of the New Deal outside the continental United States reveals just how little public housing officials did to create state-owned property in the first place.

Policy makers' embrace of private homeownership owed much to their deep-seated assumption that they needed to produce as much adequate shelter as possible within impossibly tight budgets. The architects, engineers, and rural sociologists who crafted housing policy in Colombia were not economists of the postwar world; they were economizers in an old-fashioned sense, accepting state revenue as a fixed, scarce resource and betraying no interest in either economic redistribution or economic growth that might channel new funds to the poor. Indeed, they were outsiders to the contagious spirit of their time: the midcentury fascination with economic growth, the belief that human welfare and social peace depended on it, and the conviction that states had the capacity and responsibility to generate it. The industrial, agrarian, and tax reforms of the Alliance for Progress all exemplified that spirit, aiming to raise productivity, expand the gross national product, and increase tax revenues. But as Kennedy himself explained in 1961, national and individual incomes remained extraordinarily limited in the short run, and the Alliance's social welfare programs had to operate within the logic of austerity. It fell to architects, engineers, and sociologists to devise policy under those punishing constraints, and their work in Colombia exposed divergent logics by which competing fields of the social sciences made policy, ultimately seeding quite dissimilar policy regimes. Working within the poorly financed social agencies of the Third World, housing planners generated a model of social welfare provision that was internally suited just as well to an era of fiscal retrenchment.[30]

In all of these ways, Ciudad Kennedy sat at the crossroads of political-economic orders and illuminated rival possibilities inherent in midcentury developmentalism. Those possibilities only multiplied as Bogotanos began arriving in the neighborhood.

———

The Colombian state had chosen community action as an instrument of governance, and in pushing costs and responsibilities onto residents, it unwittingly made its own policies susceptible to popular transformation. The

Colombians who built and populated Ciudad Kennedy arrived with their own ideas. In their hands and under their care, Bogotá's paragon of modern housing nurtured forms of economic life that its planners never anticipated and scarcely understood.

Perhaps the planners shouldn't have been surprised. During the late 1950s, US, Colombian, and OAS officials all pointed to the private home to convey the promise of capitalist development to Colombians, but their demonstrations harbored unacknowledged contradictions. In 1957, the ICT and CINVA used the CINVA-RAM to build a model Casa Campesina Inter-America (Inter-American Campesino House) in Bogotá. Ten thousand people visited the exhibit.[31] During the previous year, the US Information Agency had hired the Advertising Council to counter Soviet propaganda highlighting poverty and inequality in the United States. The Ad Council produced a traveling exhibit called *People's Capitalism* that projected a populist image of the US economic system. The exhibit featured a model of a log cabin and a script informing audiences that "this is the way Frontier Americans lived in 1825. Abraham Lincoln, like many other pioneer Americans, lived in a log house during his boyhood. In those days, all the back-breaking work was done by men and animals. In order just to survive, men and women had to work long hours." The Ad Council juxtaposed the log cabin with a model of a prefabricated suburban home in the 1950s. "This is Edward Barnes and his family," the script went on. "Ed Barnes is a typical American worker—a steel worker." According to the exhibit, scientific research, machine technology, the Declaration of Independence, and even foreign investment had increased the productivity of US industry, which had shared profits with workers to create a middle class. In the present day, US patterns of property ownership had virtually eliminated class divisions. "Nearly every American" earned some investment income, and a majority of people owned their own homes or farms. In the course of US history, the exhibit concluded, "almost everybody became a capitalist." *People's Capitalism*, with its model homes and ham-handed script, had its international debut in Bogotá in 1956. According to the US Information Agency, over 235,000 people came to see it.[32]

The two exhibits presented superficially compatible ideals, both proposing to turn Colombians into private homeowners. But the campesino smallholding and the suburban ranch house embodied quite different conceptions of the purpose of private property and the political-economic and gender systems into which it might fit. The CINVA-RAM house treated rural households engaged in subsistence production, petty commerce, and wage labor as workshops where campesinos and professional advisors would transform standards of health, education, and productivity. By contrast, the Ad Council explained that Barnes had earned enough as a millwright to move his family to "a

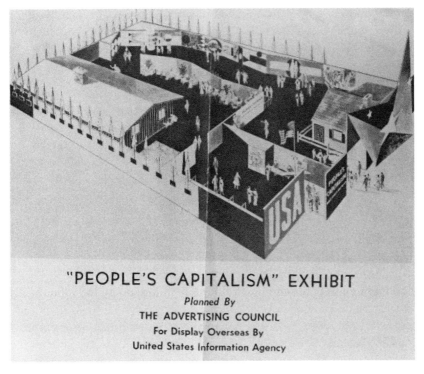

FIGURE 3.3. *People's Capitalism*, an exhibit sent around the world by the United States Information Agency, used model homes to convey the promise of capitalist development. Visitors entered at the right and immediately encountered a log cabin, said to represent the austerity of life on the North American frontier during the nineteenth century. The end of the exhibit featured a suburban ranch home, which purportedly represented the widely shared fruits of capitalist development and the conversion of the entire US population into an egalitarian community of property-owning capitalists. (Abbott Washburn Papers, Box 19, Folder "People's Capitalism Jan–Apr 1956 [4]," Eisenhower Library)

residential community," a site of leisure beyond the factory gates. Both of these homes were stylized, aspirational ideals, and during the 1960s, neither existed in Ciudad Kennedy—or, for that matter, in much of the Colombian country-side or the US suburbs. As it turned out, home buyers in Ciudad Kennedy insistently fused the two imagined types, combining social and economic practices that planners associated with two distinct historical epochs and political-economic systems. The onerous financial demands of homeowner-ship on the ICT's terms left them no other choice.

When Colombians began moving into Ciudad Kennedy in 1962, they knew that homeownership required hard work and resourcefulness. To mini-mize costs, all of the homes sat on cheap land far from the city center. In many cases, families lived in and worked on half-built houses for months while waiting for the city to install water, electricity, and sewage systems. The homes were, in the words of one CINVA researcher, "merely unfinished core shelters":

> They have silicon block walls, corrugated sheet metal roofs made of pressed asbestos cement, and prefabricated metal windows and doors. The foundations are made by filling hand-dug trenches, about twelve inches wide and twenty inches deep, with large rocks and poured concrete. The floor is pounded earth, and if a ladder to the second floor is not sufficient for the family, they must build their own stairs. The only finished materials that are provided in the basic unit are the fixtures in the kitchen and in the bathroom.

Despite the spartan conditions, Kennedy appealed to Colombians as a path to ownership. "I said to my husband, 'Dear, I am going there if I have to live in a cardboard box,'" recalls Graciela García de Avendaño. So many Bogotanos solicited housing applications that the ICT had to distribute forms in the downtown bullfighting arena. When applicants arrived at the ICT office to deliver their paperwork, they formed a line that circled the block eight times.[33] Ana Teresa Huertas de Díaz, her husband, Jeremías, and their five children did not secure a house in Ciudad Kennedy until 1966. "I gave thanks to God because we had the house," she explained forty-five years later. "My oldest daughter says the same thing, that they'll take us out of the house in a coffin bound for the cemetery, but that we won't sell."[34]

The Colombian government's inability to build publicly owned, heavily subsidized housing prevented Ciudad Kennedy from serving very poor people. The minimum income requirements for ICT mortgage loans disqualified at least half of all Bogotanos, and Kennedy therefore became a neighborhood for government employees and skilled workers looking to escape rental housing.[35] It was simply impossible to build houses cheaply enough for poor people to pay most of the cost themselves. And Ciudad Kennedy was hardly the cheapest variety of aided self-help housing; indeed, it revealed the great variety of settlements that the technique created and the range of costs involved. The residents of Kennedy were not in fact using CINVA-RAM machines to make earthen blocks but employing labor-intensive methods to assemble fairly conventional materials.[36] And although they took pride in building the core houses with their own hands, they commonly supplemented their efforts by hiring construction workers. In 1962, residents spent weekends and holidays at the building site while the ICT oversaw a corps of wage laborers during the workweek. In its materials, cost, and work schedule, Ciudad Kennedy was designed for Bogotanos with well-paying, formal-sector jobs.[37]

FIGURE 3.4. Alliance for Progress officials visit Clímaco Patiño to see a model home in Ciudad Kennedy. Patiño, far right, worked as the chauffeur to Milton Drexler, the Alliance for Progress housing advisor in Bogotá during the 1960s. James Fowler, the director of the USAID mission in Colombia, observes in the background. (Photo courtesy of Clímaco Patiño and María del Carmen Samboni de Patiño)

It was also designed for people with connections. The Díaz family received their house in 1966 thanks to Jeremías's job as a police officer; the original plan for Kennedy earmarked units for members of the police and military. María Ester Ramírez and her husband worked for the National Registry of Civil Status, and she recalls the 1960s as a time when patronage and clientelism served her family well: "Before, for example, to get a job, I would go to a magistrate's office, or I would go to the President's office, and I would say, 'I am so-and-so, I work in this or that,' and right there they would give me a job. . . . Now you can't do that, and I have a daughter who works in the presidential house!" Clímaco Patiño Sepúlveda worked as a driver for the ICT, and during the 1960s, the institute loaned him out to the US embassy. There he became the chauffeur for Milton Drexler, a veteran of Puerto Rico's self-help housing program and the US housing advisor to Colombia under the Alliance for Progress. Patiño, his wife, María del Carmen Samboni de Patiño, and their two children would have been unlikely candidates for ICT housing without their relationship to Drexler and the institute, since the application process gave priority to large families.[38]

Owning a home in Ciudad Kennedy gave residents more than a place to live. Families used the property to augment their incomes, renting out rooms and entire houses in violation of ICT rules. In fact, the Patiños first moved to Ciudad Kennedy during the early 1960s as illegal renters before qualifying for a mortgage in 1965. Graciela García de Avendaño's husband, an ICT security guard, built three apartments inside their house and rented them to other families. The Díazes, living in military housing, covered their mortgage payments by renting out the living room. When María Ester Ramírez and her husband traveled to La Guajira for a work assignment, they rented their house for use as a store. By the early 1970s, more than a quarter of homeowners in Ciudad Kennedy rented out rooms or entire houses, and at least 13 percent of families lived with people unrelated to them.[39]

Houses doubled as workplaces and businesses, likewise violating ICT rules that designated them as purely residential spaces. In 1966, one-third of families in Superblock 8-A took in laundry, operated small workshops, or ran stores out of their homes.[40] María Ester Ramírez, in addition to her job in the National Registry of Civil Status, ran an ice cream shop out of her house. Alcira Peñuela de Guerrero moved to Ciudad Kennedy as a ten-year-old in 1962, settling in barrio Tequendama. Her father was a skilled ironworker, and he established a shop where he taught his sons the trade. Peñuela and her neighbor Aura Morena de Fajardo became part of a group of women and children who knit sweaters in an old-fashioned sweated labor operation. A woman from the United States whom they knew as Doña Bertha supplied the wool, paid residents by the piece, and then marketed the sweaters. During Tequendama's first years, only one of Peñuela's neighbors owned a television set. He ran a small business of his own, charging neighborhood children admission to watch programs and renting them bicycles to ride.[41]

Growing vegetable gardens, raising livestock, running businesses, and renting rooms, the residents of Ciudad Kennedy did more than bend their homes to their needs. They suggested a reason that Colombians in postwar cities idealized homeownership. Most observers have regarded that desire as so natural as to require no explanation, but it had clear social and historical roots. When the ICT began soliciting applications for Ciudad Kennedy, most Bogotanos had been born in rural areas. While many if not most housing recipients were already living in the city, the ways that they used residential property recalled the long history of campesino demands for land as a source of income and autonomy.[42] That old ideal turned out to be more than a vestigial feature of rural life. It was a necessity of urban existence, sustained and invigorated by the costly proposition of homeownership. Despite the ICT's efforts to functionally separate urban space, divide home from work, and establish sup-posedly modern forms of economic and social organization, the demands of private homeownership breathed new life into strategies of economic survival and social mobility that planners increasingly denigrated as backward.[43]

The residents of Kennedy looked just as insistently to the national govern-ment as an economic lifeline. When they first moved in, Ciudad Kennedy lacked all sorts of public services and institutions. Aura Morena de Fajardo walked more than three miles a day to drop her children off and pick them up from the private bus line that took them to their old school in the center of Bogotá. "I did third grade in the living room," recalls Alcira Peñuela. "Every family made a room available, and every room had a class. A [public school] teacher would come, teach the class, and leave." As services became available during the 1960s and 1970s, these families eagerly took advantage of them. To this day, they speak highly of the governments of Alberto Lleras Camargo and John F. Kennedy and praise the local schools, police, and other state institutions in their communities. Morena took classes in doll making, painting, and crafts at the Servicio Nacional de Aprendizaje (SENA), which enabled her to become a vendor selling stuffed animals and dolls. Carmen Samboni enrolled in secre-tarial courses at SENA in order to get a job with the ICT in 1974. Peñuela recalls buying groceries from a truck sent by the Instituto Nacional de Abastecimien-tos before supermarkets opened in Ciudad Kennedy. Both she and the Díazes' daughter, Elizabeth Torres, fondly remember meals at the John F. Kennedy School, whose cafeteria was open to the public and served "a delicious lunch."[44]

These homeowners developed the identification with the state that the ad-vocates of self-help housing hoped to inculcate in them. They also came to identify with one another. The experience of auto-construction every week-end and holiday forged lasting class ties among people who shared nothing in particular but their income levels, varieties of employment, age, and access to patronage. "We all cooperated to build the houses," explains María Ester Ramírez. In barrio Tequendama, Peñuela recalls that after the early days of construction, "there was a lottery to distribute the yards, because that wasn't enclosed. There was just one yard for twenty-five families. . . . We were a single group of people." Peñuela married one of her neighbors; she and Morena list other marriages within the neighborhood and note that "the Gómezes are married to all of the block." The children in Peñuela's generation created what she describes as a joint savings fund made up of equal monthly deposits from each person; they divide the earnings every December. Within and beyond barrio Tequendama, all of these residents vividly remember weekends spent working collectively on their homes. They describe local stores selling to them on credit when they lacked cash, and they insist that there was no crime what-soever in Ciudad Kennedy during much of the 1960s.[45]

Idyllic memories of Ciudad Kennedy's early years are dubious history. By 1964, residents were in fact writing directly to the president to report crime and demand local police forces.[46] Rather than unvarnished truth, these stories are fascinating evidence of class formation that took place in Kennedy's super-blocks. By the mid-1970s, most ICT recipients in Kennedy identified themselves as "middle class," and decades later, they universally describe the trajectory of the neighborhood in terms of decline and insecurity. Ciudad Kennedy experienced the array of problems during the 1970s and 1980s that other areas of Bogotá did: residents recount stories of muggings, murders, and drug dealing. Their understanding of these events is colored by the origins of their neighborhoods as socially segregated communities. The 1970s saw the growth of new neighborhoods around the original ICT developments, including both formal settlements and informal ones launched by people too poor to qualify for ICT housing. "There are drug addicts around here," says Ana Teresa Huertas de Díaz, describing her neighborhood in 2011. "I go to the police gymnasium, and the *comandante* gets us together there so that we can serve as informant guides." Morena recounts the growth of poorer, illegal neighborhoods during the 1970s and says that her block now experiences "terrible insecurity." In Ciudad Kennedy, class segregation is remembered as safety, community, and well-being.[47]

For these homeowners, the identifications forged in Kennedy's neighborhoods nurtured a tightly constrained sense of social solidarity. "Thank God unions were never founded here," exclaims Clímaco Patiño. His neighbors concur; they were not union members, and they do not consider unions to have had any significant influence among the people they knew.[48] By the 1980s, Juntas de Acción Comunal in the neighborhoods of Cuatro Puntas, Pío XII, and Las Américas were organizing to expel poor Bogotanos who had begun squatting in public parks. Years later, JAC leader José Elías Calderón Cabrera recalled the effort with pride. "I'm pleased because that green space, which was almost a zone of disposables [a derogatory term for the poor], almost a garbage dump—it is a great satisfaction to me to see how it is today." José de la Cruz Acevedo Hurtado explained that his neighborhood junta had worked with police, city authorities, and Acción Comunal to drive out "black people" whom he deemed a source of crime and violence.[49]

Living in Ciudad Kennedy gave thousands of public-sector employees and skilled workers access to property ownership, state services, and forms of income, credit, and investment. In at least some cases, the experience also taught them to fear and despise the poor, and they in turn became objects of envy and resentment by both political radicals and mainstream development theorists. The Central Nacional Provivienda, a housing organization that mobilized

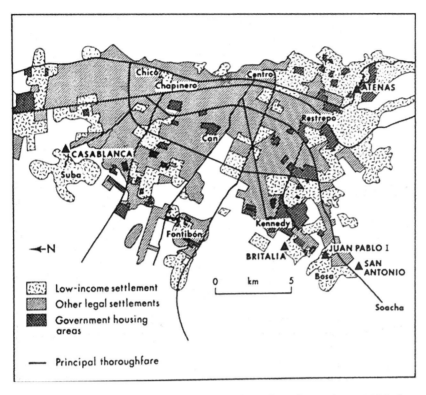

MAP 3.1. Bogotá during the early 1980s. Adapted from Alan Gilbert and Peter M. Ward,
Housing, the State, and the Poor: Policy and Practice in Three Latin American Cities
(Cambridge: Cambridge University Press, 1985), 63.

squatters to win public services and land titles, denounced ICT developments
as manifestations of the National Front's clientelism and disregard for the
poor. In February 1971, the organization helped establish an illegal settlement
in Kennedy that became the neighborhood of Nuevo Chile, named in honor
of Salvador Allende's socialist government.[50] A year later, Martín Reig of the
National University derided ICT housing as "a magnificent business" for residents but "a bad business" for "The Nation."[51] As community action boards
cleared squatters out of Ciudad Kennedy during the 1980s, geographers Alan
Gilbert and Peter M. Ward saw the perversity of a program that had made
miserly promises in order to reach the poor, and then failed to reach them at
all: "It is a sad situation to say that if poverty forces people to build their own
houses, many households are too poor to do even that." Ciudad Kennedy had
generated the very inequalities, social animosities, and political conflicts that
the National Front had set out to defuse, or at least to politically neutralize.[52]

In 1961, when the Kennedy administration had begun making plans for the Alliance for Progress, Arthur Schlesinger Jr. famously advised the president that Latin America needed a "middle-class revolution" or it would face a "workers-and-peasants" revolution. Ciudad Kennedy encouraged that process of middle-class formation, transforming the fortunes and solidarities of a thin stratum of working-class Bogotanos.[53] But the cultivation of a self-identified, home-owning middle class had consequences Schlesinger never imagined. Not only did it breed conflict, but it also inculcated social relationships and economic practices that defied planners' expectations. Residents survived by combining skilled, formal-sector employment outside the home with subsistence production, informal work, and small-scale proprietorship in the home. They formed households that quite often looked nothing like nuclear families. Paid and unpaid labor by women and children made ends meet, and "overcrowding" generated the illicit rental income necessary to cover mortgage payments. In Aura Morena's family, a wife's informal earnings from knitting sweaters were precisely what made the home conform to the image of modern domesticity, a place where a male breadwinner joined his family after work to watch television:

> I remember that my husband used to arrive home and the distraction was to go out to the IRIS theater.... I would say, "Where is he going every day?" He said, "But what am I doing here sitting like an idiot?" and would leave. So, one day a man came in a car advertising televisions with no down payment.... I got the television, and when Pedro got home at 5 p.m., he said... "Where did that television come from? You're going to pay for it."... I said, "Leave it there. I'll watch it. I'll pay for it." Later, he stopped being angry and would come home to watch the telenovela and wouldn't go out. And I told him: now you see, now you get it.[54]

Kennedy's residents never wrote economic treatises, but their lives communicated a naturalized sense of the private home as a source of income and autonomy, a site of labor and leisure, a link between formal and informal sectors, a foundation of political citizenship and class belonging, and a place where nonnuclear households could deliver security for parents and children.

―――――

Lauchlin Currie did write economic treatises, and in the 1960s he presented his own prescription for the private home: he proposed to situate it alongside a new system of public property. An old New Dealer, Currie drew his own lessons from the Roosevelt years, and concluded that self-help housing and land reform—flagship projects of the National Front—were stumbling blocks on the path to prosperity. In a country where housing policy was mainly a debate about how to develop and use private property, Currie became a standard-bearer for a different kind of mixed economy—one that included expansive state ownership of valuable urban land. He never got quite what he wanted.

In an earlier life, Currie had been one of the most influential Keynesians in the United States. Born in 1902 in Nova Scotia, he had received his undergraduate degree from the London School of Economics and earned a PhD in economics from Harvard in 1931. He remained there as an instructor until 1934, when he and his former classmate, Harry Dexter White, were snatched from Cambridge to join the Roosevelt administration. There they worked for the Treasury and Federal Reserve and served as members of the Freshman Brain Trust. In Washington, Currie began to anticipate arguments that appeared in Keynes's 1936 *General Theory* and became the intellectual leader of a small group of advisors urging FDR to use deficit spending to reactivate the US economy. "In Washington, there are people who call shy, retiring Mr. Currie the most powerful man in the Government," *PM* newspaper reported in 1941. Sensationalism sold newspapers, but by all accounts Currie exercised more influence than any other economist in shaping Roosevelt's understanding of the Great Depression. In 1936, he became one of six special White House aides to FDR, and he went on to administer Lend-Lease in China during World War II.[55]

Currie's prominence in the Roosevelt administration soon gave him an international career. In 1944, he attended the Bretton Woods conference that designed the World Bank and International Monetary Fund. Five years later, the World Bank chose Colombia as the site of its first comprehensive country survey and selected Currie to chair the mission. Currie produced a doorstop of a book describing and offering recommendations for every sector of the Colombian economy. The 1950 report became a touchstone in one of the monumental transformations of the twentieth century: the construction of the economy as a nationally bounded space susceptible to statistical and mathematical representation, an object of specialized disciplinary knowledge, and an entity that could grow if states administered that knowledge properly.[56] With the report filed, Currie remained active in Colombia, participating in government discussions of it and aiming to shape its implementation.[57] He simultaneously found himself the target of McCarthyist attacks at home. Based on his wartime work in China, Currie was accused of having been a communist spy. The notion would have amused any communist in Colombia and has been vigorously contested by historians and colleagues. Nevertheless, Currie recognized that the Cold War had transformed Washington, and in 1952, he decided to remake his life abroad. By 1958, Currie had lost his US passport, dissolved his marriage, started a new family in Bogotá, and taken on Colombian citizenship.[58] Today he is forgotten in the United States—an example of the power of McCarthyism to erase people from history. But he became one of the most influential economists, political advisors, and public intellectuals in twentieth-century Colombia. In the memorable dictum of President Virgilio Barco (1986–90), "there are two kinds of economics in Colombia: that before Currie and that after Currie."[59]

Settling in Colombia in 1952, Currie became a presidential advisor for the second time in his life. For two years, he and Albert Hirschman served as the foreign members of Colombia's National Planning Council, which advised the president on economic matters. But Currie grew restless during the Rojas years. Like many planners, he considered Rojas hostile to technical expertise, and like Hirschman, he left the council in 1954. Moving to the town of Albán in Cundinamarca, Currie became a dairy farmer for the rest of the 1950s, and there he began to transform common ideas in development economics into quite unusual recommendations for Colombia. Currie's experience as a farmer reinforced his impression that there was no future for most Colombians in the countryside; small farmers could not compete with large-scale, capital-intensive agriculture, and he considered it socially destructive for them to do so. Like many early development economists, Currie looked at Colombian campesinos and saw the unemployed from the Great Depression. Their marginal productivity was so low that he considered them functionally jobless. He believed, then, that a basic problem of Colombian economy was disguised unemployment, and that the New Deal might offer applicable lessons. His solution was to move campesinos into cities and put them to work in construction, transportation, services, and industrial jobs.[60]

None of those ideas would have shocked any development economist, but as Currie spun them out into policy recommendations, he set himself against the signal projects of the early National Front. In 1961, at the height of enthusiasm for land reform, Currie published *Operación Colombia*, a book-length economic plan that proposed to accelerate urban migration and liquidate small farmers. His idea made no sense to leaders of the National Front, their supporters, or even their critics, nearly all of whom believed that the countryside was emptying too quickly and that uncontrolled urban growth *was* the problem to solve. But Currie argued that cities were in crisis simply because urban planning was all wrong. Redistributing rural property to keep unproductive campesinos on the land would only prolong the country's suffering. Instead, Colombia needed to provide housing and jobs for urban migrants. Here Currie broke the conventional boundaries of development economics and crafted his own theory.[61]

The core of Currie's argument was a critique of aided self-help housing. Currie assailed Ciudad Kennedy, calling it a waste of public resources that actually restricted the supply of housing and jobs. While the ICT's housing projects appeared cheap, Currie noted that they bore steep hidden costs. Ciudad Kennedy was inexpensive because it sat on marginal land, far from jobs, poorly served by public transportation, and lacking public services. Whatever Colombians saved on land purchases they lost in extending public infrastructure. Currie further criticized the disguised costs of auto-construction, arguing that residents' unpaid labor was not in fact free. It had a high opportunity cost, since it took workers away from paid jobs that contributed to economic growth. And at times, self-help produced shoddy houses that required repair and renovation.[62] Beyond matters of cost, Currie contended that the ICT fed economic inequality by allowing middle-class borrowers to hoard public resources. The ICT extended mortgage loans at rates below the general rate of interest, providing a hidden subsidy to middle-class borrowers. That subsidy systematically decapitalized the agency, constraining its growth and preventing it from serving a wider public interest.[63] Furthermore, the ICT's home-ownership programs allowed individual property owners to capture rising land values rather than channeling them back to the ICT for reinvestment. In Currie's view, Ciudad Kennedy residents reaped undue windfalls from self-help housing. They could and should pay more for shelter, freeing up public subsidies for truly low-income people.[64]

Currie proposed that the Colombian government reimagine housing as an instrument of macroeconomic policy. His basic insight came from the New Deal, when the US government had used construction to stimulate economic recovery. On that basis, he argued that in Colombia, housing construction could be a leading sector spurring development; concentrated investments in home building could fuel all kinds of other economic activity. Construction would create well-paying jobs, and the income that workers earned would increase demand for consumer goods and housing itself. Meanwhile, the construction sector would create demand for building materials and equipment. In other words, it was counterproductive to evaluate housing policy based on its up-front, monetized costs. Paying more to build housing through the formal construction sector would spur economic growth, and the benefits of growth would far exceed the illusory cost savings of auto-construction.[65]

Currie took aim at everything CINVA and US housing advisors had taught Colombian policy makers since the early 1950s. Looking beyond specific policies, he contested policy makers' understanding of economic analysis itself. Indeed, Currie was doing battle with an old idea of economy as the economization of scare resources and popularizing an idea of *the* economy as an object that the state could manage and make grow. The engineers, architects, and sociologists who dominated CINVA and US housing missions had made clear their own ideas about the nature of economics; from their perspective, simple cost accounting was the major economic consideration in housing policy. CINVA had in fact offered classes on housing economics since 1951. They were a minor part of the curriculum, and they taught students about the costs of construction.[66]

In arguing about home building, then, Currie presented the Colombian public with a new understanding of the nature, purpose, and purview of his discipline. He brought to public life a battle roiling in the cloistered world of the academy. During the 1940s, Colombian universities had begun establishing freestanding economics faculties outside schools of law and administration. University reform aimed to conjure a new kind of economist: a credentialed disciplinary specialist with wide responsibilities for national planning. Currie played a crucial if unusual role in that project. The shadow of McCarthyism trailed him even in Colombia, where the Rockefeller Foundation financed some of the top economics programs and blackballed him. But in 1960, Currie was one of only two Colombian citizens with a doctorate in economics, and his wide experience gave him unparalleled renown as an exponent of the emergent discipline.[67] From beyond the academy, his 1950 World Bank report and *Operación Colombia* shaped the direction of university research; indeed, as Currie critiqued self-help housing in the early 1960s, a new generation of economists began compiling Colombia's first national labor statistics to determine whether cities could absorb the urban workforce he proposed to create.[68] At times, he intervened directly in fledgling economics faculties. When the Colombian Association of Universities faced the task of accrediting new programs in 1964, it sent Currie to evaluate them. When the left-leaning Universidad Nacional needed a dean for its economics faculty in 1966, Currie filled the role for a year. During the same historical moment that Currie intervened in housing debates, he wrote iconoclastic essays on economics education and embarked on a thirty-year mission to retrain Colombian economists.[69]

From Currie's perspective, the chief problem afflicting new economics programs was their confusion about the definition of the field. Surveying programs in Bogotá and Medellín during the 1960s, he argued that they combined three distinct disciplines: economics, management, and accounting. Currie worked from an understanding of discipline as subjective as any other, but he conveyed an important truth: Colombian universities had become crossroads where self-identified economists from many national and intellectual backgrounds found themselves face to face, struggling to arrive at shared conceptions of the field's scope, the identity of an economist, and the nature of an economic question. Currie gave voice to one powerful impulse in that debate, calling for the expulsion of accountants and managers from the profession.[70]

Currie's intervention in housing policy represented a parallel effort to shape Colombians' understanding of discipline and profession. Simple cost accounting, in his view, was not economic analysis. Thinking as an economist meant looking at an entire nation as a set of related sectors and devising a strategy by which they could interact to produce economic growth. That idea gave economists a fundamentally new position in society. Economics, according to Currie's definition, was not an accounting tool for urban planners to deploy but a discipline that adjudicated social disputes. Economists' concern with maximizing growth gave them a global view of society that could produce optimal policies for all. Architects and engineers might be able to wring a great deal from a tiny budget, but only economists could grasp the entirety of material life—that was the economy, supposedly—and use that totalizing knowledge to harmonize the interests of all people. Economists could ensure that goods existed in the right amounts and fell into the right hands. They could see that varied areas of activity fed one another to impel new production, consumption, and trade. Currie expressed the essential spirit of midcentury macroeconomic planning, depicting economists and growth as servants of an imagined general interest. In doing so, he recast his own disciplinary colleagues as the rightful masters of architects and engineers—older, more established professional communities.

Currie brought an economist's sensibility to housing policy, and he brought the spatial imagination of an urban planner to the field of economics. Indeed, his original contribution to development theory turned out to be his urban plan. Developed over the 1960s and 1970s, it began with the proposition that the state should foment construction on expensive, urbanized land, not wetlands outside the city limits. Furthermore, officials should stop building communities without public parks, offices, and other nonresidential spaces. Currie derided Ciudad Kennedy as a working-class "dormitory," marred by class segregation and a striking lack of employment and recreation.[71] Currie went on to warn Colombian policy makers against what he considered the mistakes of US urban planning. Embracing emergent critiques of urban sprawl, automobile dependence, segregation, and single-use zoning, he cited Jane Jacobs on the value of density, and he studied British New Towns of the 1940s, Singapore's planned cities of the 1960s, and the metropolitan regions of Paris, Vancouver, Stockholm, and Rotterdam.[72] Currie saw in all these places the possibility of small-scale, mixed-use design that allowed growing populations to fulfill their needs close to home. During the 1960s, he had no trouble finding such models; they were proliferating across Europe, North America, and the

Third World, where many critics of high modernism embraced the village as a fundamental unit of planning.[73]

Drawing on a world of experiments, Currie constructed his own high-modernist plan for Colombia, and in the 1970s, he gave it a name: cities-within-cities. Currie proposed that the state create new publicly owned, mixed-income, mixed-use neighborhoods in the central city. The unruly megalopolis would be reborn as a decentralized collection of dense, walkable communities. Some low-income people would find housing in the new developments, but many units would go to those with middle and high incomes. The rest of the urban poor could "filter" into decent vacated housing elsewhere. As long as construction outpaced the formation of new households, Colombia's housing supply would increase, and living conditions might improve for everyone.[74]

Among all the urban plans in Colombia, Currie's was the only one to call for large-scale public property ownership. He proposed to create a new set of public enterprises—"public urban corporations"—that would own the cities-within-cities, hire private contractors to build everything in them, and then rent property to tenants. These corporations promised to become characteristic features of the decentralized state whose construction Currie had long advanced. Currie had conducted seminal research for the creation of the Corporación Autónoma de los Valles del Magdalena y del Sinú (CVM), the CVC's counterpart in the riverine regions of the Atlantic coast.[75] Turning his attention to cities, he now proposed that regional development corporations and city governments jointly form the public urban corporations. The CVC and its counterparts would prevent urban sprawl by safeguarding rural land for agriculture. Meanwhile, urban corporations would create meticulously planned neighborhoods that matched the local labor force to the supply of jobs and services. More than housing agencies, they were to be far-reaching development authorities that could buy land, expropriate property, build roads, operate bus lines, receive international loans, and purchase utility services to resell at their own rates. At the national level, both urban and regional corporations would operate under the National Planning Department, harmonizing spatial planning with macroeconomic planning.

In a country where the concepts of social justice and progressive redistribution were powerfully tied to dreams of small property ownership, Currie's defense of public property was strikingly novel. State ownership appealed to him partly as a social good and more importantly as a practical necessity for integrated planning. State enterprises had fundamentally different motives from private real estate developers, he noted; they needed to cover costs, but they did not need to maximize profits. As a result, they alone could be relied on to implement a plan that prioritized national economic growth, local social integration, economic redistribution, and physical density over the pursuit of spectacular returns. A nonprofit, public developer would have the latitude to set rents in accordance with local wages, allowing workers to live near their jobs. It could use revenues from high-end properties to subsidize low-income units nearby. It might choose to build day care centers, public schools, and playgrounds to help women work outside the home. And as it captured rising land values, it could reinvest them in social services or hand them to the National Planning Department to build new cities-within-cities.[76]

Private homeownership retained a place in Currie's plan; it simply lost pride of place as the iconic product of Colombian housing policy. Currie considered the private home a legitimate counterpart to publicly owned cities-within-cities, suitable for the wealthy and for any Colombian living outside dense urban centers. He therefore coupled his urban plan with a new housing finance system designed to accelerate home building and bring homeownership within reach of those Ciudad Kennedy had never served. Beginning in *Operación Colombia* and extending into the 1970s, he argued that the main obstacle to residential construction was a lack of credit available to those who wanted to buy a house. His proposed financing system, which eventually acquired the name UPAC, aimed to remedy that problem. UPAC stood for *unidad de poder adquisitivo constante*, or "constant purchasing power unit." Behind the unwieldy jargon lay a relatively simple idea. Currie believed that an untapped supply of private savings existed in Colombia that the state could channel into housing construction. The supply was untapped, he thought, because high inflation discouraged people from saving; if they deposited money in a bank, the rate of interest they earned would be lower than the rate of inflation, and so the real value of their deposit would fall over time. Therefore, Currie imagined a new kind of savings account in which the rate of interest remained constant but the value of the deposit itself rose daily with inflation. Adjusting the principal would preserve the real value of deposits and make saving an attractive option. A public regulatory board would oversee individual lenders, which would create accounts, use the deposits to provide mortgage loans to home buyers, and thus channel private savings into housing construction. Currie's idea drew on the work of Irving Fisher, a pioneer in the construction of price indexes during the 1920s, and UPAC resembled indexed savings systems established in Brazil and Chile during the 1960s. By the 1970s, indexing had become a common tool for coping with inflation in Latin America.[77]

In Colombia, the politics of Currie's plan were mercurial, and he struggled to find supporters. Currie was no leftist and had nothing to do with Colombia's socialist or communist organizations. He kept his distance from CEPAL, dismissing Latin America's leading economic planners as inward-looking protectionists deploying flawed quantitative techniques.[78] He found little sympathy within the Liberal Party, whose leaders carried the banner for aided self-help housing and agrarian reform. The Kennedy administration, too, backed land reform; when Currie met with Walt Rostow in 1961 to discuss *Operación Colombia*, his ideas fell on deaf ears.[79] Currie's opposition to land redistribution set him against Colombian campesino organizations, and his proposal to create urban jobs even alienated organized labor. He considered union wages excessive overall and demanded that union members tighten their belts to free up national investment for urbanization. Union wages would fall in the short run, but formal employment in construction would grow, offering higher pay than agricultural work and raising the national standard of living. Labor leaders were unimpressed.[80]

During the 1960s, the only defenders Currie could find were capitalists. The business association representing the construction industry, CAMACOL, spied in his ideas a new way to identify its pursuit of profit with national development. Needing supporters, Currie eagerly allied himself with the group. It was in fact CAMACOL that published *Operación Colombia* in 1961. The next year, it hired Currie to conduct research on the construction sector.[81] In short order, Currie transformed the gremio's reasoning, much as the CVC had altered the arguments of Valle's large landowners. Founded in 1957, CAMACOL had always rhetorically linked its fortunes to the fate of the nation, but in terms quite different from Currie's. It had originally called for new government investment in public works and factories of all kinds, justifying those expenditures as instruments to pacify the country, improve public health, and foment industrialization. Housing figured as a vital social need that CAMACOL could fulfill, but it had no evident relationship to any other economic goal. Indeed, CAMACOL discussed the construction of factories separately, arguing that they had special importance for Colombia's drive to industrialize. Echoing most development theory of the time, CAMACOL in the 1950s imagined national development as a balanced process in which every economic sector grew in perfect proportion to the others.[82] But during the 1960s, CAMACOL spoke a new language. Echoing Currie, its reports and public statements depicted construction as a leading sector and an engine of economic growth. Gone was the idea that Colombia needed widely dispersed public spending; an investment in construction would redound to the entire nation. As CAMACOL became Currie's champion, it popularized this strand of professional economic thought.[83]

Currie could not get anywhere as an advisor during the 1960s, when land reform and self-help housing were national priorities. But he did spend the decade turning Colombian academics toward his questions. Currie became a mentor to the Grupo Integración, a study group of young, college-educated economists founded in Bogotá in 1964. At the same time, he used his one-year deanship at the Universidad Nacional to foster research after his own heart. In 1966, Currie became the first director of the university's development research center, the Centro de Investigaciones para el Desarrollo (CID). The institute turned academic convention on its head by placing an economist, Currie, at the helm of an interdisciplinary staff researching policy of all kinds. CID became a haven for urban research in the tradition of *Operación Colombia*. Virgilio Barco, then mayor of Bogotá, gave CID its first external contract, enlisting the institute to assess development plans for the city. Under Currie's direction, that study became the first of many promoting cities-within-cities.[84]

The allies and intermediaries that Currie cultivated ultimately determined the fate of his proposals. They included the businessmen and young economists he met during the 1960s as well as Conservative Party leaders. Indeed, Currie's ideas found their way into government during the 1970s, when he gained the ear of Conservative president Misael Pastrana (1970–74). Pastrana is remembered as the president who reversed Colombia's 1961 land reform, purging INCORA officials and repressing the national peasant league that his predecessor, Carlos Lleras Restrepo, had established.[85] Currie's urbanization program, founded on an explicit critique of agrarian reform, appealed powerfully to the new government. Pastrana chose one of Currie's protégés, economist Roberto Arenas, as director of the National Planning Department, and Arenas recruited his mentor to join him in government. In 1971, Currie reemerged as a presidential advisor for the third time in his life and spent the next ten years at the National Planning Department. The ideas he had first presented in *Operación Colombia* became the basis of Pastrana's national economic plan, the Plan of the Four Strategies.[86]

From Currie's perspective, a dream seemed finally at hand. Pastrana allowed him to design a city-within-a-city in a sector of Bogotá called El Salitre and used executive powers to establish the UPAC system in 1972. Yet the endeavor turned out quite differently from Currie's original plan. Initially, the Pastrana administration authorized the government's middle-income mortgage lender, the Banco Central Hipotecario, to create indexed savings accounts. But the agency hardly advertised the program and attracted few depositors. Currie rescued the experiment by convincing the administration to let private banks participate in the UPAC system. It was a controversial decision. "The private sector was not in good repute," Currie later recalled, and it only looked worse after the 1973 coup in Chile. "One ran the risk of being identified with Milton Friedman and the Chicago School, which had become dirty words." Currie balked at those comparisons. In his view, the very essence of the mixed economy was the state's mobilization and regulation of private capital to serve the public good. There was nothing sinister to him about giving responsibility to the institution most likely to fulfill it; developmental states had always grown by inventing new articulations of public and private activity. "The fact that there are abuses and that there are some things that the search for higher incomes does not provide satisfactorily . . . does not relieve us of the responsibility for understanding the functioning of a mixed economy, and of utilizing its potentialities when it appears efficient to do so," he argued.[87] Currie was certainly right that private interest made the UPAC system work. By the end of Pastrana's term, private banks throughout Colombia had created "savings and housing corporations," private subsidiaries that administered indexed savings accounts and channeled private deposits into housing loans.[88]

The UPAC system got off the ground thanks to private banks that recognized it as a profitable opportunity. By contrast, the city-within-a-city at Salitre stalled for over a decade. It turned out that the state was not up to the task that Currie had set it, hamstrung by changes in presidential administration and mounting political crises of the 1970s and 1980s. The public urban corporation never came to be. Meanwhile, there was no strong private-sector interest in establishing the neighborhood; the property, after all, was supposed to be publicly owned. By 1976, the construction firms in CAMACOL had developed their own variant on Currie's views. They embraced his calls for downtown construction "on a human scale" but balked at the idea that private capital should be nothing but a contractor to state developers. The government's first priority should be the growth and protection of the private sector, CAMACOL explained.[89] As Currie's allies interpreted his ideas, they began bending his program to their purposes and exposed a profound irony of economists' pursuit of public influence. As Currie's public stature grew, he lost the power to dictate the application and meaning of his work.

In 1987, the plan for Salitre finally went ahead with one decisive modification: the government ceded landownership to private developers. With public ownership excised from Currie's plan, private industry and the country's existing mortgage lenders eagerly built Salitre as a luxury development, casting aside the idea of creating mixed-income complexes where high-income tenants would subsidize their low-income neighbors. The developers kept the rest of Currie's plan and proudly advertised Salitre as a dense, walkable, mixed-use neighborhood where Bogotanos could "live very well without going very far."[90] Poor Bogotanos had no place in Salitre but simply had the opportunity to vie for vacated apartments elsewhere as rich Bogotanos moved into new buildings on expensive urban property. This was one form of gentrification, and emblematically, President Virgilio Barco hailed Salitre in 1987 as the next generation's Ciudad Kennedy, a model for housing Colombians in the 1980s.[91] It was an ironic outcome, and one that Currie found thoroughly distasteful. He had been glad to let commercial banks provide indexed savings accounts and enter the mortgage industry, but he had never intended to replace

self-help housing with an even less egalitarian system of urban homeownership. The country's most renowned economist had transformed the logic of
housing debates and in the process lost control of his own ideas.[92]

Currie's long years of writing and advising never produced the system of
public property he imagined, but instead multiplied Colombia's systems of
private homeownership. The businessmen and politicians who claimed his
ideas selected among them, sorted them from one another, and redeployed a
few to produce a gentrification program that Currie could only lament. Social
mediators and intellectual popularizers, these Colombians kept the private
home right where they thought it belonged: at the center of the national economic order.

———

The transformation of Colombian housing policy lay bare the many futures
that Depression-era policies seeded. New Dealers interpreted their past in
divergent, unexpected ways, some adapting US public housing law to foster
private homeownership, others invoking the history of public works to legitimate state-owned rental property. Colombia's agrarian reform of the 1930s
nourished popular visions of the private home that violated the stylized categories of midcentury social theory, melding home and work to create a middle class that planners considered frighteningly close to a peasantry. Colombians who conceived of private residential property in profoundly different
ways all availed themselves of every resource at their disposal to craft a proliferating universe of private homes. The distance between any two could be
quite small—a difference in the construction system or in the use of a
bedroom—but the change in social implication and economic order was vast.

In all this work, one of the strangest paradoxes turned out to be Lauchlin
Currie's relationship with businessmen. As he strove to distinguish economics
from cost accounting and business administration, he depended on businessmen to interpret and popularize his ideas. In the end, they bent his project of
elevating economists toward their own end of elevating themselves in policy
debates. The conjoined ascent of economists and businessmen in public life,
their instrumental reliance on one another, and their persistent tensions
turned out to be characteristic contradictions of the mixed economy. In a
world where every policy depended on crafting some functional articulation
of public and private initiative, economists who considered themselves public-
minded planners could never disentangle themselves from businessmen pursuing private interest, and Currie could never enforce his imagined boundary
between fields of knowledge and professional jurisdictions. While Currie
faced that paradox in policy making, others discovered it inside the academy.

PART II

Stewards of the State

4

Economics as a Public Mission

"WHAT IS ECONOMICS?" asked John M. Hunter in 1960. The thirty-nine-year-old Illinois native spoke as director of Colombia's first economic research center and addressed readers of one of Colombia's premier journals of economic research, the *Revista del Banco de la República*. Hunter supervised research on many subjects, but of the three articles he published in the journal, two simply set out to define his own discipline. Questions about the nature and purpose of economics dogged him every day, and he was hardly alone.[1] During the years after 1945, Colombian universities established freestanding economics programs where none had existed before.[2] To be sure, there had been men called economists in Colombia for decades; they were brilliant lawyers, engineers, businessmen, and politicians who made national economic policy and taught occasional courses in political economy on the side. But the crisis of the 1930s had inspired a new regard for economic expertise as a specialized form of knowledge, and Colombians set out to create a new kind of economist to steer the state. The invention of economics as an independent discipline, a nineteenth-century process in the United States and much of Europe, was thus a twentieth-century phenomenon in Latin America, born of new visions of national development and spearheaded by renowned men in business and government. The project produced an outpouring of writing on the definition of discipline and profession, some of it in scholarly journals, most of it in interoffice memos, student manifestos, diplomatic cables, and grant applications. Explaining the scope of the field, the identity of an economist, and the realms of life in which practitioners could claim authority became a consuming preoccupation for members of a nascent profession. These questions formed the subtext, and sometimes the text, of every hiring decision, national statistical survey, and senior thesis in Colombia.

For Hunter and his contemporaries, economics came to be defined not by any specific methodological or theoretical orientation but by a proclaimed public purpose: it was knowledge for state planning and for national development. The ideas of public and private came to ground conceptions of

discipline and profession in Colombia, with economists associating themselves with the tasks of statecraft and an imagined public interest. In doing so,
they distinguished themselves from business administrators whom they associated with purely private pursuits. Yet that definition created maddening,
intractable problems in a mixed economy. As economists searched for self-
definition, they found themselves asking the same thorny questions that
echoed in the halls of the CVC, ICT, INCORA, ANDI, and Asocaña. What
should be the status of their own academic institutions in the system of public
and private sectors, and how should they relate to the varied groups exercising
public powers in Colombia, whether national planning agencies, regional development corporations, or private gremios that wielded regulatory powers,
generated national income, and spoke unabashedly for private interests? How
might economists secure their own professional autonomy, and how did that
autonomy harmonize with the wider interest of Colombian society? In practical terms, was national development simply a mass of business and regional
development projects to which economists should apply themselves, or were
local and private pursuits diversions from the general interest? Ultimately,
what did it mean to be the analyst, strategist, and guardian of the public good
in a society where the very concept of the public seemed nothing but porous
borders, ragged edges, and wheels within wheels?

Two economics faculties captured the lion's share of international aid after
1945, and they reflected the structure and paradoxes of the emergent developmental state. Both presented themselves as foils to the country's flagship public university, the Universidad Nacional in Bogotá, whose law faculty had
trained Colombia's top economic policy makers since the nineteenth century.
The Universidad de los Andes, located in Bogotá, was a private institution that
forthrightly aimed to displace the Nacional as the country's preeminent source
of economic policy makers. Across the country in Cali, the Universidad del
Valle was no private contender for public authority but rather a regional public
university that proposed to relocate planning functions to the subnational
level, just as the CVC had. These two institutions expressed the twin impulses
toward regional and private delegation that the CVC's charter had contained
and that defined both the decentralized state and the mixed economy at midcentury. Their position in society made them emblematic institutions of their
time, bound economists to regional and private projects in inescapable ways,
and endowed the economics profession with a distinctive regional division of
intellectual labor that mirrored the spatial distribution of state functions. Historians of economics and sociologists of professions have long described national economics professions as creatures of the states that conjured them and
whose activities they aimed to shape. But they generally treat the state as a
monolith, when the developmental state was in fact a shape-shifter.[3] In

postwar Colombia, economics came to bear the unmistakable marks of the mercurial state that gave it life.

———

Located in the capital city and tied to leaders of the National Front, the Universidad de los Andes moved with remarkable speed to overtake the Nacional as Colombia's leading source of state planners. Its economics faculty simultaneously became a battleground, riven by conflict over the proper relationship of economists to the state and private capital, and over the proper distribution of responsibilities between public and private institutions. By the 1960s, economists at los Andes proposed to resolve all of these questions at once by identifying themselves as disinterested guardians of the public good, private universities as guardians of their professional autonomy, and both as unrivaled guides for the national government. In doing so, they built a private institution capable of making and unmaking the midcentury state.

Los Andes was a young university, established in 1948 by a worldly group of Bogotanos to train *técnicos* for government and business. Twenty-five-year-old Mario Laserna, known as the university's founder, was the son of a wealthy businessman. Born in Paris, he had attended elementary school in New York, graduated from Bogotá's most selective private high school, the Gimnasio Moderno, and earned a BA in mathematics from Columbia University. His Ivy League pedigree earned him grotesque adulation in Colombia: on his eightieth birthday, an associate boasted that Laserna's college friends had been "the rich, the famous, the intelligent and the aristocrats."[4] Laserna's fellow founders included classmates from the Gimnasio Moderno and older men of comparable social station. Hernán Echavarría Olózaga, the first dean of the Faculty of Economics, belonged to a prominent family of industrialists in Medellín and had studied for two years at the London School of Economics. Since returning to Colombia in 1930, he had managed large-scale textile operations, served as a cabinet minister under Liberal president Alfonso López Pumarejo, and published seminal accounts of modern macroeconomic theory for Colombian readers.[5]

Laserna, Echavarría, and their collaborators considered economics training practical preparation for policy making and business administration, which they considered twin foundations of economic development. Fomenting development was in fact the university's animating purpose, and they believed that Colombia lacked a critical prerequisite: a depoliticized, technically trained elite that could rationally direct public and private affairs. The university presented itself as "a point of connection between Colombian youth and the technical and scientific advances of the rest of the world."[6] The school's international vision was fixed intently northward. Since the colonial period, Colombian universities had adapted European institutional forms and intellectual currents, but los Andes shifted Colombians' sights across the Atlantic to the United States, a country long considered an industrial powerhouse but a laggard in cultural sophistication. In 1945, as the ruins of prewar Europe smoldered and US universities emerged as world leaders, Laserna promised to fashion los Andes' curriculum after that of his alma mater, Columbia. Where Latin American and European universities had traditionally offered specialized five-year programs of study, los Andes instituted a four-year curriculum with some liberal arts requirements. To be sure, a college education at los Andes provided professional training far more specialized than anything found in New York City. After completing a handful of courses in contemporary civilization, the humanities, science, Spanish, and Colombian history, students took no electives outside their majors. The amalgamation of US and Latin American systems nevertheless struck Colombians as thoroughly *gringo*. The fields of study were equally distinctive. Initially, los Andes comprised just a handful of faculties or "professional schools": architecture, economics, chemistry and chemical engineering, electrical engineering, mathematics and languages, and a general program of liberal arts and sciences. The inclusion of economics was remarkable in 1948. The field had none of the prestige of architecture or engineering and attracted just four of the eighty students who enrolled in the first class.[7]

Los Andes distinguished itself, most importantly, as a private, secular institution. Its founders had established the university with their own money; at the outset, they owned the school and Laserna was the largest investor. They imagined los Andes as an alternative to both the Nacional and the Catholic universities that had proliferated in Latin America since the 1930s. Objective knowledge, they asserted, could never come from institutions whose leaders were political or religious appointees.[8]

The defense of private, secular education was in part a reaction against real interference by politicians in the academic affairs of the Nacional. A telling incident occurred during the infancy of the university's economics program. In 1945, the Nacional had begun a pioneering reform of economics education, creating the Instituto de Ciencias Económicas (ICE) within its Faculty of Law. Its director, Antonio García Nossa, brought together the professors already teaching at the Nacional with distinguished members of a political economy program that he had led at Bogotá's Escuela Normal Superior. He planned to convert ICE into a full-fledged faculty but quickly ran into opposition beyond the university. García was a well-known socialist, an advisor to Jorge Eliécer Gaitán's populist movement within the Liberal Party, and a veteran of Colombia's indigenous and student movements. In the waning days of the Liberal

Party's sixteen-year ascendancy, the thirty-three-year-old radical on the fringes of the party had managed to become the flag bearer for economics at the country's top university. However, his opponents in both major parties made ICE a target of such vitriolic attack that García was forced out of the Nacional in 1949. Three years later, the university expanded ICE into an independent Facultad de Ciencias Económicas, but García had no place in it.[9]

The idealization of private education was just as much a reaction against student movements that flourished at the Nacional. Throughout Latin America, public university students asserted the right to participate in academic and administrative decisions, and they made themselves heard through strikes when formally excluded from university governance. Students' demand for codetermination had roots in the university reform movement that had swept the continent during the early twentieth century. That movement had focused on the quality of authority and intellectual exchange within universities. Students criticized the power of church and state officials to dictate academic standards and decried lecturing and memorization as authoritarian styles of teaching. They argued that universities had failed to fulfill their public mission as engines of social change and crucibles of a distinctively Latin American politics and culture. To realize these goals, they needed to become protected spaces for debate among students and faculty, insulated from substantive intervention by church and state officials. In place of political or religious authority, students presented their own movements as instruments of reform and governance. Beginning in 1918 at Argentina's Universidad de Córdoba, students throughout Latin America won representation on university committees and achieved varying degrees of influence in curricular and administrative matters. At the Nacional during the 1940s, student representatives worked with a rector or president, Gerardo Molina, who had himself come out of the student movement of the early twentieth century.[10]

The founders of los Andes shared the fear of church and state power that had animated the university reform movement, but they imagined reform quite differently. Rejecting the earlier movement's ideal of a university as a wellspring of secular, pan-Hispanic politics and culture, the new reformers saw it as an incubator of universalist technical knowledge. They saw student organizing as just one more threat to objectivity and professional autonomy. The fear of Latin American student movements reflected the reality that, at times, they did endanger academic freedom by demanding the firing of professors they considered incompetent. However, los Andes' leaders were at least as frightened by leftist political organizing at public universities. In 1960, the president of los Andes' Consejo Directivo enlisted his colleagues in an effort to "control [communist] infiltration" on the campus. Behind closed doors, the rector volunteered that he knew an "active group of young people" distributing anticommunist literature, and the president committed to fund the organization. Publicly, meanwhile, the school's leaders promised to create a depoliticized campus, free of both public authority and student organizing.[11]

The defense of private, secular education finally drew strength from the experience of La Violencia and Colombia's years of dictatorship. As political parties became vehicles of assassination, as politics came to appear as nothing more than ruthless partisanship, and as democratic rule temporarily came to an end, politics lost legitimacy and the idea of technocracy acquired new appeal. The creation of los Andes was one expression of a nationalist, developmentalist, technocratic impulse to make the country governable, reasonable, and prosperous once again. That same impulse underlay the birth of the National Front in 1958; indeed, the university rector from 1954 to 1956 was none other than Alberto Lleras Camargo, the first president of the coalition government. A towering figure in the Liberal Party, Lleras never abandoned politics as a vocation, but he and his contemporaries appreciated the dangers of political mobilization. Within los Andes and the National Front, they sought to banish the explosive element of partisan competition, scrupulously including both Liberals and Conservatives in positions of leadership. Just as important, they took a benign view of private mobilization by organized, reform-minded capitalists. Emblematically, when los Andes' board considered naming Lleras rector, they met in the headquarters of the commercial Bank of Bogotá and wrung their hands in worry that Colombians might see the university as a Liberal outpost. When Lleras became head of the party in 1956, he dutifully resigned as rector to protect the university's "nonpolitical" reputation.[12]

Intellectually, the economics faculty was a fairly ecumenical place during the 1940s and 1950s. Its heterodoxy owed little to the founders. Although they considered themselves defenders of free thought, los Andes' leaders drew a hard line against Marxists and communists, and both Echavarría and Lleras Camargo disparaged CEPAL—the intellectual center of import substitution industrialization—as a hub of small-minded nationalists. Both men spent the 1950s begging Point IV and the Rockefeller Foundation to send US professors to counteract the UN agency's influence in Latin America.[13] Nevertheless, during the mid-1950s, the chair of the economics faculty was one of Colombia's leading *cepalinos*, Jorge Méndez Munévar, who argued for a wide-ranging curriculum exposing students to competing schools of thought. Méndez secured his position because, like Echavarría, he was one of the few Colombians who had studied economics abroad, earning a master's degree from Princeton during the 1940s. He had come away convinced that his education had not prepared him to understand Colombia, and as a professor, he introduced students to development economics by way of *cepalino* structuralism.[14] Méndez's capacious vision of a heterogeneous curriculum became an inescapable reality within Colombia's early economics programs, since all of them drew their instructors from a small pool of eclectically trained part-timers. Méndez himself had offered economic policy classes at the Nacional under Antonio García in 1949. Later, he taught economic theory at Laserna's alma mater, the Gimnasio Moderno, which had established a business administration program with help from J. Anton de Haas of Harvard Business School. During the late 1950s, one of los Andes' celebrated achievements was its absorption of that program, which Méndez arranged. Hard theoretical and methodological distinctions simply did not exist between Colombian economics programs during these years because individual professors taught in so many of them.[15]

Los Andes' private, secular status and the international standing of its founders made it an object of fascination for US funders. During the 1950s, the university approached Point IV, the Rockefeller Foundation, and Nelson Rockefeller himself, all of whom leaped at the chance to help the school. Responding to a 1954 entreaty from his friend Alberto Lleras Camargo, Nelson Rockefeller donated $100,000 for the construction of campus buildings and convinced the Kress Foundation to extend a grant. Four years later, he established the University of the Andes Foundation, a nonprofit organization that channeled corporate donations to what Standard Oil's company magazine termed "a struggling little school in Bogotá."[16] As chairman, Rockefeller recruited board members and staff with remarkable stature in business and government. Economist Adolf A. Berle, a veteran of FDR's Brain Trust and former ambassador to Brazil, became the foundation's president and donated much of his personal library to los Andes. Publishing giant Henry Luce served on the board alongside Peter Grace, the president and CEO of W. R. Grace. Diplomats Norman Armour and Spruille Braden had been authors of US policy in Latin America from the occupation of Haiti to the 1954 coup in Guatemala. Together, board members promoted los Andes as "a symbol of what a *private*, democratically oriented university can contribute to the development of our hemisphere" and promised that private money would safeguard "academic freedom." Major donations came from mining and petroleum firms with investments in Latin America, and while their contributions were modest by US corporate standards, they guaranteed los Andes a steady stream of dollars.[17]

Taking the school's claims at face value, US observers made the idea of a private university in Latin America into a cause célèbre in the United States. In 1956, Point IV sent economists H. K. Allen and J. F. Bell from the University of Illinois to evaluate the school, and they returned singing the praises of private funding and control. These two professors from a public university equated los Andes' independence from church and state with a commitment to "Freedom of thought and investigation."[18] Four years later, Adlai Stevenson visited los Andes with former Senator William Benton of Connecticut. In their eyes, the university's quiescent student body, drawn from Colombia's richest families, testified to the superior quality of private education in Latin America. "There are no students on the university council," Benton marveled, "and the students are given no legal rights of any kind over the operation of the university." Stevenson declared los Andes a "remarkable and novel institution" and convinced the Field Foundation to fund the university.[19]

The Rockefeller Foundation ultimately became the major benefactor of the economics faculty. In 1956, the foundation was searching for a Colombian university to support when Mario Laserna came to the United States to raise money. There he met the foundation's assistant director for social sciences, Montague Yudelman. Born in 1922 on a sheep ranch in Matatiele, South Africa, Yudelman had earned a PhD from Berkeley in 1952. He had gone on to work for the Food and Agriculture Organization of the United Nations in Rome, won a Ford Foundation grant to research economic development in Central Africa, and served as a member of the World Bank's 1955 agricultural mission to Colombia. He met Laserna a month after joining the foundation in 1956, and the young Bogotano convinced him that los Andes was the only school in the country "giving some serious attention to the social sciences" as independent disciplines.[20] Yudelman immediately visited Bogotá to inspect the university.

Foundation officials shared a great deal with the founders of los Andes, not least their anticommunist politics. The foundation itself had become a target of McCarthyist investigation during the 1950s and responded by blacklisting applicants and entire fields of research that it considered vulnerable to political attack. In 1958, when los Andes considered hiring Lauchlin Currie, Rockefeller's director for social sciences gravely warned that the foundation would first need to investigate the old New Dealer, los Andes never pursued the matter. Throughout the 1950s and 1960s, foundation staff routinely subjected academics to anticommunist vetting while condemning students and administrators at Colombia's public universities for comparable violations of academic freedom.[21] But the foundation's social science staff had no fear of CEPAL and indeed of most economists who could find jobs in creditable universities, Washington, or any of the capitalist multilateral agencies. When Yudelman arrived in Bogotá, he immediately investigated Jorge Méndez, whom anticommunist officials in Point IV considered "overly sympathetic to socialism and statism."[22] Yudelman spoke with businessmen on the board of trustees and solicited assessments from Albert Hirschman and his consulting partner George Kalmanoff. No one thought highly of Méndez, but they expressed none of the virulent anticommunist antagonism of US aid officials. Yudelman concluded that Méndez was not "top-notch, though fairly good by Colombian standards, which are low." As his appraisal suggested, Yudelman differed from

Point IV officials only in his superior ability to identify communists. The foundation's staff of social scientists knew the field of economics well enough to understand that *cepalinos* were strategists of capitalist development.[23]

In late 1956, the foundation agreed to finance the creation of an economic research center at los Andes, the Centro de Estudios sobre el Desarrollo Económico (CEDE). The first order of business was finding an economist to direct it. Méndez insisted on hiring a foreigner with no prior relationship to Colombia. As Yudelman explained, La Violencia had left divisions so deep that any director's "past associations . . . would be introduced as 'evidence' of bias whenever controversial subjects were examined." The Rockefeller Foundation delegated the search to MIT's Center for International Studies, a hub of modernization theory and a notorious collaborator with the CIA. MIT economist Everett Hagen flew to Bogotá in 1957 and on his return cast a wide net, looking for any US, European, or Australian economist with a reputable doctoral degree and an interest in working in Colombia. The young man he finally found was neither a renowned Cold Warrior nor an eminent academic. John M. Hunter, born in 1921, was a Harvard PhD who had taught at Michigan State since 1950. He had written a dissertation on economic development in Cuba and spent the previous academic year in Vietnam as a professor and government advisor. In April 1958, the Rockefeller Foundation gave los Andes a grant to hire Hunter for two years, and he became the first director of CEDE.[24]

Private funds enabled los Andes to create Colombia's first and most prestigious economic research center. CEDE opened its doors in September 1958 with a modest staff. Hunter and two full-time Colombian professors oversaw a handful of undergraduate research assistants and thesis writers. Indeed, student research represented the bulk of the center's early output. As the only institution of its kind in the country, CEDE initially attracted undergraduates from universities throughout Colombia who came to Bogotá during their final year to work under Hunter's supervision. Los Andes hired the top graduates as professors—they were, after all, some of the country's best-trained professionals in the field—and the Rockefeller Foundation sent some to the United States for graduate study on the condition that they return as faculty. Los Andes thus became the first university in Colombia whose economics professors overwhelmingly held at least undergraduate degrees in the discipline. Foreign graduate training in turn allowed CEDE to become a Colombian-led institution after just four years. Hunter and his successor, Wallace N. Atherton, a labor economist from Michigan State, each directed the center for two years but insisted on hiring a Colombian as quickly as possible. Their colleague Jorge Ruiz Lara assumed leadership in 1962 after completing a PhD at the University of Illinois, supported in part by a Rockefeller Foundation fellowship.[25]

From the start, CEDE's directors faithfully recapitulated the university creed, celebrating private financing as the basis of independent thought and, in Hunter's words, "the search for truth." But CEDE's actual experience belied the claim. Hunter, Atherton, and Ruiz all struggled to pursue what they saw as legitimate economic research in the face of their sponsors' competing demands. By the end of its first year, CEDE had become a place where proponents of economics in Colombia battled to answer two interrelated questions: what qualified as economic research, and what was the proper relationship between economists, capital, and the state?

Hunter knew before arriving in Bogotá that he would need to establish a shared definition of economics with his Colombian colleagues. Several months earlier, he had met with leaders of the university and economics faculty, who shocked him by proposing that CEDE tackle what he considered problems of business administration. "I tried to make it perfectly clear to them that I was not interested in becoming a director of a business consulting firm," Hunter wrote to the Rockefeller Foundation. Nonetheless, by the end of his first semester, he complained that "a substantial portion of the University budget is now begged largely from business" and "the independence of the University is more apparent than real." Yudelman, visiting the campus in December 1958, lamented that Hunter "has had to rebuff several influential Colombians who wished to use the CEDE for personal interest research projects."[26]

The program of study reflected the same conflation of fields and purposes. Straight into the late 1960s, students chose one of two specializations: economics or management. The programs of study were virtually identical, diverging only in the final year of coursework, and all graduates received degrees designating them as economists. Every student took classes in accounting, and management students could choose among twenty-four electives covering topics from time-and-motion studies to tax law to advertising. The remainder of the curriculum accorded with trends in the US economics profession. Students took English, mathematics, macroeconomic and microeconomic theory, money and banking, public finance, agricultural economics, sociology, and specialization courses in international trade, development economics, labor economics, and the history of economic thought. To Hunter, like Currie and indeed many US observers, this was not a curriculum but a messy agglomeration of disciplinary and national traditions.[27]

Hunter set out to teach Colombians the difference between economics and business administration. Just as Yudelman disparaged "personal interest research projects," Hunter argued that "CEDE's principal interest is the wellbeing of the community before the wellbeing (or profits) of a particular firm." He at once defined and defended economics by identifying it with the general interest, resorting to the same strategy of legitimation that Lauchlin Currie used to promote El Salitre over Ciudad Kennedy. Like Currie, Hunter identified material scarcity as Colombia's pressing problem and insisted that experts with a global view of society could channel scarce resources to their most productive use. As he argued, since the time of Hume, Smith, Ricardo, and Mill, economists had concerned themselves with "the efficient use of resources on the part of society, and that type of efficiency is inextricably associated with notions of well-being." Businessmen, like economists, dealt with production and consumption and needed to study many of the same subjects. But their motives differed. "The primordial interest of the manager is maximizing the profits of a firm," explained Hunter. "This in no way presents our manager as a simple villain," he added. Calling on classical and neoclassical theory, he explained that the pursuit of profit drove each capitalist to produce "according to the express desire of consumers" by lowering prices and improving quality. "Only chaos could arise if he renounced his interest in profits," he assured. Capitalists were perfectly fit to produce goods and services.

Only economists, however, could guarantee consumers access to the variety of products that they wanted. Hunter depicted the economist as a planner and regulator, checking the allocation of investment between sectors and measuring the volume and distribution of total consumption. In a world run by businessmen, he suggested, people might walk into stores to find nothing but shoes, and capitalists might build monopolies or fight interminably over whether to manufacture or import automobiles. "In these and other disputes," Hunter wrote, "the economist is the technically competent person called to represent the interests of the consumer, and in a broader sense the entire society." He implored Colombians to stop referring to businessmen as economists, warning that the practice allowed legitimately self-interested men to masquerade as disinterested arbiters of the general welfare.[28]

"It was decided," Hunter wrote at the end of two years in Colombia, "that CEDE would not do 'business' research but would restrict itself to 'economic' research."

> This is not an easy distinction in some cases; but, crudely put, we decided not to do research which was primarily designed to improve the profit and loss position of a single firm. Undoubtedly, however, more financial support would have been forthcoming from this type of research.

Indeed, Hunter's distinction between economic and business research won favor among CEDE's staff without substantially altering what he described as the "the vocal and monetary demands of industry." The center grew increasingly vulnerable to those demands as revenue from contract research rose from 20 percent of its budget in 1960 to 66 percent in 1962, surpassing both

Rockefeller and general university funds. In response, CEDE's leaders struggled to assert professional autonomy over economic research. Hunter unsuccessfully sought to create endowed chairs for professors, and the university lawyer confronted one private funder that declined to pay after objecting to the results of a study. CEDE further resolved to maintain control over publication rights after a conflict with the national Bankers Association. The business group had commissioned the first interindustry wage study in Colombia but refused to sanction its publication. "What they had wanted," Atherton explained, "was a brief for a strike then in prospect. So this study is still locked in a safe; but no more contracts like this will be undertaken."[29]

CEDE turned to foreign foundations to finance research that no business would support. Atherton and Ruiz pitched two studies to the Rockefeller Foundation that, to them, exemplified economics in the public interest. The first revealed just how similar "economic" and "business" research could be. Jorge Ruiz Lara proposed to design "an econometric model of the world demand for Colombian coffee." During the late 1950s, coffee production expanded worldwide, provoking intense competition among national producers and forcing each one to lower its prices. Colombia derived nearly 70 percent of its export revenues from coffee, and deteriorating prices dealt a devastating blow to national income as well as the livelihoods of individual growers. To stabilize prices, coffee-producing countries negotiated agreements setting national export quotas. Within Colombia, it then fell to one of the country's most powerful gremios or business associations, the Coffee Growers Federation, to establish a market-clearing price: the value needed to be high enough to convince growers to meet the quota and low enough for international buyers to consume the entire amount. The federation had played a leading role in regulating the price of coffee since the Depression and war years, when the national government responded to collapsing international demand by granting the organization powers and funds to buy, sell, and store the crop. During years of expanding global demand, the federation had no trouble setting prices, but during the crisis of the late 1950s and early 1960s, its prices failed to clear the market, and the country's coffee exports actually fell below its quotas. Ruiz promised to analyze the determinants of global demand for Colombian coffee to help the federation set prices that would enable the country to sell more coffee.

In Ruiz's view, a research project to protect over two-thirds of Colombia's export income clearly represented work in the national interest. "Any mistake in the coffee policy," he wrote to the Rockefeller Foundation, "is likely to retard the economic development of the country." At the same time, he and Atherton realized that the private federation ought to sponsor the research out of its own self-interest. It very nearly did so. However, according to Atherton, the federation's top leaders opposed the project because they misunderstood a few aspects of it. They wrongly believed that CEDE wanted them to disclose data that they considered proprietary, and, in Atherton's view, some foolishly doubted the value of "new-fangled quantitative economics." Lower-level federation officials admired the initiative, and Atherton and Ruiz felt certain that their superiors would come around once they saw the results.[30]

Foundation funds, in this case, allowed CEDE to do work that its staff believed private enterprise should and would eventually finance for self-interested reasons. At that point, CEDE would not be boosting the profits of a single firm but would unquestionably be supporting those of the country's largest coffee growers, whose interests the federation chiefly represented. For those who believed in the promise of a mixed economy, economic research invariably served both public and private interests, and Atherton and Ruiz obscured this fact by focusing on a commodity with outsized national significance. Under Hunter's definition, CEDE assigned only the exceptionally narrow problems of single firms to business consultants while associating broader business interests with the public interest and granting them intellectual and ethical legitimacy as economic concerns.

CEDE's depiction of economists as defenders of the public interest could justify research for gremios, and it simultaneously allowed the center to assume what many considered state responsibilities. Alongside Ruiz's study, CEDE proposed a second project to compile Colombia's first labor statistics. Studying the labor force had become a national priority in 1961, when Lauchlin Currie had published *Operación Colombia*, an early version of the plan that President Pastrana adopted during the 1970s. The report proposed moving Colombia's rural poor into urban jobs to spur economic growth and identified housing construction as a leading sector. Economists at los Andes insisted that the national state needed data to assess the proposal. Were the ranks of the urban unemployed already large enough to provide the workforce that Currie envisioned? Could cities absorb any more workers, or would new migrants simply find themselves destitute?[31]

"The carrying out of such a study by a private organization may seem peculiar," Atherton acknowledged. In fact, CEDE was openly competing with a government agency, the Departamento Administrativo Nacional de Estadística (DANE). In 1961, both had produced pilot studies of the urban unemployment rate, DANE through a census of the municipio of Fusagasugá, and CEDE through a senior thesis surveying three neighborhoods in Bogotá. Neither had the resources to extend its research; according to Atherton, DANE "has too small a budget even to tabulate the data they have already collected." A 1962 grant from the Rockefeller Foundation allowed CEDE to begin regular surveys of urban employment, unemployment, and wages. The effort began in

FIGURE 4.1. CEDE economists visit the home of an unemployed worker in Bogotá as part of an effort to compile the country's first labor statistics. CEDE was a private research center at the Universidad de los Andes that openly competed with the national government to establish itself as a source of basic economic data. (RF RG P, Series 311S, Box 81, Folder 1644)

Bogotá and the nearby city of Girardot, and with help from economists at regional universities became a privately led national initiative generating labor statistics for the country.[32] In short order, young US-educated professors at los Andes used the data to establish labor economics as a field independent of labor law. The noted economist Miguel Urrutia, after earning a BA in economics at Harvard and working briefly for CAR—the CVC's counterpart in the Bogotá savanna—began his academic career at CEDE, where he produced seminal publications measuring employment and unemployment.[33]

Compiling labor statistics was one of CEDE's signal achievements of the 1960s and exemplified the role that the center hoped to play in public policy making. At the end of Hunter's first year in Bogotá, he had argued that only a private research center could "attack problems of long-term significance and importance, and dedicate all the time necessary to their study." By contrast, he claimed that "government research, by its very nature, is inclined toward immediate problems." For Hunter and his colleagues, compiling macroeconomic statistics was a perfect example of research with long-term significance. In Colombia and much of the Third World, economists during the early postwar decades considered data collection an indispensable first step toward any kind of economic analysis and threw themselves into assembling figures on production, employment, prices, wages, and other basic indicators of national economic performance. CEPAL's reputation in Latin America rested largely on its early leadership in measuring gross national product and training government officials to maintain and interpret national income accounts. In Colombia, the UN agency did just this kind of work with the National Planning Department and wrote the ten-year plan that Colombia adopted under the Alliance for Progress.[34]

At los Andes, however, economists insisted that a private research institute, rather than a state agency, should do this work. In 1962, their argument did not rest on any evidence that CEDE was best qualified for the task. During its first four years, the center's reliance on thesis writers and private contracts limited it to narrow topics that undergraduates could tackle in a few months. Students had collected small data samples on subjects including the potato market in Bogotá, public housing quality, and interlocking directorates among Colombian firms. These studies were empirical, nationalist, and technically modest, requiring no complex mathematics, and in those respects resembled the labor statistics initiative. But they in no way established CEDE's superiority to DANE. Rockefeller Foundation officials, like los Andes' founders, believed for their own reasons that a private university could best generate knowledge for policy making. When local businessmen failed to perform their idealized function as scholarly patrons and the center was proving its boosters wrong, the foundation fulfilled its own prophecy by funding CEDE rather than DANE, making the private university a recognized source of basic research.[35]

By the mid-1960s, CEDE had used funds from the Rockefeller Foundation and Population Council to launch studies of employment and unemployment, urban demographic growth, household income and expenses, and urban and regional planning. These were vital areas of knowledge at a time when millions of rural migrants were poorly housed and underemployed in Colombia's cities. CEDE's leaders believed that the government needed to solve public problems but did not trust the Nacional or state agencies to do much of the work of policy making. Throughout the 1960s, they made sense of radical student movements at the Nacional and errors in CEPAL statistics that the National Planning Department used by dismissing public-sector research as irredeemably flawed. They joked that unreliable data was "*muy cepalina.*" Deans Hernán Echavarría and Oscar Gómez told Rockefeller officials that the Nacional employed no real economists; the program there was "very bad and without the possibility of improvement." In their view, los Andes existed not to eliminate the state but to appropriate central functions until the public sector learned to emulate a private research institute. In 1966, Dean Eduardo Wiesner explained that "once other national entities have shown interest in [CEDE's areas of expertise], CEDE will hand over to them its documentation and move onto other fields."[36]

The central bank and National Planning Department did take an interest in CEDE's labor statistics initiative and financed it when the Rockefeller grant expired. By the late 1960s, Carlos Lleras Restrepo's National Planning Department likewise relied on CEDE to forecast population growth and predict its effects on employment. Only during the 1970s, when CEDE had secured its reputation as an authoritative source of knowledge and begun new lines of research did it finally transfer responsibility for labor statistics to DANE. CEDE thus established itself as an intellectual pioneer and the state as a laggard. The image of the private research center as an unencumbered, dispassionate innovator guiding and reforming the state obscured CEDE's actual dependence on public agencies and foreign foundations to finance projects that businessmen obstructed. But the limits to professional autonomy in public institutions allowed the center's economists to celebrate los Andes' private status in every annual report, even as they inundated the Rockefeller Foundation with complaints about their own local patrons.[37]

At los Andes, the quest for professional autonomy gave rise to the first arguments for privatization among the new generation of Colombian economists. Their position was at odds with what most observers have regarded as their economic ideas. During the 1960s, it was an article of faith among many economists that only the state could spearhead projects that undergirded development but promised no short-term profits. Economists commonly assigned infrastructure development and some types of heavy industry to the public sector in order to facilitate private investment in other areas. At los Andes, economists likewise discussed their own research as a product that had long-term significance for national development but could never attract investors with short-term interests. Strikingly, however, they concluded that private financing and administration were the proper foundations of economic research in the public interest. Economists' experience of professional formation led them to unorthodox ideas about the responsibilities of public and private institutions.

Over the course of the 1960s, los Andes became the country's leading source of economic planners. The young economists who flooded government agencies in turn became symbols of educational progress, enlightened government, and bourgeois internationalism under the National Front. Jorge Franco Holguín assumed leadership of the National Planning Department in 1958, plucked from his teaching post at los Andes by incoming president and former los Andes rector Alberto Lleras Camargo. The thirty-two-year-old economist had studied at Oxford and Harvard Business School and proudly belonged to no political party. As he explained to the New York Times, his was "a technical, not a political appointment"; his only subjective commitment was "to avoid socialism in Colombia." The *Times* lavished him with praise. Not only did Franco support "favorable treatment of oil companies and other foreign capital," but he also played golf, lived in "a modern split-level house," and enjoyed music that was "either very classical, like Bach, Mozart and Vivaldi, or very, very modern."[38]

By the mid-1960s, los Andes' early graduates were old enough to take office themselves. Eduardo Wiesner had written his senior thesis under Hunter in 1960 and earned a master's degree from Stanford on a fellowship from the Rockefeller Foundation. After working at CEDE for two years, he became national budget director in 1964 and returned to los Andes the following year as dean of the economics faculty. Jorge Ruiz Lara left his job as director of CEDE in 1964 to take charge of the National Planning Department, and the next year he became an advisor to the national Monetary Board. When Carlos Lleras Restrepo took office in 1966, he immediately offered jobs to seven economics professors at los Andes. Charles Hardin of the Rockefeller Foundation congratulated CEDE in 1964 on the "great honor" of being "raided by the Government of Colombia." Atherton delightedly observed that he had always expected CEDE to attain public influence, and "the time has come."[39]

The Universidad de los Andes produced Colombia's top economic policy makers from the 1960s straight through to the twenty-first century.[40] Throughout those years, the school's defining characteristic was never doctrinal uniformity but the simple fact that the economics program responsible for launching economists into government had as its founding myth the superiority of the private sector as the guardian of free thought and the public good. Postwar economic planning in Colombia grew hand in hand with the transfer of intellectual authority to a private university and the delegitimation of both public institutions and political decision-making. The university's position in Colombian society, rather than a marked theoretical or methodological bias in the curriculum, made it the premier source of state planners during the 1960s and an emblematic feature of the mixed economy. Decades later, the economists who took the midcentury state apart came from the very same economics program, and the school's unchanged position in Colombian society made it a potent symbol of neoliberalism.

———

In the capital city, Colombian economists aspired to steer the ship of state, and by the 1960s, that had come to mean influencing national policy from the remove of a private university. In the provincial outpost of Cali, exercising public power meant something different. Charles M. Hardin of the Rockefeller

Foundation put it bluntly in 1963, noting that the CVC "is *the* government here." In a country as balkanized as Colombia, the national government did not look to Cali for economists to lead the finance ministry, the central bank, or the National Planning Department. The autonomous regional corporation was the national institution that most powerfully defined the public interest in the Cauca Valley; it possessed the ability to conjure a discipline and define its work. It was a peculiar sun to orbit. Not only did the CVC define planning in regional terms, but it also equated regional development with business development. For decades, economics in the Cauca Valley meant research for agribusiness, sponsored by a public university in the name of the public good. As Cali's economists set about answering the CVC's questions, their work presented the same problem that bedeviled economists at los Andes. Was economics anything more than a grand business consultancy? Did there exist a public purpose apart from private interest?

The CVC clamored for economists during its early years because it lacked the most basic information about the Cauca Valley. In 1956, William Hayes hunted fruitlessly for measures of productivity on local sugar plantations, and Bernardo Garcés Córdoba resorted to collecting data from his own panela mill. The CVC produced estimates of coal production, prices, and consumption that year by interviewing four businessmen and local officials. As late as 1964, Garcés contrived land value figures based on personal observation.[41] During the 1950s, the corporation began approaching the World Bank, the United Nations, Point IV, the Caja Agraria, the National Planning Department, and the Rockefeller Foundation with research proposals and requests for economists. They knew that extensive cattle ranches lay in the valley and crops in the mountains, but they needed data to determine their extent and ideal redistribution. Before building drainage and irrigation works, they wanted to know the production costs and profitability of all sorts of crops. And they wanted economists to redesign the agricultural marketing system to ensure uniform quality, long-distance distribution, and fair, stable prices.[42] By the decade's end, Garcés told the Rockefeller Foundation that the best way to support the corporation was to fund an economics program at the local university.[43]

Montague Yudelman of the Rockefeller Foundation responded. He had already met Garcés and Hayes in 1955, when he had worked with the World Bank's agricultural mission to Colombia. The CVC struck him as "one of the most exciting experiments in economic development in Latin America" and an ideal partner for a new economics faculty.[44] There was, moreover, a promising new university in Cali. The Universidad del Valle was nearly as young as los Andes, founded in 1945 with a developmentalist mission. Its founders were the same local elites who supported the CVC; the corporation itself had a seat on the university governing board, and the rector was the poet Mario Carvajal, a partner in Carvajal & Cía. and the uncle of CVC board member Manuel Carvajal. Although the school was public, it was created by the Valle legislature, which made it a departmental institution separate from the national university system. And unlike the Nacional, it had no long-standing intellectual tradition or student movement to contend with. Early on, UniValle had established programs in engineering and architecture, and it boasted medical and nursing programs led by US-trained doctors. Physicians Gabriel Velásquez Palau, Alfonso Ocampo Londoño, and their colleagues had introduced US-style medical education to Colombia and won support from the Rockefeller Foundation in 1953. By the end of the decade, the foundation considered Uni-Valle the best medical school in Latin America "by a wide margin."[45]

In 1957, the Rockefeller Foundation sent Albert Hirschman to UniValle to scout out the prospects for social scientific research. Hirschman knew the school's backers from his past work with the CVC, and he came away so impressed that he personally drafted a funding request for the rector to mail to New York.[46] The foundation waited until one last piece fell into place. In 1958, thirty-eight-year-old Antonio J. Posada arrived in Cali and spearheaded the creation of a new Faculty of Economic Sciences. A native son of the Cauca Valley, Posada had spent most of two decades in the United States and Bogotá, and he returned with valuable connections. In all likelihood, Posada was the first native-born Colombian to earn a doctorate in economics. After graduating from the Nacional's engineering faculty in 1944, he had traveled to the University of Wisconsin to study in the Department of Agricultural Economics, a stronghold of the original institutionalist school. The Wisconsin faculty had shaped US agrarian policy during the Progressive and New Deal eras, and by the postwar period, some of its members had become curious about the Third World. Posada and his advisor, Kenneth Parsons, conceived of his dissertation as the first modern economic survey of Colombian agriculture. In a waking enactment of every graduate student's worst nightmare, Lauchlin Currie and the World Bank published an incomparably grander survey of the entire Colombian economy two years before Posada finished.[47] But it turned out that no one cared. After receiving his PhD in 1952, Posada quickly found a job with the Organization of American States and spent the Rojas years in self-imposed exile in Washington.

With the fall of the dictatorship, Posada returned to Colombia. He spent a year as secretary general in the Ministry of Agriculture and in 1958 decided to cast his lot with his old associates in the Cauca Valley. Returning to Cali, he accepted two part-time jobs, becoming the first dean of a new economics faculty as well as the CVC's first staff economist. As the faculty began its first semester in 1958, Posada and Garcés again approached the Rockefeller

Foundation with a proposal to fund an agricultural census of the Cauca Valley. Officials in New York were impressed, and in October 1959 they gave UniValle its first social science grant.[48]

The faculty grew rapidly, fueled by an influx of international funds. Initially, Posada scoured the Cauca Valley and recruited the most qualified professors he could find. Six had completed coursework for undergraduate or master's degrees in economics, one was a Princeton-trained demographer, and the rest were local businessmen and lawyers, CVC officials, a Spanish statistician, an aging geography and accounting professor, and an assortment of US social scientists visiting Cali on Rockefeller and Fulbright fellowships.[49] By 1961, Rockefeller Foundation officials realized that it would take UniValle years to train a full cohort of credentialed economists. They decided to bridge the gap by sending foreign professors who would assure "quality on the one hand and freedom from leftist ideas on the other."[50] UniValle became one of just ten universities worldwide that participated in the foundation's University Development Program. The distinction guaranteed $155,000 for Posada's economics program alone, and over ten years, it paid the salaries of sixteen economists, nearly all of them foreigners.[51] The UN Food and Agriculture Organization (FAO) agreed in 1961 to send economists, agronomists, and extension experts to work jointly with Posada's faculty, the CVC, and the National University's Faculty of Agronomy, located in nearby Palmira.[52] And that same year, Wayne State University sent Luigi Laurenti, a young Berkeley-trained economist. Laurenti arrived in Cali just after publishing a landmark study of housing discrimination under Jim Crow. *Property Values and Race* challenged the logic of redlining by showing that property values did not fall as commonly expected when African Americans moved into white neighborhoods. When the book hit the shelves, the Federal Housing Administration immediately tried to hire Laurenti, and so did Wayne State. Its economics department had recently received a Rockefeller grant to send faculty to UniValle and offered him the first visiting position. Having made his contribution to fair housing, Laurenti decided to learn something new.[53]

From the start, UniValle's economics faculty served as an extension of the CVC. The collaboration began in 1959, when Posada's initial crop of faculty worked with CVC staff to produce the first agricultural census of the Cauca Valley. Funded by the Rockefeller Foundation, the CVC, business associations, government agencies, and Posada himself, the census provided the basic data on land use and ownership that underlay all of the CVC's rural projects of the 1960s. Indeed, the first fruits of the census were the agrarian reform plans for RUT and La Victoria–Cartago. Posada and his colleagues wrote the plans' economic sections that proposed to eliminate "anti-economic" minifundia, evaluate the abilities of small farmers, and force the majority into wage labor. They estimated the rising income that drainage, irrigation, new crops, and mechanization could produce, which demonstrated that loans would pay for themselves and expand the national income. Posada's staff of economists did the intellectual work of identifying dispossession with the national interest.[54]

The questions that the CVC asked in the 1950s became UniValle's during the 1960s. Agricultural production and marketing studies became the faculty's bread and butter, dwarfing all other areas of research for over a decade. Interestingly, this work thrived across an economics faculty that divided internally into several administrative and academic subfields. The institutional fracturing began quite unexpectedly in 1962, when students did the unthinkable: they went on strike. The uprising began in the economics faculty, where undergraduates demanded the dismissal of a professor whom they considered incompetent. It quickly spread across the university. The strikers identified powerfully with Posada's curriculum and the university's mission, but they argued that UniValle had failed to live up to its promise. Posada defied them, declaring that students had no right to dictate hiring and firing decisions. But in mid-April, the university fired the professor at the center of the conflict, and the entire economics faculty resigned in protest.[55] The result was a mad scramble to reconstitute the economics program and the first real debate about economics education at UniValle. Posada's incomparable stature had allowed him to design a program with little negotiation. When he left, taking with him virtually everyone in the region with any relevant credential, the field's very definition went up in the air. For two years, a dizzying parade of local businessmen, los Andes graduates, and foreign visitors struggled to keep the program afloat while the CVC, the FAO mission, and US foundations hunted for permanent replacements.[56] By 1966, that search produced a completely reorganized program. Thematically and institutionally, it was divided in four parts. A new four-year undergraduate economics curriculum promised to place new emphasis on industrial economics. A pathbreaking master's program in industrial management turned UniValle into the first Colombian university to formally separate management from economics and grant an MBA degree. An economic research center, the Centro de Investigaciones Económicas (CIDE), aimed to give UniValle the broad public influence that los Andes exercised through CEDE.[57] Finally, agricultural economics became a fairly autonomous unit with a dedicated cadre of professors and graduate students collaborating closely with the CVC, the FAO mission, and the Faculty of Agronomy in Palmira.[58] The Ford Foundation financed the management program while the Rockefeller Foundation took responsibility for the rest.[59]

On paper, this new structure seemed to resolve the tension that wracked los Andes; it ennobled management as a field in its own right, and in doing so, it promised to emancipate economics and nurture a range of subfields within it. Yet the institutional division at UniValle proved a distinction without a difference. Every piece of the new faculty came to operate as a consultancy for the CVC and for agribusiness. Paradoxically, by 1967, UniValle had become the institutional prototype for economics faculties across Colombia, which began to split in half, separating management from economics. But internally, UniValle professors worried that economics had lost its identity as a social science and become a crude form of technical assistance to capital. In the Cauca Valley, the CVC's fusion of local business and government, and its identification of productivity with the public interest, made it virtually impossible for economists to define a distinctive public purpose and professional identity.

Agricultural economics was inseparable from the CVC's program by design and circumstance. In the wake of the 1962 strike, the corporation hired Posada, Laurenti, and three of their Colombian colleagues as full-time researchers, putting them to work on land reform studies.[60] From their posts at the CVC, Laurenti and Posada continued to train and organize economists in the academy. Posada founded the Cauca Valley chapter of the Colombian Society of Economists in 1963, Laurenti served as president in 1965, and both supervised senior theses at UniValle. Along with members of the FAO mission, they directed students toward precisely the questions that Garcés had posed during the 1950s. At the height of the CVC's land reform efforts, UniValle students produced research on the production costs and prices of crops, food marketing systems and consumption patterns, and the national demand for sugar. Nearly all theses were simple efficiency studies; students conducted fieldwork throughout the Cauca Valley to determine the prevailing methods of production and marketing and recommended reforms to raise productivity and efficiency. The money for field research came from the CVC, INCORA, agribusiness firms, and gremios.[61]

Thesis writers at UniValle wholeheartedly embraced the drive for productivity and profitability as a path to prosperity. Carlos Enrique Solorzano studied agricultural marketing in RUT in 1965, by which time many young people had left the region. He lamented that the area's remaining small farms lay "in the hands of old and tired people who use anachronistic techniques, harming national progress and development." In 1964, the Quaker Oats company funded research by Cesar Tulio Ayora and Hernán Morales to determine whether it was "economic" to grow corn in RUT and La Victoria–Cartago. These students and their classmates forthrightly recommended Taylorist restructuring of the labor process and the consolidation of property, firms, and services as efficiency measures.[62]

The CVC hired the top thesis writers, at once establishing a career path for agricultural economists and making it possible to implement large-scale

projects. In one dramatic example, the corporation's overhaul of food marketing began with a 1963 thesis on livestock marketing that it financed with the
Fondo Ganadero.[63] The corporation hired two of the coauthors, Oscar Mazuera and Tomás López, gave them scholarships for graduate studies in the
United States, and promoted them within the corporation.[64] Mazuera worked
in the CVC's research division, taught at UniValle, supervised undergraduate
research on La Victoria–Cartago, and eventually became executive director of
the corporation from 1976 to 1991.[65] López led the CVC's regional planning
division during the mid-1960s, taught simultaneously at UniValle, joined the
National Planning Department under Carlos Lleras Restrepo, and became
vice minister of agriculture in 1970, negotiating national financing agreements
with the CVC.[66]

Meanwhile, Posada and Laurenti became public crusaders for the CVC and
leading intellectual authors of dispossession. In 1962, Posada presented the
RUT proposal to INCORA's board just days after resigning from UniValle.[67]
Over the course of a year, he conducted the research and negotiations that
convinced INCORA to finance the land purchases for the project. Posada
wrote the CVC's application to the Inter-American Development Bank when
the corporation needed funds for RUT in 1964, and two years later he produced the CVC's progress report and proposal for La Victoria–Cartago.[68]
Meanwhile, Posada and his wife, public administration specialist Jeanne Anderson Posada, furnished the corporation with its finest piece of propaganda
in 1966.[69] *The CVC: Challenge to Underdevelopment and Traditionalism* was a
book-length celebration of the Cauca Valley program as a triumph of comprehensive regional planning and rational public administration. Published simultaneously in English and Spanish, it grew from a 1963 agreement with Antonio
Posada's former professors at Wisconsin. Agricultural economist Raymond
Penn had led a group of social scientists and legal scholars in establishing the
Wisconsin Land Tenure Center (LTC) in 1962. Funded by USAID, the center
aimed to shape land reform initiatives under the Alliance for Progress, and
Penn hired Posada to write the first title in its book series.[70] Lilienthal, Laurenti, and Garcés commented favorably on the manuscript, and Penn declared
it a "landmark in the economic literature."[71] The CVC proudly distributed
copies to visitors, government officials, foreign news services, and international development agencies.[72]

While Posada, Laurenti, Garcés, and the FAO mission shaped UniValle's
research from beyond the university, they also convinced the Rockefeller
Foundation to restore agricultural economics within the faculty. From 1966 to
1971, the foundation sent an old friend of the CVC to UniValle to oversee the
field. Gerald I. Trant of the University of Guelph had worked at the Faculty of
Agronomy in Palmira during the 1950s while pursuing his doctoral degree at

Michigan State. Having supported the CVC's early initiatives, he returned an eager collaborator.[73] Trant dismissed large-scale land redistribution outright, calling it unnecessary at best and an invitation to revolution at worst. He and his students at UniValle spent five years churning out studies aimed at raising agricultural productivity, efficiency, and profits within the existing land tenure system.[74]

But it wasn't just agricultural economists who did this work. Agricultural marketing and production studies attracted researchers across the economics faculty, including those in CIDE and the industrial management program. The prevailing definition of regional development in the Cauca Valley pulled scholars of every stripe into a remarkably uniform research agenda.[75]

Luis Arturo Fuenzalida had the wildest career at UniValle, and his trajectory illuminated the mechanisms that could lead even quite orthodox neoclassical economists into what CEDE termed "business research." Fuenzalida was neither a management professor nor an agricultural economist: he was one of the Chicago Boys. In 1956, economists at the University of Chicago had begun training Chilean students at Santiago's Universidad Católica, using funds from Point IV and the Rockefeller Foundation. During the 1970s, the Latin Americans they educated infamously became advisors to the military dictatorship of Augusto Pinochet; they designed a radical liberalization program that leveled the labor movement and produced two deep recessions in the space of a decade. Fuenzalida counted among them. He had spent the late 1950s and early 1960s at Chicago, and during the 1980s he became Pinochet's budget director. But until Pinochet seized power in 1973, Chicago graduates in Chile were quite marginal figures who struggled to influence national policy and often accepted temporary positions abroad.[76] When UniValle fell to pieces in 1962, the Rockefeller Foundation drafted them to fill the empty seats. Four Chicago-trained Latin Americans served at UniValle between 1963 and 1968, all of them recommended by Arnold Harberger, the principal mentor to Latin American students at Chicago. Sergio de Castro, who became Pinochet's minister of economy and of finance, arrived first in 1963, followed by Fuenzalida, Alberto Musalem of Argentina, and Rodrigo Núñez of Panama. Taking up jobs in every part of the faculty, these professors made Chicago the single most powerful intellectual influence at UniValle.[77]

Fuenzalida became the Chicago School's longest-serving and most influential representative. From 1964 to 1967, he served as a founding member of CIDE and taught students of every variety, from undergraduates to top executives in the industrial management program.[78] Yet he and his colleagues never made UniValle into anything like Católica or Chicago. Like their own professors, they presented neoclassical theory as the proper basis of economic policy, and they taught core classes on monetary theory, fiscal policy, international trade, macroeconomics, and microeconomics. Musalem in particular encouraged research on the Colombian money supply, inflation, and trade.[79] But Chicago-style instruction in theory and policy hardly dominated the curriculum. Like los Andes, UniValle's program of study included a wide variety of courses in the history of economic thought, agricultural economics, and applied subjects that prepared students for jobs in agriculture and industry.[80]

Fuenzalida's stature at UniValle grew not from his theoretical convictions but from a particular set of research skills he had acquired at Chicago—qualities rarely noted in histories of the school. When Arnold Harberger recommended Fuenzalida to the Rockefeller Foundation, he argued that CIDE should conduct "basic research," and that his former student was the man for the job. "He is not a flashy econometrician but the kind of good, solid worker who would get at the basic facts and data," Ralph K. Davidson of the foundation explained after speaking with Harberger.[81] While the Chicago School is remembered for its exceptional theoretical commitments, Harberger and his students also distinguished themselves for their willingness to do work that many US economists regarded as tedious and professionally unprofitable, including data analysis that mattered tremendously in Latin America. As Harberger recalled years later, his relationship with Rodrigo Núñez led him to take up a fifteen-year consultancy with the government of Panama, producing annual income and outlay projections. "I was long since a full professor at Chicago, crossing my fiftieth birthday during this period, yet I dutifully sat down year after year with reports of Panama's comptroller, digging into the history and prospects for each of maybe 100 or more rubrics of expenditure," he explained. "The lesson here is that you learn a lot by digging into a country's data in a serious way."[82]

Fuenzalida brought that intellectual style to UniValle, and it delighted everyone. CIDE briefly joined los Andes' labor statistics initiative in 1965, and Fuenzalida and two colleagues produced the first estimates of Cali's unemployment rate.[83] He simultaneously wrote some of CIDE's first feasibility studies, assessing the profitability and marketing prospects of a host of agricultural commodities. Fuenzalida catered unabashedly to agribusiness, calculating rates of return on the assumption that crops would grow on large farms using machinery, fertilizers, genetically engineered seeds, irrigation, herbicides, and pesticides.[84] His work earned accolades from university and Rockefeller Foundation officials as well as the CVC and local capitalists, who by 1966 began hiring him for private consulting jobs. Fuenzalida was soon devoting nearly all of his time to private consulting and university administration. By the end of 1966, he was teaching just one class in the industrial management program and let it be known that he preferred to give up teaching entirely. In the context of all this work, Fuenzalida's one seminar presentation on monetary and trade policy—central interests of the Chicago School—was a forgettable event that generated little enthusiasm among his colleagues. In a country as fractured as Colombia, Cali was simply the wrong place to study policy issues that required action in Bogotá. The research that Fuenzalida did for the CVC and related business groups was the sort of work that allowed economists to rise in the Cauca Valley.[85]

UniValle's economics program followed the same course that Fuenzalida did. CIDE survived for less than three years before budget shortfalls convinced the faculty to shut it down in 1967. During its brief existence, the research center produced two labor statistics surveys and a study calculating the Cauca Valley's gross regional product. This was the sort of work that everyone in Colombia regarded as "economic" research, although many at UniValle justified it as the basis for feasibility studies. In the rest of its work, CIDE operated as a research service for agribusiness. As promised, it churned out feasibility studies for prospective investors wondering whether they should build a slaughterhouse in Buga or whether to sow 10,000 hectares of cacao in Urabá.[86] By 1966, Eduardo Wiesner of los Andes ridiculed UniValle's research center as a money-making enterprise that contributed nothing to economics.[87]

Consulting for the CVC, agribusiness firms, and prospective investors became a consuming preoccupation at UniValle because faculty could not say just what else an economist should do. While Fuenzalida's private contracting appalled many of his colleagues—it seemed so shameless to quit the classroom for lucre—the fact was that his peers had considered very similar work a thoroughly respectable activity for years before he arrived. Since the 1950s, research for the CVC had held the same appeal in Cali that government planning and coffee research did in Bogotá. The CVC had absorbed all sorts of intellectuals who differed over means and ends but who ultimately concluded that no institution in the Cauca Valley better represented the public interest. When Posada first joined the CVC, he disagreed with Garcés's economic liberalism. The executive director of the CVC believed in free trade and argued that Colombia's comparative advantage lay in agriculture. By contrast, Posada's dissertation had taken the structuralist view that primary export economies were doomed to "economic dependency." Yet he acknowledged that in the short run, agriculture supported 70 percent of all Colombians, and Garcés's proposals to diversify agricultural production could make the experience of "dependency" less acute. The dissertation called for many of the same productivity measures that the CVC endorsed, and as Posada worked inside the corporation, his views aligned ever more closely with Garcés's.[88]

The researchers at the Wisconsin Land Tenure Center had likewise made common cause with the CVC despite evident disagreements. LTC's founders saw themselves as advocates for campesinos and defenders of both growth and redistribution. They sent interdisciplinary teams of researchers across the Americas to study methods of peasant organization, land titling, and agricultural extension, and by the late 1960s developed a jaundiced view of INCORA.[89] But the professors who reviewed Posada's manuscript in 1965 had had little direct contact with the CVC, and the book hardly mentioned the problem of displacement within its land reclamation projects. It did detail a litany of CVC policies that anyone involved in agrarian reform could support, from rural electrification to crop diversification to agricultural extension. From the remove of Wisconsin, the program looked fine indeed.[90]

Most interesting was Luigi Laurenti, who regularly disagreed with Garcés but faithfully served the corporation. Laurenti worked for the CVC for several months after the 1962 strike, returned to UniValle to complete his teaching contract, and rejoined the CVC as a World Bank consultant from 1963 to 1965.[91] Like the professors from the Land Tenure Center, Laurenti took an interest in small property owners as well as the drive for productivity, and he ultimately sacrificed the first commitment for the second. Laurenti's ideas for Colombian smallholders echoed his commitment to fair housing. In both the United States and Latin America, he insisted that broad access to small property ownership was consistent with prosperity for the entire society. In 1964, after conferring with Joseph Thome of the Land Tenure Center, Laurenti proposed that INCORA formalize land titles for campesinos in the Cauca Valley as a productivity measure; proof of ownership would allow them to obtain credit for technical improvements.[92] In a separate project to design an efficient food marketing system, he considered organizing farmer and shopkeeper cooperatives. He further suggested that farmers in RUT grow crops for subsistence as well as sale. In all these cases, Garcés rejected or modified Laurenti's proposals, retaining productivity measures while slashing protections for small property owners. Laurenti conceded without any apparent fight, and the two maintained an excellent relationship. By 1965, Laurenti was working not only for the CVC but also for a local business committee, JUCODA, that published an investors' guide for RUT and a new agricultural census of the CVC's land reclamation areas.[93]

For Laurenti and Posada, context was everything. In the Cauca Valley, the CVC was the institution battling cattle barons in the name of productivity. In their own ways, both men embraced that goal and identified growth with the general interest. In an ideal world, they each hoped to couple the pursuit of productivity with other commitments, whether land redistribution or industrial protection. But in the world that existed, the autonomous regional corporation was unquestionably the most commanding champion of the politics of productivity, and it articulated the relationship between growth and the public interest in clarion terms. Choosing sides was easy.

Unlike Posada and Laurenti, Fuenzalida contracted chiefly with individual firms and investors, bypassing the CVC. His proximity to private capital and his flight from the classroom made his colleagues sit up and take notice. This, they insisted, was not research in the interest of students, the university, the mythic public, or anyone but Fuenzalida and his clients. Herbert W. Fraser, a Swarthmore economist who taught at UniValle from 1965 to 1967, assailed the faculty's absorption in "academically trivial, but possibly lucrative contract research." He admired Fuenzalida's keen mind but derided him and the dean as "operators rather than academics." No one at UniValle ever attacked Posada in those terms. The interposition of the CVC between researchers and investors could give quite similar work very different casts. The corporation's account of the relationship between the public good and private interest—an account contested so vigorously by campesinos and cattlemen—made sense to many economists until their colleagues began drawing salaries directly from private capital and the undergraduate program could scarcely meet its teaching obligations. Fuenzalida appeared a hired hand; Posada a paragon of professionalism and public-mindedness.

No one protested the narrowing of economics more furiously than Herbert Fraser, but even he had nothing to suggest. In Fraser's view, the problem was intellectual. He admired theoretical work above all else but conceded that theory was not necessarily what the Cauca Valley needed or what aroused the curiosity of his students and colleagues. He doubted, too, that anyone on campus, including himself, was up to the task of designing research more sophisticated than Fuenzalida's. As Fraser observed the discrepancies between Colombian reality and the models in US textbooks, he stood stunned at the difficulty of applying anything he knew. "It takes either ability bordering on genius, or extensive and imaginative training, to adapt the models learned to Colombian phenomena," he lamented. Fraser implicitly identified the chasm separating his colleagues from a figure like Currie, whose talents lay precisely in adapting theory, synthesizing knowledge across disciplines, and observing Colombian society. Such thinkers were hard to come by in any country.[94]

By the late 1960s, economics in Cali had become largely indistinguishable from business consulting. For reasons institutional and intellectual, both had become narrow forms of technical assistance to the CVC and the constellation of landowners and investors that surrounded it. It was a remarkable fate at the university that had invented the Colombian MBA program, promising to separate the disciplines at last. Disentangling economics from management, distinguishing public from private—both were easier said than done.

———

UniValle and los Andes expressed the peculiarities of the decentralized state and the mixed economy. The state's structure, its definitions of the public interest, and its spatial distribution of functions made the discipline of economics a pastiche of odd subfields with a distinctive intellectual geography. Agricultural economics ascended in Cali not because there were farms there—there were farms everywhere in Colombia—but rather because the CVC had wrested control over agrarian policy from Bogotá and made it an object of regional statecraft. Economists in Bogotá competed to compile labor statistics because the national state had to decide what to do with Currie's proposals. In both cities, economics faculties persistently turned out accountants and managers because no arm of the state could separate business development from national and regional development.

By the 1960s, both UniValle and los Andes had found themselves in the same impossible position, articulating boundaries between disciplines and sectors that they could never enforce. While the fusion of business and economics agitated Hunter, it furnished opportunities to others. During the 1960s, the university programs training economists to steer the state came to double as places where a new generation of industrial managers formed and organized themselves. By the 1970s, they emerged as economists' twins, marching out of the same academic institutions to claim the same role in public life. Corporate managers, they insisted, were the true guardians of the public good and the proper stewards of the state.

5

Management as a
Universal Technique

"IN THE PAST we have thought of business education as something oriented almost exclusively towards the management of an enterprise," Reinaldo Scarpetta wrote to his friend David Lilienthal in 1968. "We have become aware of how essential it is for these [business] schools to turn to ... the management of knowledge and education, health, social security and of public affairs." Scarpetta was closing in on five years as dean of the economics program at the Universidad del Valle in Cali. His chief accomplishment—indeed, his sole priority—had been the establishment of the graduate program in industrial management. By 1968, that program had become more than a service to local business. It had transformed Scarpetta into a globe-trotting evangelist for business education and for businessmen themselves. Managers, he argued, were the men called to tackle the wide-ranging problems of postwar societies. Managerial knowledge had come into the world a creature of the modern corporation, shaped to its requirements, but it now stood as a universal technique, its applications limitless. Government itself, Scarpetta declared, was simply "people managing public affairs."[1]

Scarpetta was a booster and a propagandist, not a historian. His portrait of his own time occluded a long history of businessmen and economists comparing the capitalist firm to the state, management to government.[2] It wildly overstated the novelty of businessmen assuming public functions. But Scarpetta's declaration of purpose did reveal something essential about the 1960s. His claims resembled those that Latin American economists made for themselves and dramatized the professional competition that economists came to face from managers who taught and studied in the same university programs. The postwar attempt to form a new economics profession produced an increasingly self-conscious generation of businessmen who rejected economists' account of them as narrowly self-interested masters of the shop floor and the corner office. If Colombia's new economists defined themselves by reference to an idealized boundary between public and private, managers pugnaciously resisted the constraints that vision imposed on them, and generated their own rival account of the relationship between private interest and the public good. Laboring alongside and against economists, they spent the postwar years fighting to establish their own field's public mission, their status as a profession, and their jurisdiction within the developmental state.

Scarpetta's effort to define and defend managers flowered at the Universidad del Valle, but its lasting consequences lay beyond the school. He and his colleagues drew an international procession of businessmen and academics to Cali and became restless institution builders forging new circuits between US and Latin American business schools, management associations, think tanks, and governments. Over the course of two decades, the networks forged in Latin America came to serve many functions. Initially, they promised merely to formalize and systematize management education itself. Ultimately, they pursued wider public and political ends. Turning outward from the university, the founders of Colombia's first MBA program battled to elevate managers in public life, popularized a deeply antidemocratic vision of government as management, and fought for economic liberalization on the international stage.

———

The management program at UniValle was a magnetic force during the 1960s. It grew by drawing in international funders and faculty, and in the process it became a crossroads for every tendency in postwar management education and business mobilization. The unlikely man at the center of the force field was Reinaldo Scarpetta. A young industrial manager originally from Bogotá, he had never set out to run a university program. He became dean in 1963 because no one else wanted the job. The student strike of 1962 had left UniValle's economics faculty without its founder, Antonio Posada, and he had resigned along with virtually everyone in the Cauca Valley who held any relevant degree. The university and the Rockefeller Foundation scoured the United States and Colombia for any economist willing to replace him. Over the course of eighteen months, at least forty candidates rebuffed the offer, and foundation officers admitted defeat.[3] Abandoning hope of hiring an economist or even a social scientist to lead the faculty, they turned to a circle of fifteen to twenty young, foreign-educated businessmen who called themselves the Tuesday Night Group. Henry J. Eder was an engineer trained at MIT and the son of CVC founder Harold Eder. Samir Daccach, a graduate of Georgia Tech, managed his family's textile company in Cali and was the former general secretary of the CVC. The group's members played polo, belonged to the exclusive Club Colombia, and considered themselves natural successors to Garcés and his generation in directing the development of the Cauca Valley. Once a week, they invited a guest to the club—the archbishop, a general, a presidential candidate—and asked, "What problems are you creating that we have to solve?" Well aware of US disciplinary categories, they did not for a moment consider themselves economists, but in 1963 they promised that they could find a dean for UniValle. Seeing no alternative, the Rockefeller Foundation and the university accepted the offer.[4]

The Tuesday Night Group attained influence for the same reason that the CVC's founders had during the 1950s. Cali was a rapidly growing city but a hamlet in comparison to Bogotá. In the capital, the presence of the national government gave rise to a much more complex ruling class; los Andes found itself surrounded by a considerable variety of business groups, government agencies, international advisors, and educational institutions. In Cali, the national government exercised little direct power, large-scale economic activity took fewer forms, and a well-organized segment of an extraordinarily small capitalist class could capture a great deal of the national and international assistance that did flow to the region. The very structure of a small, socially segregated city nurtured connections between ambitious local businessmen and foreign backers. The Rockefeller Foundation discovered the Tuesday Night Group because Daccach lived next door to a member of the foundation's field staff.[5]

In November 1963, the Tuesday Night Group selected one of its own members as the new dean of UniValle's economics program. Reinaldo Scarpetta was the charismatic young manager of Industrias Metálicas de Palmira, a steel products manufacturer owned by the Eder family. Twenty-seven years old, he had a BA in industrial management from Georgia Tech, a flare for self-promotion, and absolutely no interest in economics. "My intention," he explained four decades later, "was to take over the school of economic sciences and destroy it."[6] What could appear cartoonish anti-intellectualism was in fact a strategic posture that he and his peers used to advance a rival professionalization program. Scarpetta saw UniValle as a propitious vehicle for management education initiatives that he was already promoting as vice president of the Colombian Institute of Management (INCOLDA, Instituto Colombiano de Administración). A private business organization, INCOLDA trained managers and anticommunist union leaders, and Scarpetta was just one of the group's officials who shaped Colombian economics education. Hernán Echavarría, the dean of los Andes' economics faculty during the late 1950s, was president of the group. In 1961, Scarpetta had persuaded professors from Georgia Tech's school of industrial management to advise INCOLDA, and when the Tuesday

Night Group became involved at UniValle, he immediately solicited their help in remaking the economics program.[7]

The Rockefeller Foundation understood Scarpetta's motives and recruited US economists to check his influence. While no social scientist wanted the deanship, the foundation found willing candidates for visiting professorships that made UniValle a crossroads for competing visions of management. The first to arrive was Laurence deRycke of Occidental College, who spent eighteen months at UniValle from the fall of 1963 to 1965. DeRycke became Scarpetta's chief sparring partner and collaborator in launching the business program. Indeed, Scarpetta was able to establish a business school in Cali largely because the economist tasked with disciplining him supported the endeavor.

DeRycke arrived as a veteran ally of US business associations, anticommunist organizations, and government agencies engaged in the project of "selling free enterprise." That public relations campaign of the 1940s and 1950s had blanketed US schools, workplaces, and churches with booklets and cartoons contesting the claims of industrial unions and the left. Inveighing against taxation, regulation, labor mobilization, and the welfare state, the materials cast US industrial capitalism as a nineteenth-century liberal dream under fire. Profits had grown dangerously slim, they warned, but if workers collaborated with management to raise productivity, profits could rise again and deliver benefits to all.[8] DeRycke played an essential role in these campaigns as an economist lending his authority to corporate executives. During the late 1940s, he had found himself appalled by the "protectionist attitude" of unions demanding wages that kept pace with inflation. He decried the rising tide of tariffs, exchange controls, and quotas that regulated international trade. "Both labor and management have taken another step away from that risky, flexible, competitive system, whose watchword is opportunity and whose goal is more and more goods of better and better quality for more and more people at cheaper and cheaper prices," he warned in 1948. DeRycke's articulation of the liberal creed distinguished him from the National Association of Manufacturers (NAM), which eagerly supported trade protections that benefited its members. But his contempt for "state control" won him friends in the early Cold War.[9] A 1952 speech to railroad executives on the "American Private Enterprise System" earned him an award from the right-wing Freedoms Foundation.[10] The State Department sent him to India in 1959 to lecture on the US economy.[11] And from 1952 on, leading business associations including NAM and the Committee for Economic Development (CED) enlisted him to craft economics curricula for US public schools. DeRycke conducted summer workshops for high school teachers on the West Coast, coauthored a classroom economics reader titled *Business Enterprise in the American Economy*, and took a year-long sabbatical in 1953 to serve as CED's assistant field director.[12]

DeRycke was thus deeply entangled with US business organizations that understood economics as a political weapon. According to NAM, "anti-business sentiment" among industrial workers stemmed not only from the "efforts of union leaders" but also from "economic illiteracy" seeded in youth. Economics, in this view, was not so much a field of inquiry as a set of facts about business under capitalism that could inoculate Americans against the perils of economic planning, socialism, and communism. A 1959 test that NAM administered to high school students in four metropolitan areas presented no problem-solving questions whatsoever, but simply evaluated students' beliefs. Did paying taxes benefit the country? Should Social Security benefits rise? What were the causes of inflation? How large were corporate profits, and what did it cost a business to create one job?[13]

DeRycke never wrote anything as crude as NAM's exams, but he regarded businessmen as legitimate partners to economists in safeguarding "free enterprise" and molding the minds of the public. He had in fact acquired his earliest training in business administration, earning a BBA and MBA at the University of Oregon during the late 1920s and early 1930s. "I know that there is more than one approach to economics," he wrote to the Rockefeller Foundation in 1964. "I came to the discipline via Philosophy, Mathematics, Law, Accounting, and the MBA."[14]

Among US executives, the men deRycke knew best were the trustees of CED, a business think tank that presented itself as a public-minded engineer of economic growth and a moderate alternative to NAM. Founded in 1942, CED was forged in wartime struggles to reconstruct US capitalism and made its name diverting the proposals of industrial unions, consumer advocates, civil rights activists, communists, and left-liberal economists. It championed a constrained version of Keynesianism that came to prevail in the United States by the 1950s, in which the federal government sustained economic growth with fiscal and monetary policy but disavowed wider obligations to regulate capital. According to CED's trustees, growth itself could generate prosperity and social peace by raising employers' profits and workers' incomes at the same time. Anointing businessmen as strategists of growth, and bringing them together with economists to issue policy statements, CED cast corporate executives as disinterested guardians of the public good in a society beyond ideology. "CED believes there is a general interest, and a truth independent of class interest," explained research director Herbert Stein in 1962. "I think it's very important that we as a group think of ourselves not as 'right,' 'left,' 'conservative' or 'radical' but as 'responsible,'" argued Paul G. Hoffman, the president of Studebaker and CED's first chairman.[15]

DeRycke prided himself on his work with CED, and he arrived in Colombia prepared to cooperate with the businessmen of the Cauca Valley.[16] To be sure, deRycke disliked the idea of a manager directing an economics department and balked at what he considered the confusion of disciplines within UniValle's undergraduate program. But he respected management training and described business administration as a legitimate form of "applied economics" suitable for graduate study.[17]

Together, deRycke and Scarpetta negotiated the curricular reform that divided UniValle's faculty into an undergraduate economics program, a graduate program in industrial management, and a research center. For deRycke, the reorganization promised to clarify the identity and primacy of economics while fostering cooperation with businessmen. For Scarpetta, it offered a way to fund business education at a time when he lacked the leverage to abolish economics teaching entirely. With the curriculum in place, each man raced to line up faculty and funders to enforce his half of the bargain.[18]

DeRycke's vision of management as an applied social science resonated with the Ford Foundation. That institution had spent the 1950s reinventing US business schools and saw in UniValle an opportunity to extend its campaign overseas. In the United States, Ford had pushed universities to place economics, applied mathematics, and the quantitative social sciences at the center of the curriculum. This was a dramatic departure from past practice. Since the founding of the Wharton School in 1881, US business schools had sought to transform management from a pedestrian vocation into a prestigious profession. During the Gilded Age, that meant locating business programs within research universities, urging faculty to publish in scholarly journals, and replacing narrow vocational training with wider coursework in the liberal arts and humanistic social sciences. By the 1930s, industrial psychology and human relations represented the cutting edge of business education, and top-tier business schools depicted managers as more than mere technicians; they were purportedly public-minded professionals who understood workers, harmonized their interests with those of capital, and thereby turned the beastly modern corporation into an engine of peace and prosperity. That definition of management was always more aspirational than real, and the Second World War did away with it entirely. As the federal government grew and corporations became sprawling conglomerates, professors in business schools, like their peers in economics, found themselves called to act as planners. The tools that commanded respect were now linear programming and other forms of applied mathematics that modeled and coordinated the internal activities of massive organizations. During the 1950s, the Ford and Carnegie Foundations championed a new conception of business administration as an outgrowth of economics and the quantitative social sciences. Ford began funding the country's elite graduate programs, Carnegie took charge of undergraduate education, and together they popularized the new notion of "management science." Sidelining psychology and empirical research, they insisted that business professors could devise prescriptions for the firm from social-scientific models. Foundation grants rapidly transformed the business schools at Carnegie Tech, Harvard, Columbia, Chicago, Stanford, Berkeley, UCLA, and MIT. By the 1960s, their professors increasingly held doctorates in economics and other social sciences, published in disciplinary journals, and ran doctoral programs alongside the traditional MBA course.[19]

UniValle struck Ford officials as an auspicious standard-bearer for "management science." Here was a Latin American university pairing an undergraduate economics major with a graduate MBA program. Scarpetta never for a moment considered economics the foundation of business administration, but his deal with deRycke looked good on paper, and he gladly accepted the foundation's money.[20]

For his part, Scarpetta looked to his alma mater. Georgia Tech's school of industrial management lay beyond the Ford Foundation's reach. It belonged to the third tier of US business schools that Ford hoped would emulate the elite institutions it funded. As it turned out, the grants that Ford and Carnegie doled out during the 1950s created two worlds of business schools in the United States: the small circle of direct beneficiaries and the great majority of schools that never looked anything like them.[21] Scarpetta was a typical product of US business education during the 1950s, not an aberrant one, and he brought to UniValle the people he knew best: the same Georgia Tech professors he had recruited to advise INCOLDA since 1961. Chief among them was Roderick F. O'Connor, an academic of no repute at home but a beloved figure among Cali's businessmen. A clinical psychologist by training, O'Connor was a throwback to the interwar era when industrial psychology and human relations had reigned supreme in MBA programs.[22] He was certainly conversant with new directions in the field; when planning UniValle's new curriculum in 1963, he and deRycke lauded the Ford Foundation's 1959 report *Higher Education for Business*, and O'Connor argued for an MBA program that rested on "an excellent course in economics." But O'Connor could never teach that class. His authority in Cali rested less on disciplinary specialization than on his connections overseas, his charismatic defense of managers as historical protagonists, and his genuine enthusiasm for local ventures. "As a person," observed Vincent Padgett of the Rockefeller Foundation, "Roderick O'Connor combines the American stereotype of the hardheaded businessman with the American stereotype of the evangelist." By the mid-1960s, Padgett met Colombian capitalists who named O'Connor as "the only American they would consult on any problem."[23]

O'Connor and his colleagues at Georgia Tech became Scarpetta's advocates in negotiations with the university and the Ford and Rockefeller Foundations. All of them in turn became UniValle's conduits to foreign business schools, sending the dean on junkets throughout the hemisphere to recruit faculty members. By 1965, Scarpetta had met with Chileans from the Universidad Católica as well as Peruvians from ESAN, a brand new business school tied to Stanford and funded by the State Department. In Mexico, he traveled to the Instituto Tecnológico de Monterrey (ITESM), a private polytechnic founded by industrialists in 1943 to counter left-wing public universities. He flew to Chicago and stayed with Arnold Harberger, the chief mentor to the Chicago Boys. And he began discussing student exchanges with Chilean and Peruvian businessmen who ran their countries' productivity centers, the equivalents of INCOLDA.[24]

The harvest Scarpetta reaped reflected the fractured nature of the discipline. On the one hand, he drew in stars from the Ford Foundation's firmament. George Lodge of Harvard Business School, Ezra Solomon of Stanford, and Howard Johnson of MIT's Sloan School of Management all joined an advisory board to the management program, and Solomon came to Cali as a visiting professor in 1967. A Chicago-trained economist, he was known for his pioneering work applying neoclassical theory and mathematical expression to the study of finance. Scarpetta hired two Chileans from Católica: marketing professor Sergio Muñoz held an MBA from Chicago, and finance professor Hans Picker had studied at Northwestern on a Point IV scholarship. As US-trained faculty arrived in Cali, the Ford and Rockefeller Foundations sent UniValle's own professors to study at Ford-funded US business schools. By 1970, three had trained at MIT, two at Harvard, and six at Stanford, where Ford financed a new institute expressly to educate foreign business professors.

Yet Ford's influence at UniValle masked intellectual heterogeneity. Stanford professor David Faville taught alongside his colleague Ezra Solomon, but the two shared almost nothing intellectually. Trained in the 1930s, Faville was an old-style marketing specialist whose publication record consisted entirely of empirical case studies. Meanwhile, Peter Drucker's work constituted "the very foundation of the Program," according to associate dean Alvaro García. Drucker visited Cali to lecture and lead seminars during the management program's first year, and his 1954 book, *The Practice of Management*, was required reading.[25] Drucker was anything but a quantitative social scientist. Born in Vienna in 1909, he had come of age in the interwar crisis that shaped his compatriots Karl Polanyi and Friedrich Hayek. The problem that consumed him was the rise of fascism, and the fate of Nazi Germany forced him to ask whether democracy and social peace could survive industrial capitalism. During the 1930s, Drucker approached those questions through philosophy, law, and social theory, which eventually led him to the study of management. Like US business school deans of the Gilded Age, Drucker believed that the industrial corporation, directed by managers rather than owners, had never acquired social legitimacy. Managers appeared to shareholders and workers as usurpers exercising undue influence over enormously powerful institutions. Analogizing the corporation to the state, he argued that managers had never secured the consent of the governed, and he made it his life project to rehabilitate the corporation as a social and political institution. Working at cross-purposes to the Ford Foundation in the postwar era, he sustained a view of managers as masters of social organization who needed to make their mission known. For Drucker, that meant reorganizing the firm internally to cultivate consent among workers. Like Lilienthal, Drucker argued for "decentralization" and "federalism" within the corporation, welfare capitalist programs to encourage identification with the firm, and participatory procedures that enlisted workers in solving problems set out by management. For Drucker, legitimation also meant communicating the social value of managerial authority to the public. His fame owed much to the accessibility of his books and their engagement with meaningful questions of politics and philosophy. Drucker cast managers as men who recognized the humanity of workers, entrusted them with responsibility, and united battling social classes around shared goals. He spoke in plainly political terms, contending that managers transformed firms from authoritarian institutions to democratic ones. It was a striking sleight of hand that conflated participation with democracy; in Drucker's view, workers should never choose the firm's objectives or elect their own supervisors but should merely devise ways to achieve ends that management defined. As misleading as the argument was, it firmly aligned Drucker with the prewar human relations tradition and distanced him from neoclassical economists who promised to channel resources efficiently under any social or political system.[26]

The meeting of all these professors in Colombia exposed stark disagreements over the nature of management in the United States. It simultaneously made UniValle a premier destination for *vallecaucano* businessmen. The Cauca Valley's business elite had supported Scarpetta in establishing the industrial management program, and the participation of US professors persuaded major corporations and gremios, as well as the CVC, local government, anticommunist unions, and the university itself to send top officials for master's degrees. What began as a program for senior executives in 1964 grew over five years to include night classes for middle managers and certificate courses administered by INCOLDA. By 1969, nearly one thousand Colombian businessmen, public officials, and trade union leaders had enrolled in the courses.[27]

The management program in turn became the anchor for a growing network of institutions linking the Cauca Valley to US business groups and foreign aid programs. In 1963, the Peace Corps began sending young businessschool graduates to teach at UniValle and work as management consultants for the CVC, INCOLDA, and other business organizations.[28] MIT's Sloan School established its own fellowship program under which MBA candidates from Harvard and MIT worked for the CVC and other development institutions.[29] And in 1964, David Rockefeller of Chase Manhattan Bank led a group of businessmen in founding the International Executive Service Corps (IESC). Known as the "Paunch Corps" and funded by USAID, IESC was a Peace Corps for retired corporate executives who became volunteer management consultants in the Third World. Its leaders asserted that managers possessed universally applicable knowledge and shipped US retirees abroad with virtually no training. The volunteers tended to avert disaster because the companies that received them were some of the largest and most familiar in the Third World. In Cali, USAID's money went to assist Carvajal & Cía., Colombia's first multinational corporation and the family business of Manuel and Mario Carvajal, founders of the CVC and UniValle. While working with major corporations in Colombia, IESC representatives appeared at public events and fund-raisers with O'Connor, INCOLDA leaders, and UniValle officials to promote management education and consulting programs.[30]

IESC represented yet one more view of management and its uses converging in Cali. While the Ford Foundation and Peter Drucker fought over management's status as applied economics or social engineering, IESC's founders cared not at all about doctrinal debates. They embraced management training of any kind as a tool to remake the state, redirect public revenues, and redefine international assistance. IESC had grown from a campaign that David Rockefeller and Peter Grace of W. R. Grace had launched in 1961 to transform the Alliance for Progress. US foreign aid, they insisted, should prioritize growth over social reform and operate through private firms rather than intergovernmental loans. Rockefeller and Grace spoke not for US business consultants like David Lilienthal but for foreign direct investors and bankers who feared that government loans, public enterprise, and an expansion of social services might threaten private business development. Indeed, they began organizing in 1961 after the Brazilian government expropriated a subsidiary of International Telephone and Telegraph (ITT). Rockefeller and Grace argued that public officials across the hemisphere should stop trying to deliver social services or redistribute wealth themselves. Instead, governments should offer economic incentives to US corporations to develop Latin American infrastructure, manufacturing, and even health care and housing projects at a profit.

President Kennedy gave Rockefeller and Grace formal posts within the Commerce Department; in 1962, they became co-chairs of the Commerce Committee for the Alliance for Progress (COMAP). That government body became the seed of Rockefeller's independent Business Group for Latin America (BGLA), which in 1965 became the Council for Latin America (CLA). These institutions regarded the year 1963 as a watershed, when both the incoming Johnson administration and the OAS's Inter-American Committee on the Alliance for Progress embraced their recommendations and began to elevate private investment as a primary instrument of development policy. For the remainder of the 1960s, CLA and its member corporations played significant roles in diverting US and multilateral loans from Latin American governments to businesses promising to foment growth in the region.[31]

The International Executive Service Corps was one of the first fruits of their campaign. Rockefeller issued a call to organize the program in 1963, and the next year, USAID made it a reality. IESC funneled US government funds directly to Latin American business ventures, and channeled it through the US private sector. While USAID provided two-thirds of the group's funding between 1964 and 1967, operational decisions fell to a private board of businessmen that included Rockefeller, Sol Linowitz of Xerox, Philip D. Reed of General Electric, C. D. Jackson of Time Inc., and William S. Paley of CBS. For their part, corporations in the Third World had to pay a fee to receive volunteers. IESC president Frank J. Pace Jr. celebrated the organization as a pioneering "private-public" experiment; his colleague Frank B. Elliott trumpeted that IESC had replaced "government to government" assistance with "businessman to businessman" aid.[32]

For IESC, management training represented a tool to legitimate US foreign investors, build up Latin American corporations, and establish both as instruments of development policy and recipients of foreign aid. The group's founders harbored no particular preference for the type of education that UniValle offered or the specific managerial advice that volunteers gave. They valued the symbolism of private capital serving public functions, controlling the disbursement of government revenues, and mediating between states and societies. IESC depicted businessmen as statesmen, and it suggested that cultivating corporate management was a form of aid as vital as public-school teaching or community action.

As UniValle became a crossroads for competing US projects of managerial development, Colombians put the school's offerings to their own uses. Despite the best efforts of the Ford Foundation, management theses at the school tackled eminently practical problems without resort to complex mathematical techniques. Students designed and evaluated accounting systems for local sugar mills and public utilities. They undertook project planning within the rubric of the CVC's program, crafting private investment proposals to expand sugar production and estimating the costs and benefits of land reclamation.[33] To the extent that UniValle graduates came away discussing ideas, economic theory was never their focus. In 1966, Bernardo Garcés Córdoba emerged from UniValle's executive training course preaching the gospel of Peter Drucker.[34]

At UniValle, management and economics thus answered the same questions that local property owners and the CVC posed. For many faculty members, the arrangement appeared to diminish economics, but it ennobled management. Indeed, while economists struggled to define a public purpose, the graduate management program built on local consulting work to assume broad public functions. Managers' claims began to expand in 1965 and 1966, when Scarpetta spearheaded a reorganization of UniValle's finances and administration. The former industrial manager treated the public university as an ordinary business enterprise that simply needed to control costs and produce saleable goods. He analyzed UniValle through the generic categories of "personnel, accounting and financial controls, and general services," and under his watch, the university hired "the industrial relations manager of a large metal-working firm for personnel; an industrial engineer and former plant manager for systems, procedures, and services; and a del Valle–Chicago trained economist to manage budgeting and control." Scarpetta decentralized university financial systems, giving division deans considerable responsibility for raising and disbursing funds. As he explained, devolving financial responsibility would force deans to "sell services and procure donations" and teach them to "value [their] money and check expansion." These reforms expressed what he called the "Druckerian Liturgy" of management by objectives: top administrators defined overarching goals, enlisted deans to implement them, and imposed new financial pressures to force compliance. In all this work, Scarpetta spoke not a word of the school's intellectual aims, nor did he consider the effects of budgetary constraints on the quality of education.[35]

While Scarpetta devolved some financial responsibilities to deans, he transferred the university's central fund-raising activities to a new, private financial institution that he created and directed. The Fundación para la Educación Superior (FES), established in 1964, was a nonprofit fund manager that solicited and administered all private and semipublic donations to the university. The board consisted of the usual assemblage of local businessmen, who maintained that they could manage money more effectively than the university did and widen its donor base. In 1968, Scarpetta supplemented FES with a second financial institution, the Fund for Multinational Management Education (FMME). Incorporated in New York, FMME raised money from US multinationals expressly for UniValle's management program. The founding board members included university officials, David Lilienthal, Peter Drucker, CVC founder Manuel Carvajal, and Bernardo Garcés Córdoba, who by that time had become Colombia's minister of public works. Lilienthal personally donated $25,000 to get FMME off the ground, David Rockefeller gave $15,000, and CLA beat the bushes among US investors in Latin America. Scarpetta spent much of his tenure as dean traveling to Bogotá and the United States to beg money from businessmen.[36]

FES and FMME were sophisticated financial institutions that offered lucrative services to investors. They turned the act of donating to a public university—ostensibly a profitless act of philanthropy—into a gainful source of capital and easy credit for corporations. When a US multinational wrote a check to FMME in New York City, it received a tax exemption for contributing to a nonprofit foundation. FMME then transferred the funds to FES, which made a loan of equal size to the corporation's local subsidiary in Colombia. As the subsidiary repaid the loan, its interest payments were treated as tax-exempt donations, thanks to FES's nonprofit status. At the end of the process, the US multinational had secured two tax breaks and a cheap loan simply by shifting capital from one division of the company to another. FES, meanwhile, used the interest payments to fund management education at UniValle. When a Colombian institution donated to FES, the procedure was similar: FES issued a loan in the same amount to the donor and used the tax-exempt interest payments to fund the management program. "This, as you know, is something few managers will turn down in credit-tight Colombia," Scarpetta explained to Lilienthal in 1969. By 1970, W. R. Grace, IBM, International Paper, Quaker Oats, American Standard, the CVC, and wealthy men across the Cauca Valley had all availed themselves of these banking services. Union Carbide donated enough to FMME to establish its own endowed chair of management. Like the University of the Andes Foundation, FMME dealt in donations that were modest by US corporate standards, but the sums were substantial for Colombian universities and subsidiaries.[37]

FES and FMME embodied the pervasive doubling of public and private interest and the conjoined growth of public and private institutions within the mixed economy. Corporate managers claimed new authority through the growth of the public university. Multinational corporations enriched themselves by the very same process.

During the late 1960s, UniValle's management program became central to the university's conception of its public purpose and the public that it served. The school had initially attracted the Rockefeller Foundation for its developmentalist mission, exemplified in the 1950s by the medical school's public health programs. A decade later, university leaders began touting the industrial management program as a key contribution to the Cauca Valley and its people. Alvaro García, the director of the graduate program in 1965, declared that educated businessmen constituted the driving force of development, and that development "spreads its benefits in all sectors, raising the standard of living of all income categories." Alfonso Ocampo Londoño, a founder of the medical program, became university rector in 1966. He argued—and UniValle grant proposals faithfully reiterated—that the school had developed "closer ties with our community" during the 1960s, thanks in no small part to the industrial management program. In this telling, the businessmen enrolled there were "community leaders" who "provided a bond between the University and its environment." By the end of the decade, officials explained that UniValle had moved beyond training professionals to become "an agent of development of the community and of the region."[38]

The rector's identification of managers and private capital with "the community" was typical among university leaders. After meeting with local capitalists and university officials to discuss plans for CIDE in 1964, deRycke delightedly reported that there was enormous "grass roots enthusiasm" for a research center. By that time, he had already spoken with Drucker, who conveyed his congratulations to O'Connor: "What you and your friends are doing down there is, I am convinced, tremendously important, precisely because it is a project of the Colombians themselves and carried through by the local community rather than done *for* them from the outside." FMME documents opened with stirring words from Lilienthal: "There is managerial talent in every village of the world and in every block of our cities. Finding that talent, believing in it, giving it the chance is the secret to development." UniValle's backers painted the Cauca Valley's richest men as humble local heroes and the university as a grassroots institution simply for being Colombian. Recounting the origins of the industrial management program, García explained that "there emerged a development plan based on the faith that Colombians could do this for themselves." By the end of the 1960s, management education at UniValle had become an Orwellian symbol of grassroots development and community participation.[39]

Looking out from Colombia, Drucker, O'Connor, and CLA became propagandists for UniValle abroad. While local businessmen articulated general aspirations to power, US supporters cast them specifically as masters of counterrevolution in an age of decolonization and global Cold War. Enno Hobbing of CLA profiled Scarpetta as one of the "modernizers of Latin America":

The driving spirit of the Valle school is stocky, restless Reinaldo Scarpetta. By 1962, when he was twenty-six, Scarpetta had been through Georgia Institute of Technology, had worked for W. R. Grace and Company, and had become the successful manager of a Colombian metallurgical plant. But as he looked around him, he was uneasy. The countryside was wracked by

political strife, and refugees were pouring into his pleasant, subtropical native city of Cali. The Communist challenge of Fidel Castro hung in the
air . . .

"Suddenly, being a hot-shot young executive didn't seem very important
to me," Scarpetta says. "My contemporaries and I had to get ready for our
turn at the leadership of our society. If we didn't learn how to manage the
forces of change, we would be swept away by them."

O'Connor depicted the Tuesday Night Group as skillful Cold Warriors who
recognized the social dislocation wrought by incipient economic growth and
the potential that it created for "revolutionary upheaval." As he explained, Uni-
Valle's management program had made Cali's businessmen into talented top-
down revolutionaries who accelerated and controlled national development.
The "revolutionary master's degree program" had incited "growth fever" in the
Cauca Valley and vindicated management education as an urgent requirement
for all of Latin America.[40]

Peter Drucker featured Scarpetta in his books and in a "warning to the rich
white world" that he issued in *Harper's* in 1968. Drucker was less a Cold Warrior than an old-style theorist of race war. This essential feature of his thought
has escaped scholars who examine only his writing on the North Atlantic.
"The newest and greatest threat abroad in the world today may well be the
threat of a war of the poor and largely colored peoples against the rich and
largely white," he argued in 1968. "Ideally, man will find ways to make poor
countries richer. Alternatively, the rich countries will not be allowed to remain
rich." Like Scarpetta, Drucker took the view that economic development required nothing but some "local, responsible initiative." Managers became heroic figures by that logic, uniquely positioned to remake their societies and
prevent a global rising of "colored peoples." The pressing task was to produce
them, and Drucker hailed UniValle's management program as a global model.[41]

Ironically, the management program acquired extraordinary public significance as its own academic offerings sank into mediocrity. By 1968, top executives had stopped enrolling at the school, research contracts were drying up,
and professors themselves believed that their curriculum did not merit the
conferral of a master's degree.[42] The coursework diverged decisively from the
Ford Foundation's vision. In 1967, R. K. Ready of the foundation's field staff
held out great hope for UniValle but considered the professors "by and large
still weak."[43] The program's deterioration made its institutional supremacy that
much harder for economists to swallow. Throughout the late 1960s, Scarpetta
spent lavishly on the graduate program while starving the research center and
undergraduate major that were supposed to provide its disciplinary foundation. Rockefeller officials begged him to finance statistical compilation or new

teaching materials on the Colombian economy. Herbert Fraser, a visiting economist from Swarthmore, filed outraged reports that Scarpetta remodeled his office while failing to pay faculty on time. Undergraduates rarely completed reading assignments because the dean refused to create an affordable system for ordering textbooks. As of 1967, Fraser had never seen students discuss texts in class, and his fourth-year students had no experience analyzing articles that presented contradictory points of view. Far from defining the management program, the economics major had become a creature of it, channeling students into business careers that required little in the way of social-scientific erudition.[44]

As the management and economics programs declined, their leading figures left the university. Visiting economists deRycke and Fraser were both gone by 1967, their contracts expired. The Chicago alumni dispersed one by one, and Scarpetta spent most of 1968 away from Cali rustling up money for FES and FMME. By the fall, he saw student protests brewing and preemptively resigned as dean in January 1969. Departing in a blaze of bluster and jargon, he declared his intention to establish new programs "for nation-state multinational corporation relationships of the future."[45]

Under Scarpetta's watch, the cultivation of managers had eclipsed the training of economists as the defining public project of the combined faculty. Businessmen in the Cauca Valley had bound an extraordinary range of US institutions to the project, including foundations, universities, think tanks, and business associations that disagreed irreconcilably over curricular matters and the proper hierarchy of disciplines. Yet all the ferment over doctrinal issues came to very little. Scarpetta and his colleagues exercised decisive and indeed widening influence over the university's direction, and Scarpetta considered curricular debates a waste of breath. "I ran del Valle as you would a military campaign or a corporation," he explained forty years later. "I was not the least bit concerned with final verities or eternal truths."[46] The Colombians who led the graduate program were pursuing something else entirely; they made the school an object lesson demonstrating the capacity of managers to direct public institutions. University reform became a vehicle for a wider, outward-facing political project to elevate managers in public affairs and multiply the realms of life in which they could claim authority. In time, that project led them out of the university entirely.

———

The lasting legacy of UniValle's academic program lay beyond the academy because as soon as Scarpetta left campus, students laid waste to it. The destruction was furious and total, and for the university's founders, the reckoning was public and humiliating. UniValle's student movement had changed dramatically over the course of the 1960s. The strike that emptied the economics faculty in 1962 conveyed students' frustration with its failure to live up to its own promises. At the decade's end, students rejected Scarpetta's program outright, along with the capitalists who had built it and the US institutions that backed them. This was a movement that spoke in revolutionary terms, criticizing the curriculum as an expression of imperialist and capitalist class power. The most striking feature of that critique was its appeal to the notion of the public. Indeed, the students who revolted during the late 1960s and early 1970s expressed a resolute conviction that they could separate the public university from the private interests and institutions that pervaded it. As they fought to pry the public loose from the private, they revealed their essential membership in the society they condemned. Decrying the influence of private capital, these students on the far left of Colombian politics adopted the very same strategy that CEDE's leaders and Lauchlin Currie had before them: they called for a new birth of economics as an alternative to management, and they defined the field by an idealized identification with public rather than private interests.

The student movement of the late 1960s gave voice to widely shared grievances—indeed, the very concerns that professors raised behind closed doors for years. Throughout Scarpetta's term as dean, professors had struggled to safeguard teaching and institutionally supported research in the face of private consulting that consumed economists' time. They deplored having to teach from US textbooks for lack of comparable Colombian publications, and when he left, they demanded Rockefeller Foundation funds to develop teaching materials "incorporating the Colombian frame of reference." They tried to revive CIDE and establish a research program that did more than bring in money. Yet they imagined no forms of research beyond production and marketing studies, and they struggled to define work whose value exceeded its benefits to corporate clients and FES.[47]

While professors agonized in faculty meetings, left-wing students made those concerns into topics of open debate on campus. To be sure, radicals represented a minority of the student body, and that was particularly true in the economics faculty, which disproportionately attracted students with narrow professional aspirations. But even undergraduates who professed to have entered the university simply to "improve my position" and become "qualified personnel" took issue with the quality of instruction and the relevance of foreign teaching materials.[48] Those grievances made the economics program an epicenter of student organizing. Emblematically, the other wellspring of protest was the medical school, known for its ties to US foundations and flagship development projects. The uprisings began in 1968, four months before Scarpetta resigned, and were led by the elected student government, the

Federación de Estudiantes de la Universidad del Valle (FEUV). Throughout the month of September, students issued statements denouncing what they called the "privatization of the public university." To a remarkable extent, the student movement described UniValle exactly as Scarpetta did; students simply deplored what he celebrated and cast as private what he called public. FEUV assailed the influence of the Tuesday Night Group, FES, and regional business associations. Students quoted chapter and verse from Roderick O'Connor and denounced Scarpetta's reorganization of UniValle's administration. "The university's activity and production are organized in the same way as in a business," they argued. "Teaching is oriented by an obsessive criterion of economic gain. . . . The directors of the University only understand community to mean the part of society that holds power, that is to say the part that concentrates and controls capital and exploits the popular mass through private enterprise." For FEUV, the school's systematic entanglement with private capital had stripped it of any claim to be public at all.

Students likewise denounced US influence as incompatible with education in the national interest. They singled out the university's relationship to the Rockefeller Foundation and US universities, and criticized foreign teaching materials and academic traditions as useless for understanding Latin America. US-trained Colombians, visiting professors, and "deans who travel monthly to the United States" had all produced "an elite with a colonized and foreign mentality."[49] In some respects, students misunderstood the ways that US institutions exercised power in Colombia. They believed, for instance, that the Rockefeller Foundation wielded ultimate authority at UniValle and that local capitalists did its bidding. In fact, the record of skirmishes between foreign backers and local boosters laid bare the decisive power of Colombians over the university and their skill in capturing international aid. Students likely misinterpreted the significance of the Peace Corps, as well. Knowing that volunteers sent reports to Washington, they portrayed them as covert agents supporting US military and intelligence operations. The central event of the 1968 protest was an occupation of the Sociology Department to demand that professor Luis H. Fajardo stop training volunteers and that the administration expel the North Americans from campus.[50]

Despite any quibbling, FEUV captured the undisputed truth that businessmen had powerfully shaped the university and bent foreign aid to their ends. That argument resonated with students, professors, and even Rockefeller Foundation officials. Between 1968 and 1970, student mobilization provided the impetus for the university to address concerns that had previously lived and died in interoffice memos. The faculty secured funds to write new textbooks in 1969, and after a one-day strike in 1970, UniValle agreed to hire four new economics professors to alleviate chronic understaffing, strengthen

FIGURE 5.1. A 1964 poster displayed near the Universidad del Valle in Cali presented what
were then the claims of communist youth, and what became the claims of the student
movement at large by 1968. "The Peace Corps. What they are: 1. An international affiliate of
the FBI-CIA. 2. A camouflaged military corps for setting up and supporting dictatorships.
3. The oligarchies' Yankee mercenaries. What they do: 1. Hatch coups d'etat. 2. Defend Yankee
interests. 3. Prepare assassination attempts against democratic and nationalist leaders."
(Hoover Institution, John S. Applegarth Papers, Box 4, Folder "Communist Party
in Colombia")

teaching on Colombian economic issues, and introduce students to Marxist
theory. Foundation officials even conceded the legitimacy of students' interest
in studying socialist economies.[51]

These conflicts came to a head in 1971, when economics students demanded
the appointment of Bernardo García, a Marxist economist teaching at the Nacional, as dean of the division. Rector Alfonso Ocampo Londoño refused, the
economics and management students went on strike, and the entire university
shut down for two weeks as students and professors in other faculties walked
out in solidarity. Students called for citywide solidarity among "revolutionary
forces, popular sectors, students, [and] cultural workers." Their statements
denounced local employers battling unions and backed local teachers and students protesting the privatization of a public night school. Appeals for class
solidarity went hand in hand with merciless sectarianism: FEUV publicly

assailed unions and political tendencies that it deemed counterrevolutionary, and its "Polemic #1" instructed students on the views they should take of campesinos, teachers, unions, and unemployed workers as either revolutionaries or reactionaries.[52]

After two weeks, the governor of Valle turned the strike in Cali into a national upheaval. He ordered the army and police to occupy the campus, where they killed a student, injured many others, and set off violent protest in the city. Students nationwide launched sympathy strikes that shuttered universities across Colombia. The city of Cali was put under curfew, and the national government declared a state of siege. The crisis only subsided over the course of a year with Ocampo's resignation as rector, the departure of nearly the entire economics faculty, and finally a second occupation of the campus by the army in April 1972. By 1974, a genuine revolution had occurred in the university and the economics program. The visiting professors of Scarpetta's era were long since gone, and so were nearly all of the Colombian faculty who had studied in the United States on Ford and Rockefeller scholarships.[53]

Foundation officials could hardly believe the fate that had befallen the school. Both Ford and Rockfeller had begun winding down their support after Scarpetta's departure, and Rockefeller closed its last grant in 1976. As it prepared to withdraw from Cali, the foundation asked Luis Arturo Fuenzalida and Alberto Musalem to evaluate the fruits of their labor. The Chicago alumni flew to Colombia in 1974 and 1975 and found the university unrecognizable. They proudly observed that they had educated a crop of successful local elites. Fuenzalida's 120 former students occupied "top executive positions in private enterprises, in public agencies or in government. Even some of the less promising students (even one which I flunked for three consecutive years!) have prospered and progressed." As for the current students, they bewildered Fuenzalida. "Students refuse to study economic theory, reject mathematical analysis of Economic problems, oppose the 'marginalist school,' and reject the idea of efficiency, alternative cost, general price stability, and many other 'monuments' of economic theory," he wrote. "What can be done with such students? How can they be pacified or disciplined or persuaded to get in line?"[54]

The economics and management programs founded in the 1950s had crumbled to dust, leaving other projects in their place. First was a new struggle to define economics yet again as a genuine foil to business administration. The strikes of 1970 and 1971 had given rise to study groups among Marxist students and professors, and debates about the nature of economics erupted within student governing bodies. Strike organizing had in fact offered students an intellectual environment that the economics and management programs never did. As students sought to redefine economics, they bore down on the opposition between public and private. The same movement that character-ized the interpenetration of private capital and public education as privatiza-tion fervently believed that there must be an economics befitting a genuinely public university; there must be a science of development independent of capitalist class interest. Inspired by Louis Althusser's distinction between sci-ence and ideology, students and dissident faculty dismissed "marginalist dogma," "Keynesian dogma," and other non-Marxist schools of thought as mystifying apologetics for existing forms of capitalism. They never quite de-fined science, but they rhetorically associated it with democracy, anti-imperialism, and humanism. They linked it to intellectual and revolutionary motives rather than profit-making ones and cast it as contrary to technocracy. Ultimately, the student movement understood science not in terms of meth-odological or substantive content but in terms of social and political character; scientific work accorded with their notion of revolution.[55]

This inchoate, optimistic, deeply frustrated search for a new economic sci-ence found expression in the aftermath of the strike, as students and professors began drawing up encyclopedic lists of classes that the economics program should offer. Curricular reform became a utopian search for a rational, inter-nally coherent, totalizing view of society, and in that respect, UniValle's radi-cals resembled the country's archetypal economists: the professors at los Andes. The faculty there believed that the economist, armed with macroeco-nomic statistics, possessed a complete, systematic image of society and its options and could harmonize interests through a single comprehensive plan. In the Cauca Valley, students lambasted Colombia's national planning institu-tions, and living so far from the capital, they could hardly expect to work as national planners themselves. But they revealed their aspiration to replace the planners by articulating a remarkably similar concept of economics. Curricular reform proceeded from the assumption that it was possible to break down all of human life into clearly defined subfields of economics and logically explain the relationships between them. This inspired, agonizing style of course plan-ning extended well into the 1980s, as economists at UniValle tried repeatedly to arrive at a global view of "Colombian reality" and a discipline beyond class interest.[56]

No one ever came up with an economics curriculum that fit the bill. Some, like professor Edgar Vásquez, turned to writing social and urban history to capture the complexity of Cali's social relationships. Others stood back, scru-tinizing the intellectual traditions that had produced them, and became emi-nent analysts of all they had disavowed as students. Few outside Colombia have ever heard of the Universidad del Valle or the strikes that leveled it, but every scholar of development has reckoned with their best-known alumnus, Arturo Escobar. It was UniValle's student movement of the late 1960s and early

1970s that set the young chemical engineering major on a path to become an anthropologist. Two decades after graduating, he published his first book, *Encountering Development*. Like the student movement of his youth, Escobar characterized development as an imperial practice that facilitated foreign intervention by representing postcolonial societies as backward and Western ones as models. At the same time, the book moved beyond the movement's fascination with Marxism to offer a critique of Enlightenment reason. Abandoning the search for a new science of development, Escobar put the entire intellectual project under glass. Vigorously debated at the time and still read decades later, the book became a classic of postcolonial studies.[57]

During the late 1960s, the founders of the management program let their critics have the university. Scarpetta was through debating course requirements. During his final year as dean, he was looking outward, working to elevate industrial managers in public life. In the course of Scarpetta's fund-raising trips, he became a roving propagandist for the idea of management as a universal technique that could rationalize any institution, from the business corporation to the state. Scarpetta articulated a brazenly antidemocratic vision of government as management, and he made the case together with US businessmen and boosters who had backed his program, from David Lilienthal to the leaders of the Council for Latin America. For all of these men, UniValle became evidence of corporate managers' fitness to steer public policy.

Scarpetta metamorphosed rapidly from a local booster to an influential spokesman for management in the Americas. His transformation began close to home with an effort to institutionalize business education in Colombia. UniValle's restructured economics faculty became a national model in May 1965, when Scarpetta and several professors presented their formula of an undergraduate economics program, graduate management program, and economic research center to a meeting of Colombian economics schools in the city of Paipa. Organized by the Association of Colombian Universities, the meeting concluded with a unanimous decision to adopt UniValle's paper as a statement of policy on economics teaching and an agreement to bring a revised version to a meeting of Latin American economics schools in Mexico City in June.[58] By 1967, los Andes had begun to imitate UniValle, establishing separate graduate-level courses for business executives, government officials, and university administrators.[59] While serving as dean at the Nacional that same year, Lauchlin Currie led a committee in recommending that the university emulate UniValle and los Andes in creating a US-style graduate program in business administration.[60] By the 1970s, Colombian business administration professors began meeting independently of economists, and in 1982 they established their own professional association, the Asociación Colombiana de Facultades de Administración. The birth of the graduate business school in Colombia began with UniValle.[61]

Looking out from Colombia, Scarpetta gathered the deans of Latin American business schools in Cali in 1966 to establish a new international association, the Consejo Latinoamericano de Escuelas de Administración (CLADEA, Latin American Council of Business Schools). Initially based in Cali, CLADEA represented the new generation of Latin American institutions supported by the Ford Foundation, the US government, the Council for Latin America, and top-tier US business schools. Its early members included UniValle, los Andes, ITESM in Mexico, ESAN in Peru, Católica and the Universidad de Chile, and the Instituto Centroamericano de Administración de Empresas (INCAE) in Nicaragua, which Harvard Business School and USAID had helped establish in 1963. CLADEA's first executive director was UniValle professor Hans Picker, a Northwestern-trained Chilean whom Scarpetta had hired away from Católica. As Scarpetta explained to the Ford Foundation, CLADEA's inaugural meeting in Cali was a "Latin American 'good guys' conference."[62]

CLADEA served both narrow professional functions and broad political ones. On the one hand, it promised to systematize business education, establishing a stable, internationally recognized distinction between economics and management. Those fields' rivalrous entanglement had troubled professors far beyond Colombia. When Harvard Business School faculty first visited Central America in 1963, they sounded like economists arriving in Colombia, except that they saw the negative image of the same photograph. "The programs in business administration are primarily 'macro-Economics,' with soupçons of law and statistics and accounting," they lamented. CLADEA promised to help business-school deans harmonize curricula, organize campus exchanges, and plan conferences demarcating business administration as an autonomous field and a bona fide profession. Moreover, CLADEA turned a small group of deans into missionaries within the hemisphere. In 1969, when the Association of Caribbean Universities decided to reform Jamaican management education, they turned to CLADEA and hired Scarpetta as a consultant.[63]

More importantly, CLADEA provided deans with a platform from which to project a vision of businessmen as leaders in public affairs, popularize a flattened notion of government as management, and portray the for-profit corporation as a general model of social organization. This was the moment when Scarpetta began to refer to government as "people managing public affairs." In CLADEA's literature, the association itself—a consortium of academic institutions—appeared no different from General Motors, its member schools equivalent to national corporate subsidiaries, and students something like cars rolling off an assembly line. "Tantamount to a multinational knowledge company with twelve operations in eight countries," read an early brochure, "the product it [CLADEA] sells is progress through education of present and future public and private managers."[64]

The reference to "public and private managers" was typical. "Management education is not just for business but for other socioeconomic institutions as well, and surely includes government," declared R. K. Ready, a Ford Foundation representative in Cali who sang CLADEA's praises in the *Columbia Journal of World Business*. Ready held a doctorate from Harvard Business School and taught at UniValle during Scarpetta's tenure. Like many US professors, he found himself intellectually unmoored in Latin America and began to think deliberately about the vistas of his field. "Management education builds from general propositions about the institutional structure of the society in which the particular managers work," he explained. By necessity, Latin American business schools had to evaluate the applicability of US curricula and "look hard at their indigenous conditions and priorities." For Ready, that process of self-examination revealed the systemic interconnection of business and government and the limits of training managers purely for the private sector. Addressing US readers, he argued that the same lesson should apply at home, since "the distinctions between private and public and profit and welfare" had become "increasingly blurred" there, as well. Management education should teach students to "see themselves in more than one, preferably in three or four, kinds of institutional structures, i.e., government, agriculture, education, health sciences and services, etc., as well as private industry." CLADEA, Ready concluded, was "the major indigenous force" transforming "schools of business management" into "schools of management, without an adjective."[65]

Ready and Scarpetta were hardly the first people to make this imaginative leap. Lilienthal and the CVC's Colombian founders had seen the corporation as the state's structural analogue. Neoclassical economists held the same view throughout the twentieth century. In the United States, at least four public universities had reorganized themselves in the 1940s according to the guidelines in Peter Drucker's *Concept of the Corporation*.[66] The birth of the industrial corporation in the late nineteenth century had radically transformed human relationships, and with them the ways that human beings imagined social and political order. An institution that shaped so many of a person's daily interactions and conditioned access to so many of life's necessities had a profound effect on the mind and the eye; it provided a lens through which to see other institutions. But if CLADEA's equation of the state and the firm lacked originality, it mattered in its time. US and Latin American business education had in fact focused on the industrial corporation in the past; only after graduating did students cross boundaries between public and private sectors. Moreover, the founding of Latin American economics programs had aimed to distinguish the corporation from the state. A new generation of economists had posited that these two institutions required different forms of knowledge handled by separate professions. The deans in CLADEA resuscitated an embattled idea. Revanchist and futurist at once, they breathed new life into an old notion, and shrouding its past, they declared it visionary.

CLADEA's depiction of businessmen as statesmen spoke to David Rockefeller's Council for Latin America. The two institutions became close partners, and they prioritized one preeminent public mission for businessmen: crafting a liberal international economic order. CLA's primordial purpose had been to make Latin America safe for foreign direct investment. By 1969, it celebrated CLADEA and UniValle for producing research that convinced the Colombian government to loosen regulations on foreign investors, allowing them to repatriate a rising share of profits instead of reinvesting them locally.[67] CLADEA focused, too, on shaping the process of Latin American economic integration. This was a knotty, ambiguous task. During the 1960s, CEPAL considered integration a tool to make import substitution industrialization possible; most countries' internal markets were too small to support a steel industry, but a larger regional market could solve the problem. Over the course of the 1960s, Latin Americans created three major free-trade agreements within the hemisphere: the Latin American Free Trade Agreement of 1960, the Central American Common Market of 1960, and the Andean Pact of 1969. While they varied in their terms and consequences, all expressed a vision of trade liberalization quite different from CLA's: they aimed to displace foreign investors within Latin America, and they complemented national policies that regulated trade with other world regions. From CLADEA's perspective, however, liberalization was on the table and awaiting definition. In 1968, it announced its intention "to convince the Latin American businessman of the ultimate wisdom of integration" and put those men at the helm of international economic policy making. "Latin America will be integrated by businessmen— public or private—exchanging goods and services for profit."[68]

The Fund for Multinational Management Education followed CLADEA's trajectory. Founded as a vehicle to finance UniValle's management program, it became an international lobbying organization for economic liberalization, collaborating with CLADEA and CLA. FMME continued funding business education until 1973, channeling US corporate donations to CLADEA affiliates and sending Latin Americans to US business schools and corporate training programs. It shuttled Roderick O'Connor and others across the hemisphere to run joint trainings for "private sector managers" and "public sector managers." Most interesting, it began organizing international conferences that built relationships among businessmen and government officials in the Americas. This was a class formation project designed to cultivate social identification between corporate executives seeking deregulation and public officials who negotiated with their firms. A typical event occurred in Ecuador in 1976, where FMME organized a role-playing game: representatives of government and multinationals "reversed their roles as they simulated the negotiation of foreign investment contracts." FMME convened these meetings together with a new organization that it financed and got off the ground, the Washington-based International Management and Development Institute (IMDI). Their politics were clear as day. When Chileans elected Salvador Allende in 1970, FMME stopped working in the country. Meanwhile, FMME eagerly collaborated with the Brazilian, Ecuadorean, Paraguayan, Uruguayan, and Peruvian military dictatorships, as well as the hemisphere's most stiflingly compromised democracies. Their measure of a government was the degree to which it taxed, regulated, or nationalized foreign capital; they prized liberalization without regard for democracy. By those criteria, president Henry R. Geyelin declared the seminars of 1971 and 1972 successes: "It is unlikely that through any other means Peruvian Coronels, Brazilian Technocrats, Colombian Congressmen, Mexican PRI Party Leaders, Ecuadorean Army and Navy Leaders and Venezuelan Presidential Candidates could have gotten together to talk openly (for periods ranging from one to two weeks) with US and Latin Business Leaders and with members of major international banks and agencies."[69]

After 1973, FMME became something broader and simpler: a global lobbyist for multinational corporations fighting regulation. Abandoning management education as such during these years, it reorganized itself in response to efforts by the UN, OECD, and ILO to create codes of conduct governing multinational corporations. "At this time, critics of the MNE [multinational enterprise] are dominating the debates," warned an FMME fund-raising script from the mid-1970s. "This is true because business has not effectively organized to deliver credible information on its activities and programs." FMME first went to war against the New International Economic Order (NIEO), a project that Third World governments advanced within the United Nations. Inspired by CEPAL's Raúl Prebisch, these states demanded a new trade and investment regime that would raise the incomes of primary commodity producers. Economist Jack Behrman of FMME considered the proposal unfit "even for serious debate," and FMME put its business school connections to work, furnishing US corporations and trade negotiators with opposition research. The organization presented itself as a middleman helping clients purchase knowledge. "FMME will select the researcher, provide the funds, and make the necessary arrangements with government bodies and corporations," the 1975 annual report explained. When the State Department's trade negotiators went to the United Nations Conference on Trade and Development (UNCTAD) negotiations in 1976, their official briefing book came from FMME.[70]

FMME simultaneously targeted individual governments. In Egypt and Mexico during the 1970s, the organization dangled the promise of technology transfer before public officials, promising that free trade zones and foreign concessions would benefit domestic capital. Turning the claims of dependency theorists on their heads, FMME explained that foreign investment did not displace local business but nurtured it. "Early in the sixties, a number of developing country experts began to argue that it was not so much in the area of capital, but in technology, that they were most dependent," noted FMME's Harvey Wallender in 1979. "We need in Mexico between 25,000 and 30,000 managers . . . and it will not take place through education alone, but through a combination of education, training, and technology transfer."[71]

During these years, the Latin Americans who had built FMME remained on the board, but they handed the reins to staff from the United States, creating the impression that the organization and its liberalizing project originated solely in the North Atlantic. Its wider, more tangled roots were nevertheless spelled out on letterhead, clearly legible to anyone who cared to read the words. Scarpetta served on the board throughout the 1970s, and staff members including Jack Behrman, Henry R. Geyelin, and Harvey Wallender came straight from Kennedy's Commerce Department, IESC, CLADEA, and Rockefeller's CLA. David Lilienthal served as FMME's chairman until the end of 1975.[72]

Colombia's attempt to fashion a new economics profession had come to quite unexpected ends. By the 1970s, increasing numbers of Colombians held degrees in the field, and the Universidad de los Andes had trained a new generation of policy makers. But the country simultaneously produced economists who burst the field's boundaries, as well as businessmen who competed with them for authority in public life. The unanticipated project of professionalizing managers prevented economists from monopolizing policymaking knowledge and simultaneously made Colombia a crossroads for rival visions of management itself. As it happened, Colombians never had to settle on a single account of the field and its purview. Instead, they tapped the resources of foreign foundations, universities, business associations, and think tanks to build institutions of their design and battle for influence in public life. Their work revealed contradictions at the heart of the developmentalist project: public university development enriched private capital, ennobled corporate managers, and produced institutions that went on to battle rival national development programs emanating from the Third World. Their work also revealed one way that Latin American institution building shaped the North Atlantic. By the 1970s, Colombia's capitalists had become international philanthropists in their own right, financing IMDI in Washington and bequeathing FMME to North Americans, who used it to lobby their own government and multilateral agencies.

As FMME's trajectory suggested, the mobilizations of Latin American businessmen entwined with those of capitalists in the United States. Moreover, as Laurence deRycke's career reminds us, US business mobilization had broad goals and a long trajectory. For decades after Second World War, the institutions that converged in Cali—US business associations from CED to CLA, business schools of every rank and style, foundations and think tanks—battled at home to explain the virtues of "free enterprise" to North Americans. That battle reached fever pitch during the 1960s and 1970s. These were years of crisis across the globe, and in domestic affairs, the key challenge for businessmen was neither the NIEO nor the rise of economists. It was a rising of social movements. Facing off against popular mobilizations, US executives embarked on a search for new strategies of legitimation, and that search came to involve the very same groups laboring on behalf of management in Latin America. As they grasped for power at home, US businessmen found standard-bearers among veterans of the Third World.

PART III

Looking Outward

6

The Great Society as Good Business

WHEN DAVID LILIENTHAL sailed to Colombia in 1954, he had gone looking for the influence he had lost in the United States. Marginalized in Washington, the old New Dealer found what he was seeking abroad and spent the rest of his life touting his Third World experience to remake his reputation at home. By the early 1960s, Americans were listening.

The voice they heard was that of a businessman working in an unusually auspicious field: economic development. The transformation of the Third World—real and imagined, pursued and dreaded—inspired worldwide fascination during the 1960s, and North Americans who had tired of the old TVA chairman clamored to hear from the chairman and CEO of the Development & Resources Corporation. Lilienthal seized the opportunity. He spent the "development decade" interpreting foreign societies to US audiences and fashioning wisdom for the US government from his work overseas. If the New Deal had been his teaching tool in Colombia, the CVC became his instructional aid at home. Lilienthal derived a distinctive lesson from the corporation's achievements: he argued that they testified to the statesmanship of Colombian managers and the talents of his own private consulting firm. It was a self-serving message, but Lilienthal aimed to do more than pat himself on the back. He intended to remake the state. Writing to Senator Jacob Javits of New York in 1960, Lilienthal argued that overseas development programs had demonstrated the necessity of "marshaling private corporate activity" to fulfill public needs.[1] Businessmen working for profit had proven their worth as public stewards in the Third World and now stood ready to assume government functions of all kinds at home. "For almost 20 years I was a public servant, the head of two large publicly owned corporations, and for the last 17 years I have been in private business," he explained in 1967, writing in the official journal of the US Civil Service: "What I have found and what I am sure others have observed is this: that the concept of public service is no longer one confined to those engaged in some form of government service . . . [T]he emerging concept of the businessman as a leader in public affairs may prove to be *one of the most important American ideas of the 20th Century.*"[2]

Lilienthal's celebration of businessmen as public stewards suggested an essential irony of midcentury state-building. The CVC had broadened Bogotá's responsibilities by handing them to the capitalists of Cali. They in turn had nurtured Lilienthal's for-profit consulting firm in the name of national development. Within a decade of the corporation's founding, Lilienthal was redeploying those facts, calling on the US government to fulfill its own widening obligations by delegating them to private capital. As he left Colombia, he carried with him the CVC's incipient impulse toward privatization. Finding ever more uses for private, for-profit contracting, Lilienthal cast the fusion of business and government as the fulfillment of his long crusade against state centralism.

Lilienthal's message became a powerful weapon at home. When he returned to the US public eye, businessmen who had long shaped and implemented domestic policy faced a grave crisis of legitimacy, and Lilienthal cast his lot with corporate executives desperately seeking a place in the Great Society. His influence was hardly unusual; as businessmen recoiled from public rebuke during the 1960s, some of their most effective defenders came from the margins of the nation. Corporate executives who had spent the early postwar decades wringing profits from international development, military, and Indian policy brought a distinctive perspective to insurgent demands for social justice, state action, and community control at home. To survive and thrive in an age of social upheaval, they understood, businessmen needed to enter the state, conduct its work, and map their profit-making activities onto the demands of social movements. Lilienthal belonged to a cohort of skilled institution builders, publicists, and political strategists who carried that lesson from the supposedly "underdeveloped" world to domestic business associations, government advisory boards, and community action programs of the 1960s. As far as these men were concerned, grand questions about the role of the private sector in public life had been resolved by the time the War on Poverty began, and the Great Society seemed an opportunity to consolidate their gains across domestic and international spheres.

By the late 1960s, the confluence of foreign and domestic business mobilization had made the War on Poverty into many things: the high-water mark of US antipoverty policy, a platform from which corporate executives fought for authority in public life, and an incubator of entirely new forms of for-profit contracting within the US welfare state. The Johnson years are often remembered as a moment when the federal government began funding community action programs that allowed poor people's organizations to design and implement public policy on their own behalf. But businessmen turning homeward embedded a second form of devolution in the War on Poverty: this was the moment when the US government awarded its very first for-profit contracts to business corporations to run domestic training and public education programs. The federal government had long relied on for-profit contracts to conduct foreign affairs and build infrastructure, but the social services targeted by the Great Society had generally stood apart as protected realms of nonprofit activity. The War on Poverty set off a race among industrial firms to establish themselves as for-profit educators and redefine the worldly activities that could be objects of capital accumulation. It simultaneously set off explosive conflicts between for-profit contractors and those they promised to serve, from Native American women on the Navajo reservation to unemployed youth in Job Corps camps nationwide. By the decade's end, veterans of foreign policy had carved out a lasting niche for private capital within the welfare state and taught US businessmen at large to explain their public mission in dramatically new ways.

———

David Lilienthal's phone rang incessantly during the 1960s. He received invitations to cabinet meetings, gained entrée to corporate boardrooms, and addressed university symposia. In every context, he rehabilitated himself by recounting the accomplishments of his foreign clients. In 1962, Rutgers University invited Lilienthal to give a lecture on urban development in the Third World. While D&R had virtually no experience in urban policy, he gamely delivered a talk on the CVC's transformation of Cali. Making the most of his status as an interpreter of little-known places, Lilienthal retold the story of displaced minifundistas as a glorious modernization tale. He began by casting the extraordinarily rich Cauca Valley as a sleepy backwater breaking with archaic "traditions." He then redefined the purpose of Colombia's agrarian reform, depicting it merely as a productivity measure. Making no mention of the reform's redistributive goals, Lilienthal explained that the CVC's program had increased the yield of vegetables and propelled the growth of new food-processing plants in Cali. Peasants, he continued, awakened to the promise of wage labor in the emerging metropolis and poured out of the countryside to seek work. These "hard pressed but ambitious people" eagerly built their own homes through self-help housing programs, and the city's dynamism spilled over to transform higher education at the Universidad del Valle. "The quiet little local university of fine traditions but limited resources was reborn almost overnight," he marveled.[3]

Foreign advisors never had the power to unilaterally remake societies, but they did have the power to tell stories as they wished back home. Lilienthal mobilized the tropes of modernization theory to explain the recent history of the Cauca Valley, and in doing so, he denied the very facts that had drawn him to the region in the first place. As Lilienthal knew, the "quiet little local university" in Cali had no timeless "traditions" to shed; the departmental government had established it in 1945 to foment development. Lilienthal himself had arrived in Cali nine years later because the city's cosmopolitan capitalists had invited him there, and he had yoked his fortune to theirs because the Colombians seemed so likely to produce a triumph. Just as Lilienthal reduced the Cauca Valley to his audience's image of "backwardness," he papered over the explosive conflicts erupting across the countryside as he spoke. In Lilienthal's telling, the consolidation of capitalist agribusiness was a purely consensual process, undertaken against all odds and realized with extraordinary speed. The coercion and dispossession involved in producing a wage labor force became invisible.

Stylized as they were, Lilienthal's tales of Colombia burnished his image at home and gave him a platform to discuss the topic that remained closest to his heart: management. He had little interest in bringing land reform or new food-processing plants to the United States. Instead, Lilienthal presented the CVC and D&R as proof that a new kind of manager had appeared on the world stage: a moral hero fit to resolve the crises of postwar societies. He insisted that he had met such managers in the Third World, including the "young business and professional men living in Cali, chief city of the Cauca Valley." Manuel Carvajal was, in his words, a "modern businessman and patriot," a founder of the CVC and manager of Colombia's first multinational corporation. Lilienthal described the postwar "manager-leader" as historically unprecedented in his social vision, practical talents, and human sympathy. He combined "in one personality the robust, realistic quality of the man of action with the insight of the artist, the religious leader, the poet, who explain man to himself." The new manager was no bean-counting authoritarian, but a "humanist" and a charismatic protagonist in the drama of public life.[4]

Pointing to himself, the chairman and CEO of D&R argued that such men also existed in the United States. "Some eleven years ago, I proposed the founding of a private development company operating on a business basis, that is to say for a profit or loss, dependent upon its own revenues and capital, but a corporation with public objectives," he explained in 1966 at the Carnegie Institute of Technology's Graduate School of Industrial Administration.[5] Working within flagship government programs across the Third World, D&R had tested and proven "the thesis that there is no good substitute for the balance sheet and income statement in the discipline they provide."[6] The pursuit of profit improved government, he argued, and the boundary between capital accumulation and public service had largely dissolved.[7] "I think we tend to over-emphasize the difference between public and private activity in this [development] field," Lilienthal explained to *International Management* magazine in 1961:

> MR. L[ILIENTHAL]: The so-called public aid programs are essentially financing rather than operating programs. What these programs spend money for, in good part, is goods and services supplied by private firms.
>
> IM: Enter Development & Resources Corp.?
>
> MR. L.: Exactly.[8]

At one level, Lilienthal told the unvarnished truth. Development and foreign aid programs, like so many public initiatives, characteristically involved private, for-profit contracts; the state enlarged its capacity by underwriting the growth of private enterprise. D&R's history illustrated the pattern. During the 1950s, Lilienthal and the Colombian leaders of ANDI had fought to remake public enterprise in the image of the private-sector corporation. The CVC, a public development corporation, had emerged from that effort and in turn became D&R's gateway to government contracts in Colombia and Iran. By the early 1960s, D&R's experience selling services at a profit to foreign governments had given it the credibility to do the same at home, starting in US foreign aid programs. In 1961, Lilienthal had memorably rebuffed President Kennedy's invitation to serve as assistant secretary of state for Latin America, preferring to work as a contractor in Washington. Soon enough, the Peace Corps hired D&R to produce manuals for agricultural programs and train volunteers for assignments in Brazil, Colombia, India, Malaysia, Morocco, and Nigeria. In 1966, the Johnson administration awarded the firm its most notorious development assistance contract, sending Lilienthal and his colleagues to undertake TVA-style development in the Mekong Delta at the height of the Vietnam War. By the decade's end, under the auspices of government aid and development programs, D&R had worked on every continent except Antarctica.[9]

In Washington, those for-profit contracts extended a very old tradition of state-building. Since the nineteenth century, the US government had relied on private enterprise to implement military plans and erect physical infrastructure of all kinds; for-profit contracts had produced the most emblematic expressions of the national state. During the Gilded Age, the navy had amassed an arsenal of torpedoes and complex weaponry through profitable contracts with arms manufacturers. The Panama Canal acquired massive lock gates, electrical equipment, mechanical parts, and locomotives from corporations across the United States. When the Great Depression struck, the Public Works Administration (PWA) spent two years building bridges, dams, and airports by private contract, ending its experiment only when Harry Hopkins's Works Progress Administration (WPA) replaced the agency in 1935. For the remainder of the decade, the WPA defiantly insisted on overseeing its own projects, prompting one trade journal to lambast Hopkins as "The High Prophet of No Profits." Hopkins's critics ultimately won the day when mobilization for the Second World War transformed the New Deal state. During the 1940s, the WPA reverted to for-profit contracting, and across the postwar era, public works and government construction became reliable sources of business for builders. As for D&R, its contracts followed a particularly lucrative template long established among US military and public-works contractors. "Cost-plus" contracts guaranteed private firms the full cost of production as well as sizable profits. Since the First World War, the military had used these arrangements to equip armies in wartime, develop factories and research installations in the Sunbelt, and construct a network of bases across the globe. Cost-plus agreements, and for-profit contracts more generally, had built the US state, and during the mid-1960s, they delivered profits of $3 to $5 million per year to D&R.[10]

While D&R's contracts were thoroughly conventional features of US statecraft, Lilienthal put them to novel political use. In a decade's worth of speeches and articles, he described mundane contract relations as evidence that managers had developed a new social conscience. He concluded that businessmen deserved genuinely new authority in public life and insisted that the same lesson should apply across the First and Third Worlds. "US ghettoes are underdeveloped countries right next door to rich, powerful, mature economic regions which tend to dominate them," Lilienthal explained in 1968. "I am convinced that private business is the most effective catalyst in this area both at home and abroad." Equating the problems of poor countries with those of poor communities in the United States, Lilienthal proposed to widen the scope of for-profit contracting from public works, military activities, and foreign aid to the full range of social services that dominated domestic antipoverty policy. Surveying the challenges facing the United States in 1966, Lilienthal called for managers to assume responsibilities both deeply familiar and shockingly novel:

> Now it is a broader concept of the manager as a leader of men and as a do-er that more nearly fits the needs of the crisis areas that confront us all: the areas of violence and war, of widespread hunger, of filthy streams, of poisoned air, of cities that are unlivable and need to be rebuilt, of educational and medical services, outmoded, that must be retooled, of poverty that brutalizes and must be overcome, of bitterness and violence between black

and white people—and so on down the long and stern agenda of crises that challenge this generation of men.

As to all these great on-going ventures of mankind, it is my profound conviction . . . that it is the manager as leader who must become the central figure.

Lilienthal's list of "crisis areas" suggested several radically new roles for corporations and their managers in US public life. What exactly would it mean for capitalists to "retool" US education as a lucrative business venture, or to quell "violence between black and white people" as a for-profit activity?[11]

In the past, businessmen had participated in providing education, poor relief, and other forms of social welfare and public order through nonprofit charities, foundations, and civic organizations. They understood these activities as necessary but unprofitable endeavors that made capital investment in other sectors possible. During the antebellum period, philanthropic funds and public revenues together established the country's first public reformatories for orphans, neglected children, and youth convicted of crimes. Throughout the nineteenth and early twentieth centuries, poor relief and humanitarian aid fell as heavily on the YMCA, Catholic charities, and Red Cross as on any level of government. Meanwhile, municipal coalitions of businessmen eagerly campaigned for government spending on public hospitals, schools, parks, libraries, and museums. They hoped that these institutions would prepare children for industrial labor, imbue private property with economic value, and create the conditions for economic growth. Businessmen had always considered these services essential to their own pursuit of profit, but they had not considered them sources of capital accumulation in themselves.[12]

When Lilienthal hailed corporate managers as heroes of the postwar world, then, he redefined the realms of life in which the profit motive should apply. It was an audacious move during the 1960s. Lilienthal returned to the US public eye just as businessmen, corporations, the profit motive, and the very pattern of US economic growth faced crises of legitimacy. As Lilienthal lionized the CVC at Rutgers in 1962, Michael Harrington's best-seller *The Other America* exposed grinding poverty at the heart of a growing economy. Rachel Carson's *Silent Spring* revealed the deadly duplicity of the chemical industry, and Students for a Democratic Society's Port Huron Statement condemned postwar prosperity as soulless and unjust. Across the 1950s and 1960s, the black freedom movement put private employers, banks, and the real estate industry on public trial for racial discrimination. The escalating war in Vietnam incited censure of military contractors, and a new generation of Marxist economists and anticapitalist student organizations charged that the US economy relied systematically on war and imperialism to expand and survive. The very crises that allowed Lilienthal to reenter US politics made his message more than an anodyne celebration of managerial talent; he returned to public life doing battle with contemporary social movements.

A devoted polemicist, Lilienthal spent the 1960s searching for just the right phrase to describe his vision of private capital fulfilling ever more public purposes. He applauded "business statesmanship" and proclaimed D&R "a public-private enterprise." Management, he wrote, was a "high form of leadership" akin to "community mobilization."[13] During his 1966 lectures at Carnegie Tech, Lilienthal coined the term that every business journalist and aspiring MBA used by the century's end: "social entrepreneurship." The concept captured a genuinely novel idea that the public responsibility of business was not to produce quality goods, raise productivity, hire without discrimination, pay workers well, reduce pollution, contribute to charity, pay taxes, or bow out of war making—the motley claims of contemporary social movements and an earlier generation of managers. Rather, its responsibility was to apply existing strategies of capital accumulation to the widening array of problems that social movements had forced onto the national agenda. Lilienthal's perspective deflected public criticism of the firm, closed off debate over its core operations, and instead proposed to create new markets in which corporations could operate. When he published his Carnegie Tech lectures as a book in 1967—he called it *Management: A Humanist Art*—conservatives and the business press immediately recognized its value. Mary Bennett Peterson, a right-wing advocate of deregulation and privatization, applauded Lilienthal in the *Wall Street Journal*. "Business opportunities—indeed profit opportunities—to improve the human condition are endless," she argued. "These include providing for the two-thirds of the world population that is ill-fed, ill-clothed and ill-housed; in the US rebuilding blighted urban areas, controlling air and water pollution, waging a real war on poverty, ameliorating tension between our black and white citizens, educating the uneducated and semi-educated, and so on." Lilienthal, she declared, had delivered a brilliant retort to student radicals. "Perhaps if there were more David Lilienthals . . . businessmen might not so often be regarded as conformist, egotistical, money-grubbing and just plain dull, and the word on the campus today might be a bit more favorable," she concluded.[14]

Just as Lilienthal's book appeared in 1967, D&R returned home and entered the Great Society. The Johnson administration and Congress spent the mid-1960s eviscerating the Alliance for Progress and shifting funds to the War on Poverty. Capitalizing on six years of experience in US foreign aid programs, D&R's managers eagerly bid for contracts in urban redevelopment, presenting their new focus as "a logical extension of our existing activities."[15] From

California to suburban Detroit to Puerto Rico, D&R shaped domestic policies on energy, land, and water use. The company's work in metropolitan New York alone suggested its sprawling reach. In 1967, the Jamaica Community Corporation, founded by civil rights activists in Queens, hired D&R to advise on two initiatives: a campaign to win jobs for African Americans at the new JFK airport and a plan to create a multiservice center under HUD's Model Cities program. Two years later, the Commerce, Labor, Industry Corporation of Kings (CLICK), a community organization charged with bringing industry to the decommissioned Brooklyn Navy Yard, asked D&R to plan the rehabilitation of five waterfront buildings. Mayor John Lindsay enlisted D&R and Lilienthal to help redevelop Welfare Island in 1968. When the city suffered electricity shortages during the late 1960s, Con Edison solicited D&R's proposals for reforming the metropolitan energy system. D&R's Gordon Clapp went on to conduct the official state investigation of the 1977 New York City blackout. Across the Hudson River, meanwhile, D&R advised the state of New Jersey on managing water resources and redeveloping the Meadowlands during the late 1960s.[16] By the early 1970s, D&R's clients included every sort of institution wielding public power in the United States, from HUD and the EPA to private utility companies to local community organizations administering federal antipoverty grants.[17]

Curiously, in all of this work, D&R never ventured far from the traditional domains of for-profit contracting. The firm remained focused on engineering and planning services, not education or policing. D&R was less an exemplar of Lilienthal's most ambitious claims than a platform from which he pronounced them. It established him as an authority fit to speak on the most riveting problems of the day: development and poverty. And almost in spite of the firm's old-fashioned work in infrastructure, energy, and foreign policy, D&R provided the raw material from which he crafted a story about managers as public servants for a new era.

The lesson that Lilienthal drew from the Third World was peculiar; it testified less to incontrovertible truths about Colombia or his firm's activities than to his status as a businessman. The former TVA chairman had chosen that path a decade earlier, and he fully inhabited the role in the 1960s. In the interim, a great deal had changed. As the book review section of the *Wall Street Journal* made clear, Lilienthal now possessed something that most of his peers at home lacked: plausible stories of managers acting as agents of social progress. The old New Dealer spent the 1960s patching those tales together from bits of his life, polishing them to a sheen, and presenting them as gifts from the Third World to the disgraced businessmen of the First. Reentering the US public eye, his significance went far beyond D&R's rather conventional domestic business activities. Lilienthal became a prolific propagandist for private capital as the guarantor of human well-being and a spokesman for managers seeking legitimacy and power in the Great Society. It turned out that the very resources he had brought to Colombia's capitalists a decade earlier—his name, his reputation, and his storied past—could prove equally useful at home.

———

Lilienthal's trajectory was hardly unique. While he delivered speeches during the 1960s, other businessmen working at the purported margins of the nation—in Indian affairs, overseas investment associations, and military projects—did the practical work of burrowing into the welfare state. Arriving by separate routes, they converged in the War on Poverty's job-training and education programs and became living embodiments of Lilienthal's new manager. Redeploying policies and political strategies they had crafted in foreign and imperial contexts, businessmen remade social policy at home.

Many came from Latin America. In 1963, the businessmen that David Rockefeller had organized to transform the Alliance for Progress had convinced the Johnson administration to channel foreign aid through corporations and semi-private organizations like the International Executive Service Corps. The strategy that US investors honed in the Third World—supporting aid and demanding that it flow through and to the private sector—found new use within the War on Poverty. Curiously, historians have never connected these two arenas because businessmen's mobilization in Latin America became so thoroughly associated with a harrowing right turn in regional politics. US and multilateral agencies reduced and rerouted their development loans just as Latin American governments launched scorched-earth counterinsurgency campaigns and democracy came to crisis in much of the continent. The 1964 military coups in Brazil and Bolivia inaugurated a new era of authoritarian government in the region, and by 1967, the foreign investors in Rockefeller's CLA had become infamous collaborators with Latin American militaries.[18] In Colombia, CLA participated in the government's counterinsurgency war against the FARC by financing the Federación Nacional del Sector Privado Para la Acción Comunal (FEPRANAL). Founded in 1962 by right-wing anticommunists in Bogotá, FEPRANAL was a private business association that promoted community action as an austere method of social welfare provision. During the late 1960s, it operated as an adjunct to the Colombian army, organizing self-help housing and infrastructure projects in areas that soldiers had cleared of guerrillas. According to CLA, FEPRANAL's work was a model of "private sector service to the public sector." In neighboring Brazil, Enno Hobbing of CLA praised the 1964 military coup, labeling it a "revolution" and applauding the "civic responsibility" of Brazilian businessmen who "willingly left their offices for government assignments."[19] As he wrote those words in 1967, Brazil's military dictatorship was ratifying a new constitution, press law, and national security law that banned strikes, regulated "freedom of thought and information," ended direct election of the president, and curtailed civil liberties in the name of wiping out internal enemies. By the start of 1967, Brazil's military courts had registered 353 reports of torture.[20]

As CLA collaborated with counterinsurgency and dictatorship abroad, the organization sounded for all the world like David Lilienthal. Both insisted that businessmen had become the hemisphere's great public servants. Hobbing of CLA explained that the 1959 Cuban revolution had convinced US corporations that "they would have to do more than tend to business." During the 1960s, they had "invested much more heavily than before in education" and had helped Colombia develop the continent's most "comprehensive business-supported community development effort." To be sure, D&R's experience differed from CLA's. Lilienthal initially cooperated with the Rojas dictatorship and maintained a long partnership with the Shah of Iran, but his activities never intersected so directly with Colombia's counterinsurgent warfare of the late 1960s or the authoritarian governments that arose in Latin America after 1964. By contrast, Hobbing was a CIA agent and veteran of the 1954 coup in Guatemala. Despite those differences, Lilienthal and Hobbing drew the same lesson from Latin America and spoke in unison at home.[21]

These men's activities throughout the Americas reveal something rarely noted about their politics. CLA's cooperation with Latin American generals spoke less to any coherent preference for military authority than to the parasitism of business mobilization during the heyday of developmentalism. Across the hemisphere, these US businessmen made a place for themselves within every anticommunist state project that would have them. In doing so, they presented themselves as the world's public servants and laid bare a deeply amoral indifference to democracy and widely shared standards of justice.

That very indifference allowed many to enter the Great Society as eagerly as they facilitated cataclysmic violence and repression in Latin America. In 1964, the Johnson administration remade the Alliance for Progress, established the International Executive Service Corps, and announced the War on Poverty. Rockefeller's assemblage of businessmen began plying the same tools across the US state, championing foreign and domestic spending while mobilizing to channel the funds through business institutions. In the spring of 1964, the Business Group for Latin America (soon to be CLA) urged Congress to sustain funding for the Alliance for Progress just as Sargent Shriver invited several of its member firms to join a new Business Leadership Advisory Council to the War on Poverty. Corporations already active in BGLA quickly made the transition. David Rockefeller himself, as well as executives from IBM and

Sears, Roebuck, advised Shriver in 1964. By 1967, CLA and the Business Leadership Advisory Council had grown thoroughly intertwined, with common members including Bank of America, Brown & Root, Chrysler, Dow Chemical, Kaiser, and Pan Am.[22]

US foreign investors entered the War on Poverty in lockstep with military contractors, who drew on their own experience in foreign affairs. Within the Business Leadership Advisory Council, Brown & Root, Dow, IBM, and Kaiser fell into both categories, and from the earliest days of the group, Shriver invited Douglas Aircraft, Litton Industries, the Manufacturing Chemists Association, the Olin Corporation, the Pittsburgh Chemical Company, and the Utah Mining and Construction Company. These electrical, chemical, aerospace, engineering, and construction outfits lived and died by defense contracts and had long operated across the fictive boundary between domestic and international affairs. As the War on Poverty began, they saw the same opportunity for profit in the growing welfare state that CLA's foreign investors did and made their way into social policy.[23]

John Rubel, a forty-four-year-old vice president of Litton Industries, became their foremost spokesman. Rubel had been assistant secretary of defense under Robert McNamara during the Kennedy administration before accepting a job with Litton in 1963. He considered the Pentagon's for-profit contracting system a model for the rest of the federal government. In April 1964, he proposed to Shriver that the War on Poverty emulate the military and space programs by devolving responsibilities to for-profit corporations. "I think the country has a lot to gain by broadening the spectrum of possibilities open to advancing industries," he explained. "I would like to see social service in many forms become the direct concern of private business and industry."[24]

For Rubel, the War on Poverty's manpower and education programs seemed natural objects of capitalist enterprise. Many corporations already offered vocational courses to the public through private, for-profit subsidiaries. As Shriver explained in 1965, "Litton Industries . . . has trained more than 20,000 people for jobs in the last three years. More than 2,000 of these came from the ranks of the unemployed." Furthermore, a number of military contractors manufactured classroom electronics that they promised would revolutionize teaching. During the 1950s, IBM, RCA, General Electric, AT&T, and other electronics firms had begun collaborating with psychologists associated with Harvard's B. F. Skinner. Known as radical behaviorists, these researchers argued that teachers working with a classroom full of students could never effectively address the needs of each one, and that children did better learning individually from "teaching machines" and "programmed" texts. Programming broke subjects down into sequential bits of information that students read silently or listened to through headphones. At each step, the student had to respond to a question to demonstrate comprehension, and at longer intervals, children took standardized tests to measure their proficiency in the subject. To motivate pupils without the social routines of a classroom, psychologists paired programmed materials with extrinsic rewards, offering children free time, toys, food, and other prizes for correct answers and completed tasks. These techniques were enormously controversial, assailed by critics as rote learning and rejected by many teachers as affronts to their unions and professional autonomy. Decades of research found them no more effective than traditional teaching techniques. But during the early postwar decades, behaviorist technologies fascinated government officials. By the early 1960s, federal science and education grants had sent behaviorists to test their tools among some of the country's most vulnerable and stigmatized populations, including adults in psychiatric hospitals, boys in juvenile detention centers, and preschoolers on Indian reservations. Meanwhile, industrial corporations had begun manufacturing the equipment that psychologists needed, and some developed programmed texts for their own corporate training programs. In 1964, Rubel held up electronics firms as authorities on education and cast the War on Poverty as a perfect laboratory to refine and popularize behaviorist techniques.[25]

Rubel promised, finally, that military contractors could rationalize the manpower program by bringing the Pentagon's "systems approach" to the welfare state. Systems analysis was an improvised fusion of game theory, linear programming, and ordinary layman's logic that had purported to optimize military planning by the 1960s. Originally developed at the RAND Corporation during the 1940s and 1950s, it had found its most famous application within McNamara's Department of Defense. McNamara hired analysts from RAND and private industry to create a new Program Planning and Budget System (PPBS), which allowed the Pentagon to assess each military expenditure in terms of long-term and short-term objectives, measure "inputs" against "outputs," and consider trade-offs and alternatives. Systems analysis was never as systematic as its champions suggested, but the Kennedy and Johnson administrations delighted at the idea of a scientific, apolitical, efficient procedure for modeling complex decisions and allocating resources. Rubel promised to apply the same principles to job training and education. "The input—the raw material—that is fed into this machine is people," he told Shriver in 1964. "The output is people. It is the function of this machine to transform these people." In his view, the for-profit corporation was not a specialized instrument of economic production, but rather a generic vehicle for organizing any complex process. Military contractors could design national training and education initiatives, efficiently distribute tasks by contract, deploy new teaching technologies in the classroom, rigorously measure results, and use that hard data to refine the program.[26]

Shriver seized on the idea and hired Rubel to rustle up support among businessmen. Some initially balked at the very idea of a War on Poverty, while others hoped merely to secure new fiscal and trade policies. Rubel spent the spring of 1964 redirecting their aspirations, encouraging corporate executives to imagine themselves operating social welfare programs at a profit. Those experienced in foreign affairs quickly recognized the opportunity. By May 1964, Westinghouse Electric Corporation and Republic Aviation both wanted to bid for job-training contracts. Management Technology Inc., a defense contractor, offered to manage the entire War on Poverty at a profit. Shriver's staff, still working in the Peace Corps offices, hosted rounds of meetings with businessmen and psychologists to plan curricula and recruit contractors. By 1965, both Shriver's Office of Economic Opportunity (OEO) and military contractors had hired some of the country's leading behaviorists. Enticed by the promise of federal funds, Litton, Westinghouse, Xerox, RCA, Thiokol, and other veterans of foreign policy began launching for-profit educational subsidiaries in 1965, staffed them with Skinner's colleagues and protégés, and bid for work in the War on Poverty.[27]

Industrial firms never ran the entire War on Poverty, but with Shriver's support, they took charge of its manpower training programs. Job Corps, established within the OEO in 1964, offered free residential education and job training to unemployed youths. Modeled in part on the New Deal's Civilian Conservation Corps (CCC), Job Corps diverged from the CCC and most OEO programs by operating entirely through private contract, and chiefly through for-profit contracts with corporations. By 1967, industrial giants directed three-quarters of all urban Job Corps centers nationwide. As Shriver boasted, "Their names read like a who's who in American industry: Xerox, IBM, Brunswick, RCA, Litton, AT&T, G.E., Westinghouse to name a few right off the top."[28] In 1966, the Bureau of Indian Affairs began contracting with industrial firms to open employment training centers in California, Mississippi, and New Mexico. And in 1968, the Johnson administration created Job Opportunities in the Business Sector (JOBS). Funded by the Department of Labor, JOBS offered lucrative contracts to industrial corporations to train unemployed workers under twenty-two and over forty-five years of age. Like the International Executive Service Corps, the program channeled federal funds through a private business association, the National Alliance of Businessmen (NAB). Formed at Johnson's invitation, NAB was chaired by Henry Ford II, an early member of the Business Group for Latin America. Together, these programs made US manpower policy a path to training and education for unemployed Americans as well as a new source of profit for military contractors and US foreign investors.[29]

FIGURE 6.1. A 1965 Job Corps brochure shows corpsmen using teaching machines in class. The OEO maintained that new technologies developed by radical behaviorists and industrial corporations could educate youth who had struggled in conventional classrooms. (OEO brochure, *Is There a Job in Your Future?* University of Virginia, Special Collections, Alice Jackson Stuart Papers, Box 38, Folder "Kilmer Job Corps Center, Edison, New Jersey, 1965-66, n.d.")

As they moved into social policy, these firms brought a portfolio of contracting and budgeting procedures with them. Cost-plus and other for-profit contracts guaranteed surpluses over and above expenses, and the Pentagon's budgeting and planning system, PPBS, became the standard procedure for the entire federal government in 1965. Over the remainder of the decade, state and local governments took notice and began applying the system to their own public services. By 1970, three-quarters of states required school districts to use PPBS or were considering doing so.[30]

Firms experienced in foreign and imperial affairs brought one last form of experience to the War on Poverty: some had already run training programs in Indian country. The architects of Job Corps later described the New Deal's public CCC camps as their inspiration, but programs of the 1960s more closely resembled, and indeed incorporated, privatized initiatives that the Bureau of Indian Affairs (BIA) had launched on a very small scale during the Eisenhower administration. In the years after World War II, the US government had set out to dissolve tribes as political entities, first by relocating residents of reservations to surrounding cities and towns, and ultimately by adopting a policy of termination in 1953. Termination promised to abrogate a century of US treaty obligations that had established tribes as sovereign nations entitled to land and federal subsidies. The policy resurrected ideas from the late nineteenth century, when the 1887 Dawes Act had put reservation lands up for sale and the Indian Service launched social welfare programs designed to break up kinship networks, undermine tribal affiliations, and assimilate Native Americans into US society. The Roosevelt administration had temporarily reversed those policies, signing the 1934 Indian Reorganization Act to strengthen tribal governments and launching an "Indian New Deal" that directed social spending to reservations. But the Truman and Eisenhower administrations reneged on those promises and made industrial policy a new instrument of termination. The BIA promised to prepare Native people for jobs in US cities by bringing manufacturers to reservations, where firms established factories and trained workers. From 1954 to 1960, BIA commissioner Glenn Emmons and Congress created wide-ranging economic incentives to attract private industry. Notably for the future of the War on Poverty, the BIA allowed firms to hire Native workers at half the minimum wage while federal job-training funds paid the rest. As of 1960, only four factories had materialized on reservations, but the policies of the 1950s established a pattern of federally subsidized, for-profit contracting for manpower training that shaped the Great Society.[31]

The path from termination policy to the War on Poverty went through Indian organizations themselves. The BIA had courted private capital for the purpose of dissolving Native communities, but tribal leaders turned industrial policy into a nationalist tool to reconstitute reservations. Self-consciously echoing Third World nationalists, they declared industrial production a foundation of sovereignty and identified themselves as "underdeveloped" societies on a path of modernization. Washington financed factories as nation-building instruments in Puerto Rico and the Third World, they argued, and factories should serve the same function in Indian country.[32]

The incoming Kennedy administration responded. "What we are attempting to do for those in the underdeveloped area of the world, we can and must also do for the Indians here at home," declared the government's 1961 Task Force on Indian Affairs. The government spent the early 1960s redeploying Eisenhower's reservation industrialization programs as nation-building initiatives. In an extraordinary recognition of tribes' political status, the 1961 Area Redevelopment Act (ARA) and Manpower Development Training Act (MDTA) channeled federal industrial, training, and infrastructure funds to tribes as well as state and local governments. Within four years, twenty-five factories operated in Indian country, employing nearly 1,700 Native workers. When the Johnson administration crafted the Economic Opportunity Act in 1964, the BIA helped shape the legislation, and BIA commissioner Philleo Nash hailed Indian training programs as models for the nation. Indian country, he argued, had shown the United States how to transform the poor and jobless into "self-supporting, self-sustaining, contributory members of our great society."[33]

For the remainder of the decade, the War on Poverty built out private industrialization and training initiatives in Indian country. The Economic Development Administration (EDA), created within the Commerce Department in 1965, inherited the ARA's responsibilities for financing industrial development on reservations. The OEO trained tribal leaders to pitch investment proposals to corporations, teaching them to compete with states and localities that had long lured private capital with public subsidies. Beyond reservations, the BIA's new employment training centers in California, Mississippi, and New Mexico operated by for-profit contract with industrial corporations.[34]

Several of the military contractors that ran Job Corps centers after 1964 had won their first manpower training contracts from the BIA during the Kennedy years. From their perspective, the War on Poverty did not exactly invent a new pattern of private contracting. Instead, it brought a fledgling Indian policy to the entire United States. The electronics manufacturer RCA immediately made the leap from Indian country to Job Corps. Since its founding in 1919, the firm had operated a for-profit subsidiary, RCA Institutes, which offered vocational training through daytime, evening, and correspondence courses. In 1962, RCA won a BIA contract to train nearly one hundred Alaska Natives as electronics technicians in New York and then employ them at RCA facilities fulfilling defense contracts in Alaska. The project failed; it required trainees to relocate within Alaska, and most refused to do so, returning home within a matter of months. Nevertheless, RCA went on to win contracts within the War on Poverty. By 1967, it operated the McCoy Job Corps Center for men in Sparta, Wisconsin; the Keystone Job Corps Center for women in Drums, Pennsylvania; and a BIA employment training center for members of the Choctaw tribe in Mississippi. It produced instructional materials for Job Corps conservation centers. And it contracted with the Department of Labor to deliver on-the-job training to television servicemen and NASA employees. Because the Labor Department program required a background in electronics, the Department of Health, Education, and Welfare (HEW) gave RCA another contract to provide one month of training to prospective applicants.[35]

As RCA traveled from Indian country to the heart of the welfare state, US foreign investors did the same. In 1965, the very first Job Corps contract went to International Telegraph and Telephone (ITT), an original member of CLA and a notorious ally of the Brazilian military dictatorship. When Job Corps began, ITT was also a military contractor facing declining income from its defense work, and it eyed the welfare state as a new source of revenue. The firm capitalized on its experience shaping the Alliance for Progress and its relationships in Washington. An ITT subsidiary, the Federal Electric Corporation (FEC), already supplied electronic communications systems to the federal government and trained public-sector workers to operate them. Based on that experience, FEC won an OEO contract to run the Kilmer Job Corps Center in New Jersey. "Service is FEC's business—from helping make war on unemployment to helping defend the Free World," ITT announced in the pages of *Foreign Relations* and the *Financial Analysts Journal*. The twenty-two-month, $11,250,000 contract charged FEC with teaching English, math, and vocational skills to 2,500 young men. It guaranteed $541,000 in profits for the company.[36]

For corporations experienced in winning military contracts, federal manpower programs promised moral absolution and a new stream of government revenue. "Have you ever given serious thought to how those people live who have not been as fortunate as we are?" asked Thiokol vice president Robert L. Marquardt in 1970. He spoke as a chemical and aerospace executive, and addressed the readers of a trade journal, *IEEE Transactions on Aerospace and Electronic Systems*. In 1965, Thiokol had named Marquardt head of its newest division, Economic Development Operations, which bid for contracts in the War on Poverty. "Company leaders recognized Thiokol's responsibility in helping to solve some of the massive social problems confronting the country," Marquardt explained. By 1968, Thiokol boasted a Job Corps Center in Clearfield, Utah, and a BIA Employment Training Center and Indian Police Academy in Roswell, New Mexico. Meanwhile, HUD had sent Thiokol to develop low-cost homeownership programs in Gulfport, Mississippi, and Raleigh, North Carolina. For Thiokol, like ITT, the War on Poverty came at a propitious time. The company's aerospace and defense sales had peaked during the early 1960s and began declining in 1965. For the remainder of the decade, its Economic Development Operations constituted a small part of the firm's earnings but grew in absolute and proportional terms, rising from 2 percent of revenues in 1966 to 6 percent in 1970.[37]

By 1965, US foreign investors, military contractors, and veterans of Indian industrialization had broken open federal training and education programs to for-profit contractors. Traveling by separate roads from the apparent edges of the United States to the center of domestic policy making, they adapted familiar patterns of private delegation and set off an epochal transformation of the welfare state. "A marvelously revolutionary decision is being carried out by the

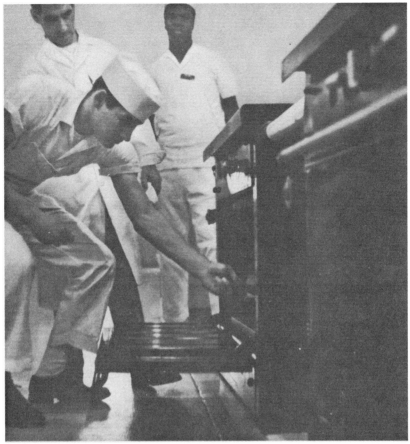

ITT is teaching Mike Fontenot how to bake a cake.

When Mike's completed his cook's training he can take an advanced course leading to a successful career as a pastry chef.

A successful career—that's one big reason for the Kilmer Job Corps Center in New Jersey, operated for the U.S. Office of Economic Opportunity by Federal Electric Corporation (FEC), an ITT subsidiary.

Instruction is offered in over thirty trades, ranging from pastry baking to automotive mechanics to offset printing. Eventually Kilmer will graduate 2,500 young men a year.

FEC is well qualified for the Kilmer project, having also trained thousands of men for highly technical jobs around the world. Some handle communications and instrumentation to track spacecraft and missiles. Others installed the largest communications system in Europe for the U.S. Air Force. Still others operate and maintain the strategic Distant Early Warning (DEW) Line which stretches from Alaska to Greenland.

Service is FEC's business—from helping make war on unemployment to helping defend the Free World.

International Telephone and Telegraph Corporation, New York, N.Y.

FIGURE 6.2. ITT, a military contractor and founding member of the Council for Latin America, announces its new role as a for-profit federal contractor operating the country's first Job Corps camp. (*Foreign Affairs*, July 1966, A-13)

Johnson administration," declared conservative *Los Angeles Times* columnist Roscoe Drummond in March 1965. ITT had just opened the Kilmer Job Corps Center in New Jersey, and Litton Industries was beginning work at the Parks Center in Pleasanton, California. "Business building ships and tanks at a profit? Obvious. Business building social welfare at a profit? Ridiculous!" Drummond proclaimed with ironic delight. "But it is not ridiculous to the Johnson administration, which views business as an ally, not an enemy." The welfare state had finally taken a lesson from the foreign policy establishment, he explained, harnessing "the motive power of profit to generate social progress."[38]

———

Treating job-training programs as sites of capital accumulation, corporations set off systemic conflicts between the pursuit of profit and the needs of trainees. When contractors bid to operate training centers, their budgets included profit as a line-item expense charged to the government, which diverted a portion of federal antipoverty appropriations from instruction itself. When money was short, profit turned out to be a non-negotiable priority. In 1967, the OEO cut funds for the McCoy Job Corps Center in Wisconsin, and RCA scaled back services while preserving profits. Terminating its subcontract with the University of Wisconsin, which had provided reading and math courses as well as counseling, RCA promised to offer its own pared-down versions of those services. "This new and more austere program provides for fewer corpsmen, a reduced staff, and fewer buildings than originally contemplated," explained Harry Mills of RCA. The contract with Wisconsin illuminated the divergent concerns that a for-profit electronics manufacturer and a nonprofit educational institution brought to the War on Poverty. During Senate hearings, the chancellor of Wisconsin's University Extension program, Donald R. McNeil, protested on behalf of students. "Education is expensive," McNeil told senators. "No matter what it costs society to retrieve these young men and make them productive members of society, I think society has to pay that cost." McNeil was, of course, defending the university's expiring contract, and his paternalistic views of trainees would likely have appalled them. But having no interest in profit, he aligned the university's interest with students' access to federal resources. Indeed, Wisconsin championed a variety of student needs that the OEO slighted. In 1967, the agency proposed to send migrant farmworkers from the Southwest to the university for a high school equivalency program. Wisconsin officials objected that the budget failed to include winter clothing for students, and they forced the OEO to renegotiate the cost.[39]

Job-training programs in fact seeded multiple conflicts between trainees and for-profit contractors. For light industry especially, these programs

subsidized a hunt for low-wage, nonunion labor that was leading manufacturers out of northern cities and across the globe. Among historians, RCA has
become a symbol of twentieth-century capital flight that devastated major US
manufacturing centers and hobbled the labor movement. Following the enticements of government subsidies and fleeing union organizing drives, the
corporation blazed a trail out of Camden, New Jersey, during the 1940s, moving its lowest-paid assembly jobs through the Midwest, the Sunbelt, and finally
across the Mexican border in 1968. Five years later, Mexico's maquiladora zone
bustled with 168 electronics assembly plants, where young women worked for
US multinationals that had followed the same path as RCA.[40]

Indian country and the War on Poverty form a forgotten part of this story.
"Indian Country Is a Frontier Again," announced the US Chamber of Commerce magazine *Nation's Business* in 1969. From 1961 to 1970, tribal governments and Washington brought over 150 new factories to reservations by offering job-training funds, defense contracts, new plants, infrastructure, loans,
housing, social services, expedited licenses and permits, and the tax-free status
of reservation land itself. At least five tribes built full-scale industrial parks.
Footloose electronics firms responded with special enthusiasm, and their assembly plants became prototypical examples of industrialization in Indian
country. Emblematically, in 1966, RCA itself applied unsuccessfully to operate
the BIA training center in Roswell, New Mexico. The company hoped to enter
the nonunion Southwest and considered BIA vocational programs a path to
cheap labor and subsidized infrastructure.[41]

An electronics assembly plant on the Navajo reservation ultimately brought
the contradictions of the War on Poverty's for-profit job-training programs to
national attention. The Navajo reservation is often remembered as the site of
ambitious community action programs during the War on Poverty; in 1965,
the federal government created an Office of Navajo Economic Opportunity,
and Native people used the agency to establish new higher-education programs and push back against the paternalism of the Bureau of Indian Affairs.[42]
But that same year, the Fairchild Camera and Instrument Corporation also
opened a transistor assembly plant in Shiprock, New Mexico.[43] The factory
was nonunion, and indeed, the tribal government had gone to great lengths to
broadcast its hostility to organized labor. In 1960, the Navajo Nation had at-
tempted to defeat an organizing drive among uranium mill workers by arguing
that 1935 National Labor Relations Act—the federal law that established US
workers' right to organize—did not apply to the reservation. The National
Labor Relations Board protested, and the Washington, DC, circuit court ruled
against the tribe in 1961. But the case sent a signal to employers.[44] The Navajo
Nation subsidized Fairchild by building an industrial park for $844,000, draw-
ing on its own funds and a loan from the EDA. It was a high price to pay for

Indian Country Is a Frontier Again

FIGURE 6.3. An article in the magazine of the Chamber of Commerce announces
government subsidies, including federal job-training programs, designed to bring industrial
firms to Indian reservations. The illustration depicts Navajo workers at the Fairchild
transistor assembly plant in Shiprock, New Mexico. (*Nation's Business*, September 1969, 76.
Courtesy Hagley Museum and Library)

jobs; the tribe's interest payments to the EDA and the foregone interest on
tribal funds exceeded the rent that Fairchild paid. Over the course of a decade,
the BIA, Department of Labor, and other federal agencies contributed nearly
$3 million in on-the-job training funds, which allowed Fairchild to pay new
hires just half the minimum wage. Another $5.5 million in federal monies paid
for infrastructure and buildings.[45] At its height in 1969, the plant operated
around the clock and employed 1,130 people, virtually all of them Navajo. Fairchild boasted that it was "the largest non-governmental employer of American
Indians in the United States" and called the Shiprock plant one of its best facilities, both in terms of quality and productivity.[46]

As electronics manufacturers had long done, Fairchild sought out vulnerable workers and chose women in a racialized community ravaged by joblessness. In December 1965, the Navajo reservation's unemployment rate stood at 44 percent, and the company availed itself of entrenched inequalities that made stressful, low-paid operative jobs some of the best opportunities available to local women. "It was tedious work under a microscope," explained Jim Tutt, a Navajo process engineer. Assembling transistors and integrated circuits required dexterity and unremitting concentration. Peering through microscopes, workers soldered layers of metal onto silicon wafers, some "no larger than the head of a pin." The company invoked racial and gender stereotypes to explain its policy of occupational segregation and the high quality of Shiprock's output. Nimble fingers suited women to operative tasks, Fairchild claimed, and "innate Navajo skill" conditioned workers for "precision assembly."[47]

By the end of 1966, as many as eighty women were arriving in Shiprock every month from other parts of the reservation. Taking up jobs at the transistor plant, they did what Navajo men and women had done for decades, channeling their earnings to extended family networks. Before the Great Depression, Navajos had survived as sheep herders, but three decades of US policy making had reduced the size of herds and brought mining and energy companies to the reservation, where they tapped uranium deposits for military production and mined coal to power southwestern metropolises. During the postwar years, young men and women commonly left home for periods of time to work for wages on and off the reservation. Families sustained reservation life by supplementing dwindling herds with industrial labor and pooling resources within sprawling family networks.[48]

Yet the jobs at Fairchild were never designed to support far-flung families. They hardly supported workers themselves. Public subsidies met the company's requirements while disregarding employees' most elemental needs, including housing and child care; the Fairchild experiment showed just how austere social welfare provision could be within the Great Society's manpower programs. In September 1966, nearly 25 percent of the company's 492 trainees lived in motels and ate in restaurants. Others lived in Farmington, New Mexico, and commuted sixty miles a day. Some local families took in workers and wound up sending their own children to the Shiprock boarding school, an extraordinary step given the reputation of Indian boarding schools as agents of empire and abductors of children. In fact, when Fairchild signed its lease in 1965, Shiprock parents were mobilizing to clarify the circumstances under which government authorities and local missionaries could remove children to foster homes or put them up for adoption against their parents' will. As

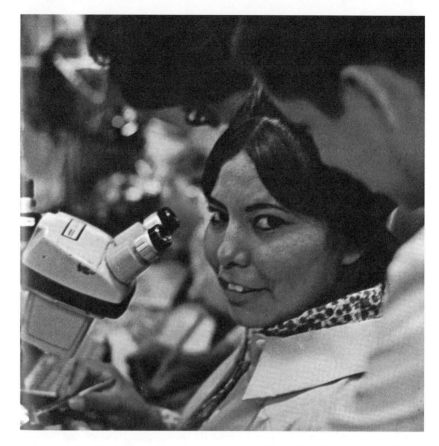

FIGURE 6.4. Fairchild hired Navajo women to assemble semiconductors, arguing that their "traditional" skill as weavers suited them to repetitive, stressful operative jobs. (Shiprock commemorative brochure, 1969, Computer History Museum)

migrants flooded the town, local welfare officials clamored for new housing, social workers, interpreters, special education teachers, juvenile justice services, a child care center, a nursing home, and mental health programs. The BIA's Branch of Employment Assistance rejected those requests, maintaining that social welfare was the responsibility of other BIA offices and private agencies. Not until 1971 did the federal government pay for 250 new single-family homes and apartments at Shiprock. The $4 million home-building program was the largest such initiative ever financed by Washington on a reservation. Characteristically, the federal government built the units under contract with the William Lyon Development Corporation and subsidized the firm's labor costs with job-training funds.[49]

Fairchild was lured to Shiprock by the promise of cheap labor, and its low wages put women in the untenable position of denying relatives income that they expected. Federal agencies and tribal governments in turn became the firm's partners in fraying the economic ties and social obligations that bound Navajo families together. In 1966, Vinita Lewis of the BIA balked at the social conflicts she saw erupting in Shiprock, and she struggled to understand them. Lewis did not perceive the economic function of extended family networks, nor did she recognize their thoroughly modern status as adaptations to twentieth-century public policies. Instead, she saw only that Fairchild employees could barely afford "rent, food, clothing . . . baby sitting, transportation . . . personal hygiene and health care." "Some trainees are now facing neglect charges in the Shiprock District Court because they have left children to be supported by their mothers, sisters, or other close relatives," she observed. Lewis hoped for new housing and social services, but she directed much of her ire at "errant unemployed husbands" and "clan relatives" who harassed hardworking wives, girlfriends, and daughters for money. Condemning the Navajo family as unfit for modern life, Lewis unwittingly revealed the unbearable strain that job-training policies placed on workers and their relatives.[50]

By 1975, workers had begun to organize a union at Fairchild. They decried inadequate health services and layoffs that had begun after the 1973 recession. Moreover, they argued that the company abused the wage subsidies that federal job-training programs provided. The details of the training program became national news in February 1975, when workers invited members of the American Indian Movement (AIM) to Shiprock, and AIM launched an eight-day occupation of the factory. As AIM leaders publicized the workers' grievances, they exposed the perverse incentives that for-profit manpower programs had given employers. Because Fairchild could pay trainees half the minimum wage, the company preferred them to permanent employees, and AIM alleged that managers contrived reasons to fire workers once they completed training. US manpower policy had become a dead end for Shiprock workers and had shielded Fairchild from federal wage-and-hour laws for nearly a decade. Daniel McDonald, the BIA's director of Tribal Resources Development, publicly conceded that running a purportedly transitional two-year job-training program for "nine years across the board is too long." In fact, in the course of the occupation it became clear that the BIA and Fairchild had already come to blows over the program. The BIA considered its permanent status an embarrassing liability and had warned that the wage subsidies would soon end.

With subsidies about to dry up and a union organizing drive gathering strength, Fairchild did what electronics manufacturers had always done in those circumstances: it shut the factory and moved production. The 1975 AIM occupation gave the company a pretext to argue that its lease had been violated, absolving it of any responsibility to continue operations in Shiprock.[51] The plant closure lay bare the precarity of any gains that workers and tribes could attain under the federal government's for-profit training programs. By some measures, reservation industrialization delivered real benefits to Native people. Over the course of the 1960s, unemployment fell on most reservations, women's labor force participation increased, and median incomes rose for both men and women. Yet those measures of success masked a profound contradiction. Native people seeking jobs depended on programs that corporations used to undermine the long-term prospect of stable, well-paying employment in the United States.[52] Antipoverty policy had exploited and abetted a notorious pattern of capital flight, and it ultimately exposed workers to the devastating consequences of that practice.

———

The corporations that left communities like Shiprock in the lurch found one final, bitterly ironic way to capitalize on midcentury social policy: they returned to some of the same places as for-profit educational contractors, promising to fix their tax-starved public schools. RCA, whose flight from Camden during the 1940s had devastated the city's tax base, reemerged in 1970 as a for-profit contractor to the city's school system. Based on its Job Corps experience, the company won a three-year contract worth $285,000 in federal and state funds. RCA and a slew of subcontractors set overall priorities for public education in Camden, redesigned curricula, and retrained teachers and administrators. On RCA's watch, Camden adopted behaviorist technologies to "individualize" instruction and thus created a new market for programmed texts and classroom electronics. Meanwhile, the entire experiment became an object lesson suggesting that the role of RCA in social policy was not to pay taxes but to receive public revenues as a for-profit contractor delivering services.

In Camden, RCA mapped its profit-making activities onto African American struggles for quality education, imbuing school reform efforts with contradictory purposes. Capitalizing on black activists' seething frustration with a racist school board, the company presented itself as an alternative source of authority and expertise. For-profit privatization was not a solution that African American parents devised, but in 1970 it struck some as the least bad option on offer. "We had very little faith in the Camden school system and we figured RCA would keep them honest," explained Jessie Tilghman, a mother of eight, longtime PTA member, and president of Camden's Community Advisory

Council. Inside the schools, RCA and its subcontractors presented their own solution to complaints about large class sizes. Rather than hire more certified teachers, they introduced massive "open classrooms." In one such room, two "master teachers" and nine paraprofessional aides worked with 115 students. The arrangement did reduce the ratio of children to adults from thirty to twelve, but it yoked that reform to the deprofessionalization of teaching. From RCA's perspective, social mobilization created pressure that the company could turn to its own ends: undermining teachers' unions and professional autonomy, creating new markets for industrial products, and challenging the identification of nonprofit, public administration with the public interest.[53]

Between 1967 and the early 1970s, RCA, Westinghouse, GE, and Thiokol all parlayed their job-training experience into public education contracts. Some, like GE and Westinghouse, worked their way into urban school decentralization experiments of the Johnson years. The Nixon administration offered wider opportunities. In 1969, the city of Texarkana, Arkansas, used federal funds to sign a "performance contract" with Dorsett Educational Systems, a small educational technology firm that manufactured teaching machines. The contract charged the company with teaching remedial courses to roughly 350 students and calibrated Dorsett's compensation to standardized-test scores. Performance contracting—outsourcing functions to private industry and paying on the basis of quantifiable results—had originated in the Department of Defense, and its inauguration in Texarkana extended the tradition of building the welfare state by borrowing managerial and contracting practices from foreign policy agencies. The Texarkana experiment eventually became a fiasco, as teachers under pressure to raise test scores leaked exam questions to students. But in 1970, the pay-for-performance principle fascinated the Nixon administration. Based on the Texarkana model, the OEO signed performance contracts with six for-profit corporations in 1970, sending them inside eighteen public-school districts across the country to teach reading and mathematics. Other federal agencies subsidized twenty more performance contracts in schools that year, and HEW hired the RAND Corporation—the intellectual author of systems analysis—to evaluate them as possible models for national school reform.[54]

Many of the performance contractors came straight from the Great Society's manpower programs. Just as the War on Poverty had given veterans of Indian industrialization policy a vast new landscape in which to work, Nixon's OEO gave Job Corps and BIA contractors unprecedented access to public schools. Westinghouse, a longtime OEO job-training contractor, won one of the agency's six performance contracts in 1970 to teach students in Gilroy, California. Thiokol supplemented its Job Corps and BIA training centers with performance contracts in Dallas, Texas, and Shreveport, Louisiana.

According to a study of twelve early performance contracts, for-profit firms spent 15 percent of their budgets on audiovisual materials and books, while ordinary public schools spent just 1 to 2 percent. Meanwhile, contractors spent only 55 percent of their budgets on teachers' salaries, far less than the 70 to 75 percent that public schools did.[55] As for-profit corporations made themselves the face of the welfare state and channeled social spending into poor communities, the beneficiaries of the War on Poverty became difficult to discern.

———

It was one thing for a businessmen's vanguard to make a place for themselves in the War on Poverty. It was another for US businessmen at large to celebrate the idea. In 1964, very few corporate executives talked about themselves the way veterans of foreign and Indian affairs did. Instead, they hailed their companies' core productive activities as foundations of a good society. Private enterprise generated jobs and economic growth, they insisted; the modern corporation had made the American standard of living the envy of the earth; and material abundance stood as the foundation of human welfare and social peace. By the early 1970s, US businessmen had begun to speak in a different register. It wasn't just that growth had failed in so many of its promises. Devoted ideologues like David Lilienthal had labored to consolidate a new mode of argument among their peers. This work did not happen in job-training centers, on Indian reservations, or in the offices of the OEO. It happened in business associations.

When the first Job Corps centers opened in 1965, David Lilienthal was paying no attention. He had become entangled with another group of businessmen: the two hundred trustees of the Committee for Economic Development. In 1962, Fred Lazarus Jr., the president of Federated Department Stores, had invited Lilienthal to join CED, and Lilienthal had eagerly accepted, saluting the organization as a model of "business statesmanship."[56] By the summer of 1965, Lilienthal's colleagues had become anxious men lashed by public criticism, and he agreed to chair a new subcommittee to write a brief in defense of the modern corporation. Over the next five years, Lilienthal worked as a spokesman among US businessmen, collaborating with executives across economic sectors and political parties to articulate a novel vindication of managers and firms as guardians of the public interest. Sidelining traditional claims that industrial production raised living standards or that private philanthropy cared for the poor, Lilienthal's committee championed incipient efforts by US corporations to resolve social crises for profit. At the end of long deliberations, nothing impressed them more than the War on Poverty's training and education programs. Lilienthal had returned home a messenger in search of a project, and the businessmen entering federal manpower programs provided one.

Lilienthal's committee transformed the politics and rhetoric of an organization that had long celebrated businessmen as heroic strategists of economic growth. Indeed, when CED stalwart Laurence deRycke had left Occidental College for Cali in 1963, the organization had sounded nothing like Lilienthal, who had just joined. For that matter, Lilienthal in 1953 had not sounded like Lilienthal in 1963. His book *Big Business* had defended the corporation by arguing that it worked as a vehicle of economic production; massive conglomerate firms met consumers' desires and thus proved trust-busters wrong. During the mid-1960s, that argument missed the mark entirely, as public criticism focused not on the supply or quality of goods but the justice of a consumer-capitalist society. CED's portrait of capitalists harmonizing social interests through the pursuit of growth became an object of ridicule among social movements, and trustee Raymon H. Mulford, chairman of the glass manufacturer Owens-Illinois, feared for the authority of businessmen and the respectability of capital accumulation itself. "Fewer outstanding young men are being attracted to business careers, preferring what they have learned to believe are the nobler professions or occupations—law, medicine, Peace Corps, government, education," he lamented in a 1965 commencement speech at Ohio's Bowling Green State University. Mulford gave voice to widespread concern within CED that too many Americans, especially young people, considered the pursuit of profit a ruthless endeavor, an engine of exploitation, and a handmaiden of war. "We must define an ideological purpose which is both true and which has a deeper appeal than just that of making money," he wrote to Lilienthal.[57]

In 1965, Mulford joined Lilienthal's committee and took up the challenge of explaining the virtues of capitalist enterprise to the public. With mild amusement, CED president Alfred C. Neal charged the group with nothing less than "salvaging the intellectual legitimacy of the large American corporation." Lilienthal worked doggedly to mute CED's traditional claim that growth made for social peace. Instead, he proposed that the committee evaluate business "as a social institution," indeed "as one of the *principal means of improving the quality of life in the United States and the world.*" In more direct terms, he advised Neal that CED should publicize corporations' involvement in development and antipoverty programs and identify new social problems that businessmen could resolve for profit.[58]

It took Lilienthal two years of hard labor to retrain the committee's focus, because Neal and many of CED's economic advisors considered it intellectually vacuous. Neal was an economist who moved in the same world that the Ford Foundation did, conceiving of business as applied economics. Lilienthal's committee became a battleground for the same dispute raging at the

Universidad del Valle, with managers fighting economists to define their nature and purpose. Neal lined up a remarkable group of scholars to address the committee. Over the course of 1966 and 1967, the group summarily dismissed the recommendations of two rising stars of new institutional economics, Oliver E. Williamson and Alfred D. Chandler, as well the dean of the Carnegie Tech Graduate School of Industrial Administration, Richard M. Cyert. Hailing from Ford-funded institutions, all of them urged the committee to address a roiling academic debate over the theory of the firm, which probed the corporation's actual functioning, its efficiency, and its contribution to human welfare. Neoclassical theory, ascendant in US economics departments after World War II, depicted a perfectly competitive economy in which many small firms jockeyed for advantage, each single-mindedly strove to maximize its profits, and the rigors of competition encouraged efficiency and innovation. The firm in neoclassical theory enjoyed secure private property rights, ready access to information, and the capacity to make and enforce contracts effortlessly. Elegant as it was, the theory failed to account for basic features of industrial capitalism. Massive corporations dominated the US economy after World War II, and they insulated themselves from competition and risk by operating across economic sectors, tapping government subsidies, and deploying sophisticated marketing techniques. The gulf separating theory from reality turned the internal workings of the firm into a burgeoning field of research.

CED's economic advisors proposed that businessmen contribute something to this debate. Cyert and Williamson believed that the only social obligation of firms was to operate efficiently and improve their performance over time. They modestly proposed that firms might not in fact do those things, and they explicitly ruled out government regulation as a solution. Instead, they invited CED to ask whether existing norms and relationships within the private sector led firms to prioritize efficiency and innovation. If not, what new "self-enforcing controls" within the private sector might discipline management? Perhaps, Cyert thought, stockholders or "a new profession of management analysts" might conduct "management audits" and certify corporations that operated well.[59]

In the context of contemporary public debate, the proposal was politically innocuous. But for businessmen reeling from public criticism, the idea of a management audit appeared threatening and insulting. "It seems to assume that business is trying to keep important matters secret that the public is entitled to examine," Fred Lazarus protested to Neal. "I think this line of thought is useless, and if it is the best the committee can do, it should disband." Rejecting new institutional economics, CED's businessmen held fast to familiar, politically useful mythologies of their work. Lilienthal received regular missives from committee members rehearsing tenets of classical liberalism and modernization theory. Businesses "tend to be self-regulating in the end," contended Edward W. Carter, president of Broadway-Hale Stores. The pursuit of profit and "freedom of choice" had yielded a thriving assortment of large and small firms in the United States, wrote S. Abbot Smith of the Thomas Strahan wallpaper company.[60]

Lilienthal and the CED committee assumed the same anti-intellectual posture that made Reinaldo Scarpetta so confounding to the Rockefeller Foundation. Like the Cauca Valley's capitalists, they took an instrumental view of economic thought, embracing ideas that confirmed their own, disregarding others, and proudly defining themselves against economists as pragmatic men of the world. They exemplified one impulse operating at cross-purposes to the Ford Foundation in both business schools and business associations during the postwar years. Although the foundation succeeded in transforming a small number of elite universities, it never substantially altered the rest. The parallel disputes unfolding simultaneously within the Universidad del Valle and CED suggest one reason that Ford's efforts came to so little. Anti-intellectualism among businessmen could appear mere buffoonery to economists, but it served a valuable function in deflecting political threats. In Colombia, managers' scorn for economic theory struck a blow to a rising profession claiming status within the state. In the United States, it shielded embattled firms and managers from scrutiny. Lilienthal revealed the manifold uses of stubborn intellectual refusal as he dismissed every economic argument he encountered during his years at CED. In 1971, he received a letter asking whether he agreed with Milton Friedman or Paul Samuelson in the widening debate on "corporate responsibility." Friedman held that business had no responsibility but to maximize profits. Pure competition, the drive for efficiency, and the pursuit of profit could themselves eliminate poverty, pollution, and discrimination, he insisted. Samuelson, meanwhile, argued that corporations should adopt social and environmental policies, and that government should tax and regulate firms in the public interest. Read against Lilienthal's speeches, Friedman's position seemed to concede that businessmen were men in gray flannel suits, living without philosophy, consumed with balance sheets, and insensitive to public concerns. Samuelson, meanwhile, suggested that the pursuit of profit competed with the public good and that business could not regulate itself. Lilienthal replied simply by mailing one of his recent speeches that declared businessmen magnanimous public servants doing the work of government. His argument deliberately sidestepped the economists' debate. In the 1960s and 1970s, that evasive maneuver performed a political function that businessmen appreciated and economists failed to comprehend.[61]

In that sense, businessmen's anti-intellectualism was no mark of mental incapacity or general hostility to authoritative knowledge. Rather, it was a strategic posture through which businessmen communicated convictions of their own. Lilienthal and his peers were men who cared to write CED reports, address commencement ceremonies, and administer university programs. They valued ideas, and they forced their own into public discussion by dismissing economists' pursuits.

Set against social movements and their own economic advisors, CED's businessmen found much to like in Lilienthal's alternative. Presenting the corporation as a for-profit social problem solver protected their core activities from inspection, cast them as agents of progress in an age of crisis, and perhaps most important, distilled increasingly common ideas. Committee member Walter H. Wheeler, chairman of the postage machine manufacturer Pitney-Bowes, wrote to Lilienthal that in 1966 alone, he had read a dozen articles broadcasting similar ideas from members of CLA, NAM, the Chamber of Commerce, the Conference Board, and the Jaycees. *Newsweek* had just profiled what it called "the new businessmen": executives of Chase Manhattan Bank, Ford, Kaiser, Pan Am, and Xerox who embraced foreign aid and domestic social programs not as philanthropy but as profitable business opportunities. "You can't separate me as a businessman from me as a human being," Sol Linowitz of Xerox had declared to the magazine. Wheeler passed a bibliography to Lilienthal, who made a point of reading a recent speech by George Champion, chairman of Chase Manhattan Bank. "For thirty years, I've listened to business complain that government was competing in their activities," Champion had told Rutgers University's Eighteenth Annual Business Conference in 1966. "I'd like to live long enough to hear government bureaucrats complain that *business* is competing in *their* activities." A few months later, in 1967, both Wheeler and Neal joined Shriver's Business Leadership Advisory Council and began attending meetings with the military contractors and foreign investors that had become mainstays of Job Corps. They signed up just in time to hear GE chairman Gerald L. Philippe deliver a report on the first year of the Job Corps Center in Clinton, Iowa.[62]

Wheeler and Lilienthal recognized a common strategy emerging in reaction to federal policies and social movements of the 1960s, and they conceived of the CED report as a grand statement of ideas percolating in business journals and conferences. While Lilienthal battled to keep the economists at bay, the committee became a correspondence society in which businessmen shared news of corporations competing with and entering the welfare state. As chairman, Lilienthal did not exactly corral his colleagues; he read the news with them and became their authoritative, eloquent, and indefatigable spokesman.

For the men on Lilienthal's committee, and for the wider reading public, businessmen's foreign and domestic activities appeared as two expressions of a single sensibility. *Newsweek*'s 1966 profile of the "new businessmen" applauded the winnowing of the Alliance for Progress in sterilized terms. Chase Manhattan Bank, in this telling, became an intrepid protagonist of US development assistance because the company had a policy of opening branches in "small countries." *Look* magazine ran its own profile of "Big Business Do-Gooders," which highlighted the International Executive Service Corps alongside for-profit education programs at home. "Even the National Association of Manufacturers, once mossback Mecca, runs schools for Harlem dropouts. . . . Rich corporations nurse the poor and tool up a private Peace Corps. Capitalism, some think, has flipped its money-lovin' wig."[63]

The articles, speeches, and memos that crossed Lilienthal's desk pointed insistently to training and education as tasks that private capital had mastered. George Champion of Chase Manhattan Bank described corporate training programs as the seedbed from which firms could assume wide responsibilities for education. "Taken as a whole, US companies are far ahead of those anywhere else in the world in the training of staff and line people at all levels," he explained in 1966. CED chairman William C. Stolk identified Job Corps contracts as models for a thoroughgoing reinvention of social services. "If Litton and ITT can run education and job-training camps for the Job Corps—why should not every corporation find an area of social improvement that matches its capabilities," he asked the National Association of Business Economists in 1968. Every firm in the country could establish a "public business group" held to the same standards of profitability as its "manufacturing and marketing" groups. "This approach completely changes the meaning of corporate execution of its social responsibilities," Stolk announced. Philanthropy, he suggested, might soon yield to what Lilienthal had recently labeled social entrepreneurship.[64]

These ideas united veterans of the New Deal with men often regarded as their opponents. Committee member John J. Corson, like Lilienthal, was an old New Dealer who had spent his life moving between government and business. During the 1930s and 1940s, he had worked for the Social Security Administration and United States Employment Service, and in 1951, he became a management consultant with McKinsey and Company. In Corson's view, public administration required the same skills that corporate management did, and he spent the 1950s working to integrate the two realms. In 1952, he wrote a book, *Executives for the Federal Service*, as well as a report to the Ford Foundation; both lamented businessmen's reluctance to work within the state, urged federal agencies to adopt new management training programs, and proposed aggressive recruitment efforts within the private sector. Two years later, he joined the Commerce Department's Business Advisory Council, a headhunting committee that identified corporate executives fit for department vacancies. Throughout his life, Corson defied anyone to name a private-sector firm that operated more efficiently than Social Security did. Yet writing to Lilienthal in 1966, he just as eagerly celebrated incipient business initiatives attacking unemployment, redeveloping cities, and designing new instructional materials for public schools. He encouraged his colleagues to consider ways that they could claim new responsibilities for financing medical research, ensuring access to health care, and improving public education. An undying defender of the New Deal, Corson believed in a mixed economy that used state action to stabilize private spending. That faith harmonized with others less often remembered: he considered public administration a species of business administration and thought that many tasks could fall to either sector, or to some combination of the two.[65]

Yale economist Henry C. Wallich echoed Lilienthal and Corson, urging the committee to devise ways for private capital to fulfill "collective wants, i.e. social insurance, health, education." Unlike his colleagues, Wallich spoke as a Republican, a veteran of Eisenhower's Council of Economic Advisors, and a critic of the War on Poverty. He read into Lilienthal's idea an aggressive critique of the public sector. "We now have Medicare because the market failed to develop a sufficiently good insurance system," Wallich wrote to Neal in 1966, bemoaning the 1965 law that provided public health insurance to senior citizens. "There is still time to prevent health care for all age brackets from becoming public, if the market will provide a system." Walter Wheeler of Pitney-Bowes agreed. During the 1950s, his company had turned to welfare capitalism to curb union mobilization and had proudly adopted fair hiring measures before the 1964 Civil Rights Act mandated them. Wheeler had eventually testified in favor of that landmark law, convinced that only state power could discipline recalcitrant employers. But he continued to champion voluntary private action as the first and best solution to social ills. He described Lilienthal's initiative as a necessary restraint on the expanding "action of government," which he traced back to the New Deal.[66]

Lilienthal's committee spent more than five years producing a major report, *Social Responsibilities of Business Corporations*, which appeared in 1971. Leading the group during its pivotal first two years and continuing on as a member, Lilienthal played a key role in sidelining CED's economic advisors and producing a statement that endorsed private capital's ability to provide public goods at a profit. Emblematically, he resigned the chairmanship in 1967 to attend to D&R's new contract in Vietnam; the final report obliterated the distinction between the state and its for-profit contractor by noting simply that Lilienthal "went into government service."[67]

The economists left one mark on the document. They furnished CED with an antidemocratic account of government as management—the very same idea that Scarpetta, FMME, and CLADEA articulated in Latin America. It was a notable point of agreement among managers and economists who disagreed on so much else. When economic advisors Cyert, Williamson, and Hans Thorelli looked inside the "black box" of the firm, they found not a unitary entity pursuing the single goal of profit maximization but a complex aggregation of workers, managers, stockholders, customers, suppliers, and even neighbors pressuring the company to pursue divergent goals. Thorelli and Neal described the modern corporation as a "political community" or "political institution" made up of competing interests. Managers, they contended, performed an essentially political function, harmonizing demands and securing consent for a shared program. That view obscured the fact that the firm's "constituents" did not enjoy rights of democratic citizenship; they did not elect managers and possessed none of the protections against them that the Constitution gave US citizens against the state. If the firm was a polity, it was not a democracy. But that fact hardly mattered to CED's businessmen. They recognized in the economists' argument an alluring depiction of themselves as statesmen already doing the work of government. The final report owed virtually nothing to economic theory, but it faithfully conveyed one point: "The chief executive of a major corporation must exercise statesmanship in developing with the rest of the management group the objectives, strategies, and policies of the corporate enterprise. In implementing these, he must also obtain the 'consent of the governed.' "[68] Equating management with government, CED cast the for-profit firm as a potential model of state authority. Executives, meanwhile, became men with constituents and studied capacities for governance.

Channeling all these influences, the final report called for the privatization of education, worker training, health, transportation, and urban redevelopment. "Government at all levels seems likely to function best as a market creator, systems manager, and contractor of social tasks rather than an actual operator of every kind of public service," CED contended. "Business, with its profit-and-loss discipline . . . is a proven instrument for getting much of society's work done." The committee cautioned that corporations would only unleash their "power and dynamism" for a reasonably assured profit. Government needed to offer incentives—cash subsidies, tax breaks, loans, credit guarantees, and insurance policies—that would make "social activities" as profitable as other fields of investment. Corporations were not charities.[69]

By the time the report appeared in 1971, businessmen had already made remarkable inroads within the welfare state, and the CED report did more than demand privatization; it applauded half a decade of progress. Members of the committee had long praised Job Corps in meetings and conferences, and the final report paid tribute to JOBS. It went on to celebrate the

FIGURES 6.5 AND 6.6. In 1970, Thomas J. Houde, an art teacher and union activist in the New Haven public schools, assailed performance contracting in cartoons published by the American Federation of Teachers. (Courtesy Danielle Slouf)

educational performance contracts that the OEO signed in 1970.[70] These were fighting words. By the time the report appeared in 1971, performance contracting had become a lightning rod for public debate. "Westinghouse, Borg-Warner, and all the rest of the military-industrial complex are not moving on the public schools because they have developed an aching social concern," insisted Emanuel Kafka of the New York Teachers Association. "They are closing on the minds of children now for the same reason they have produced napalm and Thalidomide, and polluted our rivers, our air, and our entire environment. They are driven by an insatiable hunger for constantly bigger profits." The American Federation of Teachers (AFT) published a book of political cartoons assailing performance contracts as assaults on professionalism and job security in education. "None of our teaching machines have tenure!" the fictional Ajax Learning Corporation announced in its pages. In New York City, Al Shanker, president of the AFT's United Federation of Teachers, denounced the Learning Foundations performance contract in the Bronx as unjust and even illegal. Teachers in the school reportedly sabotaged the experiment by throwing equipment out of second-story windows and advising children not to deliver questionnaires to their parents. At the end of the year, many students failed to show up for the company's standardized tests.[71] Amid the conflict, CED's trustees made their allegiances known, celebrating performance contracting as a flawless test of the profit motive in education.

In 1971, David Lilienthal signed the statement. The report's examples of for-profit educational contracts embodied the concepts of "social entrepreneurship" and "business statesmanship" that he had brought to the committee. Moreover, they gave his once-idealistic calls and curious references to the Third World a new vividness and a sense of imminent, local reality. The old New Dealer had come a long way by walking a continuous path. And he and his fellow signatories—executives from fourteen manufacturing, energy, retail, and financial corporations—had found something to like in the War on Poverty that others had missed.

Given the conflicts it provoked at the time, it is curious that businessmen's mobilization became recorded mainly in business publications, leaving hardly an imprint on the general public image of the Great Society. One reason, of course, was that in the moment and in retrospect, the phenomenon of for-profit contracting seemed a small piece of a much larger program. Capitalists constituted one distinctive group among many that met inside the state, and their immersion in a wider social project was inevitable to the extent that they aimed to reproduce within the welfare state class relations that prevailed beyond it—the very class relations that the welfare state was designed to modify and stabilize. In fact, businessmen distinguished themselves even among veterans of foreign and imperial affairs, many of whom labored elsewhere in the

War on Poverty and saw quite different promises in it. During the years when Lilienthal turned homeward, so did a great many veterans of postwar development programs whose motives, experiences, and final destination differed from his. While corporate executives flocked to US public schools, a generation of self-help housing veterans set their sights on farm labor camps and public housing projects. Moving into US cities and rural communities, they promised to give shelter to North Americans.

7

The American Dream
Comes Home

IN 1972, DON TERNER imagined a new household appliance. In his mind, it was a box about the size of a washing machine, and it would duplicate the functions of a municipal water and sewage system. Purifying and recirculating water within the home, the machine would allow low-income homeowners worldwide to live in locales that public infrastructure did not reach. Across the First and Third Worlds, he explained, "the concept of dweller autonomy . . . appears to offer one of the few hopes for truly broad-based housing improvement."[1]

As he wrote, the thirty-three-year-old architect straddled a historic divide. The idea of a consumer product replacing inadequate state infrastructure was the stuff of libertarian dreams; it harmonized with calls to privatize core functions of the midcentury state. But Terner never saw himself as an opponent of welfare and developmental states. He was in fact a social democrat who believed in a progressive income tax and thought the federal government should act as an employer of last resort. After working in low-income housing development for seven years, Terner simply despaired of the state ever living up to its responsibilities. He imagined himself mending a ragged system of social welfare provision, and he approached the task with tools he had honed as an architect in Latin America.[2]

Terner had begun his career there during the second half of the 1960s, working in Colombia, Argentina, Peru, and Venezuela. By 1968, he had conducted research for the OAS in Bogotá and managed private construction projects in Lima, Caracas, and the new steel city of Ciudad Guyana, Venezuela. He was one of a generation of architects who become transfixed by informality in Latin American cities, viewing it as eminently useful and even ennobling to the poor. Squatters, he marveled, enjoyed genuine control of their environment; they designed homes according to their own priorities, free from the coercive power of private developers and the state. The proper role of architects, he concluded, was to provide adaptable plans and materials that preserved residents' latitude as homebuilders while improving the health, safety, and social integration of their neighborhoods. As US cities burned in the summer of 1968, Terner thought he understood the crisis. He proclaimed in the pages of *Architectural Digest* that "the American Negro in the urban ghetto" suffered worse injustices than Latin American squatters. Both faced poverty and segregation, but only African Americans lived under the thumb of private slumlords and miserable public housing authorities. He announced that he and his colleagues had begun adapting an architectural system they had created for Venezuelans to serve black residents of Detroit.[3]

Terner was describing a "slum upgrading" system, one of many forms that self-help housing took in Latin America during the 1950s and 1960s. The plan for Detroit never went anywhere, and neither did the water treatment machine. But both dreams suggested the possibilities that flowed from austere homeownership programs in the Third World.

Terner and his collaborators from Latin America spent three decades spinning out those possibilities at home and ultimately became protagonists in refashioning the US welfare state. Their ability to ply their tools within the United States depended on a striking change in federal policy. During the 1930s, the Roosevelt administration had financed self-help housing in Puerto Rico, but until the 1960s, the federal government generally circumscribed its growth on the mainland. Meanwhile, self-help housing circled the globe, traveling from the First World to the Third to become an emblematic instrument of postwar nation building. Its global transits ultimately transformed the possibilities of statecraft at home. Three decades after the New Deal, US officials no longer encountered self-help as an aberrant imperial policy but as a celebrated instrument of US foreign aid and a deeply researched object of US expertise. Meanwhile, the task of domestic governance had changed. The Great Depression had long since passed, and with it policy makers' concern for reviving the construction industry and reigniting growth. The problem of poverty had become a narrower problem of transforming poor communities, and policies once rejected held new promise. The result was an unannounced but decisive change in the minds of federal officials. Across the United States, scattered communities of North Americans had tried to enlist Washington in self-help housing projects before the 1960s, often taking inspiration from foreign experiments in the North Atlantic and the Third World. Their entreaties mainly fell on deaf ears until the 1960s, when they encountered a converted audience in the capital. First in Indian country and then across the United States, federal agencies began to respond. They funded growing numbers of self-help projects, publicized their work, and transformed struggling private experiments into nationwide antipoverty policy.

The sea change in Washington opened a new career path for Don Terner and for a generation of architects and community workers who had cut their teeth abroad. During the 1960s, they reintegrated themselves into an unruly US public, and into enduring domestic debates over the proper roles of voluntarism and government action in social welfare provision. At a moment when criticism of public housing was as much the province of the left as of the right, they found unexpected allies and strange bedfellows across the political spectrum. Terner and his cohort never remade the US welfare state just as they wished but rather did what US advisors had done abroad: they inserted themselves into local power struggles, chose their allies, and became subject to processes of social mediation that determined the final meaning of their work. Together, they and their compatriots translated foreign experience, amalgamated it with existing strands of domestic policy, and remade their own landscape and political economy.

―――――

During the 1940s and 1950s, self-help housing seemed to go everywhere except the US mainland. The policy found champions worldwide because it resonated with so many visions of political-economic order and asked so little of the state. Self-help housing became a colonial and anticolonial policy, an instrument of European reconstruction, a Cold War aid program, and an adjunct to Third World industrialization. In Latin America, the Centro Interamericano de Vivienda y Planeamiento (CINVA) and the State Department promoted the policy, and Colombia and Peru produced landmark developments. The British Colonial Office sponsored self-help in Africa and the Indian subcontinent until independence, at which point some former colonies embraced it as a nation-building instrument. Both the United States and Britain promoted the policy through the Caribbean Commission and made Puerto Rico a celebrated regional model. By 1960, the United Nations, too, had thrown its weight behind aided self-help.[4] As ubiquitous as the program became, it acquired a distinct association with the Third World during these years, and for good reason: governments there deployed it on a massive, unprecedented scale. Between 1961 and 1963, Colombia's auto-construction program produced over 39,000 units of housing, more than Canada's "Build Your Own Home" initiative produced in three decades.[5]

In all these peregrinations, the US government played a peculiar role: it was a leading promoter of self-help housing abroad but a wary opponent at home. On the mainland, the federal government sanctioned a few isolated experiments before the 1960s, but the policy's principal champions were dissidents and outsiders: Quakers, African Americans, and Native Americans, many of whom belonged to their own international circuits and set out to repatriate the lessons of foreign and imperial statecraft. Following their own tangled paths through domestic and international affairs, they ultimately carried the policy home from the Third World.

Their agitation began long before the 1960s. During the pit of the Great Depression, Quaker activists launched some of the country's first organized self-help housing programs, taking inspiration from Europe. The Society of Friends was a transatlantic institution par excellence; during the 1920s, British Quakers had admired Vienna's self-help housing initiative and publicized it internationally.[6] In the United States, the American Friends Service Committee (AFSC) took up the idea. Founded during the First World War, the AFSC was a Quaker organization committed to pacifism, racial integration, and economic equality. Its work drew on a religious conviction that an inner light shone in each person, and community action became one of its chosen instruments to foster individual dignity and social ties. Quakers' opposition to war further inspired a cautious view of state power, and the AFSC took interest in social welfare policies that relied on mutual aid and cooperative enterprise. Channeling all those impulses, the AFSC tried to insert self-help housing into the federal Subsistence Homesteads Program, a back-to-the-land scheme created by the National Industrial Recovery Act in 1933. At a time when New Dealers subscribed to widely varying interpretations of the Depression's cause, the homestead program reflected a belief that industrial growth had simply reached its end in the United States. The agency's backers depicted a portion of the unemployed as economically superfluous, never again to find industrial jobs in cities. They promised to resettle those workers in new rural communities, where they would devote themselves to subsistence agriculture and cooperative enterprise. The AFSC was eager to participate, having developed similar homesteads in Wales and administered a federal child feeding program in Appalachia in 1931. The Quakers took charge of creating the Cumberland Homestead in eastern Tennessee, and for a year they applied the principle of self-help. Residents built their own homes but received only one-third the wage that the government allotted for construction workers. The AFSC set aside the rest of the wage and returned it to the government to cover the cost of the houses; when the families bought their homes from the government, they paid only a fraction of its value from their reduced wages. The practice of reserving and returning wage payments gave the Cumberland homesteaders an experience of sweat equity and mutual assistance, but when the federal Resettlement Administration inherited the program in 1935, it put a stop to the experiment. The agency's labor staff argued that self-help undermined its effort to raise and enforce wage standards, and the US Comptroller General swiftly came to their aid, finding in 1935 that the AFSC's practice had no basis in US law.[7]

From that point until the 1960s, Quaker activists found it virtually impossible to secure federal support for self-help housing and deliberately financed projects with private money. In 1937, they founded Penn-Craft, a utopian community for unemployed mine workers in western Pennsylvania. Racially integrated, run through deliberative democracy, and buzzing with dozens of committees and associations, Penn-Craft comprised fifty homesteads built through unpaid collective labor, a 100-acre community farm, a cooperative store, and a knitting mill that produced sweaters. It was what the government called a subsistence homestead, but its original funding came from major corporations and private foundations; US Steel was the largest donor, contributing $80,000.[8] During the 1950s, the AFSC brought self-help housing to North Philadelphia, where it organized low-income families to buy and renovate rundown buildings with sweat equity. In that case, they did manage to get the Federal Housing Administration to insure private mortgage loans, but only after a team of twenty-eight lawyers spent years pleading their case. Simultaneously, two African American civic organizations in Indianapolis seized on self-help to combat discriminatory lending practices. Flanner House and the Board for Fundamental Education joined together in 1950 to build the Flanner Homes, which put property ownership within reach of African Americans systematically shut out of the mortgage market. The success of the project ultimately helped convince local banks and builders that African American were creditworthy.[9]

By the 1950s, these organized self-help housing communities had become many things: collectivist dreams, refuges from global economic collapse, affronts to Jim Crow, and pathways to commercial lending. They were in every case exceedingly small, private experiments of no interest to the state. Indeed, when Penn-Craft organizers sought guidance during these years, they went not to Washington but to Nova Scotia, where the provincial government had operated a self-help housing program since 1938.[10]

In a few cases, the federal government did sponsor owner-building on the US mainland, but it often did so reluctantly, seeking to contain private initiatives that had gotten away from policy makers. The Housing Act of 1954 formalized and regulated do-it-yourself construction that had flourished without government sanction in the postwar suburbs. As federal officials realized, North Americans had taken out home improvement loans under Title I of the 1934 Housing Act and used them for purposes far beyond the law's intent. The new 1954 regulations recognized amateur building not to encourage it but to constrain it, and the result of the law was a decline in Title I insured loans.[11]

In other cases, federal support for owner-building was small-scale and haphazard. Before the 1960s, the largest experiment with federally sponsored self-help housing was the small rural program that the Farmers Home Administration (FmHA) initiated in 1949. It certainly signaled a new possibility in US housing policy, but it was nothing like Ciudad Kennedy or even US policy in Puerto Rico. The federal government did not organize, supervise, or even require volunteer labor. Instead, FmHA Section 502 simply provided loans to farm owners and allowed them to build or renovate their housing as they saw fit, whether by hiring contractors, contributing their own labor, or combining the two methods.[12]

The federal government's relationship to self-help housing changed dramatically during the 1960s. What had largely existed as an imperial and foreign initiative with only equivocal state sanction on the mainland became a national antipoverty policy in the space of just a few years. The growth and transformation of self-help housing began on Indian reservations, the same places where for-profit job training had taken off.[13] The process owed to the demands of Native people, who learned about self-help not from Europe or Canada but Puerto Rico and the Third World. Like Puerto Rico, reservations occupied a liminal status between foreign and domestic, and during the early Cold War, government officials routinely shuttled between the Bureau of Indian Affairs, Point IV, and the Office of the Territories.[14] Policy makers' career trajectories reflected the prevailing wisdom of the social sciences, which had long compared indigenous, imperial, and foreign societies, transposed analytic tools and concepts across their contexts, and defined the United States in contrast to them. Like imperial subjects everywhere, Native Americans put such systems of thought and governance to their own use, making claims against the US government by appropriating its terms. During the 1950s, the National Congress of American Indians (NCAI) sent a mission to Puerto Rico to study its postwar development program, Operation Bootstrap. That initiative folded the island's existing self-help housing policy into a wider drive for industrialization, infrastructure development, and new social services. The NCAI mission returned home demanding a version for themselves. Echoing their call, the Association on American Indian Affairs insisted in 1957 that Indian reservations needed a program like Point IV, which provided US development assistance to the Third World. And in 1961, as the Kennedy administration negotiated the Alliance for Progress, the American Indian Chicago Conference (AICC) issued its famous Declaration of Purpose, which suggested that the logic of foreign aid should extend to reservations: the US government should treat tribes as sovereign nations requiring economic and technical assistance. In all these invocations of foreign and imperial policy, Native leaders were hardly credulous observers of US statecraft; they appealed to it to challenge termination at home. For all of its limitations, Cold War development assistance provided a politics and language through which to reassert their national existence and right to economic resources.[15]

Native people never got an exact replica of Operation Bootstrap or Point IV, but they did get a new housing policy. In 1961, the incoming Kennedy administration began adapting international development programs on reservations, embracing the ideas of Indian organizations and incorporating leaders from the AICC. The government's 1961 Task Force on Indian Affairs highlighted Point IV and Puerto Rican policy as models for Indian country and singled out those regions' self-help housing programs as having "great potential value" for reservations. By the end of the year, Philleo Nash, a veteran of both the AICC and the task force, had become the new BIA commissioner, and the agency selected the Pine Ridge Reservation in South Dakota as the site of its first housing project. A storied location, Pine Ridge was home to the Oglala Lakota tribe and the site of the 1890 Wounded Knee massacre. The first fifty homes built there were conventional public housing, but in 1962, the Public Housing Administration (PHA) and the BIA also began sponsoring "mutual-help" housing on reservations. A self-help homeownership program, mutual-help targeted the 80 percent of Native Americans who were too poor to qualify for subsidized rental units. Tribes contributed land, residents contributed labor, and the PHA trumpeted its own cost savings as a point of pride. The first mutual-help homes went up on the San Carlos Apache Reservation in Arizona in 1963, and from the late 1960s through the end of the twentieth century, mutual-help housing accounted for the majority of federally subsidized units in Indian country.[16]

At San Carlos as in the Third World, the birth of self-help housing decisively expanded the responsibilities of the state. During the 1930s, the Indian New Deal had temporarily directed some social spending to tribes, but even under its auspices, reservations had had absolutely no access to federal housing programs. Until 1961, the agencies responsible for housing development—the PHA, FHA, VA, and FmHA—simply did not operate there. Indeed, when the Kennedy administration decided to extend foreign and Puerto Rican housing policy to Indian country, the first task facing tribes was simply to create local housing authorities, the basic institutions of the New Deal state that channeled funds to cities and towns. In a single stroke, Native housing authorities extended the reach of federal agencies and transformed the range of programs they sponsored.[17]

The homes at Pine Ridge were not only the first units of public housing ever built on an Indian reservation. They were also the first built in the state of South Dakota.[18] Those at San Carlos were some of the first in Arizona.[19] New Deal public works had touched every corner of the country—mainland North

America became dotted with federal courthouses, dams, bridges, and airports—but social welfare spending was never evenly distributed. Depression-era policy makers had given state and local governments the power to solicit or reject national funds, and local business interests often welcomed industrial and agricultural subsidies while blocking social spending. During the postwar years, Sunbelt cities became infamous for courting federal military contracts while obstructing local access to public housing, nutrition, and cash-transfer programs.[20] African Americans, Mexican immigrants, and single mothers faced systematic exclusion and harassment,[21] and when it came to housing policy, rural communities saw very little in the way of federal largesse. Washington left it to local officials to decide whether they would create housing authorities at all, and once established, those authorities had to take the initiative in applying for funds. In 1960, there were six states that had never built a single unit of conventional public housing.[22]

As Native people pursued their own national projects, then, they unexpectedly found themselves at the forefront of a second nation-building effort: the drive to make the US welfare state a truly national institution. In 1964, when Lyndon Johnson announced that the country would wage a War on Poverty, the BIA had helped prepare the legislation, and Commissioner Philleo Nash publicly hailed Indian policy as a model for the United States. "We know more about poverty than some other agencies of the Government," he wryly observed. "We have been in the business a long time and we have a lot of it."[23] Within two years, the BIA was one of four federal agencies sponsoring self-help housing projects nationwide. By 1968, a hundred such programs operated in thirty states.[24]

———

Outside Indian reservations, self-help housing became a farmworker program that promised to take federal policy out of the hands of people like Reeve H. Barceloux. In 1966, Barceloux owned an orange ranch in the fertile Central Valley of Northern California. Every year, he and his neighbors produced a bounty of citrus fruit, olives, sugar beets, and tomatoes. But they weren't entirely satisfied. Two years earlier, the federal government had abolished the bracero program, which had provided US farms with a flood of Mexican guest workers since 1942. Across California, landowners demanded that the government reinstate the program; in Salinas, canning companies threatened to relocate their operations to Mexico if the workers did not come to them. When that failed, growers tried a different strategy. "For the past twenty-five years that I have owned my ranch," Barceloux wrote to the Glenn County Housing Authority in 1966, "I have lacked sufficient help to harvest my crops." The problem was that the county did not have enough housing for seasonal workers. The solution was obvious: the government should build a migrant labor camp.[25]

As the War on Poverty began and the bracero program ended, Barceloux was scrambling to reassert his interests within the Great Society. One year earlier, growers from Glenn County had met with state and federal officials to complain of a labor shortage and demand housing that would justify a new influx of casual seasonal labor. They weren't interested in permanent homes sponsored by the FHA; they wanted temporary shelters for a more vulnerable migrant workforce. A representative from the state government advised them to form a local housing authority and apply to the OEO for funds. Six months later, that authority contacted every major grower in the area asking how much housing they needed, and Barceloux sent his reply.[26]

Barceloux's attempt to use federal housing policy and War on Poverty funds grew from decades of experience. Since the 1940s, large farmers in the United States had decisively controlled rural housing policy and had crafted it in tandem with labor and immigration laws to produce a workforce fractured along lines of race, nationality, and legal status. Initially, they had reacted against the New Deal, prevailing on Congress to liquidate the system of federally administered labor camps that the Farm Security Administration had built during the 1930s. Although the camps provided an essential service to growers, many large farmers saw the public provision of housing as an affront to their own control of labor. In 1947, the US government sold 122 camps to growers' associations for $1 each. Three years later, the last thirty-nine camps passed into the hands of local housing authorities. Having privatized most of the federal camps, growers went further during the 1950s, divesting themselves of the costs and responsibilities they had just assumed. Increasingly, they hired workers through labor contractors and renounced any obligation to house them. A few large farms still maintained bunkhouses, and growers' associations continued to run camps for guest workers. But the private housing market became the primary resource available to all other farmworkers seeking shelter.[27]

By the early 1960s, California farmers had etched their priorities into the landscape. When farmworkers went home at the end of the day, they split off in several directions. Braceros went to private labor camps, many of them converted from barns, Japanese internment camps, and army barracks. Their segregation was no accident: the US and Mexican governments structured the guest-worker program to divide braceros legally and socially from other farmworkers. Guest workers had no path to citizenship and no right to look for a new job. Their wages, housing, and medical care were governed by a standard contract that growers honored in the breach. By the 1950s, growers maintained the camps as private business ventures and ringed them with fences.

Most workers in California were not braceros, however. A small minority did live in camps run by growers or local housing authorities, but most struggled to find homes in rural communities or on the fringes of towns and cities. They were Mexican immigrants, Filipinos, African Americans, and native-born whites, all of whom found themselves wedged into segregated settlements, driven there by the cumulative pressures of occupational segregation, unequal pay, and discriminatory real estate practices. In the San Joaquin Valley, Mexicans who fared well might end up in decent homes in West Parlier, while others built tar-paper shacks in Three Rocks, an unincorporated community without water or sewage systems. Poplar was almost lily white, Teviston entirely black.[28]

This archipelago of labor camps and working-class settlements reflected and reproduced growers' power over labor. Where most farmworkers wanted permanent family housing, employers preferred temporary shelters for single men, which kept workers moving with the harvest. Limiting the size and offerings of their own camps, steering local housing authorities, and siphoning public investment away from low-income communities, ranchers systematically produced a shortage of decent, affordable housing in the country's richest agricultural regions. The resulting housing crisis made it a daunting task for any worker to leave the migrant labor stream.

When the War on Poverty began, the intertwined housing, labor, and immigration policies of the bracero era all began to change at once, and large farmers searched for a new set of policies to recreate the flow of vulnerable seasonal labor they had lost. In 1966, Barceloux and his neighbors in Glenn County conceded as little as possible while insinuating themselves into the War on Poverty. Bending to new federal expectations, they proposed to build family housing and establish it as a government concern. But they would control the housing authority, and they insisted on temporary shelters.

This was the moment and the place where the OEO began funding self-help housing. In the context of ranchers' initiatives, the federally sponsored, owner-built home—permanent and fit for a family—seemed a liberating dream for farmworkers. In the country's major agricultural regions, the growth of self-help housing promised finally to make federal policy responsive to farmworkers, rather than their employers.

The OEO's first foray into self-help housing brought it together with none other than the AFSC. The same Quaker organization that had created racially integrated communities in Pennsylvania had sent a staff member, Bard McAllister, to California's San Joaquin Valley in 1955 to organize its Farm Labor Committee. McAllister began working with the African American residents of Teviston and five other working-class communities to secure public utilities, and he found that farmworkers across the region considered housing one of their most urgent needs. McAllister had worked at Penn-Craft and visited Nova Scotia's self-help program in the 1940s. In 1959, he and the Farm Labor Committee drew up a proposal for their own self-help initiative, citing precedents in Puerto Rico, Pennsylvania, Canada, and Sweden. By the early 1960s, they were breaking ground. Initially, they found funding close to home. When the state needed to demolish condemned buildings to construct Highway 198, McAllister worked with members of the Tachi Yokuts tribe to win the contract, salvage materials, and renovate homes at the Santa Rosa Rancheria. In 1963, the AFSC launched a historic pilot project in the town of Goshen, working with Mexican-American farmworkers to build new, conventional ranch homes that had ovens, bathtubs, and running water.[29]

"We went on tortillas and beans to get the house," recalled Mrs. Jesse Ortega, who moved into her home in Goshen after living in a shack with an outhouse.[30] But the families in Goshen did not simply tighten their belts to become homeowners; they pioneered the government financing system that came to undergird self-help housing for farmworkers in the United States. For working-class people who had long built shantytowns along the sides of highways, the Goshen project transformed auto-construction from a private activity into public policy. It depended on the AFSC's deep knowledge of federal housing law. Since the 1930s, Quaker activists had searched for any federal program that would accommodate the kind of self-help programs they admired overseas. By the 1960s, they knew that the Farmers Home Administration allowed some owner-building under its Section 502 loan program. However, that program exclusively served landowners. According to the FmHA, a typical borrower in 1952 was Rama McKinney. A white farmer, married with nine children, McKinney owned 136 acres of farmland and pasture in Yancey County, North Carolina. He had used a $6,500 loan from Section 502 to build a new house and barn on his property. Day laborers had done most of the work, and McKinney's eldest sons had served as "helpers," shaving at least $1,000 off the cost of construction.[31] Nearly a decade later, Quaker activists seized on this minor strand of US housing policy. Redefining the purpose of Section 502, they turned a program for small landowners into a weapon that farmworkers could wield against large growers. In 1961, before the Goshen project began, the AFSC and other farm labor organizations had convinced Congress to make farmworkers, and not only owners, eligible for Section 502 loans. The amendment to the law said nothing about the way farmworkers would build their homes, and in Goshen, the AFSC did exactly what it had done during the New Deal: it channeled general housing funds into a self-help program that required much more extensive family labor than the McKinneys had undertaken.[32] Having pushed on every door in Washington, they finally

FIGURE 7.1. California farmworkers organized by Self-Help Enterprises choose colors for their homes. (George Elfie Ballis, courtesy Maia Ballis)

found one that opened. In 1963, the Farmers Home Administration not only allowed the Goshen project to proceed but also declared it a national model.[33]

In short order, federal antipoverty officials did the same. When the War on Poverty began in 1964, the self-help housing project in the San Joaquin Valley was a perfect match for the OEO's community action and rural poverty programs. Bypassing state and local governments that had starved poor communities, these programs forged direct ties between Washington and local community organizations that represented poor people themselves. In 1965, the first OEO grant for self-help housing went to Self-Help Enterprises Inc. (SHE), a new nonprofit organization in Visalia, California, created by the AFSC's Farm Labor Committee. Now, with FmHA loans covering the cost of land and materials, the OEO financed technical assistance that made home building possible. SHE screened participants, offered them financial counseling, guided them through FmHA loan applications, and supervised construction. By the end of the year, Self-Help Enterprises had helped other farmworker groups secure OEO grants, and the main organ of the War on Poverty declared self-help the year's "most significant breakthrough" in farmworker housing.[34]

From the perspective of the AFSC, Washington had become a new place. During the depths of the Great Depression, the Roosevelt administration had quashed the Quakers' experiments, but three decades later, the Kennedy and Johnson administrations encouraged them. In one sense, the AFSC had simply capitalized on an incipient promise within the 1949 Housing Act, putting Section 502 to work for farmworkers. Its work in the 1960s illuminated a little-seen possibility already unfolding under the auspices of the New Deal state. But as the AFSC drew out that possiblity, it also availed itself of a new outlook among antipoverty officials. Sargent Shriver's staff at the OEO knew a great deal about postwar community development programs, including self-help housing, in all the places where the US government had already promoted it: overseas, in Puerto Rico, and on Indian reservations.[35] The community action program of the 1960s created a new stream of funding that nurtured self-help housing organizations and transformed owner-building from an option available to Section 502 borrowers to an organized, federally promoted activity.

As Self-Help Enterprises began its work, the War on Poverty was reaching deep into rural communities and outward to the Third World. A generation of advisors and community workers who had come up through foreign and imperial initiatives returned home during the mid-1960s and fanned out across the mainland. Ervan Bueneman, a veteran of the Caribbean Commission's self-help housing programs, was by 1965 evaluating mutual-help housing projects near Phoenix for the BIA.[36] That same year, the AFSC and Ford Foundation gathered seventy-five veterans of Mexican, Puerto Rican, Canadian, and mainland US projects at the luxurious Airlie House, a conference retreat outside Washington, DC. Donald Hanson of the United Nations told the group about "sophisticated and beautiful two-story row houses" completed in Argentina and Chile. Richard J. Margolis, a freelance writer and consultant to the Ford Foundation, celebrated Puerto Rican programs as models of leadership development.[37] On the opposite coast, in less extravagant settings, farmworkers in the San Joaquin Valley attended orientation meetings where they heard about overseas projects before ever lifting a shovel. Walter Monash, director of the California Department of Housing and Community Development, perused a report by Margolis and wondered if self-help could work on a large scale. He decided that he should learn more about Puerto Rico.[38]

As mainland discussions made clear, Puerto Rico had become as much an object of fascination for US citizens as a model for the Third World. During the early Cold War, the federal government had imagined the territory as a showcase facing south toward Latin America, Asia, and Africa.[39] But foreign visitors were always sensitive to Puerto Rico's peculiarities; the island was, after all, a tiny imperial outpost that lived and died by US subsidies. In 1962, Bernardo Garcés Córdoba of the CVC went so far as to declare Puerto Rico "almost completely irrelevant to Latin American realities."[40] For a Colombian businessman invested in his own country's status as a showcase, Puerto Rico could only be an international oddity and a sideshow. But the island was eminently accessible to US officials, and they spent the 1960s and 1970s fashioning lessons from it, imagining it as their gateway to the world, and measuring the mainland against it. In 1976, Harold Robinson of HUD captured what had become common sense among policy makers: "Just as the Puerto Rican experience was able to be transferred to other countries, so their varied experience can be transferred back to Puerto Rico and this country."[41]

In the space of a few years, self-help housing projects had become points of contact between the First and Third Worlds and bridges between US states and territories. At the same time, these initiatives were as local as could be, and they became layered with as many meanings as there were rural political traditions in the United States.

———

From the moment of its birth, Self-Help Enterprises captured the contradictory promise of self-help housing. SHE deliberately appealed to people with divergent political ideologies; indeed, it arose from delicate alliances that only a religious community like the Quakers could forge in 1960s California. Bard McAllister was a radical pacifist and a social democrat. Born in 1918 in Berea, Kentucky, he had spent World War II as a conscientious objector working for the Forest Service in California. He recognized many of the exclusions built

into the New Deal state and insisted that farmworkers deserved the same protections that industrial workers had won during the early twentieth century:
the right to organize, a minimum wage, and full access to Social Security, unemployment insurance, and workmen's compensation. For McAllister, self-
help housing mattered because it connected farmworkers to the welfare state.
It gave them federal mortgage loans for the first time, and it turned seasonal
migrants into permanent local residents who could enroll in public schools
and qualify for social services.[42]

McAllister imagined an expansive welfare state operating in tandem with a
reorganized agricultural sector. He wanted to do away with market prices for
agricultural commodities and replace them with federally administered prices.
Planning, he argued, would guarantee farm incomes that covered production
costs, including the cost of decent wages. He also hoped to replace the precarious system of contract labor with stable, long-term employment relationships.
Working for a single employer over the course of years—a possibility for a
homeowner—would stabilize workers' incomes and provide a record of employment suitable to draw Social Security and unemployment benefits. In
1962, the Farm Labor Committee created its own experimental alternative to
contract labor, the Sequoia Farm Labor Association. A labor cooperative made
up of farmworkers, the association signed contracts with growers, distributed
the jobs among its members, and registered itself as an employer. Suddenly,
worker-members had a long-term employment relationship and access to social insurance programs.[43]

Self-Help Enterprises and the Sequoia Farm Labor Association were notably entrepreneurial solutions to the problems of contract labor, and they revealed a powerful impulse toward nonprofit enterprise and voluntarism within
the AFSC. For McAllister, that impulse was perfectly compatible with support
for unionization. Indeed, the Farm Labor Committee worked in the same
communities that produced the United Farm Workers (UFW) during the
1960s, and the organizations crossed paths on a daily basis. Graciela Martinez,
who worked as a typist for the AFSC as a teenager, recalls McAllister taking
her to the UFW headquarters in Delano, California, during the momentous
1965 grape strike and introducing her to Cesar Chavez. She soon went to work
for the UFW herself and stayed on for seven years as a paralegal. Chavez's older
brother, Richard, worked as a construction supervisor for SHE during its early
years, and throughout the 1960s, the AFSC sent the union a stream of organizers and donations.[44]

But Self-Help Enterprises was separate from the AFSC, and McAllister
knew that it could and should appeal to people who would never support a
union. The first chairman of the board, Ralph Rosedale, was a rancher and
Republican Party activist who, in his own words, served as "a bridge to

agriculture." Being a Quaker made all the difference in Rosedale's life. He was born in Whittier, California, where his grandparents attended Quaker meeting with Richard Nixon's family. "His mom made my mom's wedding cake," he recalled in 2013. When Rosedale was young, his family grew lemons, oranges, and avocados on a forty-acre farm in Yorba Linda, hiring workers during the harvest and otherwise tending the fields themselves. As Quakers, they shared more than a little with McAllister. Rosedale's father and brother had been conscientious objectors during World War II, and as a result, he ruefully recalled that his brother's name ended up on "some list" during the McCarthy era. He graduated from the Yorba Linda public schools, finished two years of junior college, and in 1953 left California to work for the AFSC in India. The California farm boy was sent to Rasulia in the state of Madhya Pradesh and given rural development jobs. He admired the Congress Party and traveled to conferences where he saw Asian and African nationalists speak.[45] At the end of two and a half years, he returned to California, bought a farm in Dinuba, and threw himself into local civic and political life, inspired by "my experience in India . . . working with an interesting government." For Rosedale, Nehru's government had cultivated no interest in socialism but instead reinforced a general belief in the value of political participation. Rosedale chaired the local Farm Bureau, which represented ranchers, and rose within the Republican Party to head the statewide County Chairman's Association. As the California party became a hothouse of the New Right, Rosedale was in the middle of it. He counted Caspar Weinberger, Pete Wilson, and George Deukmejian as friends. He worked on Ronald Reagan's 1966 gubernatorial campaign and Nixon's presidential runs. Rosedale never became especially powerful, and he never got rich; in 2013, he was working as a substitute school bus driver. He still opposed unions, the minimum wage, the federal food stamp program, and the Affordable Care Act.[46]

Through all of this, Rosedale was also a Quaker. He deplored the racism of both the Democratic and Republican Parties, and he considered social service a duty. When he returned from India in 1956, he began working with the AFSC in Pasadena, and Bard McAllister recruited him to join the Farm Labor Committee. Rosedale's job was to talk with growers and neutralize opposition to self-help housing. Unlike McAllister, he could sincerely explain the program not as a wedge to expand the welfare state but as a model of private initiative and a superior alternative to both government labor camps and public housing, which he associated with drugs and crime. He called self-help a program to build families, and he hoped that the Visalia project might end up like Penn-Craft, running entirely on private money and family labor.[47]

When Self-Help Enterprises began in 1965, Rosedale chaired a painstakingly assembled board. It included Renee Esquivel and Lilia Jimenez, two farmworkers who had built their own homes with help from the Farm Labor Committee. Howard Way was a Republican state representative and Mary Diran a Berkeley public health professor. To stave off resistance from the building trades, McAllister enlisted Larry Eigenman, a sympathetic business agent from the Carpenters Union. Howard Washburn, a construction contractor and a longtime antiwar activist, directed the organization. And Washburn recruited Samuel R. Tyson, a farmer he had known for decades as a radical pacifist and civil rights activist. Tyson's life history illuminated the range of traditions that flowed into SHE. During the 1940s and 1950s, he and Washburn had participated in ecumenical meetings headlined by priests from the Catholic Rural Life Conference, an organization that espoused a yeoman ideal and committed itself to anticommunist social reform. The conference maintained that the United States could once again become an agrarian society of small property owners, and it aimed to address rural poverty without large-scale government action. By the time he joined the SHE board, Tyson was also a veteran of the Fellowship of Reconciliation and the Congress of Racial Equality, a supporter of the UFW, and a pacifist who had spent over a decade participating in civil disobedience outside nuclear test sites in California and Nevada. He condemned war and urbanization as twin vices of the modern world and described himself as one of a generation trying to "move away from the politics of killing by moving into the country."[48]

Modern-day Jeffersonians and wage workers, social democrats and foot soldiers of the New Right: this was a group that cohered around a building program, not a larger political-economic vision.

———

The tensions at the heart of Self-Help Enterprises played out across the country during the 1960s and 1970s. They were inescapable in a program that wedded government subsidies to unpaid labor, applied federal power through private community organizations, raised living standards by breaking down public regulations, and delivered public services by expanding private property ownership. Throughout the United States, rural communities saw the welfare state grow from the point of oblivion, and yet its growth created projects that receded from the model of public housing. Self-help housing lay halfway to anything.

It was certainly never clear what the policy implied about the extent of government responsibilities. On the one hand, poor communities felt the presence of the state as a guarantor of social welfare and fought for its expansion. In Teviston, California, SHE spent decades connecting farmworkers to federal social programs. Teviston was a racially segregated, unincorporated community on the edge of Visalia. African Americans had migrated there from the South during the Great Depression, and on the eve of the War on Poverty, journalists who visited the area thought they were seeing scenes from *The Grapes of Wrath*. Two-thirds of the homes had pit privies, and the AFSC's first victory was simply winning public water service in 1959.[49] From 1965 to 1980, the staff of SHE deftly navigated a maze of government offices to bring in public funds for housing, health, nutrition, and utilities. Teviston secured federal assistance to build a new well when the water table fell below its historic level. During the early 1980s, residents who still heated their homes with propane, butane, and wood stoves began installing solar water heaters with federal money. At least fifteen public agencies were active in Teviston by that time, and SHE was backing new demands for natural gas service. SHE's reports on Teviston were chronicles of state action and testaments to a failing private labor market. In the words of one VISTA volunteer, Teviston in 1981 was "a community which revolves around the first of the month—the day the Social Security and Supplemental Security Income checks arrive."[50]

Across the country in Greenville, Mississippi, self-help housing likewise grew from a long struggle by African Americans to claim federal resources and power. In 1966, black tenant farmers erected Freedom City to survive a wave of evictions, and the following year, they won an OEO grant to finance self-help housing on the site. The founders of the 400-acre community were civil rights activists fresh from the fierce voting-rights campaigns of the early 1960s, and they grafted a new housing policy onto long-standing demands for political and social citizenship. When Freedom City began, Greenville's cotton planters were evicting activists and mechanizing production to sustain their own authority and profits. Tenant farmers facing homelessness and unemployment imagined freedom as something that lay beyond the plantation system and the political power of Dixiecrats. They dreamed of owning their own land, building their own houses, creating small industries, and governing themselves. Their vision of social order drew on a distinctive notion of autonomy rooted in the history of plantation slavery and emancipation. For a century, African Americans in the South had struggled to acquire property and create institutions of self-governance as ways of controlling their own lives and labor, and they had simultaneously demanded federal protection of civil and political rights. The call for federally subsidized homeownership in 1966 extended the political tradition of this nation within a nation; black Mississippians promised to shift Washington's allegiances, channeling state resources into institutions and property that they controlled.[51] In Greenville and Teviston, residents wielded shovels and hammers to manage and stretch the meager offerings of the state, but they consistently demanded more of government.

FIGURE 7.2. FmHA 502 loans financed rural self-help housing across the country.
(George Elfie Ballis, courtesy Maia Ballis)

FIGURE 7.3. Children jump rope in front of conventional ranch homes built by their families
with federal financing. Self-help housing created new opportunities for homeownership
among African Americans shut out of the mortgage market by redlining and discriminatory
real estate practices. (George Elfie Ballis, courtesy Maia Ballis)

At the national level, meanwhile, self-help housing advocates articulated a broad social-democratic program for the United States. Meeting in 1965 and 1969 at Airlie House, they declared their support for farmworker unionization, a full-employment policy, and federal antidiscrimination measures to make social programs genuinely accessible to Native Americans and African Americans. As the Vietnam War escalated during the late 1960s, they demanded cuts to the military budget and an excess war-profits tax to finance generous housing subsidies and a basic minimum income for all Americans. Some speakers at these meetings were old enough to regard this platform as an extension of social-democratic proposals of the New Deal era. "We have tended to abandon the substance of democracy and retained only the procedures," declared Clay L. Cochran in 1965. Cochran arrived at Airlie House that year as an economist from the AFL-CIO's industrial union department, but his career had begun in Weslaco, Texas, during the Great Depression, where he had managed a labor camp for the Farm Security Administration (FSA). In his view, the great virtues of the FSA were its direct provision of housing to the poor and its generous subsidies, which were deep enough to reach the truly destitute. The FSA became the standard by which Cochran judged rural homeownership programs after World War II, and he found them wanting. The FmHA channeled too many loans to grower associations instead of farmworkers themselves, and the terms of loans were much too punishing for the poor to qualify. As Cochran told Congress in 1970, homeownership would only be truly affordable if the government subsidized it exactly like public housing, covering the entire cost of construction and much of the maintenance cost. The conferences at Airlie House recommended that federal homeownership programs allow Americans to participate even if they could afford no down payment at all and no interest payments on their mortgages. They called for the government to subsidize administrative costs rather than pass them on to homeowners. In all, they suggested that the problems of Teviston and Greenville demanded a massive program of economic redistribution carried out through federal fiscal policy.[52]

Clay Cochran became one of the country's most visible champions of self-help housing, but he never fixated on individual homeownership or sweat equity as singular solutions to the problems of the poor. Beginning in 1965, he led a series of national rural housing coalitions that argued for self-help as one limited part of a much broader low-income housing program. The International Self-Help Housing Association (ISHA), the Rural Housing Alliance (RHA), the National Rural Housing Coalition (NRHC), and eventually Rural America shepherded self-help housing through more than two decades of congressional budget negotiations.[53] They consistently championed public housing as the cornerstone of federal policy and self-help housing as one of several adjuncts for people with incomes too high to qualify for public housing but too low to secure a conventional mortgage loan. They called for housing systems that gave residents control over their environment and maintained that in principle, residents could exercise control as renters in public or private housing, or as owners in cooperatives or single-family homes. If they were renters, the key was to transfer ownership from rural growers and urban slumlords to nonprofit organizations or government bodies that formally answered to tenants. By 1976, Rural America was backing rural rental housing as well as homeownership programs, and California farmworker organizations were winning FmHA 515 loans to allow farmworkers to buy grower-operated labor camps and convert them into cooperatives. Rural housing organizations insisted that self-help could fit into all of these ownership systems, with unpaid labor and experimental materials either generating equity for owners or reducing rent for tenants. Individual homeownership and unpaid labor figured as components of federal policy, but never substitutes for shelter built and owned by the state.[54]

Yet for every Clay Cochran who made the case for redistribution and broad public authority, there was a Richard Margolis heralding self-help housing as a model of voluntarism. Margolis's career entwined with Cochran's; they were founders of ISHA and its successor organizations, and they ultimately became the first chairman and director of Rural America. A freelance journalist and the author of books for adults and children, Margolis encountered self-help housing in 1965, when the Ford Foundation sent him to California to evaluate Self-Help Enterprises. He quickly became the country's most prolific champion of the policy, publishing vividly illustrated books and pamphlets that documented the lives of the rural poor. As a writer, Margolis's mode was pathos. He imagined himself working in the shadows of Jacob Riis and James Agee, specializing in literary portraits of children playing on dusty streets and parents struggling to make ends meet. His protagonists appeared not as members of movements or political parties, but as individuals and families fighting heroically to defend their dignity. He penned free-form poetry about a child who finally had a bathtub at home: "his teacher still calls him a dirty little Indian. / But he knows it's a lie." Echoing contemporary social science, Margolis concerned himself as much with psychological adjustment as social reform, declaring self-help "the only housing technique which . . . helps to sweep away the sickly sense of uselessness which often afflicts the poor." In place of Cochran's story of a growing welfare state, Margolis offered sentimental stories about individual striving, mutual aid, and the personal transformations wrought by private property ownership.[55]

Margolis was not as naive as his books suggested. He did believe that the process of building homes strengthened social ties, transformed psyches, and cultivated self-respect among participants. But privately, he recognized the perils of fetishizing unpaid labor, personal initiative, and mutual aid. "I think we've been captives of our own vernacular. The idea of sweat equity has mesmerized us," he warned the attendees at Airlie House in 1965. "It seems plain that a man who must stay away from his job in order to build his house needs more than his sweat—he needs cash." In Margolis's estimation, self-help housing activists were dangerously pandering to foundations when they obscured that fact. "I am a bit concerned about the word 'self-help' as a kind of coinage that we are capitalizing on more and more—the kind of coinage that buys grants," he warned.[56]

Yet capitalize they did. During the mid-1960s, self-help housing acquired an unmistakable association with fantasies of bootstrapping self-reliance. In fact, the association emerged through the very process of transplanting a foreign and imperial policy to the mainland, as policy makers and activists labored to explain self-help as a quintessentially national phenomenon. Turning instinctively to cherished myths of the US past, Margolis and others domesticated a program that had no national home and symbolically drained it of its most radical associations.

"The first step in the development of the American frontier was self-help housing," declared Robert G. Lewis of the Department of Agriculture in 1965. The mythology of the frontier infused arguments for self-help housing, although the policy had never existed in the nineteenth-century West. Homesteaders had, of course, built their own houses, but the process of construction had never been a government concern. The nineteenth-century state had been a land company that usurped territory and sold it to citizens; its characteristic tools were warfare and land surveying, not mortgage lending and architectural research. Nonetheless, the frontier proved an irresistible image. Latin American squatters, argued Don Terner after his years abroad, had the good fortune of living "at the city's effective frontier . . . untouched by many of its restrictions, services, and institutions. . . . In contrast, the American Negro in the urban ghetto, trapped within the confines of the surrounding society, is economically dependent, and has no access to any as yet undeveloped area where he can 'stake out his claim.' " In Terner's mind, eighteenth-century fears of economic "dependence" bled into twentieth-century discussions of "dependency," and hoary tales of the frontier as an unregulated space of liberty suggested solutions for the twentieth-century city. Richard Margolis extended Terner's line of thought, lamenting the declining prospects of the poor. "The pioneer had a surfeit of land; the poor man has no land at all," he protested in 1967. "The pioneer had an appreciative society cheering him on; the poor man faces an indifferent world boxing him in." In 1969, over a hundred rural housing advocates at Airlie House demanded "a 20th century 'homestead act' for housing, demonstrating at least as much faith in the common man as the Congress expressed a hundred and eight years ago."[57]

For North Americans in the twentieth century, the myth of the frontier explained a great many things: it was a story about the origins of political democracy, capitalist development, and rugged individualism. All of these associations lurked in arguments for self-help housing. Donald Hanson of the United Nations called the participatory process of "discussing, planning, and building" homes an exercise in democracy. The OEO cast unpaid construction work as vocational training generating productive workers. The BIA celebrated Native Americans' freedom to choose from "44 variations of a standard floor plan" and " 'bootstrap' themselves into better housing." The emerging image of self-help housing was one of active citizens striking out on their own and making free choices. Richard Margolis breathlessly recounted a meeting at the Rosebud Sioux reservation in South Dakota. "An elderly missionary stood in back of the room and watched the proceedings with wonder," he reported. " 'They are making more decisions tonight,' he said, 'than they have made in their entire life.' "[58]

The symbolism of the frontier heroically transmuted the harsh realities of federal programs. Obligatory, unpaid labor became a symbol of self-reliance, democracy was whittled down to a set of participatory procedures, and freedom became something like consumer choice. Many of the promises rang hollow. Self-help housing programs in fact permitted recipients very few choices; they could select among several floorplans, but they had no influence in consequential decisions about financing and eligibility. Moreover, job-training programs had limited effects in a country without a jobs policy. On remote Indian reservations, there was often no realistic prospect of finding long-term employment in construction. Some farmworkers might leave the fields, but for those who remained, the pressing problem was not unemployment but the exploitative terms of work.[59]

As US housing advocates invoked the frontier, they turned a thoroughly novel policy into a symbol of tradition and remade the reputation of a program known internationally as a hallmark of modern statecraft. Self-help housing facilitated mass urbanization in Latin America, and the architectural and engineering research behind it built the US suburbs. In Puerto Rico, self-help housing *was* New Deal public housing. Explaining the policy by reference to nineteenth-century settlers, North Americans obscured the ties that bound US rural policy to urban and suburban transformations of their own time. They painted a nostalgic picture of rural communities as worlds apart, and they resuscitated an exceptionalist view of the United States as a country apart.

If the frontier provided a captivating set of symbols, the history of slave emancipation supplied a distinctive language of private ownership and investment. "The child knows he owns the house; it's a way of owning himself," explained Margolis after visiting the Rosebud reservation.[60] The resonant language of self-ownership dated from the years after the Civil War, when triumphant Northerners had used it to explain the meaning of abolition and the ascent of wage labor. Freedpeople, they argued, were now their own property. The claim obscured the reality that human beings had ceased to be property at all; they could no longer be bought or sold by anyone. The language of self-ownership likewise masked the suffocating limits of liberty in the Gilded Age. But it grounded a new conception of freedom that relied on the metaphor of contract. As capitalism supplanted slavery, social relationships once structured by bondage became reimagined as consensual exchanges between formally equal property owners. To be free was to enter voluntarily into contractual agreements, invest one's resources, reap the rewards, and bear the risks of life in a marketplace.[61] This was a view of wage labor, of personal relationships, and of freedom itself, born of the consolidation of capitalism in a slaveholding country. A century later, the language of self-ownership and investment continued to inflect arguments for homeownership by the poor. In California, photographer George Elfie Ballis watched farmworkers put in thirty hours a week of unpaid labor on their homes. He grasped for words to dignify a punishing reality. "Families invest their evenings, weekends, days-off," he declared. "The people invest themselves."[62] Concepts that had once ennobled wage labor now concealed unpaid labor, casting work as an investment made by the owners of very peculiar property.

As Margolis and others reached into eighteenth- and nineteenth-century political thought, they drew out one particular idea that Cochran adamantly rejected: the conviction that private property was the foundation of responsible citizenship and economic stewardship. Cochran championed public, cooperative, and rental housing as well as private homeownership, but Margolis delighted in quoting and misquoting Arthur Young, the eighteenth-century British agriculturalist: "Give a man the secure possession of a bleak rock, and he will turn it into a garden; give him a nine years' lease of a garden and he will convert it into a desert. . . . The magic of ownership turns sand into gold." Margolis insisted that Latin American experience bore out Young's claim. He had never worked south of the Rio Grande, but he scoured reports by US observers and the Pan-American Union and plucked out choice examples of homeowners improving their properties while low-rent projects crumbled nearby. In Ciudad Kennedy, of course, resident labor was contractually required by the state, and housing recipients often went far beyond the planners' prescriptions. The toil that Latin Americans put into their homes—by design and against it—became, in Margolis's hands, evidence of the singular virtues of private property ownership.[63]

Beyond the level of the symbolic, self-help housing organizations went to great lengths to enlist private capital, insulating themselves from political opposition and giving banks and the real estate industry financial stakes in sweat-equity construction. In upstate New York, Better Rochester Living (BRL) got its start in 1965 with seed money from Eastman Kodak and Xerox, secured a $300,000 line of credit from local commercial banks, and recruited local savings and loan institutions to provide mortgages with 3 percent down payments—a low figure for commercial loans but a high one for self-help housing programs. They hired local realtors to show properties to public housing residents interested in sweat-equity rehabilitation. BRL's leaders frankly acknowledged the contradictions of their strategy. Commercial financing made the housing more expensive than the major federal loan programs did; bank loans were forthcoming because financial institutions saw low-income housing as a potentially lucrative investment. "We've opened up a new market for them," explained Welton Myers, a former building contractor and a founder of BRL. On the other hand, Myers insisted that working with the financial and real estate industries could ultimately change their practices, lowering down payments and forcing the private sector to comply with BRL's policy of racial integration.[64]

As self-help housing advocates pulled in opposite directions on the legitimacy of public ownership and financing, they also launched attacks on the regulatory powers of the state. Clay Cochran became a standard-bearer for the idea that Washington should determine the overall supply of housing while new local institutions controlled design and management. He eagerly read the work of Herbert M. Franklin of the National Urban Coalition, who argued in 1969 that the United States suffered from "upside-down federalism." As Franklin explained, "The central government concerns itself with the smallest operational questions—what kinds of doorknobs will be used in a project—but remains neutral on the biggest questions—to what degree a state or locality will permit subsidies to be used at all." In his view, Washington itself should establish national construction goals and provide new financial incentives to local authorities, acquiring land and paying for a full complement of public services to facilitate aggressive local action. The federal government would then act as a builder of last resort if housing authorities failed to meet national goals. While Washington's role in construction would expand, its regulatory role would shrink. It would enforce antidiscrimination measures and regulate landlord-tenant relations, but Franklin otherwise proposed to eradicate a great many zoning laws, building codes, contracting guidelines, and residency requirements that stood in the way of low-income housing development. Finally, he insisted that turning federalism right-side up meant creating a new set of local institutions that would develop housing, displacing state and local housing authorities that had generated inequalities since the 1930s.[65]

Franklin had no experience with self-help housing and was principally concerned with the crisis of African Americans trapped in devastated urban centers. But he masterfully synthesized ideas circulating within self-help housing organizations during the 1960s and 1970s. The distinctive pairing of robust federal power with new institutions of local control and sweeping deregulation appealed to farmworker organizations stymied by discriminatory local officials and FmHA building standards. As the practice of federalism became a subject of public controversy during the 1960s and 1970s, self-help housing advocates dove into the debate.[66]

Franklin's formula certainly made sense to AFSC staff in Palm Beach County, Florida. The AFSC's East Coast migrant project had turned its attention to housing there in 1969, and it immediately found itself fighting local officials who used administrative and regulatory powers to deny housing to the poor. As of 1971, FmHA programs offered the only path to homeownership for local people with annual incomes below $5,000, but Florida's FmHA staff made a point of lending to grower associations and housing authorities, not farmworkers. "We're not set up to serve everyone," explained Charles H. Little of the Gainesville office. County-level FmHA officials colluded with growers to deny employees' applications, and they offered credit on the most punishing terms permissible under FmHA legislation. They demanded large down payments when they could have demanded none, charged interest rates as high as 7.25 percent when they could have charged 1 percent, and turned away seasonal employees even if they cobbled together year-round work. These rules struck especially hard at black and Latino workers, whom employers confined to the lowest-paying, least stable jobs that Florida agriculture had to offer. Unmarried women likewise faced special hostility from FmHA officials. Florida staff members labeled them "a poor credit risk due to the possibility of pregnancy," refused to consider AFDC benefits a reliable source of income, and told applicants living in multigenerational households to evict their relatives or forego home loans. Between 1969 and 1971, Palm Beach County officials approved just five loans to single mothers.

James E. Upchurch, director of the AFSC's East Coast migrant project, described his encounters with the FmHA as object lessons in "Federal racism." Florida's FmHA officials made no secret of their bigotry, calling the first black applicant in Palm Beach County a "nigger" and denigrating the daughters of another black worker as "just prostitutes." John Stewart, the supervisor of the Palm Beach County office, told the *Miami Herald* that he was "proud to be a cracker."

While many of Florida's obstructionist regulations focused on the characteristics of applicants—their sources of income and family structures—others took subtler form as building codes and environmental regulations. "We want rural living to be as pleasant as the city's suburbs," explained FmHA state director William Shaddick in 1971. In fact, FmHA site requirements for rural Florida were often more stringent than local government standards and even FHA standards for urban areas. "In order to obtain an FmHA loan, the rural poor family must meet pollution specifications which exceed the local health department requirements," the AFSC protested in 1971. In some cases, the FmHA and local health departments prohibited applicants from building homes with septic tanks, effectively barring improvements in desperately poor communities that lay beyond the reach of public sewage systems. In Martin County, the AFSC worked with "families living in shanties, *with outdoor latrines,* who have been denied septic tank permits and new homes on the grounds that the *use of septic tanks would be a pollution hazard.*" FmHA director Shaddick asked smugly, "Shouldn't we all help solve the pollution problem?" The AFSC responded bitterly: "After being denied housing for generations," the rural poor should not have "to lead the battle against pollution."[67]

Facing systematic obstruction, Upchurch and the AFSC began walking a political tightrope, arguing for relaxed government regulations in order to raise living standards. They had no general objection to environmental protection; in fact, as energy costs skyrocketed and wages stagnated during the 1970s, self-help housing organizations made pioneering uses of solar, wind, and water power in low-income developments.[68] But they scorned regulations that systematically denied funds and building permits to the poor.

Veterans of Latin American programs became some of the most adamant critics of public regulation. Jim Upchurch was one of them. The director of the AFSC's East Coast migrant project had arrived in Florida in 1969 fresh from a two-year stint working on self-help housing projects in Mexico. Testifying before Congress in 1970, he offered a devastating comparison of the First and Third Worlds:

> I sincerely believe that the Latin American campesino is better off than the Mexican-American or Black farm workers with regard to housing. A campesino knows that his government probably will not help him to house his family, but at least he can develop some kind of shelter by making bricks with his own hands. But the American farm worker cannot do even this when his system fails him. If he tries to help himself, he is faced with a maze of local, state and federal codes and regulations.[69]

Upchurch took the same lesson from Latin America that Don Terner did when he celebrated squatters as frontier settlers. In 1968, Terner called for a new frontier in US cities while he was trying to adapt a Venezuelan slum-upgrading system in Detroit and running up against local building codes. At the time, he was working for Neal Mitchell, a young engineer who taught at the Harvard

School of Design and ran his own company, Neal Mitchell Associates. The firm marketed a low-cost, prefabricated, modular building system made of lightweight concrete that homeowners could assemble themselves. Home-building kits dated to the early twentieth century and had exploded after 1945. Mitchell declared that his product offered "flexibility of choice," allowing low-income people to build minimal structures and expand them over time. Adaptable plumbing systems, for instance, let a large family start out with just one bathroom for five bedrooms and add a second bathroom when they could afford it. "The beauty is, the choice is the owner's," Mitchell explained in 1968, casting choice as individual latitude within dreadful constraints. "In public housing, he can't modify [the unit] at all." In 1967, the Catholic archdiocese in Detroit won a grant from HUD to build seventeen units with Mitchell's system, but the city balked at the unconventional materials and the idea of owners incrementally developing housing from substandard cores. "In Detroit, we probably wanted to break every building code in the books," Mitchell explained. He blamed "our whole administrative and political system" for killing the project.[70]

Upchurch, Terner, and Mitchell became part of a cacophonous choir of antiregulatory voices emanating from self-help housing projects. Some of the loudest calls came from Indian reservations, where government officials saw painfully low building standards as financially necessary and culturally appropriate. They recapitulated the logic of housing planners in Latin America, who had taken national social spending and individual incomes to be scarce, fixed resources, and treated the unit cost of housing as the only realistic object of reform. While Clay Cochran demanded more generous federal spending, officials in Indian country frequently bore down under austere budget constraints, applying the architect's tools to more limited problems. The Fort Hall reservation in Oregon began participating in the BIA Housing Improvement Program in 1963, and by 1966, the cheap toilets that the BIA had provided were breaking.[71] That same year, Lyndon Johnson explained that self-help housing on the Rosebud Sioux reservation "will not be what we Americans have generally considered 'standard.' For example, while all will have a stove or space heater, not all will have electricity or running water." The president presented these homes as the only feasible options for Native people with annual incomes as low as $1,500 and as welcome alternatives to existing forms of shelter: "tents, automobile bodies, and substandard shacks."[72] In 1963, Alaska Natives in the village of Nunapitchuk demanded conventional tract housing, but Charles Blomfield of the Alaska state housing authority—an architect by training—explained that until they developed new income-generating industries, "we are going to have to have a simple approach geared to the existing economy." In other words, residents had to accept homes without running water or electricity, which Blomfield considered "a tremendous improvement" over existing one-room homes without indoor toilets or even pit privies.[73]

These calls for deregulation made wholly contradictory promises: some aimed to bring new public funds to farmworkers, while others proposed to let the poor make do under existing fiscal constraints. As the 1970s began, the Nixon and Ford administrations increasingly embraced deregulation as an austerity measure. Seeking to cut domestic housing subsidies and foreign aid alike, they made the United States into the world's leading opponent of international standards for low-income housing. In 1975, the United Nations created a new housing agency, HABITAT, which set about convening governments to establish global norms for housing policy. The agency's chairman was none other than Enrique Peñalosa, the former director of Colombia's land reform institute, INCORA. Like most Colombian officials of the 1960s, he subscribed to the basic philosophy of self-help housing. Speaking at American University in 1975, he frankly insisted that governments could not afford to build and maintain housing, and therefore "the houses of the poor will be built by the poor, as they always have been." Difficult as it might be, governments should encourage auto-construction by "put[ting] aside the consideration of standards and quality. The hard truth is that we must not only permit but foster the creation of what many would call substandard housing, because *substandard* is still better than *subhuman*." Strikingly, the Ford administration dismissed Peñalosa as overly ambitious. Before the 1976 HABITAT conference in Vancouver, the State Department warned the president that "if Peñalosa raises some of his favorite ideas [including] . . . the need for minimum standards in all countries," Ford should respond: "The adoption of minimum standards is not a *sine qua non* to improved quality of life. If the Conference gets into the subject at all, it ought to deal with minimum standards in qualitative terms—as goals—rather than in any quantitative way."[74]

The twentieth century is often remembered as a time when US officials and corporations globalized the concept of an American standard of living to which all might aspire.[75] But in low-income housing policy, the US government by the 1970s was principally engaged in an international effort to determine the lowest standard of living to which states could be held. The Nixon and Ford administrations extracted a punishing prescription from long debates over the obligations of the state.

———

The contradictions within self-help housing created opportunities for private capital to capture federal policy during the Nixon years, and ultimately made self-help a practice that could survive and grow during the crises of the 1970s and 1980s. Although nonprofit self-help housing organizations had spent the 1960s struggling to redirect state subsidies to poor people, elements of their program harmonized with the calls of for-profit developers, who lambasted public housing and demanded federal housing funds to support their own activities. By the late 1960s, the War on Poverty was blurring the boundary between the two strategies. HUD's Turnkey programs gave subsidized contracts to for-profit developers, which bought land and developed residential property before turning it over to homeowners or housing authorities. On Indian reservations, HUD, the OEO, and the BIA folded mutual-help construction into Turnkey projects, making residents' unpaid labor a subsidy to developers and the state as much as an equity-building strategy for homeowners themselves. Rodman C. Rockefeller's International Basic Economy Corporation (IBEC), which had spent the 1950s and 1960s developing self-help housing in Latin America, became a major Turnkey-Mutual-Help contractor on Indian reservations, and by 1967, HUD invited the company to adapt the same fusion of self-help and subsidized for-profit contracting in US cities.[76]

The Nixon administration's Operation Breakthrough went further, offering HUD contracts to for-profit corporations to test industrialized housing systems in US cities. Operation Breakthrough redirected the fascination with nonstandard building materials and the deregulation of construction that self-help housing programs had nurtured. In doing so, it opened new opportunities to globetrotting architects and engineers. Rudard Jones of the Small Homes Council, who had directed the Point IV housing mission to Colombia during the 1950s, advised HUD on Operation Breakthrough in 1972.[77] The program simultaneously created opportunities of a different sort by redirecting state subsidies from poor people to long chains of for-profit contractors. David Lilienthal's consulting company, the Development & Resources Corporation, secured HUD contracts to administer construction under Operation Breakthrough, solicited proposals from builders, and was soon awash in bids from firms alive to opportunities within the welfare state. Chemical companies that lived on lucrative military contracts were among the most eager applicants for HUD subsidies; by 1968, Dow Chemical was marketing Styrofoam as insulation, "modified cement systems" as masonry, and an entire menu of chemical products as materials for prefabricated home building. By that point, Thiokol already had Turnkey contracts with OEO and HUD in Mississippi and Louisiana, alongside subsidized manpower training and education contracts.[78] As an affordable housing policy, Operation Breakthrough became a fiasco, but it succeeded marvelously in funneling social welfare funds to for-profit corporations, many of which amplified their earnings by adapting the methods of self-help construction. Jim Walter Houses became one of the country's largest manufacturers of unfinished, prefabricated shell houses. The company deliberately organized the production process to assume relatively cheap early stages of construction while leaving more expensive later stages to home buyers. As the Rural Housing Alliance lamented in 1972, the company was profitable in part because it pushed costs onto people with little ability to pay them.[79]

As corporations bent low-income housing programs to their own purposes, the self-help housing programs of the 1960s no longer appeared austere counterparts to conventional public housing. Rather, they seemed embattled alternatives to for-profit, private development. Indeed, little else remained around them as the federal government eviscerated public housing policy. Aided self-help survived two decades of devastating blows that felled other programs. The first trial was Nixon's 1973 moratorium on subsidized housing programs, which put every bit of federal housing policy on the chopping block. Self-help housing survived in part because the War on Poverty had created precisely the kinds of institutions that could shepherd a program through the crisis. The Housing Assistance Council (HAC), created by the OEO in 1971, appealed to Nixon in his own terms, casting self-help as a policy befitting an austere state; owner-built homes cost the government less than units built by private contractors. "If there was any program that fits the President's inaugural message about self-reliance," argued Clay Cochran in 1973, "this is it and he should be made aware of that fact." Internally, HAC encouraged rural housing groups to keep their doors open by converting all kinds of low-income housing programs into self-help projects, both because some federally subsidized funds remained available during the early months of 1973 and because self-help could operate on a shoestring. By July, low-income housing groups had restored the FmHA 502 and 515 interest-credit programs through a federal class-action lawsuit, *Pealo v. FmHA*. While the moratorium cut self-help housing activity below projected levels, 1973 still turned out to be a record year for self-help housing, in which FmHA made an unprecedented 910 technical assistance loans.[80]

The attacks of the Nixon years failed to destroy self-help housing, but they made it less egalitarian. By 1974, FmHA had raised the income requirements to qualify for loans and extended fewer loans to minorities; by 1977, only 9 percent went to African Americans.[81] The widening inequities of the 1970s became acute when Reagan took office and threatened to cut all subsidized housing programs, including self-help. Rural housing advocates took desperate measures to survive. In 1981, HAC urged its member organizations to convert yet more housing programs into self-help projects. Some experimented with prison-release programs that put first-time offenders to work without pay on construction sites instead of serving jail time. In Watsonville, California, The Environmental Community Housing Organization (TECHO) intensified the exploitation of housing recipients themselves, asking them to build extra homes that it could sell to cover its operating costs. In some communities, standards that were already minimal were cut to the bone. Kentucky Mountain Housing Development developed what it called a "warm and dry" house that lacked even a flush toilet. "The house does not meet federal building standards," reported the *New York Times* in 1985. "But Hubert Allen, chairman of Kentucky Mountain Housing, said: 'If a family wants a new home but has no place to leach the effluent created by a flush toilet, why can't they at least have a warm house with running water and a bathtub?' "[82]

Ultimately, the key survival strategy of the 1980s was the turn to private and state-level financing. It was a move that self-help housing organizations seemed born to perfect, having worked for decades with pitifully limited access to the federal budget. They had survived the purportedly flush 1960s by resourcefully tapping marginal sources of public money, cobbling it together with corporate and commercial funds, and binding the two with sweat. Self-Help Enterprises became the best-known organization to survive and thrive after 1980, building high-quality homes that residents cherished. It was able to do so because it was already an accomplished, professionalized real estate developer with the specialized skills to navigate an increasingly fractured state. The organization had weathered the 1970s in part by securing hundreds of workers from the Comprehensive Employment and Training Act (CETA) for its housing rehabilitation program. By 1985, the same program relied on a patchwork of contracts with cities and counties, private utilities, and the state of California. Jim Upchurch, who had run the AFSC's East Coast migrant project in the face of FmHA obstruction, was by 2001 directing Interfaith Housing of Western Maryland, "leveraging money [to secure private loans] and going beyond dependence on government funding." Dana Jones of the Southern Maryland Tri-County Community Action Committee explained that HAC taught him to "use the local lending market": "We're cranking out a tax credit deal every year" he explained in 2001, and "doing home acquisitions with private money." Every one of these developers agreed that the new programs could not reach the truly poor: self-help housing had never been designed to do so in any case, and private creditors had no interest in taking the risk.[83]

Among the real estate developers who emerged from the world of self-help housing, the most successful was surely Don Terner, whose path out of Latin America initially led him to utter frustration in Detroit. He spent the late 1960s and early 1970s teaching city planning at MIT, developing self-help housing and utility systems with students and colleagues. He acknowledged the contradiction of a strategy that could expand state obligations to the poor or eviscerate them:

> It has been suggested that self-help is a reactionary mechanism used to . . . relieve pressure on the government . . . rather than a constructive means by which squatters may survive, improve their situation, and at the same time gain greater control over their environment, including developing power and organization to apply pressure to the government.
>
> In fact, both statements reflect reality. The first result is an unintended, but not unanticipated byproduct of the second.

In 1974, as Terner examined the state of squatter communities worldwide, he decided to live with that contradiction. The "priority of survival," he argued, had to take precedence over headier, long-term demands for economic redistribution.[84]

Over the next two decades, growing swaths of the world came to seem something like squatter settlements to Terner, and the "priority of survival" became his guiding principle. Terner responded to fiscal retrenchment in the 1970s and 1980s by holding fast to the idea that housing planners had an obligation to improve conditions in the world as it existed, constraints and all. The alternative, he believed, was to ask the poor to hold out for a political upheaval that might never come. In 1973, Terner shifted his attention from Cambridge, Massachusetts, to New York City, where he cofounded the Urban Homesteading Assistance Board (UHAB). Urban homesteading, another form of sweat-equity homeownership, allowed tenants to rehabilitate rundown buildings and buy them at reduced prices. It simultaneously gave the municipal government a way to unload abandoned buildings during the fiscal crisis of the 1970s. Lacking the money to recuperate and manage public property, the city ceded the structures to tenants. Terner soon found his way from the New York City fiscal crisis to the California tax revolt. In 1978, just months after California voters ratified Proposition 13, Governor Jerry Brown appointed him director of the California Department of Housing and Community Development. Terner did what he thought possible: he committed the state to support self-help housing, sued Orange County for failing to build affordable units, and on leaving public service, become a nonprofit real estate developer in California. Founding the Bridge Housing Corporation, Terner spent the 1980s and 1990s pioneering new methods of public-private financing that channeled government subsidies, union pension funds, philanthropic grants, commercial bank loans, and corporate investments into private, mixed-income housing. If UHAB adapted building techniques that Terner had honed in Latin America, Bridge extended the search for private resources that self-help had always required.

By 1992, the *Orange County Register* found at least one point of agreement with Terner, praising Bridge's ability to lower costs by skirting public-sector regulations, and concluding that only the private sector could successfully build affordable housing. Terner's career in California had, by that time, given him national renown. During the 1990s, the Clinton administration enlisted him to advise on housing policy in the Balkans and Palestinian territories, suggesting that policies suited to austerity at home might serve equally well in contexts of war and occupation. These activities were some of Terner's last. At the height of his career in 1996, Terner perished in a plane crash over Europe. He had been part of the business delegation accompanying Secretary of Commerce Ron Brown to Bosnia and Croatia, where he was to assist in postwar housing development.[85]

Between the War on Poverty and Terner's death, over 26,000 US households had built their own homes using FmHA Section 502 loans. Self-help remained a small program, but it had grown since the 1960s, accounting in 1996 for 1,514 new loans totaling over $100 million.[86] It had also acquired new champions and new meanings. In 1995, the Clinton administration designated Self-Help Enterprises a "Partner in the American Dream" as part of its National Homeownership Strategy. In the administration's telling, SHE's accomplishment had been to create "housing choices for people from previously underserved markets."[87] A policy born alongside public housing in the expansionary days of the welfare state now thrived under the banner of Third Way politics. A program that once brought federal subsidies to regions untouched by the New Deal now symbolized the hollowing out of the New Deal state and the rise of diminutive programs that made no attempt to replace every unit of public housing lost to demolition. The survival of self-help housing organizations and loan programs represented a nearly impossible achievement for low-income housing advocates during the 1970s and 1980s. But the broader social-democratic demands that had once surrounded the owner-built home faded from public discussion. The crises of the 1970s and 1980s had sorted out the competing possibilities that existed within a deeply ambiguous program. They had simultaneously sorted midcentury housing policies from one another, destroying those that offered deeper subsidies and redeploying their austere counterparts.

As self-help housing traversed historical epochs, it also traversed national borders, illuminating patterns by which policy and ideas moved during the postwar period. As a matter of intentional federal activity, self-help had begun as an imperial policy, flourished as a foreign policy, found its way to Indian country, and finally crossed the rural United States during the War on Poverty. Before the 1960s, the US mainland had seen only isolated, halting attempts at self-help, and the policy's growth owed much to activists who took lessons from Puerto Rico and the Third World. As a result of their work, US social policy came to resemble that in other world regions, and by the late 1960s, advisors found that they could travel in countless directions across the globe. Terner's career took him from Latin America to US cities and out again to the Balkans and Middle East. In 1967, Bard McAllister left the San Joaquin Valley for Zambia, where he spent six years developing self-help housing with the AFSC.[88] At home, talk of the frontier created an illusion that the United States was an exceptional country with traditions all its own, but the movement of people and practices belied that claim.

Of all these trajectories, perhaps the most surprising was that of Enrique Peñalosa, the first director of INCORA who wound up directing UN HABITAT in New York. The northward migration of Latin American officials was a little-noted but pervasive feature of postwar policy making. Multilateral institutions based in the United States have always responded to US government imperatives, and for good reason, most observers have analyzed them as creatures of the North Atlantic. But as Peñalosa's career suggested, they were also cosmopolitan workplaces and sites of migration. During years when US advisors moved in and out of the country, Latin Americans did the same. Setting their sights on Washington and New York, they grasped for influence of their own. In doing so, they made US cities into more than centers of US power. North American metropolises became crossroads where foreigners applied lessons they had learned at home.

8

Decentralization Reborn

EDUARDO WIESNER FIRST appeared in this story as he is generally known outside Colombia: as an IMF and World Bank economist of the 1980s and 1990s. During those years, he acquired a notorious reputation for negotiating structural adjustment programs across Latin America, and he championed new forms of decentralization that took apart developmental states. That much is known, and all of it is true. But where did his ideas come from? The interceding pages have offered what might seem incongruous glimpses of Wiesner's life before the 1980s, when he was a state planner in Colombia and the dean of a fairly ecumenical economics program in Bogotá. Wiesner was no dissident outsider to developmental state-building; he was a product of it.

Wiesner's career in Washington grew from his work in Colombia, and nothing makes that fact clearer than his decades of writing on state decentralization. During the 1990s, he distinguished himself as an authority on the subject, and he and his colleagues at the World Bank presented it as an adjunct to structural adjustment. But Wiesner's interest in the topic dated to the early 1960s, when the National Front was in its infancy and he was a young man. In those days, the CVC was new, and its founders celebrated decentralization as a way to build a developmental state. Living halfway across the country in Bogotá, Wiesner received that message. He first encountered the CVC in 1959 while researching his undergraduate thesis in economics at the Universidad de los Andes. He immediately found himself intrigued not just by the corporation's work but by the form of government it represented. Surveying the country, Wiesner counted at least fifty decentralized public agencies that had sprung up since the 1930s, the great majority of them dating to the 1950s. He decided that it was time to evaluate their performance. Did decentralization serve any purpose or should Bogotá itself do the work of government? In 1963, Wiesner produced los Andes' first economic study of Colombia's autonomous public agencies. Calculating their contributions to state revenue and expenditures, he came to the conclusion that they operated more efficiently than the central government itself. To an economist, the lesson was clear: the public interest demanded an efficient state, and under the circumstances, that meant a decentralized one.[1]

Wiesner could not possibly know it at the time, but this was the very argument that he and the World Bank would use decades later to press governments worldwide to relinquish their functions to localities, departments, and other subnational governments. His path from Bogotá to the World Bank exposed the irony of state-building in mixed economies. From the 1930s to the 1960s, delegation and devolution within and beyond the public sector permitted the US and Colombian governments to assume new responsibilities within extraordinary ideological and material constraints. By the end of the century, decentralization had been reborn as an instrument to reassign and dismantle existing state functions in an era of structural adjustment. In unforeseen ways, the state-building experiments of midcentury developmentalism forged tools that constructed a new political-economic order.

If the Washington Consensus of the 1980s and 1990s represented one conceivable endpoint of midcentury experiments in state restructuring, it was never the only one. Wiesner's arrival at the World Bank in the 1990s was in part a flight from Colombia, where the country's governors, mayors, and new social movements all claimed the concept of decentralization for themselves. Indeed, Wiesner was one of countless Colombians who reimagined and redeployed the practice over the postwar decades. During the 1980s, Colombian politics became a great contest between multiple decentralizing visions that collided with Wiesner's and swiftly transformed the state. By the century's end, the paradigmatic symbols of decentralization in Colombia were no longer the CVC or its 1954 charter but instead a new 1991 constitution and a set of surrounding laws that fused Wiesner's calls for fiscal decentralization with rival programs of political, administrative, and ethnic decentralization. Riddled as it was with contradictions, the new order disappointed many of its architects, including Wiesner himself. Like Lauchlin Currie, he had shaped public debate but lost control of his own concepts. In response, he did what Currie and Lilienthal had both done decades earlier when stymied at home: he cast his sights abroad. The World Bank had always been a vehicle through which Colombian elites pursued their agendas. Its powers had appealed to the CVC's founders during the 1950s, when they faced off against the Rojas regime. Years later, they enticed Wiesner. Having lost his battle in Colombia, he looked northward for a new station from which to make his case.

The Cauca Valley, the CVC, and the mind of one influential official were never singular origin points for the decentralizing reforms of the 1950s or the 1990s, but they are superb vantage points from which to witness new forms of state restructuring and new modes of reasoning emerge from the old.

Wiesner's career reveals the winding, tangled roots of the Washington Consensus, which extended into developmental states themselves. His career reminds us, too, that the Bretton Woods institutions—like the Fund for Multinational Management Education, the International Management and Development Institute, and other US-based institutions that pushed for economic liberalization after 1970—were products of long international exchange. Their officials and founders included Latin American elites who used relationships in the North Atlantic to advance their interests at home. They were imperial institutions, and imperial power is never simply produced in metropoles.

———

During the 1950s, the CVC was born alongside the first economics programs at Colombian universities, and as it became a model development project, it doubled as a training ground for the country's first generation of professional economists. Wiesner belonged to that cohort, and like many within it, his career extended from the heyday of developmentalism into its twilight. Traversing historical epochs, he and his colleagues drew persistently on the peculiar context of their professionalization to craft evolving prescriptions for the state.

For Wiesner, the story began at the Universidad de los Andes. He earned his undergraduate degree there in 1960, and as a star pupil, he received a Rockefeller Foundation scholarship to pursue graduate studies in the United States. After completing a master's degree at Stanford in 1962, he spent most of the next two decades back in Colombia shuttling between government and academia. From 1962 to 1982, Wiesner served as national budget director, finance minister, chief of the National Planning Department, dean of economics at los Andes, and a researcher at the university's prestigious economic research institute, CEDE. When he wrote his study of Colombia's decentralized agencies in 1963, he was CEDE's assistant director and among the most lavishly credentialed economists in the country.[2]

In those days, talk of decentralization was everywhere among economists. The CVC's counterpart in the Bogotá savanna, CAR, had forged close ties to economists at los Andes, enlisting them as researchers for its land reclamation and reform program. Oscar Gómez Villegas, dean of the economics faculty, served on CAR's board. Beginning in 1962, CEDE economists Jorge Ruiz Lara and Rafael Prieto, together with University of Oregon geographer Gene Martin, studied land tenure in CAR's jurisdiction, supported by a grant from the Rockefeller Foundation. Economist Miguel Urrutia worked for CAR studying minifundia in the municipio of Caldas, Boyacá, that same year, just before joining CEDE. As part of his job at CAR, Urrutia visited the CVC in 1962 to study its agricultural extension service. All this is to say that Wiesner's colleagues knew Colombia's decentralized agencies well, and they paid public respect to CAR, the CVC, and even the TVA.[3] In 1960, David Lilienthal sent a copy of his book *TVA: Democracy on the March* to Jorge Franco Holguín, the director of Colombia's National Planning Department and a former economics professor at los Andes. The country's top economic planner immediately read the chapter on decentralization. "The more I think about this problem," Franco wrote to Lilienthal, "the more convinced I am that for a developing economy like Colombia decentralization is imperative."[4]

When Wiesner and his colleagues thought of decentralization, their minds turned not only to regional development corporations but also to a vast constellation of public institutions growing up around los Andes—the wide-ranging entities that Wiesner analyzed in his 1963 study. During the Great Depression, Bogotá had adapted an old tradition of administrative decentralization to charter autonomous public institutions that promoted agriculture, industry, and home building. After 1950, it aggressively extended that pattern of state-building. By Wiesner's count, the number of decentralized agencies quintupled between 1950 and 1963. Across the 1960s and 1970s, these agencies' expenditures grew from 1.4 percent to 20 percent of GNP, and the executive branch of the central state came to comprise at least 105 separate public establishments, twenty state-owned enterprises, and fifteen "mixed" enterprises—all these in addition to the presidency, cabinet ministries, administrative departments, and superintendencies. By 1984, 123 agencies acted on behalf of the national government in the department of Valle alone. They ranged from IN-CORA, the agrarian reform institute, to health and education authorities, to public utilities delivering water, sewer, and electricity services.

These institutions shared broad characteristics with the CVC. All relied principally on national tax revenues and international loans, and their boards enjoyed considerable autonomy in administering those funds. Even the CVC, which collected a local land tax and charged rates for electricity, expanded during the National Front with loans from international financial institutions and foreign governments. Beyond that resemblance, decentralized agencies performed a common political function, displacing municipios and departments as public service providers and centers of power. Just as the CVC had established the natural region as a new jurisdiction in Colombian statecraft, autonomous public agencies imposed their own maps onto national space. Many, like INCORA and the ICT, operated across the entire country but organized their internal activities along lines of their own choosing. Some followed the political boundaries of departments and invited governors to join their boards, while others drew brand new maps. Both choices marginalized the local political system of the municipio, diluted departmental authority, and sidelined party organizations. At midcentury, this arrangement expressed a time-bound vision of peaceable, democratic government under the National Front; it promised to extend technically competent public administration across the country in the name of an elected national state. In a country where both governors and mayors were political appointees, Colombian municipios and departments were hardly models of direct democracy, and decentralized agencies did not exactly roll back representative government. But as the CVC's history suggested, it did insulate essential government functions from political mobilization, shift local balances of power, and allow public officials to pursue deeply unpopular policies. During the 1960s, the powers vested in the CVC had empowered a small group of capitalists to barrel over minifundistas and hostile ranchers who far outnumbered them in the Cauca Valley. Likewise, decentralized water and sewer services across Colombia raised rates that local governments had kept relatively low. The CVC and its peers defended the new structure of the state, the demotion of the municipio, and the increasingly complicated, multilayered map of the country, hailing them as triumphs of clean government over corrupt, violent politics.[5]

In 1963, as this decentralized landscape was still taking shape, Wiesner was rewriting its origins. In doing so, he began to redefine the purpose of decentralization and authorize a distinctive role for economists as disciplinarians of the decentralized state. Projecting his concern for efficiency back in time, Wiesner maintained that Bogotá must have created autonomous institutions in pursuit of that goal. The decision to restructure the state, he explained, "implied a tacit recognition that within the normal *modus operandi* of the government, such activities could not be carried on with the efficiency deemed necessary." In 1954, the CVC had certainly promised to rationalize national policy at the regional level, and Bernardo Garcés Córdoba had hailed private-sector management systems as more efficient than the procedures of public administration. But the Rojas regime had never handed over functions in the name of efficiency. At its founding, the CVC had undertaken new tasks that Bogotá did not perform and had no plan to pursue; there was no comparison of efficiency to make. Even at moments when the corporation did seize existing responsibilities of the central government, as in the 1957 usurpation of CHIDRAL, it did so to consolidate the power of a local elite, not to raise the efficiency of the hydroelectric plant. Wiesner gave decentralization a new origin story, and in doing so, he crafted a new question for policy makers: were agencies living up to their supposed mission, and what mechanisms might encourage them to do so? A decentralized system could function efficiently, he believed, but it could just as well squander resources. What if agencies did their work competently, for instance, but pulled in different directions?

From his office at CEDE, Wiesner searched for sources of efficiency in Colombia's experiment. He was looking for lessons, and he found a few. Like the founders of the CVC, he celebrated agencies' control over personnel policies, which allowed them to evade official pay scales, contain labor costs, and simultaneously attract professionals and managers with high salaries that competed with the private sector. Indeed, in 1962, the CVC exploited its liminal position in the public sector to do even more than that; it barred most of its workers from unionizing by classifying them as *empleados públicos* rather than *trabajadores oficiales*. A minority of CVC employees did belong to a union and spent years fighting that decision without success. Beyond labor relations, Wiesner explored power relations within the state and proposed that Bogotá aggressively leverage them to harmonize policies across the public sector. Many decentralized bodies, including the CVC, named governors or other presidential appointees to their boards, which allowed the central state to exercise a degree of authority. Furthermore, the central government ultimately held the purse strings, controlling the national budget and often retaining powers to review autonomous agencies' budgets and international loan agreements. What conditions might Bogotá impose in exchange for disbursements and authorizations? In 1963, Wiesner made no general recommendations, but he began to imagine a new task for economists. Someone needed to evaluate the internal functioning of the state and devise mechanisms that would induce autonomous institutions to function efficiently.[6]

Wiesner's reinterpretation of decentralization made him a foil to Lilienthal, who spent these same years drawing a different possibility out of developmentalist statecraft. The CVC charter of 1954 had made manifest twin tendencies toward private delegation and regional devolution that pervaded Colombian policymaking and defined the practice of decentralization at midcentury. Lilienthal's subsequent work within the Great Society adapted one of those tendencies: the impulse toward privatization. Wiesner, meanwhile, gave new meaning to regionalism. The CVC's founders had argued that natural regions—the river valley in their case—gave rise to shared problems and a general interest that local technocrats could best address. Wiesner gave no thought to the contours of a river valley, but his depiction of decentralization as an efficiency measure presented a new rationale for the idea that states might function best by dispersing their powers across the national territory. Devolution within the public sector became a solution to an entirely new problem, and in that sense, Wiesner made an existing practice applicable in circumstances that the CVC's founders had never considered.

Over the next two decades, Wiesner continued to study decentralization at home and abroad, becoming a keen observer of states beyond his own. He spent most of these years in Bogotá, but from 1972 to 1976, he lived in

Washington, working first for the OAS and then the Inter-American Development Bank.[7] Staffed largely by Latin Americans, both agencies were Pan-American hubs in the heart of the US capital, and they gave Wiesner a wide view of Latin American statecraft. At the OAS, Wiesner read new research by CEPAL that illuminated the explosive growth of Latin America's "decentralized sector"; from 1959 to 1970, public enterprises and "parastatal" agencies had grown more rapidly than the public sector overall. Wiesner termed these entities the "leading sector" of government and argued that effective development planning required a new understanding of the state as it truly was. He proposed that governments create a new planning tool, a "consolidated budget" that would account for every piece of the public sector, from state enterprises to municipal governments that often evaded national planning and budgeting procedures. "The basic issue is not, obviously, greater or lesser direct control of the [decentralized] sector by the central administration," he explained in 1973, "but the strengthening of conjoined and complementary action."[8]

Wiesner sensed that decentralization could breed chaos, and the CVC's experience ultimately proved him right. The proliferation of decentralized agencies at home made the corporation both a vaunted symbol of the developmental state and a perpetually endangered institution that had to defend itself from competitors. In 1968, the CVC launched a campaign to preserve what it considered the true meaning of decentralization, responding to a constitutional reform that had circumscribed its authority. Colombia's 1968 constitutional reform is often remembered as a decentralizing measure, as it established new semiautonomous national agencies with a common set of regulations, encouraged the definition of new regional jurisdictions, and devolved some health and education funds to departments and municipios.[9] However, the CVC's original powers were so vast that it experienced the measure as an encroachment on its autonomy. The reform created a new national agency, the Instituto Nacional de los Recursos Naturales Renovables y del Ambiente (INDERENA), which competed with the CVC for control of environmental management. To add insult to injury, the constitution required decentralized agencies to respect civil service regulations and submit to oversight in contracting and budgetary matters. Facing indignant protest from the CVC board, the government quickly restored the corporation's regional jurisdiction over environmental management and negotiated agreements that allowed it to continue violating public-sector wage scales and personnel procedures. Nonetheless, the CVC's leaders chafed at having to solicit national approvals and exemptions.[10] José Castro Borrero, who had known Lilienthal since 1954, moaned to him in 1971 that "centralizing measures" had "practically made [the CVC's] former autonomy disappear."[11]

The CVC board spent decades demanding that Bogotá restore their original powers and guarantee the same measure of autonomy to all the country's regional corporations (figure 8.1).[12] They simultaneously expanded their activities, claiming new turf to fend off rivals. During the 1970s, the CVC became a pioneer in the field of environmental management precisely to keep INDERENA out of its jurisdiction. Creating its own Water Pollution Control Section in 1976, the CVC became the first Colombian agency to conduct environmental impact assessments. Institutional power struggles pervaded Colombia's decentralized state; at times, they were motive forces driving the growth of state capacities.[13]

Beyond the CVC, decentralization fomented a different kind of chaos. During the 1970s, Colombia's autonomous agencies began to inspire precisely the forms of local political mobilization they had meant to tame. Between 1971 and 1985, Colombian public-sector unions and urban consumers launched two hundred civic strikes that paralyzed cities across the country. At their largest in 1977 and 1981, the *paros cívicos* became national general strikes and met with ferocious repression from the army and police. These mobilizations, which involved shifting coalitions of trade unions, neighborhood organizations, professional associations, and left-wing parties and guerrilla movements excluded from the National Front, channeled widespread discontent with inadequate public services, labor conditions in the public sector, and declining real wages among urban workers. Because decentralized agencies had assumed such wide-ranging public responsibilities, they became explicit targets of the upheavals. Some of the emblematic conflicts of the 1970s recapitulated the CVC's earlier battles and revealed the corporation's relative strength among decentralized agencies. In 1976, during a massive strike of public-sector health care workers, medical providers employed by the Instituto Colombiano de Seguros Sociales (ICSS) walked off the job. They were protesting the institute's attempt to strip them of labor rights by reclassifying them, turning *trabajadores oficiales* into *empleados públicos*. This was precisely the legal maneuver that the CVC had effected in 1962, mobilizing its ambiguous status within the public sector to bar its employees from unionizing. While the CVC had won that battle during the 1960s, institutions following the same script faced crises of legitimacy a decade later. As the sixteen-year National Front ended, the conflicts it had cultivated turned explosive. From 1974 through 1982, the Liberal administrations of Alfonso López Michelsen (1974–78) and Julio César Turbay Ayala (1978–82) issued a succession of decrees to contain and repress urban protest, culminating in Turbay's infamous 1978 Security Statute, which granted the military powers to enforce public order in cities nationwide.[14]

Eduardo Wiesner and Miguel Urrutia found themselves at the center of these disputes during the 1970s, when each served as chairman of the National

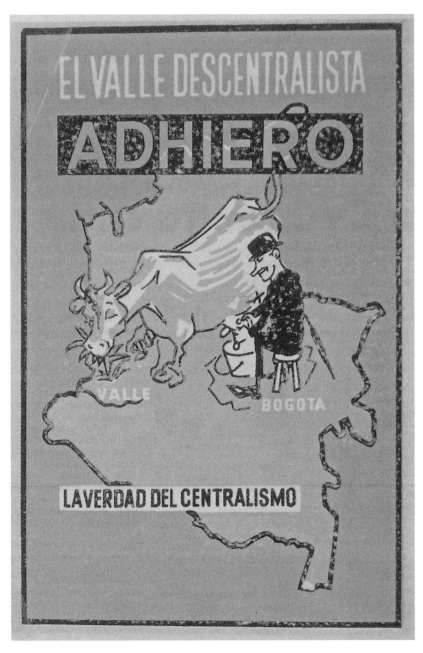

FIGURE 8.1. "I'm Sticking with the Decentralist Valley." An image from the CVC's post-1968 decentralization campaign exposes "the truth of centralism" by depicting a Bogotano businessman milking a cow symbolizing the agriculturally rich Cauca Valley.
(*Génesis y desarrollo de una visión de progreso* [Cali: CVC, 2004], 86)

Planning Department. López Michelsen appointed Urrutia in 1974, and Turbay chose Wiesner four years later. In what the CVC saw as another attack on its autonomy, the government had by that time placed the corporation under the planning department, and so these two economists automatically became chairmen of the CVC board. Both arrived as long-standing admirers of the corporation and as representatives of administrations desperately afraid that the decentralized state might collapse. Urrutia vigorously defended the CVC's autonomy in conflicts over control of the electrical sector, and throughout 1978 and 1979, Wiesner threw his weight behind an unsuccessful effort to introduce an "autonomy bill" restoring the corporation's original powers. The bill's still-birth revealed Wiesner's admiration for the CVC's antiunion record and his enduring view of decentralization as a cost-containing strategy. As he explained to the CVC's executive director, he had brought the proposed legislation to President Turbay and backed down only because he realized that releasing all regional corporations from public-sector personnel procedures would invite union mobilization and strikes, raising labor costs. While the CVC "had enough maturity to manage these situations," other regional corporations did not, and the government could hardly afford "disorderly growth in the workforce and unmanageable situations with respect to a union." According to Wiesner, decentralized institutions could only wield broad powers if they contained organized labor as effectively as the CVC did.[15]

By the late 1970s, economists trained in the 1950s and 1960s realized that the decentralized state had become a source of social upheaval rather than efficiency and order. Their disappointment emboldened them. Rather than forsake decentralization, many took up the task that Wiesner had assigned economists in 1963: they began to imagine new ways of configuring the decentralized state to make it the efficient machine they had always believed it could be. Turning over decentralization in their minds, fashioning their own wisdom from the past, Colombian economists began to adapt this characteristic mid-century practice to new problems.

There was no shortage of examples with which to reason. In 1976, Miguel Urrutia grasped for policy ideas as chief of President López Michelsen's National Planning Department. Reaching back in time, he proposed that Bogotá deal with striking teachers and doctors by taking a lesson from the old Ministry of Public Works. Since the 1930s and 1940s, that cabinet ministry had operated by private contract. Now that public services had overtaken industry and infrastructure as objects of planning, why not apply the same principle to education, health, sanitation, and every other government function? Urrutia's recommendation grew from a peculiar diagnosis of labor conflict in the 1970s. He attributed Colombia's public-sector strikes to the sheer size of the national state, reasoning that "it is very difficult to maintain good human relations in large enterprises." Looking beyond Colombia, Urrutia contended that governments across the North Atlantic faced the same problem: large bureaucracies had produced strikes in New York City, protests at the University of California, and "the events of 1968" in France. In truth, none of those uprisings owed in any simple way to the size or centralization of the state. The strikes that rocked New York in 1976 responded to devastating budget cuts imposed after the city's 1975 fiscal crisis. Students protested in Berkeley and Paris as part of international mobilizations against war and imperialism, consumer capitalism, racism, and censorship. Urrutia's judgment revealed more about the world that had formed him than the movements he was observing. To the extent that current realities shaped his thought, he was struck by the French government's *response* to May 1968: it sought to undermine student organizing by dividing the university system into smaller campuses. For Urrutia, decentralization appeared both a time-honored practice in Colombia and a manifestly useful solution to contemporary crises of public order.

Drawing idiosyncratic lessons from Colombia in the 1930s and Paris in 1968, Urrutia proposed to end his country's labor conflicts by breaking up the public sector and managing workers in smaller groups. Bogotá could either devolve responsibilities to subnational governments or, like the Ministry of Public Works, outsource functions to private contractors. Urrutia discussed both practices as forms of decentralization, explaining that in either case, the national state would finance public services while allowing others to deliver them. Municipios could run public schools, or the government could leave education entirely to private schools and offer tuition vouchers to poor families. ICSS, whose doctors were on strike as Urrutia wrote, could simply stop employing health care workers. Why not offer money to patients, "letting them choose the doctor and the quality of service?" Urrutia proposed a radical restructuring of the public sector, and yet he persistently identified the mid-century state itself as the source of his ideas.[16]

As for Wiesner, he began his ascent as an expert on state decentralization in 1981. He stepped down that year from Turbay's National Planning Department, and with it the CVC board, to become Colombia's finance minister. In his new position, Wiesner's immediate concern was the Latin American debt crisis, which he viewed through his long-standing concern with popular mobilization. Extending arguments of the 1970s, Wiesner attributed Colombia's "fiscal imbalance" to excessive government spending, which he argued had a "political origin." Pointing to a decade of urban uprisings, Wiesner held that Colombians had forced the government to spend excessively on public health, education, security, and the justice system. While he recognized the importance of those services, he accused Colombians of making unsustainable demands around "immediate, regional, sectoral, and particular interests" without considering their long-term, national budgetary implications. Wiesner never saw himself as a state killer but as a defender of a state in danger of collapse. In this context, he redeployed the idea of decentralization, heralding it as a way to attain "fiscal balance" by curbing political mobilization. His argument went beyond Urrutia's. Departmental and municipal governments should certainly channel national funds and organize services, he believed, but they should also raise their own revenues. Devolving administrative responsibility as well as fiscal obligations would limit Colombians' ability to make political demands in Bogotá and force local groups that received public benefits to face the responsibility of paying for them.[17]

Nothing outraged Wiesner more than Colombia's educational finance system, its teachers' unions, and its student movements. In his eyes, education policy had become a bastion of centralism and a dangerous stimulus to urban protest. In 1975, Congress had mandated that the national Ministry of Education begin paying a portion of secondary-school teachers' salaries. The central state pledged to increase its share of payments until eventually it contributed the equivalent of teachers' entire 1975 salaries. Freeing local governments from that expense, Congress hoped they would spend more on other educational needs, increasing total investments in schooling. Yet local governments never responded as intended. Instead, educators and their unions pushed Bogotá to increase salary payments beyond 1975 levels, and local governments failed to come up with new revenues for education. By the early 1980s, Wiesner considered teachers scandalously overpaid, Bogotá's spending uncontrolled, and other public functions starved by supposedly self-interested union members. Refusing to acknowledge any justice in the demands of organized labor, he dismissed national budget guarantees as naive encouragement to rapacious popular organizations. "For what strange reason could it be," he asked drily, "that as more resources are devoted to teachers, the more radical the union situation is in that sector, and the less public order is observed in public universities?"[18]

In 1981, Wiesner solicited the first major report recommending fiscal decentralization in Colombia. Rather than write it himself, Wiesner did what Colombians had always done: he recruited a distinguished international authority to dispense his chosen advice. Economist Richard M. Bird of Harvard Law School's International Tax Program had studied Colombia's tax system since the 1960s, and Wiesner assembled a distinguished commission of Colombian economists to work with him. The resulting study, known as the Bird-Wiesner report, indicted Colombia's existing system of intergovernmental finance and called for a new one. Bird captured the mercurial quality of state-building since the 1930s, documenting the many ways that Bogotá had expanded its functions by chartering decentralized or "parastatal" agencies. Like Wiesner, he cast

Colombia's intricate system of delegating money and power as a source of waste and disorder. Localities pushed escalating costs onto Bogotá, he explained, while failing to generate revenues themselves. Bird highlighted the CVC, as well as electrical utilities in Bogotá and Cali, as exceptions to the rule. "They have generally had a good financial record; they have received a good deal of foreign credit (for instance, from the World Bank); and they have received very little direct national budgetary support." But the rest of the "parastatal sector" demanded too much and delivered too little, Bird contended. The fiscal burdens it imposed on the nation—"direct budgetary transfers, earmarked taxes, the cancellation of debts, and loan guarantees"—had become unbearable.[19]

Wiesner publicly hailed the report as the beginning of a new era in Colombian statecraft. In doing so, he helped to consolidate a new retrospective understanding of the developmental state. "Parastatal" agencies that had once symbolized decentralization and autonomy now appeared as symbols of centralism—mere extensions of the central government, and profligate ones at that. The report identified departments and municipios as alternative entities—true representatives of decentralization—that could become primary instruments of statecraft, raising revenues and exercising power separately from Bogotá. Standing on their own feet, they would conserve resources that older agencies had wasted. Wiesner's prologue to the study associated midcentury governance with "the naïve and simplistic belief that problems can be solved by throwing money at them." In his telling, the developmental state was an improvident leviathan—labyrinthine to be sure, but all roads led to Bogotá, all money flowed from it, and all problems demanded more from it. Wiesner lauded Bird for helping Colombia dispense with these ideas. "No amount of public revenues can suffice to offset expenditures whose expansion is frequently uncontrolled and whose execution is unsupervised," he asserted. "The new idea that we wanted to bring to life was that, although the amount of government revenues is important, what really counts in the long term is the efficiency with which revenues are distributed, transferred, and used."[20]

The Bird-Wiesner report captured the ideas of economists who had grown up with the midcentury decentralized state, admired it, and honed a professionally distinctive way of analyzing it in terms of efficiency. When they found it wanting in the 1970s, they sought to design a new decentralized system that would finally live up to the promise the midcentury state had made. That very effort—to define and defend the supposedly true and best form of decentralization—made it impossible to acknowledge their analytic and political debt to the order they sought to replace.

The Bird-Wiesner report appeared in 1981, a year before Wiesner left Colombia to work for the IMF. As Western Hemisphere director of the fund from

1982 to 1987, he negotiated structural adjustment programs across Latin America. It was an infamous undertaking, not least because many of the officials sitting across the table were struggling to consolidate democracies after the fall of military dictatorships. Wiesner and the IMF spent these years winnowing the promises that democracy could make. Indeed, his most publicized act at the IMF occurred in 1984, when he flew to Argentina and personally demanded that the government of Raúl Alfonsín cut public-sector wages. Alfonsín had won election a year earlier vowing to restore labor rights that Argentines had lost during seven years of military rule. The *New York Times* devoted an entire article to the apparent puzzle of Eduardo Wiesner: how could an architect of Colombia's developmental state issue these prescriptions? Wiesner's career had in fact prepared him for the task.[21]

———

Wiesner's years in Washington were years of crisis in Colombia. National politics in the 1980s became a mad scramble for power; presidents, governors, mayors, both major parties, and the country's web of decentralized agencies all struggled to sustain themselves in the face of civic strikes, guerrilla violence, drug trafficking, failed peace negotiations, budding indigenous and Afro-Colombian mobilizations, and international pressure to cut the growing deficit. Strikingly, a remarkable number of those locked in combat believed they could realize their goals through some form of state decentralization. The conflicts of the 1980s generated multiple versions of an old midcentury practice, and by the 1990s, the collision of those competing programs remade the Colombian state. The Colombian dissidents who challenged the government during these years were not unlike Cali's businessmen of the 1950s, who had restructured the state to assign themselves coveted public powers. Likewise, the new self-styled reformers in the Liberal and Conservative Parties shared one insight of the National Front's founders, who had considered decentralization a way to extend the reach and legitimacy of a weak, embattled state. In both the 1950s and the 1980s, decentralization seemed an answer to crises of political violence, public disorder, and a lack of territorial control. The difference was this: the newfound decentralizers of the 1980s proposed to strip power from the very institutions the National Front had nurtured, reassigning authority and resources to municipios, departments, and newly defined ethnic communities. In other words, the question that consumed the country was not merely what the central government should do, but through which organs it should act and which social formations deserved political recognition. Colombian politics was a struggle between competing decentralizing visions.

Decentralization became a central object of politics because the government declared it so. Conservative president Belisario Betancur (1982–86) and Liberal Virgilio Barco (1986–90) spent their years in office advancing decentralization measures to tame the debt crisis and an increasingly brutal armed conflict. Although Colombia's fiscal deficit and international debt burden were never as large as those of its neighbors, the country suffered with all of Latin America when Mexico defaulted on its debt in 1982 and creditors cut off the entire region. Meanwhile, the constriction of cocaine trafficking in Chile during the 1970s had pushed that business northward. Colombia became a center of the international narcotics trade during the 1980s, and new urban drug cartels brought both right-wing paramilitaries and left-wing guerrillas into the work. Cocaine smuggling generated staggering levels of violence and crime, and when cartels began channeling money to political candidates, they corroded what little legitimacy the state had left. During the 1980s, these intertwined crises remade the reputation of a country once known for many things. In the postwar world, Colombia had earned fame and ignominy as a showcase of the Alliance for Progress, a model of anticommunist democracy, an exemplar of economic stability, a devoted US ally, and, of course, the home of perpetual armed conflict and attempts at pacification. During the 1980s, it acquired a narrower, almost singular reputation as a notorious international capital of political assassination, kidnapping, and corruption.

Presidents Betancur and Barco met these challenges in part with peace negotiations, aiming to demobilize leftist guerrillas in the FARC, Nineteenth of April Movement (M-19), Ejército Popular de Liberación (EPL), and Communist Party. But the talks proved spasmodic, and by 1990, only the M-19 and the EPL had laid down their weapons. The FARC and Communist Party recoiled from the peace process after thousands of their members did demobilize in 1985 to form a political party, the Unión Patriótica. Right-wing opponents assassinated as many as three thousand of the party's leaders during the next five years, making peace appear little more than a death sentence.[22]

As peace talks faltered, decentralization became the state's second chosen instrument. Both Betancur and Barco considered the 1981 Bird-Wiesner report a blueprint for ending the fiscal and debt crises. Meanwhile, reformist mayors and members of the Liberal and Conservative Parties in Congress believed that allowing wider participation in municipal politics could reestablish popular identification with the state. All of these ideas expressed a vision of decentralization quite different from Lilienthal's. Indeed, by the 1980s, the leading exponents of decentralization were no longer the leaders of the CVC but figures like Wiesner who had derived their own novel definitions of decentralization from long experience inside the midcentury state. For this generation of Colombians, municipios and departments appeared authentic alternatives to centralized power, while the paradigmatic decentralized agencies of the midcentury era seemed mere agents of Bogotá. The goal of new decentralizing reforms, then, was to transfer responsibilities away from an older set of decentralized institutions to new ones.

Betancur launched a program of fiscal decentralization, aiming to convert the Bird-Wiesner report into reality. Law 14 of 1983 reformed the tax system to raise more revenue at the municipal and departmental levels. Law 12 of 1986 devolved a growing portion of the national sales tax to municipios and charged them with administering a widening range of public programs. An austere budget slashed public-sector salaries and overall government expenditures. And the president appointed a blue-ribbon Comisión del Gasto Público, whose 1986 report extended the Bird-Wiesner recommendations. Alongside these fiscal measures, Betancur championed political decentralization. Responding to the calls of mayors, he approved a 1986 constitutional reform that ushered in the direct election of mayors for the first time in a century. A year later, President Barco accelerated the process of administrative decentralization. Decrees 78 to 81 of 1987 tasked municipios with delivering a host of public services, including water, sanitation, and infrastructure development for health and education systems.[23]

The reforms of the mid-1980s reoriented national political debate. Everyone seeking power in Colombia—from the CVC guarding its powers to popular organizations and guerrilla movements vying for new ones—had to decide whether this particular reconfiguration offered them anything. For the CVC, the answer was clear. In January 1987, the board ticked off the functions of regional corporations that Law 12 of 1986 threatened to hand to municipal governments: electrical service, reforestation, and the construction of water and sewage systems. Board members could breathe a small sigh of relief; the National Planning Department recognized the CVC's unusually strong record in delivering services and suggested that it alone might retain those responsibilities. But the law aimed to strip nearly every other regional corporation of powers that the CVC had fought tooth and nail to protect. For the CVC, the new reforms compounded old threats, and the corporation spent 1987 and 1988 securing exemptions and drafting yet another bill to restore its "lost autonomy."[24]

The CVC faced stiff competition, not only from presidents, governors, and mayors but also from emergent indigenous and Afro-Colombian movements. During the 1970s, indigenous people in Colombia, like their counterparts across Latin America, had begun to speak politically as ethnic groups and had launched their own organizations apart from older institutions of the left. The transformation of indigenous politics in the Cauca Valley was illustrative. From the 1930s to the 1960s, indigenous activists in the department of Cauca had mobilized within peasant leagues, left-wing political parties, guerrilla movements, and popular organizations sponsored by the Liberal Party. Their affiliations reflected a keen sensitivity to national policy and political institutions. In decades when the Colombian state promised land titles to smallholders, when the National Front fostered mass organization as a method of governance, and when the left proposed to mobilize rural laborers across lines of race, Cauca's indigenous activists took up their offers. But during the early 1970s, all these avenues turned to dead ends. The Conservative Pastrana government spurned the 1961 agrarian reform law, and the left-wing parties, campesino organizations, and guerrilla movements of the 1960s suffered mounting repression and internal division. In 1971, the Cauca Valley became the birthplace of Colombia's first indigenous organization, the Consejo Regional Indígena del Cauca (CRIC). CRIC's founding congress brought together veterans of an embattled left to seek a new way forward.

CRIC's pioneering innovation of the 1970s was to reformulate old claims around land and labor in ethnic terms. Muting the language of class conflict that permeated campesino and left-wing organizations, CRIC's members began to represent themselves as ethnic citizens whose distinctive history and legal status entitled them to land. Haltingly over the course of the decade, they reimagined their histories and solidarities. CRIC resurrected the memory, program, and appeals of Manuel Quintín Lame, a leader of the Nasa people who had organized uprisings in Cauca and Tolima during the 1910s. And it set to work reinventing institutions of the prerepublican past: collective landholdings (*resguardos*) and autonomous governing councils (*cabildos*). Organizers unearthed colonial-era land titles, invaded private property that they claimed as theirs, and ousted older cabildo officials who operated as party clients. By 1973, CRIC had reconstituted seventeen resguardos in Cauca; a decade later, it had extended its sights into Valle, asserting rights to fertile sugar plantations.[25]

During the 1980s, CRIC became one of a constellation of indigenous organizations throughout Colombia that claimed economic resources and political autonomy as inalienable rights of ethnicity. Their example contributed to a dramatic transformation of Afro-Colombian politics. Historically, Latin Americans had conceived of indigenous and Afro-descendant populations in different terms. In Colombian law and letters, indigenous status had defined the limits of national culture, sovereignty, and territory. Afro-descendant people had never experienced quite the same acknowledgment of difference, with all of its punishments and latent possibilities. They contended with another form of racism that denied slavery's enduring legacies in Colombian society and cast Afro-Colombians as primitive members of a mestizo nation. As indigenous organizations made gains during the 1980s and 1990s,

Afro-Colombians began to mobilize under the rubric of ethnic rights, and Colombians began to debate their status within the nation.[26]

Colombia's indigenous and Afro-Colombian organizations forged their own critiques of municipal decentralization. As power shifted from Bogotá to municipios, these social movements argued that precious resources and responsibilities were passing right over their heads. The Movimiento de Autoridades Indígenas del Suroccidente, representing indigenous people in the southwestern departments of Cauca, Nariño, and Putumayo, condemned municipios as invading powers. During the 1980s, some municipios went so far as to create new corregimientos inside resguardos, converting indigenous land into ordinary rural settlements. In the eastern department of Meta, Jorge Flórez Flórez of the Guahibo (Sikuani) people decried new mayoral elections as rigged affairs in which party leaders chose candidates, funded campaigns, and left indigenous people with only the illusion of choice. Meanwhile, newly empowered local governments hoarded resources in urban centers while starving indigenous resguardos. In Flórez's own municipio of Puerto Gaitán, indigenous people made up the majority of the population but in 1991 received just 4 percent of the local budget for electrification, housing, school buildings, water, and health centers. In the eyes of Lorenzo Muelas Hurtado, a Guambiano leader from Cauca, centralism had never gone away; the ascent of municipios had simply reproduced power relations that indigenous people had faced since colonial times. For five hundred years, "we have had to live between colonial haciendas and *municipios*," he asserted. "'*Municipio*' is contrary to countryside, to campesino, to Indians; the municipio has been nothing but an area of expansion for the center of urban power," Muelas Hurtado contended.[27]

As decentralizing reforms rained down on them, indigenous organizations recast their own demands for sovereignty as true expressions of the decentralizing impulse. "We understand the decentralization process . . . as a challenge that we must confront and conquer," declared Roque Arévalo and Joaquín Herrera of the Organización Uitoto del Caquetá, Amazonas y Putumayo. Cabildos were "public entities" that merited national resources and autonomy, they insisted. Alberto Mendoza Morales of the Asociación Nacional de Pescadores a Pequeña Escala o Artesanales de Colombia hailed the resguardo as a "model of decentralization and self-government." In fact, he suggested that it should become the prototype of political authority for all of Colombia. "The resguardo resembles a municipio, but not because the resguardo descends to the quality of the municipio," he explained. Rather, indigenous forms of collective property ethically outshone the minifundio system that prevailed elsewhere in Colombia. "The resguardo appears, then, as the model for the municipio."[28]

In 1990, these competing notions of decentralization collided when President Barco called on Colombians to rewrite the 1886 constitution. It was a desperate attempt to stabilize a state in crisis. Together, he and incoming Liberal president César Gaviria (1990–94) charged Colombians with throwing open the state and reconstructing it.[29]

The National Constituent Assembly elected in 1991 was an unruly gathering of every faction in Colombian politics. It included three indigenous delegates who spoke for a vast collection of ethnic organizations. Afro-Colombian social movements had no formal delegates but found advocates in indigenous delegates Francisco Rojas Birry (Emberá) and Lorenzo Muelas Hurtado (Guambiano), as well as anthropologist Orlando Fals Borda, a representative of the demobilized M-19. As the constituent assembly began meeting in February 1991, these three men joined a parallel three-day summit of indigenous and Afro-Colombian leaders from every corner of Colombia. Gathering in Cali, they denounced existing forms of decentralization and proposed to reinvent the practice by transferring power to ethnic communities. Trismila Rentería, speaking for the Comité de Organizaciones de Base en Buenaventura, argued that Afro-Colombians should become the CVC's supervisors and evaluators. Rojas Birry advanced a new concept of "ethnic decentralization." Anthropologists Nina de Friedemann and Jaime Arocha, pioneers in the study of Afro-Colombian history and culture, spoke alongside representatives of the country's largest Afro-Colombian organizations, Cimarrón and the Centro para la Investigación y el Desarrollo de la Cultura Negra.[30]

Meanwhile, the Colombian Federation of Mayors lobbied for its own notion of decentralization, calling on the constituent assembly to increase budget transfers to municipios. The proposal appalled ethnic organizations and regional corporations alike. In March 1991, the CVC board watched in horror as the delegates in Bogotá considered dissolving regional corporations entirely and transferring their powers to municipios. The corporation and allied delegates from Valle launched a countervailing lobbying campaign to preserve the natural region of the river valley as a jurisdiction governed by the autonomous regional corporation.[31]

Not to be outdone, advocates of fiscal decentralization made their own play for power. The delegates to the National Constituent Assembly included economist Guillermo Perry, who had served as one of the Colombian consultants to the 1981 Bird-Wiesner report. The president himself, César Gaviria, was an economist trained at the Universidad de los Andes during the late 1960s, when Wiesner had been dean of the economics faculty. As the constituent assembly met, Gaviria appointed Wiesner chair of a new national Mission for Decentralization, which formulated its own recommendations and met with delegates.[32]

Colombia's new constitution of 1991 chaotically fused these ideas, bringing within the state conflicts that had once surrounded it. At the insistence of M-19 delegates, the document provided for the direct election of governors, a measure that outraged mayors fearful of departmental authority. Nevertheless, both mayors and governors rallied around new fiscal measures that increased automatic budget transfers from Bogotá to departments and municipios alike. The payments financed education and health programs, guaranteeing that subnational governments would not receive new administrative responsibilities without revenues to cover them. Ironically, this guarantee ran against Wiesner's long insistence that Bogotá already bore too much responsibility for local spending.[33]

For their part, indigenous and Afro-Colombian communities made remarkable gains. For the first time, the 1991 constitution declared Colombia a multiethnic, pluricultural state and established that ethnic groups possessed distinctive rights to land. Indigeneity and colonialism remained fundamental concepts through which Colombians understood ethnicity, and the constitution therefore made divergent promises to indigenous and Afro-Colombian people. On the one hand, indigenous resguardos attained clear status as inalienable ethnic territory constitutive of collective existence rather than private property subject to ordinary contestation and commerce. Resguardos further became political jurisdictions entitled to national budget transfers and local autonomy; cabildos could establish their own laws consistent with the constitution, craft development plans, and veto outside proposals to exploit natural resources. By contrast, the constitution and subsequent enabling legislation, Law 70 of 1993, made more constrained offers to Afro-Colombians. They established collective property rights (rather than inalienable territorial rights) to untitled lands in the Pacific region so long as residents conformed to a defined image of ethnic difference; they had to use "traditional practices of production" and display markers of cultural distinction derived from notions of indigeneity. Beyond the Pacific, the constitution promised land and political representation to Afro-descendant Raizals who lived on the islands of San Andrés, Providencia, and Santa Catalina. Finally, the 1993 law allowed Afro-descendant people in every region of Colombia to claim the same rights as those in the Pacific so long as they resembled that region's protected riverine communities. Together, the constitution and Law 70 codified new, exacting terms on which Afro-Colombians could claim ethnic authenticity, and with it material resources and political power. In turn, it established terms on which all Colombians came to scrutinize Afro-Colombians and reconceive their place within the nation.[34]

The CVC, too, emerged transformed. Its lobbying prevented the constituent assembly from dissolving the country's seventeen regional corporations, but the constitution reinvented their purposes and powers. The document established new foundations for Colombian environmental law, and in its service, Law 99 of 1993 created a Ministry of the Environment and thirty-four new regional autonomous corporations to manage environmental affairs. The government abolished INDERENA, the environmental agency that had bedeviled the CVC since 1968, and handed its responsibilities to the ministry, which oversaw the regional corporations. The CVC and its peers thus outlived their midcentury competitor and attained status and security in the new decentralized state. But their subordination to the ministry reproduced long-standing struggles over labor, contracting, and budgeting procedures, which the CVC considered the essence of autonomy. Moreover, the 1993 law redefined the work of regional corporations, limiting them to environmental stewardship and cutting them out of electricity generation and distribution. In 1994, the CVC was forced to surrender its electricity program to a separate public utility that was quickly privatized. For an agency that had spent its formative years fighting to control the electrical sector, it was a bitter pill to swallow. The CVC had strategically fashioned itself an environmental authority in the 1970s to protect a much wider set of powers. It had never imagined that a new constitutional order might convert that newfound capacity into an exclusive mission.[35]

As the CVC's responsibilities shrank, its board grew. Law 70 of 1993, which delineated Afro-Colombian ethnic rights, required regional autonomous corporations to include a black representative on their boards if their jurisdictions included collective Afro-Colombian landholdings. The CVC held its first election for an Afro-Colombian board member in 1995, and the proceedings drew a raucous crowd of Afro-Colombian organizations jockeying for position. In the newly declared multiethnic state, the corporation had become a site of contestation, not just between former insiders and outsiders but also among ethnic citizens debating their political strategies and solidarities under the auspices of public procedures.[36]

The new decentralized state contained profound contradictions, both because it incorporated conflicting ideals and because it retained notable features of midcentury decentralization. The map of Colombia remained a palimpsest, with municipios, departments, regional corporations, and ethnic communities all stamping their jurisdictions onto the same national space. River valleys became subject to two competing logics as both regional autonomous corporations and ethnic authorities exercised powers of environmental management. Along the banks of the Cauca River and westward to the Pacific coast, the CVC never abandoned its pursuit of growth and productivity, but it faced indigenous and Afro-Colombian organizations that redefined productivity as just one possible means to new ends; in their view, the true and final purpose of development was to produce a multiethnic society.[37] In recognizing both of these political formations, the new Colombian state enshrined a doubled conception of land as ethnic territory and an ordinary factor of production; seen in light of the CVC's history, this was perhaps the most profound contradiction of the new order. Decades earlier, the National Front and the CVC had made sure that the only argument the state would hear in land conflicts was an appeal to growth and productivity. In that context, smallholders could never win property claims against large landowners armed with tractors and fertilizer. The people who lost the battles of the 1960s never fashioned a head-on critique of growth or productivity. Instead, in unforeseen and perhaps more human ways, they reacted to dispossession and defeat by reconceiving their histories and solidarities, claiming for themselves the terms of their opponents, and availing themselves of a moment of crisis to inscribe in law an alternate way of reasoning about land, one that made it possible to contest growth without ever naming it. The order that emerged in the 1990s never displaced everything that came before but instead layered institutions and logics, with ethnic groups appearing as new agents of governance alongside rehabilitated development agencies of the midcentury order. Concern for productivity never dissipated, but land redistribution became possible, at least in principle, under a coexisting rubric of ethnic rights.

———

Among the architects of the new decentralized state, no one emerged more ambivalent than Eduardo Wiesner. The question he had posed in the early 1960s—not whether to decentralize, but how to do so—had become everyone's question by the 1990s, and the collision of decentralizing visions had corrupted his program. Wiesner spent 1991 advising the constituent assembly as chair of Gaviria's Mission for Decentralization, and in 1992, the mission's final report conveyed deep concern that the new order might prove as inefficient as the old. Indeed, the Colombian state grew relentlessly under the new constitution. Between 1992 and 1998, nonfinancial government expenditures rose from 25.8 to 37.2 percent of GDP. Total tax revenues nearly doubled from 1990 to 2007, from 8.2 to 16.2 percent of GDP. And while subnational governments began to raise slightly more money on their own, their contributions fell as a proportion of overall taxation. In other words, municipios and departments came to rely on ever-growing financial transfers from Bogotá, and they spent them according to priorities dictated in the capital. The new fiscal system, Richard M. Bird lamented in 2012, was old-fashioned centralism in disguise, "delegation rather than devolution."[38]

Wiesner's inability to control the form that decentralization ultimately took gave him a special role in the post-1991 order. He became, on a permanent basis, what he had accidentally become while doing other things: an expert evaluator of the state. Looking out from the country, he parlayed his experience at home and at the IMF to become a consultant to the World Bank. There he contributed to the "second-generation" reforms of the 1990s, which complemented the IMF's harsh macroeconomic policies of the previous decade. Wiesner and his colleagues at the Bank acknowledged that structural adjustment had failed to produce growth, alleviate poverty, and reduce inequality, but they argued that the problem lay in Latin America, not in the IMF's prescriptions. According to the Bank, Latin American systems of public administration, law, and social policy had undermined structural adjustment, and the continent needed a new round of reforms to remake those institutions. Wiesner emerged in this context as an authority on two topics involved in state restructuring: decentralization and the evaluation of public administration. It was a role he was well prepared to play.[39]

Wiesner carried to the World Bank arguments he had honed over decades. In 1982, he had declared that Colombia's "fiscal imbalance" had a "political origin"; the strikes of the 1970s had driven up public expenditures and channeled them to those he dismissed as the loudest, least public-minded, and best organized. He had held fast to that conviction at the IMF, arguing in the mid-1980s that the Latin American debt crisis stemmed from deep political roots, not merely the immediate provocations of aggressive foreign lending, rising interest rates, or an international recession.[40] He arrived at the World Bank's Office of Operations Evaluation in 1993; it was a moment when the whole world seemed in flux, but his ideas held firm. As Wiesner explained in 1997, states should hold down the cost of public services by destroying the power of both political machines and public-sector unions. His definition of efficiency denied the legitimacy of collective action that increased public expenditures and recognized no ethical difference between unions negotiating decent wages and patronage networks funneling money to their members. Pointing to his old nemeses in Colombia, Wiesner condemned unionized teachers and telecommunications workers as rent seekers looting the public. Only competition could improve government services, he maintained, but public-sector workers and their employers acted as "monopolists" keeping others out of the market. Their ultimate victims were Colombia's poor, whom Wiesner said paid too much for thoroughly inadequate public services.[41] By 1998, Guillermo Perry had joined him as a consultant to the World Bank, making the very same points. In two coauthored books on decentralization and public-sector reform, Perry denounced Colombia's growing budget transfers for health and education and accused teachers' unions of pursuing narrow self-interest at the expense of schools' "clients" and "beneficiaries." His proposed solutions included school vouchers, charter schools, and merit pay that pegged teachers' salaries to test scores.[42]

These ideas defined the Bretton Woods institutions during the late twentieth century, earning them the epithet *neoliberal* and drawing throngs of protesters to their annual meetings. Seen from the vantage point of Colombia rather than Washington, DC, their origins look rather surprising. In 1982, when Wiesner left Colombia for the IMF, he had come to these convictions through his experience inside Colombia's decentralized state, initially as an admiring analyst and later a sympathetic internal critic who feared for the state's survival. He had drawn tenaciously on the concepts and institutions that surrounded him, adapting and reinterpreting the ideas that had built the midcentury state. His training as an economist in a heterodox intellectual environment had given him a rather generic interest in efficiency but no exceptional theoretical or methodological orientation. In 1982, Wiesner owned no notable debts to intellectual communities often credited with dismantling the midcentury order—the Chicago School, public choice theorists, the Mont Pelerin Society, or the wider schools of Austrian and neoclassical economics. He had lived a cosmopolitan life, but he was a homegrown decentralizer.

The Bretton Woods institutions did give Wiesner a few things: wider authority, new intellectual relationships, and with them, an altered vocabulary that made his ideas clearly legible in US policy debates. Wiesner's colleagues at the IMF included the protagonists of most stories about neoliberalism, from Jeffrey Sachs to Martin Feldstein. By 1991, Wiesner sought advice for the Mission for Decentralization from old colleagues like Richard M. Bird as well as newer acquaintances like James Buchanan, a leading exponent of public choice theory. The report extended ideas that Wiesner had developed for years but explicitly reframed them as expressions of public choice theory.[43] Wiesner's intellectual community widened once more when he collaborated with the World Bank's Operations Evaluation group in 1993. His colleagues there were new institutional economists led by director general Robert Picciotto. Working in the tradition of Douglass North, Ronald Coase, and Oliver Williamson, this group diverged from both the neoclassical and original institutionalist schools within the economics profession. Economic activity, its members claimed, was conditioned by "institutions," by which they meant all formal and informal constraints on human behavior, from laws to religious ideas. Unlike the original institutionalists, these economists barely modified neoclassical assumptions about human behavior, believing that individuals responded rationally to incentives. "Most authors," explained Wiesner, "perceive neoinstitutional economics as a broadening of the neoclassical model to deal with situational constraints." People would behave as they do in neoclassical text-books, he suggested, if their social context actually conformed to the assumptions of neoclassical theory—if they enjoyed secure private property rights and ready access to information, if they could effortlessly make and enforce contracts, and so forth. Wiesner and Picciotto granted neoclassical economists their claim that a radically competitive society could satisfy human needs, but they pointed out that no such society existed. For Wiesner, Picciotto, and their colleagues within the World Bank, that insight inspired an effort to redesign government to create the conditions that neoclassical economists assumed to exist. It simultaneously prompted them to treat government itself as susceptible to incentives and constraints and to assign economists the task of conditioning it to operate efficiently within the demands of austerity.[44]

From 1993 on, Wiesner marshaled new institutionalism and public choice theory to elaborate his long-standing position that merely devolving tax revenues to local governments did not ensure efficient public administration. He argued for conditional transfers that forced local governments to raise revenues independently in order to receive national funds. He called on national governments to impose tight fiscal controls at every level: projects should raise as much money as they spent, local governments should not issue debt under most circumstances, and national officials should not bail out insolvent local governments. His citations and vocabulary changed, but his ideas remained remarkably consistent. Indeed, new institutionalism and public choice proved natural vehicles for him because they put economists in the position that Wiesner had first imagined during the 1960s. These schools did not assume away the political environment but made it an express object of analysis and manipulation.[45]

Wiesner embraced new institutionalism and public choice in the same way that his generation of Colombian economists had always searched and selected among schools of thought, putting international intellectual currents to their own uses. The continuities in his thought suggest the genuine intellectual authorship of a Latin American official who willingly did the viciously hard work of structural adjustment for the IMF and public-sector restructuring for the World Bank—and who emerged from the experience sounding just like his North American colleagues. It suggests, too, the error that historians can commit in looking for the influence of the Chicago School, the Mont Pelerin Society, or any particular band of intellectuals to explain the unraveling of the midcentury state. Eduardo Wiesner had never been a Chicago protégé, but in the 1990s, he represented one tendency within the new institutionalist school that explicitly recognized an affinity with Chicago. "In reality there is much in common between the neoinstitutional school and the Chicago School," he explained in 1997. Both agreed that "in general, people will try to maximize their welfare or their utility in this way: they compete among themselves and generate markets and competition."[46] Wiesner did not say it, but he in fact turned the neoclassical description into a prescription; when workers did not behave as competitive, self-interested individuals but instead as union members, he gave economists the job of transforming the political economy to make collective action futile or impossible. Nevertheless, Wiesner had certainly found common ground with Chicago. Their convergence simply did not reveal influence.

By the 1990s, Wiesner's essays and books had obscured his own intellectual trajectory as well as the long history of the practice he analyzed. Invented and reinvented over time, state decentralization had come to appear utterly novel, laden with new purposes and rationales. Gone were the days when David Lilienthal had hailed the TVA as a model of decentralized public administration, or when the National Front's regional technocracies had seemed democratic innovations. The arguments of the 1950s had become politically distasteful to many, and more than that, they had become irrelevant, even unspeakable, within the prevailing terms of debate. New conceptions of decentralization, new manifestations of it, and new ways of reasoning about it, had wiped Lilienthal's ideas from public memory.

In one respect, nevertheless, Wiesner had grown to resemble the old New Dealer. When the ink dried on the 1991 Constitution and Wiesner scrutinized the fruits of his labor, he saw the failure of a cherished dream at home. Four decades earlier, David Lilienthal had seen something very similar in Washington. Looking abroad, he had become one of a generation of North Americans who traveled to Colombia in search of a place to try again. Their encounter with Latin Americans had made postwar Colombia a feverish intellectual crossroads, a showcase, a war zone, and an incubator of a new generation of state makers. In 1992, a new process of state formation had begun, and Eduardo Wiesner looked out from his own country in search of a place to get it right.

Epilogue

SORTING OUT THE MIXED ECONOMY

THE WORLD at the turn of the twenty-first century was strikingly new, but it was made from familiar materials. The conflicts of the 1970s, 1980s, and 1990s had sorted out the elements of the mixed economy, obliterating some, redeploying others, and redefining them all as features of two different historical eras. As a result, remnants of the mixed economy are all around us, generally renamed and politically resignified. If we cast our sights across the Americas, we find the landscape littered with projects whose origins this book has traced. Let us take a tour.

In Ogden, Utah, the War on Poverty is today a distant memory, but not so the for-profit contractors it spawned. In 1965, Ogden became the headquarters of Thiokol's Economic Development Operations, which for fifteen years scooped up performance contracts in public schools and ran training centers for Job Corps, the Bureau of Indian Affairs, the Peace Corps, VISTA, and the Department of Labor. The 1970s became a moment of crisis for the company, and indeed for every industrial subsidiary founded in the mid-1960s to capture new social spending. As the Great Society unraveled and school enrollments fell, education and training ceased to be boom industries; by 1980, several of Thiokol's competitors had folded, and the company's top executives wanted out. Vice President Robert Marquardt and two colleagues in Ogden arranged a buyout of their division and renamed it the Management and Training Corporation (MTC). Continuing to run Job Corps centers, they also revived a time-honored business strategy: they began hunting for new sources of public revenue, and they spied an opportunity in the country's growing network of prisons, jails, and immigration detention centers. In 1983, the Reagan administration began signing for-profit contracts with corporations to run correctional facilities, and four years later, MTC won its first such contract in Desert Center, California. By the turn of the century, MTC still did a thriving business with Job Corps, but it was mainly known as the country's third-largest private prison operator, with an archipelago of prisons, jails, and immigrant detention centers stretching from Texas to Canada and even Australia. MTC considered its work all of a piece, arguing that running a prison required the same skills the company had honed rehabilitating juvenile delinquents for Job Corps. As Marquardt's 2012 obituary declared, "Bob never lost his passion for education, rehabilitation and giving people a second chance." The company likewise redeployed Thiokol's old argument that the private sector could deliver public services more cheaply than the state. Where Thiokol had once promised that systems analysis would make education efficient, MTC promised to slash daily expenditures per inmate. Marquardt had spilled much ink in the 1960s laying out the reasons that a military contractor should administer social welfare programs; when the welfare state came undone, he and his colleagues had all the practical and ideological material they needed to make the leap into the carceral state.[1]

In Iowa City, another reinvention was underway. In 1968, Westinghouse had supplemented its training and education contracts with a spectacular capital investment; it bought a massive test-scoring facility at the University of Iowa. The Measurement Research Center (MRC) had been a nonprofit academic institution founded in 1953 by engineering and education professors who had spent years designing standardized tests, building sophisticated machines to process them, and channeling the revenues into education research at the University of Iowa. When Westinghouse bought the center, it transformed a nonprofit undertaking into a for-profit business. Like Thiokol, Westinghouse soured on education in the late 1970s and began shuttering its operations; in 1983, it sold MRC to National Computer Systems (NCS) and bowed out of schooling entirely. But the ashes of its midcentury operation became fertile ground for a new generation of for-profit education reformers. In 1983, Ronald Reagan's National Commission on Excellence in Education released *A Nation at Risk*, which argued that public schools had deteriorated calamitously since the 1960s. The report set off a wave of reform, including new standardized testing regimes in a majority of states. Every subsequent presidential administration expanded federal support for mandatory testing, and in the midst of it all, NCS cornered the market on exam scoring. Westinghouse's discarded refuse became a fabulously lucrative venture thanks to Reagan-era public policy; by 2000, it processed forty million exams a year.

That same year, the British multinational Pearson bought NCS, and the test-scoring center in Iowa became the heart of a new for-profit school assessment giant. Pearson was no veteran of the War on Poverty. It had originated as a nineteenth-century public-works contractor and diversified after World War II, acquiring new holdings in publishing and financial services. During the 1990s, it spied in US education reform just the kind of opportunity that

Westinghouse had perceived in the War on Poverty. Between 1996 and 2000, it reinvented itself as an education company, selling virtually everything but its media and textbook-publishing subsidiaries and buying NCS, HarperCollins Education, Prentice Hall, and Allyn and Bacon. In the eyes of most Americans, Pearson came out of nowhere and represented something new in education: a sprawling multinational corporation making hay from curricular standardization, testing, and assessment. But the company was in fact picking up business strategies and institutions left lying around by an earlier generation of educational contractors.[2]

Halfway across the country, Lauchlin Currie suffered his own reinvention. The eighty-eight-year-old economist arrived in Washington, DC, in April 1990 to address the Third International Shelter Conference. "I propose to discuss residential building strictly from the point of view of macroeconomics," he announced. Currie treated his audience to the same argument he had made since the 1960s, presenting housing as a leading sector that could accelerate growth in capitalist economies. During the early years of the National Front, he had made that case to criticize austere self-help housing programs; as he searched for allies, he had made common cause with Colombian building contractors who put his idea to their own use and undermined his calls for public ownership. Three decades later, Currie was still looking for allies and found them among US business groups. The sponsor of the International Shelter Conference was the National Association of Realtors (NAR), which in the 1980s attached itself to the United Nations housing program, organizing "private sector support" for homeownership programs worldwide. NAR's conference report faithfully recapitulated Currie's rationale for home building as a spur to growth. It celebrated the Colombian UPAC system, which channeled individual savings into private mortgage loans. But NAR folded those ideas into a program that Currie had never proposed. It conflated his goal of fomenting growth with the distinct macroeconomic program of the IMF, arguing that "housing-sector reform" lay "at the heart of the process of structural adjustment and growth." It went on to denounce public construction and ownership. "Governments should not be in the business of trying to produce housing, but should be involved in creating the conditions necessary to unleash the inherent energies of the private sector," NAR maintained. It put forward a hazy idea of deregulation convenient to its members, suggesting that states loosen the bounds on real estate developers while protecting investors' property rights and public subsidies. Scanning the globe, NAR hailed liberalization in the Soviet Union and China, endorsed the Reagan administration's calls for housing deregulation, and celebrated self-help in "developing countries"—what it called the "informal sector" producing housing "at the community level."

NAR's report was a feat of alchemy: it selectively appropriated Currie's ideas, tied them to contradictory impulses in self-help housing, and aligned the whole messy package with structural adjustment and dreams of postsocialist transition. The report denounced "economies that are heavily managed," but in fact redeployed ideas and policies scavenged from those economies.[3]

Farther south in Bogotá, the Universidad de los Andes became known as Colombia's neoliberal university in the 1990s. Its reputation did not reflect doctrinal or political uniformity; the school was never a University of Chicago or Universidad Católica de Chile. To be sure, los Andes continued to produce the country's top economic policy makers, including the architects of Colombia's economic "opening" of the early 1990s. But it also trained and employed leading critics of that policy. José Antonio Ocampo, widely considered the dean of Colombian economists, directed CEDE during the early 1980s and publicly deplored the Washington Consensus. Intellectually, the economics faculty would have been considered intolerably heterodox in the United States. Lauchlin Currie taught at los Andes from 1981 to 1991 and prided himself on introducing students to competing schools of economic thought. Samuel Jaramillo, one of Colombia's notable Marxists, graduated from los Andes in 1973 and has served on the economics faculty since 1976. The university's association with neoliberalism owes less to any uniformity in its intellectual production than to the very institutional attributes that originally made it an emblem of the developmental state: its private status, wealthy student body, technocratic mission, and overt rivalry with the public Universidad Nacional. By the 1990s, those facts had acquired new meaning.

Our tour could go on, but even this brief circuit suggests the parasitic quality of capitalism in the late twentieth century. Mixed economies bequeathed to the 1980s and 1990s many of the ideas and institutions that became paradigmatic symbols of neoliberalism, from private prison corporations to for-profit school assessment firms, reputedly neoliberal economics departments, and realtor associations lambasting public housing. At their birth, the arguments, policies, and organizations seen here had been instruments to build welfare and developmental states in mixed economies, and their origins remind us of the stifling limits to those states' ambitions. For decades, governments promising to extend social protection and assure widely shared prosperity operated under punishing fiscal and ideological constraints, mainly of their own design. As a result, they systematically relied on private capital to carry out new public functions. They incubated new strategies of profit making within flagship public initiatives. They endowed new local and private intermediaries with powers to generate authoritative knowledge and apply national directives. They crafted strikingly austere forms of social welfare provision to push costs and risks onto those least able to bear them. All of those practices extended the reach of midcentury states, and all found new uses after the 1970s.

Not every feature of midcentury statecraft could survive the crises of the 1970s and 1980s; the world at the end of the twentieth century was new precisely because it contained only pieces of the past. Right-wing demands for fiscal retrenchment and regressive redistribution functioned as a sieve that sorted midcentury practices from one another, imperiling or annihilating some while redeploying others. In the United States, federal budget cuts dealt a blow to conventional public housing while leaving a thin lifeline that sustained self-help housing. The Reagan administration furnished fresh opportunities to the War on Poverty's flagging for-profit contractors while attacking cash-transfer programs. In both cases, the policies that endured tended to be relatively small ones that reached fewer people, channeled less generous subsidies to the poor, and promised less progressive redistribution of income. The institutions that survived tended to be private, entrepreneurial ones that the midcentury state had cultivated, from nonprofit housing developers to for-profit corporate subsidiaries.

As these pieces of the mixed economy traversed the 1970s and 1980s, they acquired new meanings. Plucked from their original contexts, they lost their association with developmental and welfare states and appeared increasingly as manifestations of reaction. The process of sorting out the mixed economy was thus both material and symbolic; policies, practices, and institutions born together met different fates and became retrospectively reimagined as elements of two different eras and political-economic orders. In the United States, conventional public housing stands today as a symbol of Keynesianism, while its twin, self-help housing, is a marker of neoliberalism. For-profit educational contracting and state decentralization are known as quintessentially neoliberal practices, their earlier lives forgotten. That recategorization went hand in hand with the consolidation of new ideals that conferred legitimacy on worldly phenomena. Decentralization, self-help housing, for-profit contracting, and other practices once authorized by their association with the notion of the mixed economy—that vast imagined space between socialism and laissez-faire—now found legitimation through their association with "the market," the private sector, the entrepreneur, civil society, or the austere state—ideals of a different order. The decline of welfare and developmental states thus involved a profound reordering of ideals that masked continuities in practice. At the turn of the twenty-first century, the US and Colombian economies could still have been described as mixed economies, but they never were. The mixed economy had died as a legitimating concept, replaced by others equally notional and aspirational.[4]

Our understandings of the practices in this book are thus of recent vintage. They were forged in the 1970s, 1980s, and 1990s, in the very process of dismantling welfare and developmental states. Indeed, the work of political-economic restructuring involved a great deal of storytelling about what the midcentury state had been. When Eduardo Wiesner reimagined the practice of state decentralization in the 1980s, he rhetorically distinguished his version from older ones by recasting the developmental state as a centralized behemoth. Decentralization came to appear utterly novel, associated in memory with the decline of developmental states rather than their construction. Wiesner was one of many state makers who reconstructed the past in order to explain the virtues of an imagined future. Most kept a low profile: Wiesner wrote for a cloistered world of policy makers and academics. But a few pursued the status of public intellectual—Milton Friedman, Jeffrey Sachs, and Francis Fukuyama count among them—and their writings became lightning rods for public debate. We tend to remember their essays and books as polemical apologies for a new world in birth. They were certainly that. But they were also works of popular history that retold the story of the twentieth century. It is worth rereading them as such.

———

Take one exemplar of the genre: Hernando de Soto's book *El otro sendero* (*The Other Path*). Published in 1986, it became a best seller in Latin America and the United States, and popularized a right-wing, libertarian view of the owner-built private home as a novel alternative to midcentury statism. The book made de Soto a hero among defenders of the Washington Consensus and a notorious symbol of neoliberalism on the left. But it mainly reconfigured and politically resignified policies and arguments that had long existed inside welfare and developmental states.

De Soto capitalized on more than a decade of intellectual work by the United Nations and the World Bank. Both institutions had thrown their weight behind self-help during the 1970s, in the process giving the policy new names and making it even more austere. The meetings convened in that decade by the UN housing agency HABITAT addressed "minimum standards" in construction and became a crossroads for every contradictory practice in self-help housing. The earliest discussions included chairman Enrique Peñalosa, a veteran of Colombia's National Front, as well as John F. C. Turner, a British architect who had helped develop the policy in Peru during the 1950s and 1960s. Unlike Peñalosa, Turner was an anarchist. As a young man, he had admired the ideas of the nineteenth-century British socialist William Morris, a critic of industrial production who celebrated artisanship as the basis of a utopian society. Turner combined Morris's ideas with his own interest in an-archism to develop an argument for auto-construction. Self-help, he argued, gave poor people control over their environments and freedom to create com-munities that conformed to their standards of justice. During the 1950s and 1960s, Turner called on governments to channel resources directly to squatter settlements, allowing residents to upgrade their neighborhoods rather than suffer clearance and relocation. Moreover, he drew bright lines between variet-ies of self-help, condemning massive projects like Ciudad Kennedy. After all, Kennedy did not allow Colombians to renovate their existing environments but relocated them to planned superblocks. It did not authorize poor people's own forms of collective association, but demanded that they mobilize under Acción Comunal. And it did not invite residents to identify problems for ar-chitects to solve, but required them to follow plans that architects had drawn up for them. Turner's version of self-help aligned him with left-wing architects including Don Terner—the man we first met in 1968 when he tried to bring a "slum upgrading" system from Venezuela to Detroit. Both men taught at MIT during the late 1960s and early 1970s, and together with colleagues from Cam-bridge and Peru, they became coauthors of *Freedom to Build*, a 1972 book that became a manifesto for self-help housing worldwide.[5]

As Turner and Peñalosa converged in HABITAT, the World Bank articu-lated similar ideas. Robert McNamara had become bank president in 1968 and declared the old financial institution an antipoverty agency. Under his leader-ship, the World Bank began financing housing programs and appropriated Turner's ideas to condemn projects like Ciudad Kennedy. Symbolically recon-figuring flagship self-help projects as archaic expressions of improvident, over-weening states, the World Bank called for a more austere variation on a theme: governments should provide "sites and services" for auto-construction while leaving the rest to residents. Echoing Turner's libertarian rhetoric and enlisting him as an advisor, the Bank described its pared-down program as a guarantor of human freedom.[6] By the late 1970s, talk of sites and services, upgrading, and other diminutive forms of self-help pervaded international policy discussions. Synthesizing research on Colombian housing in 1977, anthropologist Susan E. Brown characterized ICT developments as "government housing" built by the state or erected through "institutionalized autoconstruction." She contrasted both methods to "progressive autoconstruction" in pirate settlements, where residents incrementally built their homes without initial authorization.[7]

When Hernando de Soto published *The Other Path* in 1986, he was a right-wing activist appropriating ideas that midcentury policy makers had authored and laid out for all to see. At the time, he was forty-five years old and had re-cently moved back to Peru after living in Geneva for more than three decades. Settling in Lima, he took up work for mining investors and established a think tank dedicated to the protection of private property rights. De Soto's Institute for Liberty and Democracy (ILD) immediately impressed Friedrich Hayek and Antony Fisher, both members of the Mont Pelerin Society. Fisher's Atlas Foundation for Economic Research funded the ILD. So did the Center for International Private Enterprise, an affiliate of the US National Endowment for Democracy and the Chamber of Commerce. Unlike Wiesner or Lilienthal, de Soto and his backers understood themselves as dissident outsiders to mid-century welfare and developmental states. *The Other Path* became an iconic statement of their ideals.[8]

Writing from Lima and purporting to speak for the poor of the Global South, de Soto offered readers a stylized history of Peru's illegal urban settlements and the government's long struggle to eradicate them. He recounted the state's efforts to evict squatters as well as attempts to legalize neighborhoods and fold them into national programs of community organization. Throughout, he showcased Peruvians' very real pursuit of private property ownership and condemned the state's failure to grant full rights to land and buildings within its legalization programs. The history of these settlements was a complicated story that others had told in a hundred ways. John F. C. Turner had lived some of that history and had perceived in squatter settlements a form of collective life concerned equally with individual autonomy and social solidarity. Residents had demanded property rights as grounds for both of those ideals. They had developed complex relations with the state, battling evictions while seeking public recognition and resources. Like the rather different tale of Ciudad Kennedy, this was a story that defied the stylized dichotomies of individualism and collectivism, public and private, state and society, legal and illegal, formal and informal. But de Soto retold it through just those binaries. In his account, residents of illegal neighborhoods became "informals," classical liberal subjects with innate propensities to truck and barter, natural tendencies to invest for individual gain alone, and irrepressible desires for property that locked them in conflict with a monolithic state. Fifty years of Peruvian history boiled down to a great clash between "the people's struggle to acquire private property" and a state demanding "socialized models of community living." In de Soto's telling, every demand for property became evidence that "informals" wanted just what he did—a state that "receded" until it did nothing but protect private property rights.

Politically, de Soto redeployed a well-worn association between self-help and democracy—a debatable idea, but a familiar one espoused by generations of anticommunist officials, anarchists, civil rights activists, Quakers, and so many others. In Peru in 1986, the argument took on special meaning. From 1968 to 1980, a left-wing military dictatorship had ruled the country and enacted many of the programs de Soto condemned. The dramatic turning point in *The Other Path* became "the advent of democratic government" in 1980; the new state finally realized "how mistaken the authorities had been" and began experimenting with titling programs without neighborhood organization. The lesson was clear: democracy, private property, and the individual pursuit of gain stood opposed to the left, the developmental state, and collective pursuits. Those dichotomies scrambled historical reality; in mixed economies, developmental states had devoted themselves to individual private property development and frequently battled the left. But such dichotomies made an eminently usable past.[9]

The Other Path was thus a work of historical reinvention. In its pages, de Soto claimed the most vanishingly austere expressions of self-help housing, embraced a few of the ideas surrounding them, and situated both in a new telling of Peru's history that affirmed the faith of right-wing libertarians. No single book did more to politically align self-help housing with neoliberalism and obliterate its developmentalist roots.

De Soto and Wiesner belonged to a cohort of post-1970s state makers who did the difficult ideological labor of sorting midcentury practices into two imagined political heaps: the Keynesian and developmentalist on one side, and the postdevelopmental or neoliberal on the other. Their work found reinforcement among businessmen, who had their own ways of remembering the past. Like Wiesner and de Soto, corporate executives and their firms emphasized the novelty of their activities after 1970. For them, a past without precedent affirmed their own account of themselves as sources of innovation and progress and concealed all record of experiments gone bust. Pearson's rendering of its history illustrates a common pattern. Today, the company's website commemorates the founding of the Measurement Research Center in 1953 but makes no mention of Westinghouse, the firm that acquired MRC in 1968 and made the genuinely unprecedented decision to use the test-scoring center for profit. A history without Westinghouse performs clear ideological functions, ennobling Pearson and masking the ignominious fate of for-profit contractors during the 1970s. But this stylized history is more than self-interested artifice; it is a readily available, believable version of the past for anyone at Pearson. When Westinghouse sloughed off its flagging educational subdivisions in the 1970s and 1980s, it noted the decision in annual reports but hardly memorialized the refuse; it spoke no more of failure. Years later, when Pearson bought National Computer Systems, Pearson executives had no reason to know or care about the shuttered educational ventures of the Westinghouse Electric Corporation. They no longer existed and could only matter to a historian.[10]

In all these instances, businessmen and economic advisors retold history in ways that obscured their debts to the mixed economy. Their memory of the 1970s, 1980s, and 1990s as a moment of cataclysmic rupture expressed their self-conceptions and the demands of their work. Curiously, their tellings of the twentieth century harmonize with some forms of historical memory on the left. Susan George's influential 1997 essay in *Dissent*, "How to Win the War of Ideas," was an early statement of ideas that a generation of journalists and scholars has since extended. Embracing the language of left-wing movements across the North and South Atlantic, George termed the new political-economic order *neoliberal* and traced its origins to ideological outsiders of the postwar moment: the Mont Pelerin Society, the Chicago School, and the web of intellectuals, businessmen, foundations, think tanks, and publications that surrounded them. Her article appeared two years after Juan Gabriel Valdés published his seminal history of the Chicago School in Chile, *Pinochet's Economists*. Both were exemplary works of their moment, and they communicated an incontrovertible truth: these figures of the right had spent decades working to undermine the redistributive policies of welfare and developmental states. They had openly deplored a wide assortment of labor, socialist, anticolonial, and social-democratic movements. And during the 1970s and 1980s, they had gone to work for right-wing governments. But these thinkers tended to take the right's account of its lineage at face value; Margaret Thatcher announced her admiration for Friedrich Hayek, and George set about showing how Hayek's ideas had attained influence. Moreover, they recapitulated the right's claims to originality, crediting it with extraordinary intellectual creativity and political autonomy across the mid-twentieth century. In these tellings, right-wing funders and institutions popularized spectacularly marginal ideas and institutionalized them in moments of crisis, displacing all that came before. If Hernando de Soto aggrandized himself as an intellectual iconoclast and policy innovator, intellectuals on the left reinforced that image.[11]

The burgeoning literature on neoliberalism is, to a significant extent, the mirror image of policy makers' and businessmen's triumphalist accounts of their own careers. The casts of characters are largely identical, as are the key historical episodes and periodization of the twentieth century. In that sense, histories of neoliberalism have performed a vital political function, constituting a powerful form of dissent. They have turned apologetics on their heads, capturing and reworking the urgent grievances of Chilean miners, socialists, and indigenous people who suffered mightily at the hand the Pinochet dictatorship. They recuperate the stories of New Yorkers who lost access to free higher education when Wall Street banks induced the New York City fiscal crisis and then shaped its resolution. They recall the enormous social cost of the 1979 Volcker shock, and the coercive power of international trade and financial institutions that finished off import substitution industrialization. These stories draw our attention to Mexican campesinos unable to make a living growing corn since the passage of the North American Free Trade Agreement, as well as US trade unionists and welfare rights activists who have seen their share of national income shrink since the 1970s. For young activists seeking the roots of contemporary inequalities and usable pasts of their own, this literature transmits valuable knowledge of the twentieth century and meaningful memory of social movements.

By its nature, it also tends to narrow our memory of the mixed economy, reducing it to those elements that the right battled and capital abhorred. That is the unintended consequence of inverting celebratory narratives and implicitly agreeing that the roots of our moment lie outside, before, and in reactions against welfare and developmental states. Both accounts lead us to remember expanding social insurance programs, progressive income taxes, strong labor unions, government-built housing, robust banking regulations, and the redistributive promises of land reform. We forget the novel opportunities that capitalists found inside the state, the austere systems of social welfare provision that flourished at midcentury, and the many uses of privatization, deregulation, and decentralization to fulfill public promises. To the extent that we do remember those phenomena, they can strike us merely as incipient manifestations of reaction, rather than constitutive elements of state-building. As the left deposits them into the category neoliberal, it contributes to the retrospective sorting of the mixed economy's contents.

A thinned-out memory is not a sin. For those seeking a more egalitarian future, it can in fact be a political asset. On the left, remembering just a few pieces of the mixed economy is often a way of claiming them as living ideals while leaving others behind. As it happened in history, Medicare came into the world alongside for-profit educational contracting; when critics of neoliberalism separate them in historical memory, they implicitly suggest that the two need not go together. During the 1960s, the notion of the mixed economy conferred legitimacy on both, but seen in the light of other ideals, they can appear wholly incompatible and might one day be sorted from each other. Packing the concept of neoliberalism with practices evacuated from the past can thus be a way that activists indicate what they take from history and what they reject—which elements deserve rebuke and which deserve a future. When Bernie Sanders spoke of renewing the New Deal in the 2016 presidential campaign, he mobilized the past in just this way—not to resuscitate every piece of the mixed economy but to propose an order more egalitarian than it had ever been. The chief consequence of his campaign was to make "Medicare for All" a political possibility in the United States.

————

Memory has its uses, and so does history. This book challenges triumphalist accounts of our moment in a different way: it takes issue with their origin stories. It begins by recasting the way that influence operated internationally. The image of intellectuals, governments, foundations, and multilateral institutions in the North Atlantic projecting power southward has been central to their own legitimation as well as their critics' denunciations. It is beyond question that power flowed in that direction. But it is equally clear that the IMF, the World Bank, and foundations and think tanks pushing liberalization after 1970—FMME and IMDI among them—were products of international exchange. Their founders and staff included Latin American capitalists, economists, university officials, and government functionaries. Their access to Latin American societies depended on those same groups, which had long enlisted foreign advisors and funders to tip the balance of power in domestic disputes. Class conflict operates within every society, and Latin American elites used North Atlantic institutions to fight their battles at home and eventually project influence abroad. These were not simply elites associated with authoritarian politics, often remembered on the left as architects of neoliberalism. Many were strategists of liberal democracy in Cold War Latin America, and they remind us of the constraints and inequities of that vision. As for US advisors, they exercised power in choosing their allies in Latin America, but they rarely imparted genuinely new ideas. Their accounts of extraordinary accomplishment overseas, and the appreciation that Latin American partners lavished on them, were often strategic claims that each made to legitimate themselves at home.

Latin Americans made their own use of US university assistance, folding foreign economists into projects that conveyed their own conceptions of national development and the public interest. The history of economics education in Latin America is often remembered as a great contest between rival schools of thought in which US universities transmitted neoclassicism to Latin America, training the intellectuals who put an end to import substitution industrialization. Yet that was hardly the only process taking place within Latin American economics faculties. For more than two decades after 1945, the first order of business was not to debate well-defined schools of economic thought—an impossible luxury in a society without naturalized definitions of discipline and profession—but to define the boundaries of the field, decide who an economist was, and determine what an economist did. That endeavor centered on the struggle to distinguish economics from management and public from private in mixed economies that relied on those dichotomies while systematically fusing them. The consequences of long attempts to clarify disciplinary and professional jurisdictions were deeply ironic: Colombian intellectuals, businessmen, public officials, and university leaders enlisted foreign allies with divergent visions of economics and management, and generally undermined their doctrinal demands. The emblematic products of foreign training were not neoclassical economists but rather institutions that reflected the structure of the developmental state: management programs and associations that assumed public functions, private and regional universities that claimed national and public responsibilities, and private business plans that were inseparable from national and regional economic plans. Economics faculties became relatively ecumenical crossroads where the Chicago Boys taught alongside Wisconsin institutionalists, *cepalino* structuralists, and European-trained Marxists. They turned out businessmen and heterodox economists who built the midcentury state and later proved as capable of arguing for fiscal decentralization and economic liberalization as anyone from the University of Chicago. If historians wish to find the direct transmission of doctrine in Colombia, they would do best to look beyond economics faculties to the wider world of popular economic thought. At midcentury, the people who learned to speak as intended were large landowners who adopted simple forms of economic reasoning to make their interests legible to the state. Land reform was a much more coercive instrument of ideological transformation than academic coursework.

Back in the United States, meanwhile, social policy was shaped by possibilities opened and foreclosed abroad. Latin American housing programs of the 1950s and early 1960s were contact zones in which North Americans and their southern neighbors amalgamated Depression-era policies, adapting them to new problems under extraordinary fiscal constraints. The New Deal went through a fiscal wringer in the Third World, which made conventional public housing unthinkable as a foreign aid policy and turned Puerto Rico's austere variants into celebrated models. The rise of self-help housing as a vaunted symbol of US development assistance ultimately altered the range of policies that officials deemed thinkable at home. Since the 1930s, federal agencies had battled virtually every group on the US mainland that had tried to use tax dollars to support self-help housing. But in the 1960s, the Native Americans, Quakers, farmworkers, and civil rights activists who pursued self-help projects found a converted audience among US officials; Washington ceased fighting them and began funding them. As in Latin America, foreign experience did not introduce unknown ideas to North Americans but tipped the balance of power in disputes of long standing.

US training and education programs exposed subtler forms of connection within American societies. Historians writing transnational studies of policy and intellectual life have tended to study direct, on-the-nose forms of connection and exchange; they show US urban planners learning from urban planners abroad and Third World revolutionaries conferring on the strategy of guerrilla warfare. Yet the distinct conceptualizations of poverty in Latin America and the United States meant that some forms of knowledge and experience could never traverse borders in any direct way. The queen of the social sciences in Latin America—development economics—faced a blocked passage back to the United States because poverty there was not generally understood as a systemic consequence of macroeconomic order, as it was in the Third World. But blocked passages could produce unexpected detours and forms of indirect connection. The professionalization of economists in Latin America inspired a powerful reaction from businessmen there, which entwined with business mobilization in the United States. Throughout the 1960s, linked networks of corporate executives and managers battled simultaneously for legitimacy across the hemisphere, cooperating to build new management education programs, think tanks, and professional associations in Latin America and asserting themselves as public policy makers in both regions. As businessmen entered the US welfare state, they forged another form of indirect connection. Having little experience in social welfare policy, they brought to it lessons on state restructuring learned in military, foreign aid, and Indian affairs. It happened that the US government functioned differently in foreign and imperial contexts, relying more extensively on for-profit contracting than it did in domestic social policy. The War on Poverty became a turning point in US history when businessmen carried contracting and budgeting practices from the edges of the state into training and education programs. In all these cases, connections within the Americas were real and consequential but have escaped observers looking only for direct exchanges between discrete fields of policy or economic thought.

Within the United States, high-level government decisions to sanction self-help housing and for-profit educational contracting never determined the way those programs unfolded. Rather, they altered the field of play for social movements, religious communities, and business organizations already battling over the place of private capital and voluntaristic self-help in social welfare provision. Local actors gave national policies meaning, and returning waves of architects, planners, community workers, and businessmen moved in their circles and applied foreign experience to their debates. In that sense, US social policy was very much like Latin American development. Foreign influence never dictated the course of national history and rarely introduced unprecedented ideas. But at times, it produced a new terrain for struggle.

US and Latin American societies were thus entwined in ways far more pervasive than stories about the southward projection of power suggest. This book offers a richer map of the hemisphere, the circuits connecting it, and the forms of exchange, collaboration, subjection, and subversion that grew from national, regional, and social inequalities. That map may accommodate exceptional cases like Pinochet's Chile, where a ruthless military dictatorship allowed a marginal group of Chicago protégés to turn national economic policy on its head. It also provides a ground to explain more ordinary cases like Colombia, where those same Chicago protégés had the mundane careers they might have had if Pinochet had never seized power—and where the political economy was nevertheless transformed. It is a map that I hope will invite new research on topics only glimpsed in the preceding pages, from the evolution of social entrepreneurship to the rise of the economic development corporation in US cities.

Most fundamentally, this book challenges triumphalist origin stories of our time by reformulating their central question. Rather than ask where neoliberalism came from, this book asks how midcentury states came into being and how they came undone. That question dislodges neoliberalism as the only conceivable endpoint of twentieth-century political economy. It also opens our eyes to features of mixed economies that we are likely to miss when we imagine them only as the antagonistic antecedents to something else, or when we ransack them for the roots of an order hardly imaginable at the time. Welfare and developmental states were profoundly contradictory formations that offered extraordinary resources to those who dreamed of social democracy and those who dance on its grave today. They generated manifold forms of decentralization, private delegation, deregulation, and austerity, nearly all of them forgotten because subsequent state makers appropriated those practices, put them to new ends, wrote them new genealogies, and branded them neoliberal. The category *neoliberal* thus contains within it policies, practices, and concepts that have crossed political-economic systems and built quite varied orders across the twentieth century. Neoliberalism is best understood as a term of its time, a meaningful epithet that conveys an important truth: the elements of the mixed economy that have survived serve novel purposes today and represent ideals distinctive to our moment.

If shards of the past lie embedded in the present, we might take a few things from history. On the one hand, we might recognize that the order we call neoliberal is itself an unruly, unsettled aggregation of practices susceptible to sorting and redeployment, much like the mixed economy from which it grew. We might follow the lead of Johanna Bockman, Arturo Escobar, and James Ferguson in presuming that our world contains seeds of multiple futures, and search the present for forms of economic life and knowledge that point a way out.[12] Just as important, we might recognize that when we take issue with neoliberalism, we are often struggling with much more enduring features of capitalism, and take aim accordingly.

NOTES

Introduction

1. David E. Lilienthal, "New Opportunities for 'Underdeveloped' America to Seize," *Smithsonian* (July 1976): 108.

2. Greg Grandin, "The Liberal Traditions in the Americas: Rights, Sovereignty, and the Origins of Liberal Multilateralism," *American Historical Review* (February 2012): 68–91; Greg Grandin, "Your Americanism and Mine: Americanism and Anti-Americanism in the Americas," *American Historical Review* 111, no. 4 (October 2006): 1042–66; Victor Bulmer-Thomas, *The Economic History of Latin America since Independence* (Cambridge: Cambridge University Press, 2014).

3. Paulo Drinot and Alan Knight, eds., *The Great Depression in Latin America* (Durham, NC: Duke University Press, 2014); Eric Helleiner, *Forgotten Foundations of Bretton Woods: International Development and the Making of the Postwar Order* (Ithaca, NY: Cornell University Press, 2014); Joseph L. Love, *Crafting the Third World: Theorizing Underdevelopment in Rumania and Brazil* (Palo Alto, CA: Stanford University Press, 1996); David Rock, ed., *Latin America in the 1940s: War and Postwar Transitions* (Berkeley: University of California Press, 1994).

4. Christopher R. W. Dietrich, *Oil Revolution: Anticolonial Elites, Sovereign Rights, and the Economic Culture of Decolonization* (Cambridge: Cambridge University Press, 2017); Johanna Bockman, *Markets in the Name of Socialism: The Left-Wing Origins of Neoliberalism* (Stanford, CA: Stanford University Press, 2011); Jeffrey James Byrne, *Mecca of Revolution: Algeria, Decolonization, and the Third World Order* (Oxford: Oxford University Press, 2016); Alice H. Amsden, *The Rise of "The Rest": Challenges to the West from Late-Industrializing Economies* (Oxford: Oxford University Press, 2001).

5. Verónica Montecinos and John Markoff, eds., *Economists in the Americas* (Northampton, MA: Edward Elgar, 2009); Michael A. Bernstein, *A Perilous Progress: Economists and Public Purpose in Twentieth-Century America* (Princeton, NJ: Princeton University Press, 2001); J. Adam Tooze, *Statistics and the German State, 1900–1945: The Making of Modern Economic Knowledge* (Cambridge: Cambridge University Press, 2001); Alan Brinkley, *The End of Reform: New Deal Liberalism in Recession and War* (New York: Alfred A. Knopf, 1995), 132–35; Colin Gordon, *New Deals: Business, Labor, and Politics in America, 1920–1935* (Cambridge: Cambridge University Press, 1994); Love, *Crafting the Third World*.

6. Meg Jacobs, *Pocketbook Politics: Economic Citizenship in Twentieth-Century America* (Princeton, NJ: Princeton University Press, 2004); Nelson Lichtenstein, "From Corporatism to Collective Bargaining: Organized Labor and the Eclipse of Social Democracy in the Postwar Era,"

in *The Rise and Fall of the New Deal Order, 1930–1980,* ed. Steven Fraser and Gary Gerstle (Princeton, NJ: Princeton University Press, 1989), 122–52; Martha Biondi, *To Stand and Fight: The Struggle for Civil Rights in Postwar New York City* (Cambridge, MA: Harvard University Press, 2003); Robert M. Collins, *More: The Politics of Economic Growth in Postwar America* (New York: Oxford University Press, 2000); Jennifer Klein, *For All These Rights: Business, Labor, and the Shaping of America's Public-Private Welfare State* (Princeton, NJ: Princeton University Press, 2003); Brinkley, *The End of Reform.*

7. Tore C. Olsson, *Agrarian Crossings: Reformers and the Remaking of the US and Mexican Countryside* (Princeton, NJ: Princeton University Press, 2017); Bruce J. Schulman, *From Cotton Belt to Sunbelt: Federal Policy, Economic Development, and the Transformation of the South, 1938–1980* (Oxford: Oxford University Press, 1991); Sarah T. Phillips, *This Land, This Nation: Conservation, Rural America, and the New Deal* (New York: Cambridge University Press, 2007); Donald Worster, *Rivers of Empire: Water, Aridity, and the Growth of the American West* (New York: Pantheon, 1985).

8. Michael B. Katz, *The Undeserving Poor: From the War on Poverty to the War on Welfare* (New York: Pantheon, 1989); Alice O'Connor, *Poverty Knowledge: Social Science, Social Policy, and the Poor in Twentieth-Century US History* (Princeton, NJ: Princeton University Press, 2002); Schulman, *From Cotton Belt to Sunbelt*; Robert O. Self, *American Babylon: Race and the Struggle for Postwar Oakland* (Princeton, NJ: Princeton University Press, 2005); Andrew Needham, *Power Lines: Phoenix and the Making of the Modern Southwest* (Princeton, NJ: Princeton University Press, 2014); Thomas J. Sugrue, *The Origins of the Urban Crisis: Race and Inequality in Postwar Detroit* (Princeton, NJ: Princeton University Press, 1996).

9. Lauchlin Currie, *The Role of Economic Advisers in Developing Countries* (Westport, CT: Greenwood Press, 1981), 59–60 and passim; World Bank, *The Basis of a Development Program for Colombia* (Washington, DC, 1950); United States Senate, Committee on Foreign Relations, *Survey of the Alliance for Progress* (Washington, DC: US Government Printing Office, 1969), 659–864; Albert O. Hirschman, *The Strategy of Economic Development* (New Haven, CT: Yale University Press, 1958).

10. Albert O. Hirschman, "The Rise and Decline of Development Economics," in *Essays in Trespassing: Economics to Politics and Beyond* (Cambridge: Cambridge University Press, 1981), 20; Albert O. Hirschman, *The Passions and the Interests: Political Arguments for Capitalism before Its Triumph* (Princeton, NJ: Princeton University Press, 2013), 3; Jeremy Adelman, *Worldly Philosopher: The Odyssey of Albert O. Hirschman* (Princeton, NJ: Princeton University Press, 2013), 477–88.

11. Sarah Babb, *Managing Mexico: Economists from Nationalism to Neoliberalism* (Princeton, NJ: Princeton University Press, 2001); Montecinos and Markoff, eds., *Economists in the Americas.*

12. Marion Fourcade, *Economists and Societies: Discipline and Profession in the United States, Britain, and France, 1890s to 1990s* (Princeton, NJ: Princeton University Press, 2009); Marion Fourcade, "The Construction of a Global Profession: The Transnationalization of Economics," *American Journal of Sociology* 112, no. 1 (July 2006): 145–94.

13. Frank Safford and Marco Palacios, *Colombia: Fragmented Land, Divided Society* (Oxford: Oxford University Press, 2002); Catherine LeGrand, *Frontier Expansion and Peasant Protest in Colombia, 1850–1936* (Albuquerque: University of New Mexico Press, 1986); Marco Palacios,

¿De quien es la tierra? Propiedad, politicización y protesta campesina en la década de 1930 (Bogotá: Fondo de Cultura Económica, 2011).

14. Robert A. Karl, *Forgotten Peace: Reform, Violence, and the Making of Contemporary Colombia* (Berkeley: University of California Press, 2017); Mary Roldán, *Blood and Fire: La Violencia in Antioquia, Colombia, 1946–1953* (Durham, NC: Duke University Press, 2002).

15. Eduardo Sáenz Rovner, *Colombia años 50: Industriales, política y diplomacia* (Bogotá: Universidad Nacional de Colombia, 2002).

16. Roberto Junguito and Hernán Rincón, "La política fiscal en el siglo XX en Colombia," *Borradores de economía*, no. 318 (Bogotá: Banco de la República, December 2004), 123.

17. Currie, *Role of Economic Advisers*, 60–62; White House Press Release, March 14, 1961, JFK Library, National Security Files, Box 215, Folder "Latin America, General, 3/8/61–3/14/61"; Michele Alacevich, *The Political Economy of the World Bank: The Early Years* (Stanford, CA: Stanford University Press, 2009), 112–46.

18. Karen M. Tani, *States of Dependency: Welfare, Rights, and American Governance, 1935–1972* (Cambridge: Cambridge University Press, 2016); Daniel R. Ernst, *Tocqueville's Nightmare: The Administrative State Emerges in America, 1900–1940* (Oxford: Oxford University Press, 2014); Gail Radford, *The Rise of the Public Authority: Statebuilding and Economic Development in Twentieth-Century America* (Chicago: University of Chicago Press, 2013); Brian Balogh, *The Associational State: American Governance in the Twentieth Century* (Philadelphia: University of Pennsylvania Press, 2015); James T. Sparrow, William J. Novak, and Stephen W. Sawyer, eds., *Boundaries of the State in US History* (Chicago: University of Chicago Press, 2015).

19. Cited in Eduardo Wiesner, "Perspectivas de la Planificación y de la Programación Presupuestaria," in *Informe Final del Tercer Seminario Interamericano de Presupuesto, Santiago, Chile, 7–11 de mayo de 1973* (Washington, DC: OAS, 1974), 36.

20. "The Goal of Management Is to 'Get Things Done': An Interview with David Lilienthal," *Columbia Journal of World Business* (November–December 1968): 57.

21. Kwame Ture (Stokely Carmichael) and Charles V. Hamilton, *Black Power: The Politics of Liberation in America* (New York: Vintage, 1992), 5.

22. Alyosha Goldstein, *Poverty in Common: The Politics of Community Action during the American Century* (Durham, NC: Duke University Press, 2012); Daniel Immerwahr, *Thinking Small: The United States and the Lure of Community Development* (Cambridge, MA: Harvard University Press, 2015); Karin Alejandra Rosemblatt, "Other Americas: Transnationalism, Scholarship, and the Culture of Poverty in Mexico and the United States," *Hispanic American Historical Review* 89 (2009): 603–41; Judy Tzu-Chun Wu, *Radicals on the Road: Internationalism, Orientalism, and Feminism during the Vietnam Era* (Ithaca, NY: Cornell University Press, 2013); Peniel E. Joseph, *Waiting 'til the Midnight Hour: A Narrative History of Black Power in America* (New York: Henry Holt, 2006); Robin D. G. Kelley, *Freedom Dreams: The Black Radical Imagination* (Boston: Beacon Press, 2002); Nikhil Pal Singh, *Black Is a Country: Race and the Unfinished Struggle for Democracy* (Cambridge, MA: Harvard University Press, 2004); Brenda Gayle Plummer, *In Search of Power: African Americans in the Era of Decolonization, 1956–1974* (Cambridge: Cambridge University Press, 2013); Daniel M. Cobb, *Native Activism in Cold War America: The Struggle for Sovereignty* (Lawrence: University Press of Kansas, 2008); Paul C. Rosier, *Serving Their Country: American Indian Politics and Patriotism in the Twentieth Century* (Cambridge, MA: Harvard University Press, 2009).

23. Immerwahr, *Thinking Small*, 138–50.

24. David E. Lilienthal, *Management: A Humanist Art* (New York: Columbia University Press, 1967), 38. The book is a published version of speeches given in 1966.

25. Quinn Slobodian, *Globalists: The End of Empire and the Birth of Neoliberalism* (Cambridge, MA: Harvard University Press, 2018); Juan Gabriel Valdés, *Pinochet's Economists: The Chicago School in Chile* (Cambridge: Cambridge University Press, 1995); Babb, *Managing Mexico*; Angus Burgin, *The Great Persuasion: Reinventing Free Markets since the Depression* (Cambridge, MA: Harvard University Press, 2012); Philip Mirowski and Dieter Plehwe, eds., *The Road from Mont Pèlerin: The Making of the Neoliberal Thought Collective* (Cambridge, MA: Harvard University Press, 2009); David Harvey, *A Brief History of Neoliberalism* (New York: Oxford University Press, 2005); Kim Phillips-Fein, *Invisible Hands: The Making of the Conservative Movement from the New Deal to Reagan* (New York: W. W. Norton, 2009); Bethany Moreton, *To Serve God and Wal-Mart: The Making of Christian Free Enterprise* (Cambridge, MA: Harvard University Press, 2009); Nelson Lichtenstein, *The Retail Revolution: How Wal-Mart Created a Brave New World of Business* (New York: Picador, 2009); Mark Blyth, *Great Transformations: Economic Ideas and Institutional Change in the Twentieth Century* (New York: Cambridge University Press, 2002); Greg Grandin, *The Last Colonial Massacre: Latin America in the Cold War* (Chicago: University of Chicago Press, 2004); Monica Prasad, *The Politics of Free Markets: The Rise of Neoliberal Economic Policies in Britain, France, Germany, and the United States* (Chicago: University of Chicago Press, 2006); Judith Stein, *Pivotal Decade: How the United States Traded Factories for Finance in the Seventies* (New Haven, CT: Yale University Press, 2011); Jefferson Cowie, *The Great Exception: The New Deal and the Limits of American Politics* (Princeton, NJ: Princeton University Press, 2016).

26. Glen Biglaiser, *Guardians of the Nation? Economists, Generals, and Economic Reform in Latin America* (Notre Dame, IN: University of Notre Dame Press, 2002).

27. Bockman, *Markets in the Name of Socialism*, 1.

Chapter 1: Decentralization in One Valley

1. David E. Lilienthal, "Shall We Have More TVA's?" *New York Times*, January 7, 1945.

2. James M. Boughton, *Silent Revolution: The International Monetary Fund, 1979–1989* (Washington, DC: International Monetary Fund, 2001), chap. 9; Eduardo Wiesner Durán, *From Macroeconomic Correction to Public Sector Reform: The Critical Role of Evaluation* (Washington, DC: World Bank Discussion Papers, 1993); Eduardo Wiesner, *Fiscal Federalism in Latin America: From Entitlements to Markets* (Washington, DC: Inter-American Development Bank, 2003), 45.

3. David E. Lilienthal to Reinaldo Scarpetta, June 5, 1969, DELP, Box 482, Folder "Fund for Multinational Management Education, 1969."

4. David E. Lilienthal to Chairman, Members of the Board of Directors, and Executive Director, Corporación Autónoma Regional del Valle del Cauca, Cali (hereafter CVC), July 14, 1955, D&R, Box 230, Folder 9.

5. Steven M. Neuse, *David E. Lilienthal: The Journey of an American Liberal* (Knoxville: University of Tennessee Press, 1996), chaps. 2–10.

6. David E. Lilienthal to Edward R. Murrow, January 14, 1950, and David E. Lilienthal, "Where Are the Places in the World," DELP, Box 308, Folder "Point Four Material, 1950."

7. "Report on Conference with Mr. Eugene Black," April 1950, DELP, Box 362, Folder "World Bank."

8. Cary Reich, *Financier: The Biography of André Meyer* (New York: Wiley, 1998), 80.

9. David E. Lilienthal to Milo Perkins, July 30, 1950, DELP, Box 362, Folder "Perkins, Milo, 1950."

10. Reich, *Financier*, 65–68, 188.

11. David E. Lilienthal, *Big Business: A New Era* (New York: Harper and Brothers, 1953), ix, 35, 52–59.

12. Adolf A. Berle Jr. and Gardiner C. Means, *The Modern Corporation and Private Property* (New York: Macmillan, 1932); Lilienthal, *Big Business*, 23–26, 153–54.

13. David E. Lilienthal, "Big Business for a Big Country" (Employee Relations Staff, GM Information Rack Service, n.d.), and Ruth Ivey, "Memorandum of Telephone Conversation with Mr. Lufkin's office," November 5, 1953, DELP, Box 310, Folder "Publication: *Big Business for a Big Country*."

14. F. A. Hayek, *The Road to Serfdom* (Chicago: University of Chicago Press, 1994), 63–79.

15. David E. Lilienthal and Robert H. Marquis, "The Conduct of Business Enterprises by the Federal Government," *Harvard Law Review* 54 (1941): 546–601; David E. Lilienthal, *TVA: Democracy on the March* (Chicago: Quadrangle Books, 1944), 138–49; David E. Lilienthal, *This I Do Believe* (New York: Harper and Brothers, 1949), 80–91. TVA officials themselves subscribed to multiple conceptions of decentralization. For their debates, see David Ekbladh, *The Great American Mission: Modernization and the Construction of an American World Order* (Princeton, NJ: Princeton University Press, 2010), 62, 287; Daniel Immerwahr, *Thinking Small: The United States and the Lure of Community Development* (Cambridge, MA: Harvard University Press, 2015), 40–43; Sarah T. Phillips, *This Land, This Nation: Conservation, Rural America, and the New Deal* (Cambridge: Cambridge University Press, 2007), 91–93; Erwin C. Hargrove, *Prisoners of Myth: The Leadership of the Tennessee Valley Authority, 1933–1990* (Princeton, NJ: Princeton University Press, 1994), 19–114; Philip Selznick, *TVA and the Grass Roots: A Study in the Sociology of Formal Organization* (New Orleans: Quid Pro, 2011).

16. General Electric, "How G-E Subcontracts Help People in Fenton, Mich.," brochure, n.d., and *General Electric Stockholders Quarterly*, October 25, 1951, DELP, Box 312, Folder "Big Business—Decentralization Chapter VIII."

17. Ralph J. Cordiner, *Developing Management Leadership for a Free Society* (New York: American Management Association, 1952); Ralph J. Cordiner, *New Frontiers for Professional Managers* (New York: McGraw-Hill, 1956), 37, 61–75, 88–90; Lilienthal, *Big Business*, 154–55; Kim Phillips-Fein, *Invisible Hands: The Making of the Conservative Movement from the New Deal to Reagan* (New York: W. W. Norton, 2009), 103.

18. In 1951, Lilienthal made what was arguably his first international advising trip, but it was an unofficial one. He traveled as a private citizen to India and wrote an article in *Collier's* recommending a TVA-style program for the Indus River. Indian politicians and the World Bank picked up the idea and credited him with it. Ekbladh, *Great American Mission*, 162.

19. "A Job for Mr. Perkins," *Time*, August 25, 1941; "The Last New Dealer," *Time*, July 26, 1943; Tharon Perkins, "Venezuela Booms," *Harper's*, December 1950, 58–66; "How Green Will My Valley Be?" *Tucson Daily Citizen*, July 14, 1954.

20. José Castro Borrero to Alfonso Bonilla Aragón, September 9, 1972, reprinted in Corporación Autónoma Regional del Valle del Cauca, *Génesis y Desarrollo de una Visión de Progreso:*

CVC Cincuenta Años (Cali: CVC, 2004), 52–53; Jairo Henry Arroyo R., *Historia de las prácticas empresariales en el Valle del Cauca: Cali, 1900–1940* (Cali: Programa Editorial Universidad del Valle, 2006), 28.

21. Oscar Almario García, *La configuración moderna del Valle del Cauca, Colombia, 1850–1940: Espacio, poblamiento, poder y cultura* (Cali: Cecan Editores, 1994); Germán Colmenares, *Historia económica y social de Colombia, Tomo II: Popayán, una sociedad esclavista, 1680–1800* (Bogotá: La Carreta Inéditos, 1979); Germán Colmenares, *Cali, terratenientes, mineros y comerciantes: Siglo XVIII* (Bogotá: Tercer Mundo Editores, Universidad del Valle, Banco de la República, Colciencias, 1997); Frank Safford and Marco Palacios, *Colombia: Fragmented Land, Divided Society* (Oxford: Oxford University Press, 2002), 44–48, 177–84, 272; Universidad del Valle, *Sociedad y economía en el Valle del Cauca*, 5 vols. (Bogotá: Banco Popular, 1983); Edgar Vásquez Benítez, *Historia de Cali en el siglo 20: Sociedad, economía, cultura y espacio* (Cali: Universidad del Valle, 2001); Nancy P. Appelbaum, *Muddied Waters: Race, Region, and Local History in Colombia, 1846–1948* (Durham, NC: Duke University Press, 2003).

22. David E. Lilienthal, *Recommendation on the Establishment of Regional Development Authorities by the Republic of Colombia: An Informal Report Submitted on the Invitation of the President of the Republic His Excellency General Gustavo Rojas Pinilla* (New York, 1954); José Castro Borrero, "Contenido Social y Económico del Plan Lilienthal," July 4, 1955, D&R, Box 232, Folder 4; INCORA Acta No. 62, August 2, 1963.

23. José Castro Borrero to Alfonso Bonilla Aragón, September 9, 1972, reprinted in CVC, *Génesis y Desarrollo*, 53; Phanor J. Eder, *El Fundador Santiago M. Eder*, trans. Antonio José Cárdenas and Luis Carlos Velasco Madriñán (Bogotá: Flota Mercante Grancolombiana, 1981), 20, 65, 76, 97, 637; Bernardo Garcés Córdoba to David E. Lilienthal, April 14, 1965, D&R, Folder 230, Box 11.

24. David E. Lilienthal, *The Journals of David E. Lilienthal, Vol. 5: The Harvest Years, 1959–1963* (New York: Harper and Row, 1964), 371; "Colombian 'TVA' Moving Along," *Courier-Journal* (Louisville), October 26, 1961; "Máximos orientadores de la CVC," *CVC: 25 Años Vitales*, October 18, 1979, D&R, Box 181, Folder 3.

25. Arroyo, *Historia de las prácticas empresariales*, 253–56; Bernardo Garcés Córdoba to Development and Resources Corp., February 22, 1956, D&R, Box 238, Folder 11.

26. "Manuel Carvajal Sinisterra, 1916–1971: Empresario social," *El Tiempo*, February 2, 1999.

27. Arroyo, *Historia de las prácticas empresariales*, 29–31, 53, 403–6.

28. Catherine LeGrand, *Frontier Expansion and Peasant Protest in Colombia, 1830–1936* (Albuquerque: University of New Mexico Press, 1986); James D. Henderson, *Modernization in Colombia: The Laureano Gómez Years, 1889–1965* (Gainesville: University Press of Florida, 2001), chap. 4; Frank Safford, *The Ideal of the Practical: Colombia's Struggle to Form a Technical Elite* (Austin: University of Texas Press, 1976).

29. Stuart George McCook, *States of Nature: Science, Agriculture, and Environment in the Spanish Caribbean, 1760–1940* (Austin: University of Texas Press, 2002), 106–39; Eduardo Mejía Prado, "Ciro Molina Garcés y Carlos Durán Castro: Gestores y científicos en el desarrollo agropecuario del Valle del Cauca," in *Empresas y empresarios en la historia de Colombia, Siglos XIX–XX: Una colección de estudios recientes*, ed. Carlos Dávila L. de Guevara (Bogotá: Norma, CEPAL, Uniandes, 2003), 1189–214.

30. CVC, *Génesis y Desarrollo*, 54–55, 57.

31. John C. Cady to Edwin G. Flittie, May 29, 1952, National Archives, College Park (hereafter NACP), RG 469, Entry 1140, Box 4, Folder "Public Administration—City Planning Community Development"; Alan Laflin to John Cady, July 14, 1952, NACP, RG 469, Entry 1140, Box 8, Folder 3.0; John C. Cady to Alan Laflin, July 14, 1952, NACP, RG 469, Entry UD889, Box 31, Folder 1; Lyall E. Peterson to Files, December 8, 1952, NACP, RG 469, Entry UD889, Box 30, Folder 2; John C. Cady to Rey M. Hill, February 6, 1953, NACP, RG 469, Entry 1140, Box 1, Folder "Correspondence Mr. Cady Aug 52–June 53."

32. Paul Oquist, *Violence, Conflict, and Politics in Colombia* (New York: Academic Press, 1980), 227; Marco Palacios, *Between Legitimacy and Violence: A History of Colombia, 1975–2002* (Durham, NC: Duke University Press, 2006), 19–20, 27–30, 63–64, 150–53; Eduardo Sáenz Rovner, *Colombia años 50: Industriales, política y diplomacia* (Bogotá: Universidad Nacional de Colombia, 2002); Safford and Palacios, *Colombia*, 246.

33. Palacios, *Between Legitimacy and Violence*, 20; Frédéric Martínez, *Nacionalismo cosmopólita: La referencia europea en la construcción nacional en Colombia, 1845–1900* (Bogotá: Banco de la República, Instituto Francés de Estudios Andinos, 2001).

34. Inter-American Housing and Planning Center, *Housing Institutions in Bogotá: Development and Administration* (Bogotá: Inter-American Housing and Planning Center, 1961); David E. Lilienthal, *Journals, Vol. 3*, 544; Marco Palacios, *Coffee in Colombia, 1850–1970: An Economic, Social, and Political History* (Cambridge: Cambridge University Press, 2002), 214–26.

35. David E. Lilienthal to Milo Perkins, June 9, 1954, and Milo Perkins to David E. Lilienthal, June 14, 1954, July 23, 1954, July 27, 1954, August 20, 1954, DELP, Box 391, Folder "Perkins, Milo, 1954"; "How Green Will My Valley Be?" *Tucson Daily Citizen*, July 14, 1954; Milo Perkins, "Grass Made to Your Order," *Harper's*, May 1955, 64–67.

36. Lilienthal, *Recommendation*.

37. Diego Tobón Arbeláez, "Aspectos Jurídicos de la CVC," *Economía Colombiana* Año 3, Vol. 9, No. 26 (June 1956), 270–74; Diego Tobón Arbeláez, *Principios fundamentales del derecho administrativo* (Medellín: Tipografía Industrial, 1939); Bernardo Garcés Córdoba, untitled document, March 12, 1963, Correspondencia, Archivo Central, Corporación Autónoma Regional del Valle del Cauca, (hereafter CVC Correspondencia).

38. The corporation's name was later changed to the Corporación Autónoma Regional del Valle del Cauca. "Corporación Autónoma Regional del Cauca Board," D&R, Box 230, Folder 9.

39. David E. Lilienthal to Gustavo Rojas Pinilla, April 27, 1955, D&R, Box 230, Folder 9.

40. Decree No. 1829 of 1955; Bernardo Garcés Córdoba, "Talk to IDE Participants, Ninth Course, Buga," February 24, 1964, D&R, Box 235, Folder 18; Lilienthal, *Journals, Vol. 3*, 488; "TVA Network of Power Lines Linking Hydro-Electric Dams," *Christian Science Monitor*, February 13, 1942.

41. David E. Lilienthal to Diego Garcés Giraldo, March 21, 1955, and David E. Lilienthal to Bernardo Garcés Córdoba, March 18, 1955, both in D&R, Box 230, Folder 9.

42. See, for instance, José Castro Borrero, "Contenido Social y Económico del Plan Lilienthal," D&R, Box 232, Folder 4; "Un 'Plan Lilienthal' para explotar el Río Bogotá proyecta el gobierno," *El Espectador*, November 5, 1954; "Que el Plan Lilienthal sea aplazado piden en el Valle," *La República*, June 22, 1956; "Pleno respaldo al 'Plan Lilienthal' ofreció ayer el presidente Rojas," *El Colombiano*, July 12, 1956.

43. Peregrino Castro Martínez and Fanny E. de Castro M. to David E. Lilienthal, June 20, 1956, D&R, Box 231, Folder 3.

44. The CVC signed additional contracts with Point IV, the Instituto Geológico Nacional, Albert Hirschman, and engineering firms in Colombia, the United States, and Belgium. David E. Lilienthal to Chairman, Members of the Board of Directors, and Executive Director, CVC, July 14, 1955, D&R, Box 230, Folder 9; "Agreement between Corporación Autónoma Regional del Cauca, Cali, Colombia and Development and Resources Corporation, New York, NY, USA," D&R, Box 231, Folder 7; Instituto Geológico Nacional to Bernardo Garcés Córdoba, August 24, 1955, D&R, Box 232, Folder 4; "Personal de la CVC," December 31, 1955, D&R, Box 236, Folder 1; Frank A. Pettit to Walter G. Stoneman, November 3, 1956, NACP, RG 469, Entry 1140, Box 20, Folder 3.0; Bernardo Garcés Córdoba to Sr. Payán, November 4, 1955, CVC Correspondencia.

45. Gordon Clapp to Bernardo Garcés Córdoba, November 17, 1955, D&R, Box 229, Folder 3; Bernardo Garcés Córdoba to David E. Lilienthal, April 1, 1956, D&R, Box 238, Folder 11; CVC Acta 67, April 16, 1956.

46. David E. Lilienthal to J. Burke Knapp, November 2, 1954, and J. Burke Knapp to David E. Lilienthal, November 5, 1954, D&R, Box 240, Folder 6; IBRD, *The Autonomous Corporation of the Cauca and the Development of the Upper Cauca Valley: Report of a Mission Organized by the International Bank for Reconstruction and Development at the Request of the Government of the Republic of Colombia and the Autonomous Regional Corporation of the Cauca* (Washington, DC: IBRD, 1955).

47. Bernardo Garcés Córdoba to Alberto Gómez Arenas, January 14, 1956, attached to CVC Acta 57, February 7, 1956.

48. David E. Lilienthal to Robert L. Garner, November 21, 1955, D&R, Box 240, Folder 6.

49. David E. Lilienthal to Robert L. Garner, November 21, 1955, D&R, Box 240, Folder 6; Frank Tannenbaum, "The Future of Democracy in Latin America," *Foreign Affairs* 33 (1955): 444; Joseph Maier and Richard Whitney Weatherhead, *Frank Tannenbaum: A Biographical Essay* (New York: University Seminars, Columbia University, 1974); Olsson, *Agrarian Crossings*, 47–55.

50. Albert Waterston, interview by Bogomir Chokel, May 14, 1985, 4, World Bank/IFC Oral History Program.

51. Harry L. Case, "Gordon R. Clapp: The Role of Faith, Purposes, and People in Administration," *Public Administration Review* 24 (1964): 86–91.

52. Lilienthal, *TVA*, xiv–xv; Selznick, *TVA and the Grass Roots*.

53. Albert O. Hirschman, *Journeys toward Progress: Studies of Economic Policy-Making in Latin America* (New York: Twentieth Century Fund, 1963), 168.

54. Bernardo Garcés Córdoba to Alvaro Ortiz Lozano, August 24, 1955, CVC Correspondencia.

55. "La financiación en el exterior puede considerarse asegurada," *Diario del Pacífico*, June 3, 1955.

56. "La financiación en el exterior puede considerarse asegurada," *Diario del Pacífico*, June 3, 1955.

57. "Rojas Pinilla puede sacar avante el Plan Lilienthal," *Relator*, January 7, 1956.

58. José Castro Borrero, "Contenido Social y Económico del Plan Lilienthal," D&R, Box 232, Folder 4; CVC, *Génesis y Desarrollo*, 96.

59. José Castro Borrero, "Contenido Social y Económico del Plan Lilienthal," D&R, Box 232, Folder 4.

60. Sáenz Rovner, *Colombia años 50*.

61. Bernardo Garcés Córdoba, "Talk to IDE Participants, Ninth Course, Buga"; Hirschman, *Journeys*, 136.

62. Lilienthal, *Journals, Vol. 3*, 483–91.

63. César Augusto Ayala Diago, *Resistencia y oposición al establecimiento del Frente Nacional: Orígenes de la Alianza Nacional Popular, ANAPO: Colombia, 1953–1964* (Bogotá: Universidad Nacional, 1996), 45; "Peron-Style Bloc in Colombia Dies," *New York Times*, February 26, 1955.

64. William J. Hayes to files, April 14, 1955, D&R, Box 228, Folder 13; 1955 contracts between Point IV and the CVC in NACP, RG 469, Entry 1140, Box 8, Folder 3.0.

65. William J. Hayes, "The Realities of the Lilienthal Plan," August 22, 1956, D&R, Box 231, Folder 1.

66. "CHIDRAL, 45 años generando progreso," *El Tiempo*, November 15, 1995.

67. The conflict over Calima, CHIDRAL, and national funding for the CVC is documented in hundreds of sources in D&R and NACP. See D&R, Box 229, Folder 3; Box 231, Folders 1–5; Box 232, Folders 2–5; Box 233, Folder 4; Box 234, Folders 4–8; Box 235, Folders 5, 11, 13; Box 236, Folders 1–2; Box 240, Folder 6. See NACP, RG 469, Entry 1140, Box 14, Folder 3.0; RG 469, Entry 1140, Box 20, Folder 3.0; RG 469, Entry 1140, Box 27, Folder "Cauca Valley Development, FY 1957/58."

68. Bernardo Garcés Córdoba to Luis Córdoba Mariño, August 24, 1956, CVC Correspondencia.

69. *Report on the Demand for Power in Cali and the Cauca Region, Prepared by Hirschman and Kalmanoff, Economic Consultants, Bogotá* (Cali: CVC, February 1956), Albert O. Hirschman Papers (hereafter AOHP), Box 37, Folder 1.

70. CVC Acta 73, June 18, 1956.

71. CVC Acta 75, July 2, 1956.

72. Bernardo Garcés Córdoba to David E. Lilienthal, June 16, 1956, D&R, Box 231, Folder 4; W. J. Hayes, "CVC Considerations and/or Arrangements to Be Established during Lilienthal Visit," July 7, 1956, and David E. Lilienthal to Bernardo Garcés Córdoba, July 12, 1956, D&R, Box 229, Folder 3; Gordon R. Clapp and David E. Lilienthal to Bernardo Garcés Córdoba, July 13, 1956, Gordon R. Clapp, "Notes on Colombian Trip," July 16, 1956, and "Copy of Cable Received October 11, 1956, Cali, Colombia," D&R, Box 231, Folder 4; CVC Acta No. 77, July 9, 1956.

73. Bernardo Garcés Córdoba to David E. Lilienthal, March 26, 1957, D&R, Box 231, Folder 4; Bernardo Garcés Córdoba, "Talk to IDE Participants, Ninth Course, Buga."

74. Unsigned letter to David E. Lilienthal, October 11, 1955, D&R, Box 233, Folder 4; Bernardo Garcés Córdoba to J. Burke Knapp, April 27, 1956, CVC Correspondencia; CVC Acta 75, July 2, 1956; Bernardo Garcés Córdoba to David E. Lilienthal, February 6, 1957, D&R Box 231, Folder 4; William J. Hayes to Carson Crocker, January 8, 1957, D&R, Box 231, Folder 4; William J. Hayes to J. F. Bell, January 10, 1957, NACP, RG 469, Entry 1140, Box 20, Folder 3.0; Bernardo Garcés Córdoba, "Talk to IDE Participants, Ninth Course, Buga"; Hirschman, *Journeys*, 137.

75. A. Groot to Carson O. Crocker, July 18, 1957, NACP, RG 469, Entry 1140, Box 27, Folder "Cauca Valley Development, FY 1957/58"; "Que el Plan Lilienthal sea aplazado piden en el

Valle," *La República*, June 22, 1956; Phillip Z. Kirpich to Bernardo Garcés Córdoba, August 2, 1956, and Leonide Hassilev to E. H. Anson, August 13, 1956, D&R, Box 236, Folder 1.

76. F. G. Steiner to AM, EHH, May 28, 1956, D&R, Box 233, Folder 4; Gordon R. Clapp, "Notes on telephone conversations with B. Knapp (WB) and Ambassador Urrutia, Colombia—CVC," July 25, 1956, D&R, Box 231, Folder 4; Orvis A. Schmidt to Bernardo Garcés Córdoba, October 15, 1956, D&R, Box 240, Folder 6.

77. Carson O. Crocker to Wyman R. Stone, January 29, 1957, NACP, RG 469, Entry 1140, Box 26, Folder 19.0.

78. David E. Lilienthal to Gordon R. Clapp, March 19, 1957, D&R, Box 231, Folder 4.

79. CVC Acta 79, July 23, 1956; and in CVC Correspondencia: Bernardo Garcés Córdoba to Alberto Gómez Arenas, June 16, 1956; Bernardo Garcés Córdoba to Alberto Acosta, July 26, 1956; Bernardo Garcés Córdoba to Mariano Ospina Navia, August 6, 1956; Bernardo Garcés Córdoba to Luis Córdoba Mariño, August 24, 1956; Bernardo Garcés Córdoba to Mariano Ospina Navia, September 25, 1956; Bernardo Garcés Córdoba to Luis Córdoba Mariño, January 21, 1957; Bernardo Garcés Córdoba to Jaime Polonia Puyo, April 30, 1957.

80. Bernardo Garcés Córdoba to David E. Lilienthal, November 6, 1956, and January 7, 1957, D&R, Box 231, Folder 4.

81. Bernardo Garcés Córdoba to David E. Lilienthal, April 27, 1957, D&R, Box 231, Folder 4; CVC Acta 87, April 22, 1957.

82. Palacios, *Between Legitimacy and Violence*, 150–54; Sáenz Rovner, *Colombia años 50*, 209–29.

83. CVC Acta 92, November 26, 1957; CVC Acta 101, May 16, 1958.

84. Bernardo Garcés Córdoba to David E. Lilienthal, December 16, 1957, D&R, Box 234, Folder 3.

85. Bernardo Garcés Córdoba to David E. Lilienthal, June 17, 1957; Bernardo Garcés Córdoba to Albert Waterston, June 25, 1957; Bernardo Garcés Córdoba to Gordon R. Clapp, January 30, 1958; Bernardo Garcés Córdoba to Albert Waterston, January 30, 1958, all in CVC Correspondencia.

86. "$2.8 Million Power Loan in Colombia," IBRD Press Release No. 567, December 15, 1958, George Kalmanoff Papers, Box 3, Folder "Colombia—Foreign Loan Data"; Bernardo Garcés Córdoba to Walton Seymour, July 2, 1963, D&R, Box 235, Folder 18.

87. David E. Lilienthal to Bernardo Garcés Córdoba, December 3, 1957, D&R, Box 231, Folder 11; Gordon Clapp, "Notes on telephone call with Albert Waterston," December 13, 1957, D&R, Box 234, Folder 3.

88. Walter Howe to William Hayes, October 19, 1955, and Bernardo Garcés Córdoba to Walter Howe, October 25, 1955, both in NACP, RG 469, Entry 1140, Box 14, Folder 3.0.

Chapter 2: Land Reform in Local Hands and Minds

1. Centro de Investigación y Educación Popular, ed., *Campesinado y capitalismo en Colombia* (Bogotá: Centro de Investigación y Educación Popular, 1981); Cristina Escobar, *Experiencia de organización campesina en el Valle del Cauca, 1960–1980* (Bogotá: Taller Prodesal, Instituto Mayor Campesino y Estudios Rurales Latinoamericanos, 1987); Luis Llorente, Armando Salazar, and Angela Gallo, *Distribución de la propiedad rural en Colombia, 1960–1984* (Bogotá: Ministerio de

Agricultura, Corporación de Estudios Ganaderos y Agrícolas, 1985); Absalón Machado, *Problemas agrarios colombianos* (Bogotá: Corporación de Estudios Ganados y Agrícolas, 1986); Marco Palacios, *Between Legitimacy and Violence: A History of Colombia, 1975–2002* (Durham, NC: Duke University Press, 2006), 182–84; Stephen G. Rabe, *The Most Dangerous Area in the World: John F. Kennedy Confronts Communist Revolution in Latin America* (Chapel Hill: University of North Carolina Press, 1999), 159; Nola Reinhardt, *Our Daily Bread: The Peasant Question anf Family Farming in the Colombian Andes* (Berkeley: University of California Press, 1988); José María Rojas G. and Luis Carlos Castillo G., *Poder local y recomposición campesina* (Cali: Fondo DRI-CIDSE UNIVALLE, 1991); Jeffrey F. Taffet, *Foreign Aid as Foreign Policy: The Alliance for Progress in Latin America* (New York: Routledge, 2007), chap. 7; Leon Zamosc, *The Agrarian Question and the Peasant Movement in Colombia* (Cambridge: Cambridge University Press, 1986). For typical treatments of the 1961 land reform in public discussion, see Antonio Caballero, "Reforma Agraria," *Semana*, March 1, 2008, and Jorge Eduardo Cock, "Reforma y contrarreforma agraria," *El Tiempo*, June 15, 2016.

2. For related arguments about landowner influence rather than resistance, see Bruce M. Bagley, "Political Power, Public Policy, and the State in Colombia: Case Studies of Urban and Agrarian Reforms during the National Front, 1958–1974" (PhD diss., University of California, Los Angeles, 1979), and Ernest Feder, *The Rape of the Peasantry: Latin America's Landholding System* (Garden City, NY: Anchor Books, 1971).

3. Transcript of Bernardo Miguel Garcés Córdoba, Fletcher School of Law and Diplomacy, Tufts University Archives; Bernardo Garcés Córdoba to the Editor, *New York Times*, May 11, 1941; and the following in CVC Correspondencia: Bernardo Garcés Córdoba to John Stovel, March 6, 1957; Bernardo Garcés Córdoba to Edward Prentise, January 26, 1961; Bernardo Garcés Córdoba to Eugene Staley, January 22, 1962; Bernardo Garcés Córdoba to Douglas Henderson, June 26, 1964; Bernardo Garcés Córdoba to Donald Lloyd-Jones, June 15, 1956; Bernardo Garcés Córdoba to Sir Edgar Vaughan, June 8, 1965; Bernardo Garcés Córdoba to L. J. Lebret, July 22, 1960; Bernardo Garcés Córdoba to the Editor, *New York Times*, March 30, 1966; Bernardo Garcés Córdoba to Carlos Sanz de Santamaría, May 28, 1960.

4. Kenneth W. Thompson to Leland C. DeVinney, September 20, 1960, RF RG A81, Box R1738, Folder "311S, Universidad del Valle, Economics, 1958–1960"; Laurence deRycke, "Memorandum of Conversations b/w Apodaca, Conger and deRycke," May 12, 1964, RF, RG A81, Box R1737, Folder "311S, Universidad del Valle, Economics, Jan–Apr 1964."

5. Bernardo Garcés Córdoba to John Conger, April 22, 1964; Bernardo Garcés Córdoba to Charles Fossum, March 21, 1963; Bernardo Garcés Córdoba to Harold Larsen, April 25, 1955; Bernardo Garcés Córdoba to William J. Hayes, June 12, 1956; Bernardo Garcés Córdoba to Jorge Mejía Salazar, July 30, 1957; Bernardo Garcés Córdoba to Luigi Laurenti, March 25, 1964, all CVC Correspondencia.

6. *Censo Agropecuario del Valle del Cauca, 1959* (Cali: Universidad del Valle, Facultad de Ciencias Económicas, 1963); Michael T. Taussig, *The Devil and Commodity Fetishism in South America* (Chapel Hill: University of North Carolina Press, 1980), 70–92; Reinhardt, *Our Daily Bread*.

7. Bernardo Garcés Córdoba, "La CVC Como Instrumento para el Desarrollo Económico y Social de Colombia," conferencia dictada en Cali, June 18, 1958, CVC Informes Técnicos; and documents in CVC Correspondencia: Bernardo Garcés Córdoba to Harold Larsen, April 25,

1955; Bernardo Garcés Córdoba to Herbert Stewart, May 31, 1955; Bernardo Garcés Córdoba to David H. Blellech, June 14, 1955; Bernardo Garcés Córdoba to Donald Lloyd-Jones, November 6, 1956; Bernardo Garcés Córdoba to Alvaro Ortiz Lozano, January 3, 1957; Bernardo Garcés Córdoba to Víctor M. Patiño, January 10, 1957; Bernardo Garcés Córdoba to Carson Crocker, January 21, 1957; Bernardo Garcés Córdoba to Marino Dávalos, March 11, 1957; Bernardo Garcés Córdoba to Marion Walker, March 11, 1957; Bernardo Garcés Córdoba to Albert Waterston, December 3, 1957; Bernardo Garcés Córdoba to John Johnston, June 4, 1958; Bernardo Garcés Córdoba to Enrique Peñalosa, February 24, 1962; Víctor Manuel Patiño to Bernardo Garcés Córdoba, December 12, 1962.

8. Shawn van Ausdal, "Productivity Gains and the Limits of Tropical Ranching in Colombia," *Agricultural History* 85, no. 3 (2012): 1–32; Shawn van Ausdal, "Pasture, Profit, and Power: An Environmental History of Cattle Ranching in Colombia, 1850–1950," *Geoforum* 40 (2009): 707–19; Bernardo Garcés Córdoba to Harold Larsen, September 19, 1955, and Bernardo Garcés Córdoba, "The CVC Land Tax," February 14, 1962, CVC Correspondencia.

9. Bernardo Garcés Córdoba to Dr. Llano, August 16, 1955; Bernardo Garcés Córdoba to Carlos A. Lombana Cuervo, October 1, 1956; Bernardo Garcés Córdoba to George Funke, March 20, 1958, CVC Correspondencia.

10. CVC Acta 81, September 19, 1956; CVC Acta 86, January 24, 1957; and in CVC Correspondencia: Bernardo Garcés Córdoba to Alberto Gómez Arenas, November 20, 1956; Bernardo Garcés Córdoba to Carlos A. Lombana Cuervo, January 29, 1957.

11. Informe CVC C-4267, Rev. 1, "Proyecto Roldanillo-La Unión-Toro: Estado y Progreso," January 1965, 4, 148, 149–57, 163–82, INAT; CVC Report C-4267, "Roldanillo-La Unión-Toro Project: Status of Development," April 1962, 4, BMC.

12. CVC Acta 102, June 3, 1958; Informe CVC C-4267, Rev. 1, 1, INAT; and in CVC Correspondencia: CVC, "Notas sobre el programa de recuperación de tierras de la CVC," August 14, 1957; Bernardo Garcés Córdoba to Philip Z. Kirpich, December 9, 1957; Bernardo Garcés Córdoba to John W. Johnston, March 13, 1959; Bernardo Garcés Córdoba to Moncada and Kirpich, September 23, 1960; Bernardo Garcés Córdoba to Arnold A. Boettcher, June 23, 1961; Bernardo Garcés Córdoba to Agustín Merea Canelo, July 15, 1961.

13. CVC Acta 129, December 9, 1958; CVC Acta 154, May 11, 1959.

14. CVC Acta 156, May 21, 1959.

15. CVC Acta 260, August 9, 1961; INCORA, *Estudio de evaluación de los proyectos de adecuación de tierras, primera fase: Estado actual de los proyectos*, vol. 3, December 1972, P-22, INAT.

16. CVC Acta 220, September 12, 1960; CVC Acta 241, February 20, 1961; CVC Acta 254, June 12, 1961; Bernardo Garcés Córdoba to Charles Fossum, February 1, 1962, CVC Correspondencia; CVC Report C-4267, 1, BMC.

17. Bernardo Garcés Córdoba to Gustavo Balcázar Monzón, April 7, 1959, CVC Correspondencia; M. C. Mirow, "Origins of the Social Function of Property in Chile," *Fordham Law Review* 80, no. 3 (2011): 1183–217; Eliécer Batista Pereira and James Iván Coral Lucero, "La función social de la propiedad: La recepción de León Duguit en Colombia," *Criterio Jurídico* (Cali) 10, no. 1 (2010): 59–90; Jorge González Jácome, "La Propiedad en el Catolocismo Social y su Lectura en América Latina en la Década de los 1960," in *Aproximación iberoamericana a la construcción de una sociedad democrática y justa*, ed. Jaime Rossell Granados, Julio Andrés Sampedro Arrubla, Jorge González Jácome, and Ildikó Szegedy-Maszák (Bogotá: Ediciones Jurídicas Gustavo Ibáñez, 2015), 197–214.

18. Catherine LeGrand, *Frontier Expansion and Peasant Protest in Colombia, 1850–1936* (Albuquerque: University of New Mexico Press, 1986); Marco Palacios, *¿De quien es la tierra? Propiedad, politización y protesta campesina en la década de 1930* (Bogotá: FCE, Universidad de los Andes, 2011).

19. Bernardo Garcés Córdoba to David E. Lilienthal, September 30, 1960, D&R, Box 182, Folder 1.

20. William A. Doebele, Orville F. Grimes Jr., and Johannes F. Linn, "Participation of Beneficiaries in Financing Urban Services: Valorization Charges in Bogotá, Colombia," *Land Economics* 55 (1979): 75; CVC Acta 100, April 24, 1958.

21. Bernardo Garcés Córdoba to Alberto Gómez Arenas, June 20, 1956, CVC Correspondencia, emphasis in the original.

22. Bernardo Garcés Córdoba to Otto Morales Benítez, July 25, 1961, CVC Correspondencia.

23. Bernardo Garcés Córdoba to Charles Fossum, July 30, 1960, and Bernardo Garcés Córdoba to José Consuegra, September 29, 1960, CVC Correspondencia.

24. Bernardo Garcés Córdoba to Carlos Lleras Restrepo, May 3, 1961, CVC Correspondencia; Robert A. Karl, *Forgotten Peace: Reform, Violence, and the Making of Contemporary Colombia* (Berkeley: University of California Press, 2017).

25. Bernardo Garcés Córdoba to Otto Morales Benítez, July 25, 1961, CVC Correspondencia; Ley 135 de 1961, Capítulo 12, Artículos 68 and 72.

26. CVC Report C-4267, "Roldanillo-La Unión-Toro Project: Status of Development," April 1962, 112, BMC.

27. Bernardo Garcés Córdoba to Barend A. deVries, November 23, 1961, CVC Correspondencia.

28. Bryon Denny to William V. Turnage, December 15, 1959, NACP, RG 59, Entry A13178, Box 13, Folder "Land Reform 59"; William V. Turnage, "Statement on Agrarian Reform," Pan American Union, April 25–30, 1960, NACP, RG 59, Entry A1 3178, Box 13, Folder "Land Reform 57–60."

29. Wymberley Coerr to Dempster McIntosh, February 24, 1960, NACP, RG 59, Entry A1 3178, Box 22, Folder "L 1.1, Folder 1, Latin America: Agriculture, Sept. 1959–Dec. 1960"; Riddleberger and Rubottom to Under Secretary, March 17, 1960, NACP, RG 59, Entry A1 3178, Box 13, Folder "Land Reform 1960."

30. CVC Acta 247, April 24, 1961; and in CVC Correspondencia: Bernardo Garcés Córdoba to Carlos Lleras Restrepo, May 3, 1961; R. J. Brady to Bernardo Garcés Córdoba, September 5, 1961; Bernardo Garcés Córdoba to Rollin Atwood, September 20, 1961.

31. Samir Camilo Daccach to Henry J. Eder, May 11, 1959, Bernardo Garcés Córdoba to Lauchlin Currie, June 8, 1959, Bernardo Garcés Córdoba to Srta. Duque, June 5, 1961, Bernardo Garcés Córdoba, two letters to Rodrigo Botero, both March 6, 1962, Bernardo Garcés Córdoba to Dr. Palacín, May 29, 1962, Vicente Aragón A. to CVM, April 24, 1963, CVC Correspondencia; CVC Acta 157, May 25, 1959; CVC Acta 292, April 3, 1962; Bernardo Garcés Córdoba to David E. Lilienthal, June 19, 1961, and David E. Lilienthal to Diego Suarez, December 20, 1961, DELP, Box 425, Folder "Re Colombia CVC 1961"; and the contents of D&R, Box 238, Folder 8; D&R Box 226, Folders 3 and 9.

32. CAR subdirector Hernando Zuleta became national director of the budget in 1962. David E. Lilienthal to Hernando Zuleta, December 19, 1962, DELP, Box 431, Folder "Re Colombia CVC 1962."

33. Miguel Fadul and Enrique Peñalosa, *La industria azucarera en la economía colombiana* (Cali: Asocaña, 1961); Bernardo Garcés Córdoba to Alvaro Ortiz Lozano, January 26, 1955, CVC Correspondencia; Montague Yudelman, "Excerpt from MY diary: Luncheon with Dr. Roberts, Dr. A. Hirschman, Dr. G. Kalmanoff," May 24, 1956, RF, RG 1.2, Series 311, Box 78, Folder 739.

34. Eugene R. Black to André Meyer, October 2, 1961, DELP, Box 425, Folder "Re Colombia CVC 1961."

35. David E. Lilienthal to JFK, January 13, 1960, and JFK to David E. Lilienthal, January 22, 1960, DELP, Box 419, Folder "Kennedy, John F., 1960", David E. Lilienthal to Jacob Javits, April 11, 1960, DELP, Box 419, Folder "Javits, Jacob K. 1960"; David E. Lilienthal to JFK, September 6, 1960, DELP, Box 417, Folder "Development and Resources Corporation 1960"; David E. Lilienthal to William O. Douglas, June 8, 1961, DELP, Box 425, Folder "Re Colombia CVC 1961"; Gordon R. Clapp to Teodoro Moscoso, November 13, 1961, D&R, Box 51, Folder 3; Bernardo Garcés Córdoba to Edward M. Kennedy, August 5, 1961, CVC Correspondencia; Bernardo Garcés Córdoba to Henry Hopp, January 23, 1962, CVC Correspondencia.

36. David E. Lilienthal to Bernardo Garcés Córdoba, February 15, 1961, DELP, Box 425, Folder "Re Colombia CVC 1961"; Robert Sargent Shriver Jr. to David E. Lilienthal, March 22, 1961, and David E. Lilienthal to Robert Sargent Shriver Jr., January 8, 1962, DELP, Box 428, Folder "Peace Corps, 1961"; David E. Lilienthal to Enrique Peñalosa, October 6, 1961, D&R, Box 226, Folder 9.

37. Bernardo Garcés Córdoba to Alfonso Ocampo Londoño, August 1, 1960, and Bernardo Garcés Córdoba to Albert O. Hirschman, February 14, 1961, CVC Correspondencia.

38. Bernardo Garcés Córdoba to Jorge Franco Holguín, August 1, 1960, CVC Correspondencia; Bernardo Garcés Córdoba to Alvaro Llorente, September 3, 1960, CVC Correspondencia.

39. CVC Acta 261, August 16, 1961; CVC Acta 270, October 16, 1961; Morris I. Stein, *Volunteers for Peace: The First Group of Peace Corps Volunteers in a Rural Community Development Program in Colombia, South America* (New York: Wiley and Sons, 1966), 7, 142.

40. Informe CVC C-4267, Rev. 1, January 1965, 147–48, INAT; INCORA Acta 12, April 23, 1962; Bernardo Garcés Córdoba to Enrique Peñalosa, June 11, 1962, CVC Correspondencia.

41. CVC Acta 296, April 30, 1962; Bernardo Garcés Córdoba to Enrique Peñalosa, June 11, 1962, CVC Correspondencia.

42. Bernardo Garcés Córdoba to Enrique Peñalosa, February 11, 1963, CVC Correspondencia.

43. INCORA Acta 21, July 16, 1962; INCORA Acta 54, June 3, 1963.

44. CVC Acta 138, January 26, 1959; CVC Acta 154, May 11, 1959; CVC Acta 325, January 8, 1963; CVC Acta 329, February 5, 1963; Bernardo Garcés Córdoba to Enrique Peñalosa, January 21, 1963 and February 6, 1963, CVC Correspondencia.

45. Victor Daniel Bonilla, "El Valle del Cauca a la Hora de su Transformación Agraria," *Tierra: Revista de Economía Agraria*, no. 6 (October–December 1967): 39.

46. Informe CVC C-4267 Rev. 1, January 1965, 5, 147, INAT.

47. Bernardo Garcés Córdoba to Carlton R. Adams, July 19, 1962, CVC Correspondencia.

48. Bernardo Garcés Córdoba to Carlos Obando Velasco, July 17, 1962, CVC Correspondencia.

49. Bernardo Garcés Córdoba to Leo L. Anderson, August 31, 1964, CVC Correspondencia.

50. Informe CVC C-4267, Rev. 1, January 1965, 5, 147–48, INAT; INCORA, *Plan de Desarrollo: Distrito de Riego Roldanillo-La Unión-Toro* (Palmira: INCORA, 1973), 21, INAT; Bernardo Garcés Córdoba to Alfonso Jaramillo Arango, July 17, 1963, CVC Correspondencia.

51. CVC Report C-4267, 116, BMC.

52. CVC Report C-4267, 102, BMC; Informe CVC C-4267, Rev. 1, January 1965, 147, 190.

53. INCORA, *Estudio de Evaluación de los Proyectos de Adecuación de Tierras, Primera Fase: Estado Actual de los Proyectos*, Vol. 3, P22-3, December 1972, INAT; Informe CVC C-4267, Rev. 1, January 1965, 147; Bonilla, "El Valle del Cauca a la Hora de su Transformación Agraria," 39.

54. Blanca Dora Holguín de Robledo, "Incidencia social y económica del Proyecto RUT (Roldanillo La Unión, Toro) en la vereda Tierrablanca, Municipio de Roldanillo, Valle" (undergraduate thesis, Universidad del Valle, 1994).

55. Guillermo Barney Materón to Personero Municipal, Roldanillo, Valle, October 26, 1962, CVC Correspondencia.

56. Bernardo Garcés Córdoba to Junta Comunal, Guayabal y El Palmar, Roldanillo, September 19, 1962, and Bernardo Garcés Córdoba to Gustavo Balcázar Monzón, November 9, 1962, CVC Correspondencia.

57. Vicente Aragón A. to Cristóbal Cadavid Z., September 9, 1963, and AMC, "Distrito de Riego Roldanillo-La Unión-Toro: Desarrollo de la Orden de Trabajo No. 1 al 31 de Dic. de 1963," CVC Correspondencia.

58. Bernardo Garcés Córdoba to Charles Fossum, December 28 1962, CVC Correspondencia.

59. Juan Pablo Alvarez V. to Rafael Pino E., January 30, 1965, CVC Correspondencia.

60. Juan Pablo Alvarez V. to María Adelina Borja viuda de García, May 31, 1963, CVC Correspondencia.

61. Juan Pablo Alvarez V. to Gustavo Salazar García, Ricardo Ramírez Osorio, and Ignacio Cruz Roldán, February 27, 1965, CVC Correspondencia.

62. Bernardo Garcés Córdoba to Luigi Laurenti, September 28, 1964, CVC Correspondencia.

63. AMC, "Distrito de Riego Roldanillo-La Unión-Toro: Desarrollo de la Orden de Trabajo No. 1 al 31 de Dic. de 1963," CVC Correspondencia; Bonilla, "El Valle del Cauca a la Hora de su Transformación Agraria," 49.

64. Bernardo Garcés Córdoba to Agustín Merea, June 27, 1964; Bernardo Garcés Córdoba to Luigi Laurenti, September 28, 1964; Bernardo Garcés Córdoba to Humberto González N., December 17, 1964; Juan Pablo Alvarez V. to Gustavo Salazar García, Ricardo Ramírez Osorio, and Ignacio Cruz Roldán, February 27, 1965, all CVC Correspondencia.

65. Juan Pablo Alvarez V. to Guillermo Becerra Navia, January 20, 1965, CVC Correspondencia; Juan Pablo Alvarez V. to Coronel Ignacio Valderrama Diaz, August 21, 1965, CVC Correspondencia.

66. CVC Acta 437, August 1, 1966.

67. Escobar, *Experiencia de organización campesina en el Valle del Cauca*, 19–21; Gonzalo Sánchez G. and Donny Meertens, *Bandits, Peasants, and Politics: The Case of "La Violencia" in Colombia* (Austin: University of Texas Press, 2001); Eduardo Pizarro Leongómez and Ricardo

Peñaranda, *Las FARC (1949–1966): De la autodefensa a la combinacion de todas las formas de lucha* (Bogotá: Tercer Mundo, 1991); Karl, *Forgotten Peace.*

68. See CVC Correspondencia: Bernardo Garcés Córdoba to José María Paredes, August 3, 1956 and November 15, 1956; Bernardo Garcés Córdoba to Coronel Antonio M. Convers Pardo, June 1, 1957; Diego Llano to Coronel Gabriel Rebeiz Pizarro, January 22, 1958; Bernardo Garcés Córdoba to Coronel Alfredo Angel Tamayo, August 11, 1959; Bernardo Garcés Córdoba to César A. Cabrera, July 18, 1960. The CVC obtained a gun for its external payor who carried cash to Cauca. Juan Pablo Alvarez V. to Señor Coronel Rumualdo Fajardo Alvarez, April 10, 1964, CVC Correspondencia.

69. Bernardo Garcés Córdoba to Alberto Bernal García, September 29, 1960; Bernardo Garcés Córdoba to A. D. Spottswood, May 21, 1962; Juan Pablo Alvarez V. to Coronel Bernardo Sánchez Salazar, December 15, 1966, all CVC Correspondencia.

70. Juan Pablo Alvarez V. to Gustavo Balcázar Monzón, September 4, 1963, CVC Correspondencia; Bernardo Garcés Córdoba to Orvis Schmidt, November 8, 1963, CVC Correspondencia.

71. Bernardo Garcés Córdoba to David E. Lilienthal, April 14, 1965, D&R, Box 230, Folder 11 and CVC Correspondencia; "Solemne Funeral de Harold Eder," *El Tiempo,* April 14, 1965.

72. CVC Acta 95, January 8, 1958.

73. Bernardo Garcés Córdoba to Comandante de la Policia Nacional, División del Valle, August 13, 1957, and September 2, 1957, CVC Correspondencia.

74. CVC Acta 103, June 23, 1958; CVC Acta 117, September 22, 1958; CVC Acta 149, April 13, 1959.

75. Bernardo Garcés Córdoba to Coronel Gabriel Rebeiz Pizarro, July 16, 1958, CVC Correspondencia.

76. CVC Acta 63, March 5, 1956; CVC Acta 64, March 12, 1956; CVC Acta 84, December 3, 1956; CVC Acta 91, October 21, 1957; and in CVC Correspondencia: Bernardo Garcés Córdoba to Ciro Velasco C., December 5, 1956; Bernardo Garcés Córdoba to Mariano Ospina Navia, January 30, 1957; Bernardo Garcés Córdoba to Albert Waterston, July 22, 1957; Bernardo Garcés Córdoba to Jorge Mejía Salazar, July 30, 1957; n.a., "Notas sobre el impuesto del 4 por 1000 para las obras de la CVC," August 14, 1957; Bernardo Garcés Córdoba to James Eder, August 22, 1957; Bernardo Garcés Córdoba to Director, *El Tiempo,* October 21, 1957; unsigned letter to Alejandro Jiménez Arango, December 19, 1958; Absalón Fernandez de Soto to Jorge Ospina Delgado, December 19, 1958.

77. Bernardo Garcés Córdoba to Alberto Lleras Camargo, July 16, 1958, and Bernardo Garcés Córdoba to Roberto García-Peña, October 21, 1958, CVC Correspondencia; and the following in NACP, RG 469, Entry 1140, Box 27, Folder "Cauca Valley Development, FY 1957/58": "Que la CVC es un producto del más férreo centralismo," *Relator,* July 1957, clipping; A. Groot to Carson O. Crocker, July 18, 1957; Carlos Aragón Cabal to Director, *El Tiempo,* September 29, 1957; Sociedad de Agricultores y Ganaderos del Valle del Cauca, "Estado del Conflicto entre la CVC y los Postulados Democráticos Colombianos."

78. CVC Acta 100, April 24, 1958; CVC Acta 131, December 18, 1958; CVC Acta 134, January 5, 1959; CVC Acta 136, January 19, 1959; CVC Acta 151, April 27, 1959; CVC Acta 155, May 14, 1959; Carlos Lleras Restrepo, *Concepto relacionado con el decreto legislativo número 0160 de 1956 (enero 31), que autorizó un aumento del impuesto predial para dotar de recursos a la Corporación*

Autónoma Regional del Cauca (Bogotá: CVC, 1958); Bernardo Garcés Córdoba to Edgar N. Langley, June 6, 1959, CVC Correspondencia.

79. CVC Acta 134, January 5, 1959.

80. Bernardo Garcés Córdoba to James Eder, August 22, 1957, CVC Correspondencia.

81. Jesús Antonio Bejarano, *Economía y poder* (Bogotá: CEREC, 1985), 198–209.

82. Antonio J. Posada F. to Albert O. Hirschman, July 1, 1963, AOHP, Box 68, Folder 8.

83. INCORA Acta 48, April 8, 1963.

84. Bernardo Garcés Córdoba to Alfonso Jaramillo Parango and Sebastian Ospina B., July 5, 1963, and Bernardo Garcés Córdoba to Alfonso Jaramillo Arango, July 17, 1963, CVC Corresponencia.

85. Enrique Peñalosa, "Réplica de Enrique Peñalosa a opositores de la Reforma Agraria," *Revista Nacional de Agricultura* 55, no. 698 (1963), reprint in Steenbock Library, University of Wisconsin; Enrique Peñalosa, "Resultados de la Reforma Agraria en Dos Años," *El Tiempo*, March 2, 1964.

86. INCORA Acta 62, August 2, 1963.

87. INCORA Acta 78, November 22, 1963; CVC Acta 334, March 26, 1963; CVC Acta 362, November 19, 1963; CVC Acta 370, February 18, 1964; Bernardo Garcés Córdoba to Eugenio Castro B., November 27, 1963, CVC Correspondencia.

88. INCORA Acta 100, May 26, 1964.

89. CVC Acta 419, January 10, 1966; CVC Acta 461, June 19, 1967; CVC Acta 506, August 12, 1968; CVC Acta 529, March 24, 1969; CVC Acta 556, October 20, 1969; CVC Acta 644, December 20, 1971.

90. Decreto 2602 de 1968.

91. Alejandro Martínez Caicedo, *El Zarpazo: Andanzas del INCORA en el Valle del Cauca* (Bogotá? 1970); n.a., "La concentración parcelaria de Jamundí: Declaración de los gremios agrarios," *Revista Nacional de Agricultura* 64, no. 773 (August 1970): 12–14.

92. By 1971, the CVC considered even that provision too strict and proposed amending the law to offer exemptions based on the expected macroeconomic outcomes of investments: landowners could escape land reform by spending money in ways that promised to generate employment and income, contribute to national agricultural production goals, or improve the national balance of payments. Ultimately, a 1973 amendment to the agrarian reform law simply eliminated the 1968 provision, and the CVC went on to negotiate ad hoc exemptions for large landowners who paid valorization taxes. CVC Acta 623, June 14, 1971; Artículo 37, Ley 4 de 1973.

93. Holguín de Robledo, "Incidencia social y económica del Proyecto RUT," 67–70.

94. Fabio Peñarete Villamil, "25 años del Instituto de Crédito Territorial," *Economía colombiana* 20, no. 58 (1964): 72.

Chapter 3: Private Homes and Economic Orders

1. Instituto de Crédito Territorial (hereafter ICT), *Informe al Señor Ministro de Fomento para su Memoria al Congreso Nacional* (Bogotá: ICT, 1962), 39–45.

2. Momacu, "El barrio verde" (unpublished manuscript, ca. 2000), BLAA.

3. Alfonso Torres Carrillo, *La ciudad en la sombra: Barrios y luchas populares en Bogotá, 1950–1977* (Bogotá: Centro de Investigación y Educación Popular, 1993); Carlos Arango Zuluaga, *La*

lucha por la vivienda en Colombia (Bogotá: Ecoe, 1981); "Adelina Suaza y Víctor Suaza, madre e hijo, Barrio Policarpa Salavarrieta," interview in *Voces del común: Testimonios de líderes comunales de Bogotá*, ed. Marta Lasprilla and Piet Spijkers (Bogotá: Departamento Administrativo de Acción Comunal, 1998), 33–60; Rakesh Mohan, *Understanding the Developing Metropolis: Lessons from the City Study in Bogotá and Cali, Colombia* (Oxford: Oxford University Press, 1994).

4. ICT, *Una política de vivienda para Colombia: Primer seminario nacional de vivienda, 1955* (Bogotá: Imprenta del Estado Mayor General de las Fuerzas Armadas de Colombia, 1956), chaps. 2, 4; ICT, "Mejoramiento de la vivienda campesina en Colombia," *Revista Nacional de Agricultura* 35, nos. 430–31 (1940): 28–29; Fabil Peñarete Villamil, "25 años del Instituto de Crédito Territorial," *Economía Colombiana* (February 1964): 71–74; Susana Romero Sánchez, "Ruralizing Urbanization: Credit, Housing, and Modernization in Colombia, 1920-1948" (PhD diss., Cornell University, 2015).

5. Romero Sánchez, "Ruralizing Urbanization," 241–55.

6. ICT, *Una política de vivienda para Colombia*, 12–13, 16–21, 25.

7. Richard Harris, "The Silence of the Experts: 'Aided Self-Help Housing,' 1939–1954," *Habitat International* 22 (1998): 165–89; Nancy H. Kwak, *A World of Homeowners: American Power and the Politics of Housing Aid* (Chicago: University of Chicago Press, 2015), 100–111.

8. Harris, "Silence"; Foreign Operations Administration, Washington, DC, airgram, December 29, 1954, NACP, RG 469, Entry 1140, Box 9, Folder 8.1; Kwak, *A World of Homeowners*.

9. Rodrigo Llorente to John C. Cady, November 21, 1952, NACP, RG 469, Entry 1140, Box 2, Folder 2, "Housing Project. June 51–June 53"; T. Wilson Longmore, "Housing," April 30, 1953, NACP, RG 469, Entry 1140, Box 1, Folder "Longmore, T. Wilson—Housing Economics, Correspondence."

10. Harris, "Silence"; Richard Harris, "Flattered but Not Imitated: Cooperative Self-Help and the Nova Scotia Housing Commission," *Acadiensis* 31, no. 1 (2001): 103–28; Tricia Schulist and Richard Harris, " 'Build Your Own Home': State-Assisted Self-Help Housing in Canada, 1942–75," *Planning Perspectives* 17, no. 4 (2002): 347–72; C. A. Sharpe and A. J. Sawyer, *Sweat Equity: Cooperative House-Building in Newfoundland, 1920–1974* (St. John's: Institute of Social and Economic Research, 2016); Richard Harris, "Slipping through the Cracks: The Origins of Aided Self-Help Housing, 1918–53," *Housing Studies* 14, no. 3 (1999): 281–309; Richard Harris, *Building a Market: The Rise of the Home Improvement Industry, 1914–1960* (Chicago: University of Chicago Press, 2012), 202–23; *Report of the Administrator of the Farmers Home Administration, 1950* (Washington, DC: United States Department of Agriculture, 1950), 16–20; *Report of the Administrator of the Farmers Home Administration, 1953* (Washington, DC: United States Department of Agriculture, 1953), 12.

11. Wilson Longmore, memos dated July 3 and July 7, 1953, NACP, RG 469, Entry 1140, Box 1, Folder "Longmore, T. Wilson—Housing Economics, Correspondence"; McMann to Foreign Operations Administration, Washington, DC, February 1, 1954, NACP, RG 469, Entry 1140, Box 9, Folder 8.1.

12. T. Wilson Longmore to Jean F. Rogier, July 3, 1953, NACP, RG 469, Entry UD889, Box 30, Folder 12.

13. Working for the ICT from 1953 to 1954, Longmore trained his Colombian colleagues to produce the country's first housing statistics and fought fruitlessly for self-help. See the contents of NACP, RG 469, Entry 1140, Box 1, Folder "Longmore, T. Wilson—Housing Economics,

Correspondence"; NACP, RG 469, Entry 1140, Box 9, Folder 8.1; NACP, RG 469, Entry UD889, Box 30, Folder 12; NACP, RG 469, Entry 1140, Box 2, Folder 2; and NACP, RG 469, Entry 1140, Box 11, Folder 18.10.

14. Jason Scott Smith, *Building New Deal Liberalism: The Political Economy of Public Works* (Cambridge: Cambridge University Press, 2006).

15. CINVA, *CINVA RAM: Máquina portatil para hacer bloques de tierra estabilizada* (Bogotá: CINVA, 1957); *Casa campesina de suelo-cemento: Juego de planos de construcción* (Bogotá: CINVA, 1957); René Eyhéralde F., *El concepto del desarrollo progresivo en el diseño de la vivienda* (Bogotá: CINVA, 1953).

16. Harris, *Building a Market*, 304–34.

17. "The Schools and Architectural Research," *Journal of Architectural Education* 1 (Spring 1947): 31; "Small House Costs Cut by Improved Building Methods," *Science News Letter* 54, no. 8 (1948): 285; Rudard A. Jones, "Your Home—1902 to 1952," *Popular Mechanics*, May 1952, 147–49; Rudard A. Jones to Walter Howe, May 17, 1955, and "Biographical Statement of Edward G. Echeverria, Planner," both in in NACP, RG 469, Entry 1140, Box 9, Folder 8.1; Rudard A. Jones, "Final Report," November 20, 1957, NACP, RG 469, Entry 1140, Box 39, Folder "Reports FY 1957–1958" (Folder 2 of 5); Rudard A. Jones, "Report of Activities, August 16–September 15, 1955," and Jones, Memo UI/ICA/6/4/56-1, both in RG 469, Entry 1140, Box 16, Folder 8.1, "Housing & Community, General, FY56."

18. T. Wilson Longmore to Agustín Amaya Rojas, April 21, 1953, NACP, RG 469, Entry 1140, Box 1, Folder "Longmore, T. Wilson—Housing Economics, Correspondence"; "Biographical Sketch, Thomas W. Longmore," NACP, RG 469, Entry 1140, Box 2, Folder 2, "Housing Project. June 51–June 53"; Jess Gilbert, *Planning Democracy: Agrarian Intellectuals and the Intended New Deal* (New Haven, CT: Yale University Press, 2015); Daniel Immerwahr, *Thinking Small: The United States and the Lure of Community Development* (Cambridge, MA: Harvard University Press, 2015), 46–53.

19. Stassen, Foreign Operations Administration, Washington, DC, airgram, September 4, 1954, NACP, RG 469, Entry 1140, Box 9, Folder 8.1; ICA airgram, October 27, 1956, NACP, RG 469, Entry 1140, Box 23, Folder 8.1.

20. Foreign Operations Administration, Washington, DC, airgram, May 5, 1955, NACP, RG 469, Entry 1140, Box 9, Folder 8.1.

21. "Genuine Aid Program," *New York Daily News*, March 3, 1957.

22. T. Wilson Longmore to George L. Reed, June 14, 1954, NACP, RG 469, Entry 1140, Box 9, Folder 8.1; Robert L. King to C. L. Williams, November 24, 1953, NACP, RG 469, Entry UD889, Box 30, Folder 12; Carson O. Crocker to Wyman R. Stone, November 5, 1956, NACP, RG 469, Entry 1140, Box 23, Folder 8.1, "Housing & Community, General, FY57."

23. Rudard A. Jones, "Final Report," November 20, 1957, NACP, RG 469, Entry 1140, Box 39, Folder "Reports FY 1957–1958" (Folder 2 of 5); William N. Womelsdorf to John Johnston, February 17, 1958, NACP, RG 469, Entry 1140, Box 39, Folder "Reports FY 1957–1958" (Folder 2 of 5); Inter-American Housing and Planning Center, *Annual Report, 1957* (Bogotá: CINVA, 1957); CINVA, *Informe del CINVA, 1958* (Bogotá: CINVA, 1958); ICT, *Informe al Señor Ministro de Fomento Para su Memoria al Congreso Nacional* (Bogotá: ICT, 1959), 10–11; CINVA, *Mesas redondas sobre el aporte de la comunidad en vivienda: Ayuda mutua y esfuerzo propio (autconstrucción); Informe* (Bogotá: CINVA, 1959).

24. Robert A. Karl, *Forgotten Peace: Reform, Violence, and the Making of Contemporary Colombia* (Berkeley: University of California Press, 2017); Caroline F. Ware, "Observaciones sobre acción comunal urbana en el Distrito Especial de Bogotá," July 1959, in Jorge Enrique Rivera Farfán, "Informe de la misión de asistencia técnica directa de la OEA a la Oficina de Planificación del Distrito Especial de Bogotá, Colombia," August 1959, Archivo de Bogotá; Elisabeth Shirley Enochs to Wyman R. Stone, August 6, 1953, NACP, RG 469, Entry UD889, Box 29, Folder 12.

25. ICT, *Informe al Señor Ministro de Fomento Para su Memoria al Congreso Nacional* (Bogotá: ICT, 1962), 39–45; ICT, *Informe al Señor Ministro de Fomento Para su Memoria al Congreso Nacional* (Bogotá: ICT, 1963), 10; Raúl Cristancho et al., *Ciudad Kennedy: Memoria y realidad* (Bogotá: Universidad Nacional de Colombia, 2003), 6–7; ICT, *Programa de vivienda de interés social dentro de la Alianza para el progreso, Préstamo DLF No. 207, Informe Final* (Bogotá: ICT, 1966).

26. ICT, *Informe al Señor Ministro de Fomento Para su Memoria al Congreso Nacional* (Bogotá: ICT, 1965), 67–68; Secretaría de Cultura, Recreación y Deportes, *Localidad de Kennedy: Ficha básica* (Bogotá, 2008).

27. Miguel Urrutia and Olga Marcela Namen, "Historia del crédito hipotecario en Colombia," *Ensayos sobre política económica* 30, no. 67 (2012): 280–306.

28. Cristancho, *Ciudad Kennedy*; ICT, *Informe al Ministro de Fomento* (1965), Peñarete Villamil, "25 años del Instituto de Crédito Territorial," 74.

29. Momacu, "El Barrio Verde," 18.

30. White House Press Release, March 14, 1961, JFK Library, National Security Files, Box 215, Folder "Latin America, General, 3/8/61–3/14/61."

31. Inter-American Housing and Planning Center, *Annual Report, 1957*.

32. Robert C. Hickok to Mr. Boerner, December 27, 1956, AWP, Box 19, Folder "People's Capitalism May–Dec 1956 (2)"; "Annex A: People's Capitalism Exhibit," AWP, Box 19, Folder "People's Capitalism May–Dec 1956 (3)."

33. George A. McBride, "A Description of Proyecto Ciudad Techo and an Analysis of Some of Its Economic Aspects," June–September 1962, 20, 41–42, unpublished report, Fondo CINVA; Graciela García de Avendaño, interview by the author, Bogotá, Colombia, February 11, 2011.

34. Ana Teresa Huertas de Díaz, interview by the author, Bogotá, Colombia, February 10, 2011.

35. Mohan, *Understanding the Developing Metropolis*, 148.

36. CINVA embraced capital-intensive techniques after the rise of the National Front. For practitioners, these different versions of aided self-help appeared deeply antagonistic. Mark Healey, "Shelter in a Time of Violence: Colombia as Unlikely Laboratory for Housing, 1951–1961" (unpublished manuscript, April 1, 2015); John F. C. Turner and Robert Fichter, eds., *Freedom to Build: Dweller Control of the Housing Process* (New York: Macmillan, 1972).

37. McBride, "Description of Proyecto Ciudad Techo," 9.

38. McBride, "Description of Proyecto Ciudad Techo," 20–21; interview with Ana Teresa Huertas de Díaz; María Ester Ramírez, interview by the author, Bogotá, Colombia, February 3, 2011; Clímaco Patiño Sepúlveda and María del Carmen Samboni de Patiño, interview by the author, Bogotá, Colombia, February 21, 2011.

39. These statistics come from surveys by John I. Laun, who notes that they are conservative, since residents likely underreported violations. John I. Laun, "El Estado y la vivienda en Colombia: Análisis de urbanizaciones del ICT," in *Urbanismo y vida urbana*, ed. Carlos Castillo (Bogotá: Instituto Colombiana de Cultura, 1977), 309, 316; interviews with Clímaco Patiño Sepúlveda and María del Carmen Samboni de Patiño, Graciela García de Avendaño, María Ester Ramírez, and Ana Teresa Huertas de Díaz.

40. Elsa Gómez Gómez, "Evaluación socio-económica del proyecto de ayuda mutua de la Supermanzana 8-A, Ciudad Kennedy, Bogotá: Estudio de caso de 28 viviendas," November 1966, chap. 2, unpublished report, Fondo CINVA.

41. Alcira Peñuela de Guerrero and Aura Morena de Fajardo, interview by the author, Bogotá, Colombia, January 31, 2011; interview with María Ester Ramírez.

42. Laun, "El Estado y la vivienda en Colombia," 324; Gómez Gómez, "Evaluación socio-económica," chap. 1.

43. CINVA visited recipients to see if they used each room as intended, saved money for home improvement, and cooperated with one another and ICT staff. McBride, "Description of Proyecto Ciudad Techo." For similar conflicts in Argentina and Brazil, see Leandro Benmergui, "The Alliance for Progress and Housing Policy in Rio de Janeiro and Buenos Aires in the 1960s," *Urban History* 36 (2009): 303–26.

44. Interviews with Aura Morena de Fajardo, January 28 and 31, 2011, Bogotá, Colombia; Alcira Peñuela de Guerrero; Clímaco Patiño Sepúlveda and María del Carmen Samboni de Patiño; and Elizabeth Torres, February 3, 2011, Bogotá, Colombia.

45. Interviews with María Ester Ramírez, Alcira Peñuela de Guerrero, Aura Morena de Fajardo (January 31, 2011), and Ana María Huertas de Díaz.

46. Jorge Nariño and residents of Supermanzana 9B to Guillermo Leon Valencia, January 28, 1964, AGN, Fondo Presidencia, 1960–1970, Transferencia 7, Despacho Sr. Presidente, Caja 153, Carpeta "Departamentos Territoriales."

47. Laun, "El Estado y la vivienda en Colombia," 313–14; interviews with Ana Teresa Huertas de Díaz and Aura Morena de Fajardo (January 28, 2011); and similar comments in the interviews cited previously.

48. Interviews with Clímaco Patiño Sepúlveda and María del Carmen Samboni de Patiño; Aura Morena de Fajardo (January 28, 2011); María Ester Ramírez; Ana Teresa Huertas de Díaz; Graciela García de Avendaño.

49. Judith Cabrera Cabrera, "Cuatro Puntas: Un sector residencial en vía de extinción," in *Bogotá, historia común* (Bogotá: Departamento Administrativo de Acción Comunal, 1998), 47–81; "José Elías Calderón Cabrera: Barrio Las Américas," in Lasprilla and Spijkers, *Voces del común*, 163; "José de la Cruz Acevedo Hurtado, Barrio Pío XII," in Lasprilla and Spijkers, *Voces del común*, 152–53.

50. "Adelina Suaza y Víctor Suaza," 33–60; Arango Zuluaga, *La lucha por la vivienda en Colombia*, 63–72.

51. Martín Reig, *La vivienda popular oficial y el desarrollo urbano* (Bogotá: Sociedad Colombiana de Planificación, 1972), mimeograph, Colección General, Archivo de Bogotá.

52. Alan Gilbert and Peter M. Ward, *Housing, the State, and the Poor: Policy and Practice in Three Latin American Cities* (Cambridge: Cambridge University Press, 1985), 129.

53. Arthur Schlesinger Jr. to John F. Kennedy, March 10, 1961, JFK Library, National Security Files, Box 215, Folder "Latin America, General, 3/8/61–3/14/61."

54. Interview with Aura Morena de Fajardo (January 31, 2011).

55. Roger J. Sandilands, *The Life and Political Economy of Lauchlin Currie: New Dealer, Presidential Advisor, and Development Economist* (Durham, NC: Duke University Press, 1990), 1–140; "FDR Injects New Life into the U.S. Foreign Service," *PM*, February 24, 1941.

56. World Bank, *The Basis of a Development Program for Colombia* (Washington, DC, 1950); Timothy Mitchell, *Rule of Experts: Egypt, Techno-Politics, and Modernity* (Berkeley: University of California Press, 2002), chap. 3.

57. Michele Alacevich, *The Political Economy of the World Bank: The Early Years* (Palo Alto, CA: Stanford University Press, 2009); Lauchlin Currie, *Informe Final del Comité de Desarrollo Económico* (Bogotá: Banco de la República, 1951).

58. Sandilands, *Life*, 141–77; James Boughton and Roger Sandilands, "Politics and the Attack on FDR's Economists: From the Grand Alliance to the Cold War," *Intelligence and National Security* 18, no. 3 (2003): 73–99.

59. Barend deVries, interview by Charles Ziegler, January 21, 1986, 15, World Bank/IFC Oral History Program.

60. Sandilands, *Life*, 159–221.

61. Lauchlin Currie, *Operación Colombia: Un programa nacional de desarrollo económico y social* (Barranquilla: Cámara Colombiana de la Construcción, 1961); Sandilands, *Life*, 204–5.

62. Lauchlin Currie, "The Planning and Administration of a New City," December 11, 1973, LBCP, Box 18, Folder "Housing Urban 1959–1993, Proyecto Salitre 74–90, carpeta #16"; Lauchlin Currie, *Urbanization Trends and Policies* (New York: UN Department of Economic and Social Affairs, 1973), 29–30; Lauchlin Currie, "According to Preliminary Calculations . . . ," January 30, 1974, LBCP, Box 18, Folder "Housing Urban 1959–1993, Proyecto Salitre 1974/90, Carpeta #17 (ene–jun 74)"; Lauchlin Currie, *Urbanization: Some Basic Issues* (New York: United Nations, 1975); Lauchlin Currie, *The Role of Economic Advisers in Developing Countries* (Westport, CT: Greenwood Press, 1981), 138–43.

63. Currie drew on Charles Richter, "Un análisis del papel del sector público en la construcción de vivienda," September 8, 1972, and other studies by Richter in LBCP, Box 17, Folder "Housing-Urban, 1959–1993, carpeta #3."

64. Lauchlin Currie, "The First New City within a City," September 5, 1974, LBCP, Box 18, Folder "Housing Urban 1959–1993, Proyecto Salitre 1974/90, Carpeta #17 (ene–jun 74)"; Lauchlin Currie, "A Fondo for Subsidized Popular Housing," September 22, 1986, LBCP, Box 18, Folder "Housing—Urban 1949–1993, carpeta #9."

65. Lauchlin Currie, "The Multiple Objectives of Urban Development," March 10, 1972, LBCP, Box 17, Folder "Housing-Urban, 1959–1993, carpeta #3"; Lauchlin Currie, "Capital and Housing," March 11, 1988, and other documents from 1988 in LBCP, Box 18, Folder "Housing-Urban, 1959–1993, carpeta #10"; Lauchlin Currie, "Macroeconomic Aspects of Housing," January 13, 1986, LBCP, Box 16, Folder "UPAC 1986"; Lauchlin Currie, "Residential Building as a Leading Sector," *Housing Finance International* 5, no. 3 (1992): 11–19; Lauchlin Currie, "Housing as an Instrument of Macro-Economic Policy," *Habitat International* 7, no. 5/6 (1983): 165–71; Lauchlin Currie, "The Interrelation of Urban and National Economic Planning," *Urban Studies* 12 (1975): 37–46; Lauchlin Currie, *La política urbana en un marco macroeconómico* (Bogotá:

Banco Central Hipotecario, 1983); Lauchlin Currie, *Taming the Megalopolis: A Design for Urban Growth* (Oxford: Pergamon Press, 1976).

66. See the following syllabi in the Archivo de Bogotá, colección general: CINVA, Serie: Enseñanza No. 4-D "Curso básico de introducción a la vivienda de interés social: D. Los Aspectos económicos, Edición preliminar," 1951; CINVA, Serie: Enseñanza No. 4-B, "Curso básico de introducción a la vivienda de interés social: B. Los Aspectos económicos, Edición preliminar," 1958; Jorge A. Videla, "Bases económicas del estudio de la vivienda," 1959.

67. Jorge Restrepo Hoyos to Montague Yudelman, October 1, 1958, and Leland DeVinney to Jorge Restrepo Hoyos, October 9, 1958, RF, RG 1.2, Series 311, Box 78, Folder 740.

68. Charles M. Hardin interview with Wallace N. Atherton, October 20, 1961, RF, RG 1.2, Series 311, Box 79, Folder 744; Jorge Ruiz Lara, "Aspectos Cuantitativos de la Operación Colombia," September 9, 1963, AGN, Fondo Departamento Nacional de Planeación, Code CONPES-6, Caja 8, Carpeta 84, Folio 22.

69. Sandilands, *Life*, 216–18; Lauchlin Currie, *La enseñanza de la economía en Colombia* (Bogotá: Tercer Mundo Ediciones, 1965); Lauchlin Currie, "La escuela de economía para graduados: Universidad de los Andes," February 24, 1964, LBCP, Box 20, Folder "Teaching 1960–1993, Carpeta #1."

70. Currie, *La enseñanza de la economía*; John M. Hunter and James Anthony Short Tenent, "The Teaching of Economics in Colombia," *Journal of Inter-American Studies* (April 1960): 189–96; Marion Fourcade, *Economists and Societies: Discipline and Profession in the United States, Britain, and France, 1890s to 1990s* (Princeton, NJ: Princeton University Press, 2009).

71. Currie, "The Planning and Administration of a New City."

72. Lauchlin Currie and Fundación Para el Progreso de Bogotá, *Estudio de Bogotá* (Bogotá: Departamento Administrativo de Planificacion Distrital, 1963), 34–40; Currie, *Urbanization Trends and Policies*; Currie, "The Multiple Objectives of Urban Development"; Currie, "The Interrelation of Urban and National Economic Planning."

73. Catherine Bauer, "Economic Progress and Living Conditions: An Argument for Regional Planning and Urban Dispersal in Develping Countries with Limited Resources," *Town Planning Review* 24, no. 4 (January 1954): 296–311; Nick Cullather, *The Hungry World: America's Cold War Battle against Poverty in Asia* (Cambridge, MA: Harvard University Press, 2010), 77–80; Immerwahr, *Thinking Small*; Priya Lal, *African Socialism in Postcolonial Tanzania: Between the Village and the World* (New York: Cambridge University Press, 2015); Stephen J. Macekura, *Of Limits and Growth: The Rise of Global Sustainable Development in the Twentieth Century* (Cambridge: Cambridge University Press, 2015).

74. Currie, *Urbanization Trends and Policies*; Currie, "The Planning and Administration of a New City"; Lauchlin Currie, *Alternativas para el desarrollo urbano de Bogotá DE* (Bogotá: Universidad Nacional, Centro de Investigaciones para el Desarrollo, 1969); Lauchlin Currie, "For Whom Should Housing Be Built?" *Habitat International* 4 (1979): 291–97; Departamento Nacional de Planeación, *Ciudades dentro de la ciudad: La política urbana y el Plan de Desarrollo en Colombia* (Bogotá: Ediciones Tercer Mundo, 1974); Currie, *Taming the Megalopolis*; Sandilands, *Life*, 245.

75. Sandilands, *Life*, 183–90.

76. Lauchlin Currie, "La creación de una empresa de desarrollo urbano," January 15, 1974; Lauchlin Currie, "Exposición de Motivos," January 16, 1974; and Lauchlin Currie, "Comments

on Terms of Reference CAN-Modelia Fontibon Area," March 20, 1974, LBCP, Box 18, Folder "Housing Urban 1959–1993, Proyecto Salitre 1974/90, Carpeta #17 (ene–jun 74)"; Lauchlin Currie to Miguel Urrutia, November 13, 1974, LBCP, Box 18, Folder "Housing Urban, Proyecto Salitre 1974/90, carpeta #18"; Currie, *Taming the Megalopolis*, 67–121.

77. Lauchlin Currie and Luis Eduardo Rosas, "UPAC: The Colombian System of Savings and Housing; A Theory Converted into a Successful Reality," 1986, LBCP, Box 16, Folder "UPAC 1985"; Lauchlin Currie, "UPAC: The Beginnings," February 10, 1983," LBCP, Box 16, Folder "UPAC 1985"; Roger J. Sandilands, *Monetary Correction and Housing Finance in Colombia, Brazil, and Chile* (Farnborough: Gower Press, 1980).

78. Lauchlin Currie, *Ensayos sobre planeacion: Introducción a una teoría de desarrollo conocida como Operación Colombia* (Bogotá: Ediciones Tercer Mundo, 1963); Lauchlin Currie, "La escuela de economía para graduados: Universidad de los Andes," February 24, 1964, LBCP, Box 20, Folder "Teaching 1960–1993, Carpeta #1."

79. Sandilands, *Life*, 203.

80. Lauchlin Currie, "La fuerza laboral organizada y la Operación Colombia," August 1, 1962, speech to the Federación de Trabajadores de Cundinamarca, BLAA.

81. Currie, *Operación Colombia*; Lauchlin Currie and Hugo Belalcazar L., *Proyecciones de la demanda de construcciones y de materiales para construcción en Colombia, para el período 1962–1970* (Bogotá: CAMACOL, 1963).

82. CAMACOL, "Memorandum sobre la industria de la construcción, presentado por la Cámara Colombiana de la Construcción al excelentísimo Señor Doctor Alberto Lleras Camargo, Presidente Electo," June 1958, AGN, Fondo Presidencia, 1950–1959, Transferencia 6, Despacho Sr. Presidente, Caja 108, Carpeta 13.

83. Miguel Lleras Pizarro, "El ahorro, la vivienda y la productividad," *Construcción Colombiana* 5, no. 17 (1965): 5–6; Centro Nacional de Estudios de la Construcción, *Oferta de edificaciones urbanas en Bogotá* (Bogotá: Centro Nacional de Estudios de la Construcción, 1977), Archivo de Bogotá, Colección General; CAMACOL Cundinamarca, "Desarrollo Urbano: 'Ciudades dentro de la Ciudad,' " XIX Asamblea Nacional de CAMACOL, October 21–23, 1976, Archivo de Bogotá, Colección General.

84. Sandilands, *Life*, 216–18; Roberto Arenas Bonilla, "Currie: El profesor visionario," unpublished paper presented at "El pensamiento de Lauchlin Currie, 1902–1993," BLAA, February 6, 2008; "Algunas Políticas del CID," LBCP, Box 20, Folder "Teaching 1960–1993, Carpeta #5"; Universidad Nacional, Centro de Investigaciones para el Desarrollo, "Informe sobre su estructura, organización y labores realizadas de enero a septiembre de 1967," October 9, 1967, LBCP, Box 20, Folder "Teaching 1960–1993, Carpeta #7"; Lauchlin Currie, "A Note on Cities-within-Cities Studies in Colombia," July 1987, LBCP, Box 18, Folder "Housing Urban 1959–1993, Proyecto Salitre 1974–90, carpeta #21"; Magda Rivera, "Departamentos en la Facultad de Ciencias Humanas: Integración para el desarrollo, 1966–1978," in *Búsquedas y logros desde la academia*, ed. Antonio Hernández Gamarra and Beethoven Herrera Valencia (Bogotá: Universidad Nacional, 2002), 104–9.

85. Leon Zamosc, *The Agrarian Question and the Peasant Movement in Colombia* (Cambridge: Cambridge University Press, 1986), 72, 97–04.

86. Sandilands, *Life*, 236–37, 324; Lauchlin Currie, "The Colombian Plan, 1971–1974: A Test of the Leading Sector Strategy," *World Development* 2, nos. 10–12 (1974): 69–72.

87. Sandilands, *Life*, 251; Lauchlin Currie, "UPAC: The Beginnings," February 10, 1983, LBCP, Box 16, Folder "UPAC 1985."

88. UPAC's development is documented in LCPB, Boxes 15, 16, 23, and 24.

89. CAMACOL Cundinamarca, "Desarrollo Urbano."

90. Lauchlin Currie, "Salitre: Basic Issues; Public vs. Private Development," June 18, 1987, and BCH brochure, "Ciudad Salitre," LBCP, Box 18, Folder "Housing Urban 1959–1993, Proyecto Salitre 1974–90, carpeta #21"; "Sector privado inicia planes en Ciudad Salitre," *El Tiempo*, February 17, 1990; "El Salitre," special section, *El Espectador*, May 17, 1990; "Vendido el 97% de Ciudad Salitre," *El Tiempo*, July 31, 1991.

91. "Ciudadelas en 20 ciudades: Barco," *El Tiempo*, July 14, 1987.

92. Lauchlin Currie, "Notes on Salitre," June 1990, LBCP, Box 18, Folder "Housing Urban 1959–1993 (Proyecto Salitre) 1974/90 carpeta #22"; "Exportaciones menores no deben sacrificiarse," *Portafolio*, September 13, 1993.

Chapter 4: Economics as a Public Mission

1. John M. Hunter, curriculum vitae, RF, RG 1.2, Series 311, Box 78, Folder 740; John Merlin Hunter, "Aspectos de una política de exportación de productos agropecuarios para Colombia," *Revista del Banco de la República* 32 (June 1959): 678–81; John M. Hunter, "Qué es economía?" *Revista del Banco de la República* 33 (March 1960): 297–300; John Merlin Hunter, "La metodología de la investigación económica," *Revista del Banco de la República* 33 (August 1960): 967–70.

2. Seventeen existed by 1965, enrolling some 1,500 majors. Beginning in 1931, the Faculty of Law at the Universidad Pontificia Javeriana in Bogotá did grant undergraduate degrees in economics. But the very idea that a law school could grant economics degrees communicated the belief that economics was not an independent discipline. In 1928, the Universidad Nacional likewise created a Faculty of Economic Sciences within its Faculty of Law, but it seems to have disappeared by 1930 without producing any graduates. As of 1945, no university in the country had an independent Faculty of Economics. Álvaro Montenegro García, "Los primeros programas de economía en Colombia," Documentos de Economía, Universidad Javeriana, Bogotá, Colombia, March 2008; Magda Rivera, "Institucionalización de los estudios económicos en la Universidad Nacional de Colombia, 1945–1952," in *Búsquedas y logros desde la academia*, ed. Antonio Hernández Gamarra and Beethoven Herrera Valencia (Bogotá: Universidad Nacional, 2002), 37; Lauchlin Currie, *La enseñanza de la economía en Colombia* (Bogotá: Ediciones Tercer Mundo, 1965), 10.

3. Marion Fourcade, *Economists and Societies: Discipline and Profession in the United States, Britain, and France, 1890s to 1990s* (Princeton, NJ: Princeton University Press, 2009); Sarah Babb, *Managing Mexico: Economists from Nationalism to Neoliberalism* (Princeton, NJ: Princeton University Press, 2001); Mary O. Furner, *Advocacy and Objectivity: A Crisis in the Professionalization of American Social Science* (Lexington: University Press of Kentucky, 1975); Michael A. Bernstein, *A Perilous Progress: Economists and Public Purpose in Twentieth-Century America* (Princeton, NJ: Princeton University Press, 2001).

4. Willy Drews, *Laserna: Crónica de una biografía* (Bogotá: Universidad de los Andes, 2003), 41–42; "University of the Andes," *The Lamp* 41, no. 3 (Fall 1959): 20.

5. "Hernán Echavarría Olózaga," *Gran enciclopedia de Colombia*, vol. 9 (Bogotá: Círculo de Lectores, 1991); Hernán Echavarría Olózaga, *Pleno empleo y otros temas* (Bogotá: Minerva, 1948); Hernán Echavarría Olózaga, *El sentido común en la economía colombiana* (Bogotá: Imprenta Nacional, 1958), Hernán Echavarría Olózaga, *Macroeconomía de la América cafetera* (Bogotá, 1971).

6. Consejo Directivo, Acta, July 2, 1953, Andes Archivo.

7. Consejo Directivo, Acta, March 9, 1949, Andes Archivo; Consejo Directivo, Acta, June 24, 1953, Andes Archivo; "University of the Andes," April 15, 1958, RFAM, RG 4, Series L, Box 254, Folder 2529; Walter Howe to Wyman R. Stone, May 13, 1955, NACP, RG 469, Entry 1140, Box 11, Folder 19.0 "Stone, Wyman R., General, FY 55"; Reinaldo Muñoz Zambrano to Walter Howe, December 14, 1955, NACP, RG 469, Entry 1140, Box 15, Folder 5.10; Gustavo Bell Lemus, Patricia Pinzón de Lewin, Lorenzo Morales Regueros, and David Rojas Roa, *Historia de la Universidad de los Andes, Tomo 1: Inicios, 1948–1977* (Bogotá: Universidad de los Andes, 2008), 64, 68.

8. Los Andes was in fact publicly subsidized, receiving 10 percent of its budget from the national government in return for adherence to national educational standards. Interviews: HMM, Montague Yudelman, Mario Laserna (Pinzón), May 2, 1956, RF, RG 1.2, Series 311, Box 78, Folder 739. Los Andes was part of what Daniel C. Levy describes as the second wave of private universities in Latin America. The first, beginning in the 1930s, consisted of Catholic universities. The second wave after 1945 consisted of "secular elite" universities. The third wave of the 1970s consisted of "nonelite secular institutions" that responded to unmet popular demand for higher education and focused heavily on job training. Daniel C. Levy, "Latin America's Private Universities: How Successful Are They?" *Comparative Education Review* 29 (1985): 444–48.

9. Herbert Braun, *The Assassination of Gaitán: Public Life and Urban Violence in Colombia* (Madison: University of Wisconsin Press, 1985), 175; Jorge Vallejo Morillo, *Cuatro economistas colombianos* (Bogotá: Norma, 2003), 137–94; Rivera, "Institucionalización de los estudios económicos en la Universidad Nacional de Colombia, 1945–1952," 29–50; Simón de la Pava S., *Antonio García Nossa: Un pensamiento revolucionario para Colombia y Latinoamérica* (n.p.: Aurora, 2004), 33–69.

10. Richard S. Pelczar, "University Reform in Latin America: The Case of Colombia," *Comparative Education Review* 16 (1972): 230–50; Rivera, "Institucionalización," 38; Raúl Alameda Ospina, "Una mirada histórica de la Facultad de Ciencias Económicas de la Universidad Nacional de Colombia: Insituto de Ciencias Económicas, 1945–1952," in Hernández Gamarra and Herrera Valencia, *Búsquedas y logros desde la academia*, 378–86; Guy S. Hayes, "A university can influence . . ." RF, RG A82, Box R1929, Folder 311S.

11. Consejo Directivo, Acta, August 29, 1960, Andes Archivo.

12. Alberto Lleras Camargo to Nelson A. Rockefeller, August 25, 1955, RFAM, RG 4, Series E, Box 23, Folder 181; interviews: HMM, Montague Yudelman, Mario Laserna (Pinzón), May 2, 1956, RF, RG 1.2, Series 311, Box 78, Folder 739; Consejo Directivo, Acta, August 19, 1953, Andes Archivo.

13. Albert O. Hirschman, Diary, September 9–10, 1957, AOHP, Box 57, Folder 10; Walter Howe, "Monthly Report June 1–30, 1956," July 6, 1956, NACP, RG 469, Entry 1140, Box 26, Folder 18.10, "Reports: Prog. Summary Monthly Reports, FY-57."

14. Jorge Valencia Restrepo, "Jorge Méndez Munévar: In Memoriam," *Desarrollo y Sociedad* 39 (1997): 1–13; Montague Yudelman, interview with Jorge Méndez, November 27, 1956, RF, RG 1.2, Series 311, Box 78, Folder 739. Méndez is often erroneously described as having earned a PhD.

15. Jorge Méndez, "Programa de política económica," 1949, ICE 1952; Jorge Méndez, "Teoría económica: Conferencias dictadas en la Facultad de economía industrial y comercial del Gimnasio Moderno," 1952, unpublished manuscript, BSE; Montague Yudelman, interview with Jorge Restrepo Hoyos and Jorge Méndez, May 24, 1956, RF, RG 1.2, Series 311, Box 78, Folder 739.

16. Interview by Norman S. Buchanan with Jorge Restrepo Hoyos, April 23, 1958, RF, RG 1.2, Series 311, Box 78, Folder 740; "University of the Andes," *The Lamp* 41, no. 3 (1959): 18–21; and the following in RFAM, RG 4, Series E, Box 23, Folder 181: Alberto Lleras Camargo to Nelson A. Rockefeller, September 17, 1954; Nelson A. Rockefeller to Alberto Lleras Camargo, December 1, 1954; Nelson A. Rockefeller to Samuel H. Kress, January 31, 1955; Alberto Lleras Camargo to Nelson A. Rockefeller, August 25, 1955.

17. The board initially included representatives of organized labor and higher education: ILGWU president David Dubinsky; United Steelworkers president David J. McDonald; and Theodore Martin Hesburgh, the liberal Catholic priest and president of Notre Dame. "University of the Andes Foundation," pamphlet, 1960, and "The University of the Andes Takes Another Giant Step in Latin America's Educational Progress," pamphlet, 1960, RFAM, RG 4, Series L, Box 254, Folder 2528; "List of Donors to the University of the Andes Foundation, Inc.," April 20, 1960, RFAM, RG 4, Series L, Box 254, Folder 2529; "University of the Andes Foundation, Contributions Received from 1961 to Date," March 1968, RFAM, RG 4, Series L, Box 254, Folder 2533; *Universidad de los Andes Boletín Informativo*, no. 4, July 1969, RFAM, RG 4, Series L, Box 254, Folder 2527.

18. H. K. Allen and J. F. Bell, "Final Report on the University of the Andes and the University of Cauca," NACP, RG 469, Entry 1140, Box 15, Folder 5.10.

19. Colombian corporations sponsored a limited number of scholarships, but in 1966, los Andes students came disproportionately from twenty-one elite high schools. William Benton, *The Voice of Latin America* (New York: Harper and Row, 1961), 133; Adlai Stevenson to Adolf A. Berle, July 5, 1960, and Maxwell Hahn to Adolf Berle, December 1, 1960, RFAM, RG 4, Series L, Box 254, Folder 2528; Consejo Directivo, Actas February 8, 1949, March 8, 1949, and October 26, 1953, Andes Archivo; Consejo Académico, Actas September 20, 1966 and October 18, 1966, Andes Archivo.

20. *The Rockefeller Foundation Annual Report, 1956* (New York: Rockefeller Foundation, 1956), xx; clipping from *Rockefeller Foundation Staff Newsletter*, July 1956, in folder "Montague Yudelman," BF; interviews: HMM, Montague Yudelman, Mario Laserna (Pinzón), May 2, 1956, RF, RG 1.2, Series 311, Box 78, Folder 739.

21. Ellen Schrecker, *Many Are the Crimes: McCarthyism in America* (Boston: Little, Brown, 1998), 407–8; Jorge Restrepo Hoyos to Montague Yudelman, October 1, 1958, and Leland DeVinney to Jorge Restrepo Hoyos, October 9, 1958, RF, RG 1.2, Series 311, Box 78, Folder 740. On Rockefeller's anticommunist vetting of professors at the Universidad del Valle, and efforts to guide Colombians away from the left through US training, see Amy C. Offner, "Anti-Poverty Programs, Social Conflict, and Economic Thought in Colombia and the United States, 1949–1980" (PhD diss., Columbia University, 2012), 282n48.

22. Carson Crocker to Washington, June 21, 1957, NACP, RG 469, Entry 1141, Box 1, Folder "Illinois University FY 1956–1958."

23. See the following in RF, RG 1.2, Series 311, Box 78, Folder 739: Montague Yudelman, interview with Jorge Restrepo Hoyos and Jorge Mendes [sic], May 24, 1956; excerpt from Montague Yudelman Diary: Luncheon with Dr. Roberts, Dr. A. Hirschman, Dr. G. Kalmanoff, May 24, 1956; excerpt from Montague Yudelman Diary, J. McCarthy, May 30, 1956.

24. Memo of telephone conversation between Montague Yudelman and Max F. Millikan, October 8, 1957, RF, RG 1.2, Series 311, Box 78, Folder 739; Everett E. Hagen to Norman Buchanan, December 14, 1957, RF, RG 1.2, Series 311, Box 78, Folder 739; interview by Norman S. Buchanan, Montague Yudelman with Dr. Everett Einar Hagen, January 17, 1958, RF, RG 1.2, Series 311, Box 78, Folder 740; Grant RF 58077, April 2, 1958, RF, RG 1.2, Series 311, Box 78, Folder 739; David C. Engerman, "West Meets East: The Center for International Studies and Indian Economic Development," in *Staging Growth: Modernization, Development, and the Global Cold War*, ed. Nils Gilman, David C. Engerman, Mark H. Haefele, and Michael E. Latham (Amherst: University of Massachusetts Press, 2003), 199–224; Nils Gilman, *Mandarins of the Future: Modernization Theory in Cold War America* (Baltimore: Johns Hopkins University Press, 2003), 155–202.

25. John M. Hunter, "Primer Informe Anual," August 31, 1959, RF, RG 1.2, Series 311, Box 78, Folder 740; CEDE, "Segundo Informe Anual," July 30, 1960, Kalmanoff Papers, Box 3, Folder "Colombia: Centro de Estudios sobre Desarrollo Económico"; Wallace N. Atherton, Vita, and John M. Hunter, "Experiences in Developing an Economic Research Center in Bogotá," unpublished manuscript, December 14, 1960, RF, RG 1.2, Series 311, Box 78, Folder 743; interview by Charles M. Hardin with Wallace N. Atherton, January 27, 1961, RF, RG 1.2, Series 311, Box 79, Folder 744; Wallace N. Atherton, "Third Annual Report," September 1, 1961, RF, RG 1.2, Series 311, Box 78, Folder 738; Consejo Directivo, Acta, September 26, 1962, Andes Archivo.

26. John M. Hunter to Norman S. Buchanan, April 4, 1958; interviews: Montague Yudelman, University of the Andes, December 1–6, 1958; John M. Hunter to Montague Yudelman, December 15, 1958, all in RF, RG 1.2, Series 311, Box 78, Folder 740.

27. "Universidad de los Andes, Facultad de Economía," October 19, 1961, RF, RG 1.2, Series 311, Box 79, Folder 744; interview by Charles M. Hardin with Wallace N. Atherton, January 27, 1961, RF, RG 1.2, Series 311, Box 79, Folder 744; Consejo Académico, Acta, March 15, 1966, Andes Archivo; H. K. Allen and J. F. Bell, "Final Report on the University of the Andes and the University of Cauca," NACP, RG 469, Entry 1140, Box 15, Folder 5.10; Lauchlin Currie, *La enseñanza de la economía en Colombia* (Bogotá: Tercer Mundo Ediciones, 1965); John M. Hunter and James Anthony Short Tenent, "The Teaching of Economics in Colombia," *Journal of Inter-American Studies* (April 1960): 189–96.

28. Hunter, "Qué es economía?"; John M. Hunter, "Primer Informe Anual," August 31, 1959, RF, RG 1.2, Series 311, Box 78, Folder 740.

29. John M. Hunter to Montague Yudelman, December 15, 1958, RF, RG 1.2, Series 311, Box 78, Folder 740; John M. Hunter, "Experiences in Developing an Economic Research Center in Bogotá," unpublished manuscript, December 14, 1960, RF, RG 1.2, Series 311, Box 78, Folder 743; CEDE, "Second Draft," n.d., unpublished manuscript, RF, RG 1.2, Series 311, Box 78, Folder 742; interview by Charles M. Hardin with Wallace N. Atherton, January 27, 1961, RF, RG 1.2, Series 311, Box 79, Folder 744; Wallace N. Atherton to Charles Hardin, May 21, 1962, RF, RG 2.1, Series 311, Box 79, Folder 744.

30. Marco Palacios, *Coffee in Colombia, 1850–1970: An Economic, Social, and Political History* (Cambridge: Cambridge University Press, 2002), 214–26, and the following in RF, RG 1.2, Series 311, Box 79, Folder 744: interview by Charles M. Hardin and Robert K. Waugh with Oscar Gómez, Wallace N. Atherton, Jorge Ruiz Lara, February 28, 1962; Wallace N. Atherton to Charles M. Hardin, April 28, 1962; Wallace N. Atherton to Charles M. Hardin, June 20, 1962; Jorge Ruiz Lara to Charles M. Hardin, June 23, 1962.

31. Lauchlin Currie, *Operación Colombia: Un programa nacional de desarrollo económico y social* (Barranquilla: Cámara Colombiana de la Construcción, 1961); Charles M. Hardin interview with Wallace N. Atherton, October 20, 1961, RF, RG 1.2, Series 311, Box 79, Folder 744.

32. Miguel Antequera, "Ocupación y desocupación en Bogotá: Los Alcázares, Quiroga, Las Ferias, agosto de 1961" (undergraduate thesis, Universidad de los Andes, 1962); Wallace Atherton to Charles Hardin, February 27, 1962, and Wallace N. Atherton to Charles M. Hardin, June 20, 1962, RF, RG 1.2, Series 311, Box 79, Folder 744; Grant RF 62085, September 21, 1962, and Grant-in-Aid GA-HSS 6456, June 3, 1964, RF, RG 1.2, Series 311, Box 78, Folder 739; Eduardo Wiesner, "Memorandum: The Activities of CEDE and the Rockefeller Foundation," October 5, 1966, RF, RG 1.2, Series 311, Box 79, Folder 746.

33. J. Hunter to M. Yudelman, March 3, 1959, RF, RG 1.2, Series 311, Box 78, Folder 740; Miguel Urrutia, "Cálculo del desempleo," *Revista del Banco de la República* 36 (1963): 739–42; Miguel Urrutia et al., *Empleo y desempleo en Colombia* (Bogotá: Universidad de los Andes, 1968); Guillermo Franco Camacho, *Investigaciones sobre desempleo en Colombia* (Bogotá: CEDE, 1964); Francisco J. Ortega and Rafael Prieto, *Investigación sobre ingreso y distribución del gasto familiar urbano en Colombia: Bogotá, Cali, Medellín y Barranquilla* (Bogotá: CEDE, Universidad de los Andes, 1967); Rafael Isaza Botero and Francisco J. Ortega, *Encuestas urbanas de empleo y desempleo: Análisis y resultados* (Bogotá: CEDE, 1969).

34. John M. Hunter, "Primer Informe Anual," August 31, 1959, RF, RG 1.2, Series 311, Box 78, Folder 740; Currie, *Role of Economic Advisers*, 72–74.

35. Guillermo Franco Camacho, *Mercado de la papa respecto a Bogotá* (Bogotá: CEDE Monografía No. 2, 1959); Eduardo Wiesner Durán, *Control personal de la economía colombiana* (Bogotá: CEDE Monografía No. 6, 1960); Rafael Prieto Durán, *Evolución de una urbanización en Bogotá* (Bogotá: CEDE Monografía No. 7, 1960); *CEDE: Décimo aniversario de su fundación, 1958–1968* (Bogotá: CEDE, 1968), 19–27, RF, RG 4, Series E, Box 23, Folder 181.

36. Margarita Fajardo, María José Ospina, Jorge Alexander Bonilla, and Fabio Sánchez, *Historia del CEDE: 50 años de investigación en economía, 1958–2008* (Bogotá: Universidad de los Andes, 2008), 11–13; Eduardo Wiesner, "Memorandum: The Activities of CEDE and the Rockefeller Foundation," October 5, 1966, RF, RG 1.2, Series 311, Box 79, Folder 746; Interview by Erskine W. McKinley with Hernán Echavarría, June, 3, 1960, RF, RG 1.2, Series 311, Box 78, Folder 743; Charles M. Hardin, interview with Wallace N. Atherton, January 27, 1961 and Charles M. Hardin, interview with Oscar Gómez, October 19, 1961, RF, RG 1.2, Series 311, Box 79, Folder 744.

37. Fajardo, Ospina, Bonilla, and Sánchez, *Historia del CEDE*, 11–13, 53–56; Eduardo Wiesner, "Memorandum: The Activities of CEDE and the Rockefeller Foundation," October 5, 1966, RF, RG 1.2, Series 311, Box 79, Folder 746.

38. "Youth Points Way for Colombia to Return to a Stable Economy," *New York Times*, January 13, 1960; interview by Montague Yudelman with Jorge Restrepo Hoyos and Hernán Echavarría, June 25, 1957, RF, RG 1.2, Series 311, Box 78, folder 739.

39. Wiesner Durán, *Control personal de la economía colombiana*; Ramón de Zubiria to Charles M. Hardin, February 21, 1964, RF, RG 1.2, Series 311, Box 79, Folder 745; Charles M. Hardin to Francisco J. Ortega, March 12, 1964, and Wallace N. Atherton to Charles M. Hardin, March 23, 1964, RF, RG 1.2, Series 311, Box 79, Folder 745; Eduardo Wiesner Durán to Ralph K. Davidson, February 16, 1966, and excerpt from James M. Daniel Diary Notes, August 31–September 5, 1966, RF, RG 1.2, Series 311, Box 79, Folder 746.

40. Luis Bernardo Flórez Enciso, "Colombia: Economics, Economic Policy and Economists," in *Economists in the Americas*, ed. Verónica Montecinos and John Markoff (Northampton, MA: Edward Elgar, 2009), 195–226.

41. Bernardo Garcés Córdoba to William J. Hayes, June 12, 1956; Llano to Kirpich, July 30, 1956; Bernardo Garcés Córdoba to Luigi Laurenti, July 28, 1964, all CVC Correspondencia.

42. Montague Yudelman to Leland C. DeVinney, June 16, 1959, RF, RG 1.2, Series 311, Box 73, Folder 698A; William J. Hayes, "CVC Job Description, Position: Economist," and "CVC Job Description, Position: Agricultural Economist," October 14, 1955, D&R, Box 236, Folder 8; and the following in CVC Correspondencia: Bernardo Garcés Córdoba to Herbert Stewart, May 31, 1955; Bernardo Garcés Córdoba to David H. Blelloch, June 14, 1955, and October 14, 1955; Bernardo Garcés Córdoba to Francisco Urrutia Holguín, January 19, 1956; Bernardo Garcés Córdoba to Alvaro Ortiz Lozano, January 3, 1957; Bernardo Garcés Córdoba to Carson Crocker, January 21, 1957; Bernardo Garcés Córdoba to John Stovel, March 6, 1957; Bernardo Garcés Córdoba to Ralph Ellis, March 6, 1957; Bernardo Garcés Córdoba to Marino Dávalos, March 11, 1957; Bernardo Garcés Córdoba to J. F. Bell, April 3, 1957; n.a., "Notas sobre el programa de recuperación de tierras de la CVC," August 14, 1957; Bernardo Garcés Córdoba to Javier Robledo O., April 4, 1959.

43. Erskine W. McKinley, interview with Bernardo Garcés, November 27, 1959, and n.a., "Cauca Valley Corporation (CVC)," August 12, 1960, RF, RG 1.2, Series 311, Box 73, Folder 698A.

44. William J. Hayes to Files, June 22, 1955, D&R, Box 228, Folder 13; excerpt from M. Yudelman diary with Antonio J. Posada F., December 10, 1958, RF, RG 1.2, Series 311, Box 73, Folder 698A.

45. Mario Carvajal, *Testimonio Universitario* (Cali: Universidad del Valle, 1969); Luis Aurelio Ordóñez Burbano, *Universidad del Valle 60 años, 1945–2005: Atando cabos en clave de memoria* (Cali: Universidad del Valle, 2007); CVC Acta 289, March 13, 1962; "Murió el ex-ministro Mario Carvajal Borrero," *El Tiempo*, April 21, 1972; Julio César Londoño, *Manuel Carvajal Sinisterra: Una vida dedicada a generar progreso con equidad* (Cali: Universidad Icesi, 2016), 30–33; Leland C. DeVinney, untitled document, March 13, 1959, RF, RG 1.2, Series 311, Box 73, Folder 698; Robert B. Watson to Joseph A. Rupert, December 19, 1963, RF, RG 1.2, Series 309, Box 7, Folder 44; "The Universidad del Valle, Pre-University Development Program, 1953–1961, second draft," June 25, 1975, unprocessed materials, RF, RG A82, Box R1929, Folder "311S, Universidad del Valle, Program Review, 1974–75."

46. Albert O. Hirschman, Diary, Brazil and Colombia, August 12–September 11, 1957, AOHP, Box 57, Folder 10; Mario Carvajal to Norman S. Buchanan, September 7, 1957, RF, RG 1.2, Series 311, Box 73, Folder 698.

47. Posada taught at the Nacional in 1949 between earning his MA and PhD at Wisconsin. Antonio J. Posada, "Programa de economía agraria y de la industria," 1949, ICE 1952; Resolución No. 125 de 1949, March 11, 1949, ICE 1949; Antonio J. Posada, "Economics of Colombian

Agriculture" (PhD diss., University of Wisconsin, 1952); Antonio J. Posada F., "Vita, 1967," LTC Box "Research & TA (by Country), Latin America (Cont), Colombia #2 of 2, Box 11 of 14," Folder "20.4-A (corresp) Posada, Antonio J., VIII"; Marvin A. Schaars, "The Story of the Department of Agricultural Economics, 1909–1972," unpublished manuscript, AEL.

48. CVC Acta 121, October 27, 1958; Montague Yudelman, interview with Antonio J. Posada F., December 10, 1958, unprocessed material, RF, RG A81, Box R1738, Folder "311S, Universidad del Valle, Economics, 1958–1960"; Montague Yudelman to Leland C. DeVinney, June 16, 1959 and Grant-in-Aid GA SS 59100, October 16, 1959, RF, RG 1.2, Series 311, Box 73, Folder 698A.

49. Alvaro López Toro, "Problems in Stable Population Theory" (PhD diss., Princeton University, 1960); Samir Camilo Daccach to Pedro Mejía Eder, March 20, 1959, and Samir Camilo Daccach to Juan Quintero Marín, March 20, 1959, CVC Correspondencia; Erskine W. McKinley, interview with Antonio J. Posada F., November 28, 1959, and Kenneth Thompson, interview with Antonio J. Posada, August 12, 1960, unprocessed material, RF, RG A81, Box R1738, Folder "311S, Universidad del Valle, Economics, 1958–1960"; CVC Acta 236, January 9, 1961; Charles M. Hardin, interview with Antonio Posada, October 23, 1961, and Charles M. Hardin, interview with A. J. Posada, October 24, 1961, unprocessed material, RF, RG A81, Box R1738, Folder "311S, Universidad del Valle, Economics, July–December 1961."

50. Guy S. Hayes, excerpt from diary with Antonio Posada, August 13, 1960, unprocessed material, RF, RG A81, Box R1738, Folder "311S, Universidad del Valle, Economics, 1958–1960."

51. Grant RF 61153, December 5–6, 1961, RF, RG 1.2, Series 311, Box 78, Folder 698; James S. Coleman, "Professorial Training and Institution Building in the Third World: Two Rockefeller Foundation Experiences," *Comparative Education Review* 28, no. 2 (May 1984): 181n2.

52. CVC Acta 270, October 16, 1961; CVC Acta 271, October 24, 1961; "El centro de formación profesional e investigación agrícola, Valle del Cauca," brochure, UV Facultad Correspondencia Caja 2, Carpeta 1.

53. Luigi Laurenti, *Property Values and Race: Studies in Seven Cities* (Berkeley: University of California Press, 1960); Charles M. Hardin, interview with David Felix and Randall Whaley, May 22, 1961, May 25, 1961, May 23, 1961, unprocessed materials, RF, RG A81, Box R1738, Folder "311S, Universidad del Valle, Economics, January–June 1961"; Victor Rapport et al. to Randall M. Whaley, March 12, 1962, unprocessed materials, RF, RG A81, Box R1738, Folder "311S, Universidad del Valle, Economics, 1958–1960."

54. *Censo Agropecuario del Valle del Cauca, 1959* (Cali: Universidad del Valle, Facultad de Ciencias Económicas, 1963); "Censo Agropecuario Preliminar del Valle del Cauca, 1959," unpublished questionnaire, AOHP, Box 40, Folder 8; Antonio Posada to Montague Yudelman, February 17, 1959, unprocessed material, RF, RG A81, Box R1738, Folder "311S, Universidad del Valle, Economics, 1958–1960;" K. W. Thompson, excerpt of diary with Antonio J. Posada F., August 12, 1960, and Antonio J. Posada to John H. Greenfieldt, December 19, 1960, RF, RG 1.2, Series 311, Box 73, Folder 698A; CVC Report C-4267, "Roldanillo-La Unión-Toro Project: Status of Development," April 1962, BMC; CVC Report C-4204, "Bugalagrande-Cartago Project," April 1962, CVC Informes Técnicos; CVC Acta No. 599, October 26, 1970.

55. Laurenti and Posada misunderstood the protest, depicting strikers as weak students or communists. In fact, a leading spokesman was Oscar Mazuera, who went on to become the CVC's executive director. "Consejo estudiantil de la Facultad de Ciencias Económicas," UV Movimientos Box 1, Folder 1; Consejo Estudiantil de la Facultad de Ciencias Económicas,

"Resolución No. 2," April 3, 1962, RF, RG A81, Folder "311S, Universidad del Valle, Economics, January–May 1962"; Luigi Laurenti to Dave Felix, April 9, 1962, and April 14, 1962, RF, RG 1.2, Series 311, Box 73, Folder 693; Bernardo Garcés Córdoba to C. Clyde Mitchell, May 8, 1962, CVC Correspondencia.

56. "Report of Robert S. Smith (Duke University) on a visit to Cali, Colombia, October 3–12, 1962," RF, RG 1.2, Series 311, Box 75, Folder 721; "Profesores de la Facultad de Ciencias Económicas, 1962–1963," unprocessed material, RF, RG A81, Box R1737, Folder "311S, Universidad del Valle, Economics (Aug–Dec 1963)," and the contents of RF, RG A81, Folder "311S, Universidad del Valle, Economics, January–May 1962"; RF, RG A81, Folder "311S, Universidad del Valle, Economics, June–Dec 1962"; RF, RG 1.2, Series 311, Box 76, Folder 721; RF, RG 1.2, Series 311, Box 73, Folder 698; Bernardo Garcés Córdoba to E. J. Gregory, June 19, 1965, CVC Correspondencia.

57. N.a., "Notes on the present and future efforts of the School of Economics of the Universidad del Valle," n.d., UV Facultad Correspondencia, Caja 2, Carpeta 1; Laurence deRycke to Kenneth Thompson, April 30, 1964, unprocessed material, RF, RG A81, Box R1737, Folder "311S, Universidad del Valle, Economics, Jan–Apr 1964."

58. Glenn L. Johnson, "A Possible Future for Agricultural Economics at the University de Valle," unprocessed material, RF, RG A77, Box R1345, Folder "311S, Universidad del Valle, Agricultural Economics, 1964–1965"; Bernardo Garcés Córdoba to Archivo, August 19, 1965, and October 4, 1965, CVC Correspondencia; Rockefeller Foundation, *Annual Report* (New York: Rockefeller Foundation, 1966), 59, 146; n.a., "Relación del período comprendido entre el 14 de agosto de 1968 y el 31 de agosto de 1973," November 12, 1973, unprocessed materials, RF, RG A77, Box R1345, Folder "311S, Universidad del Valle, Agricultural Economics, 1970–1973–75."

59. R. S. Wickham, "Summary of Ford Foundation Support of University del Valle, Cali, Colombia," January 1965, unprocessed material, RF, RG A82, Box R1929, Folder "311S, Universidad del Valle, Program Review, 1974–75"; "Colombians Supported by RF under Fellowship Program for Advanced Study in Economics and Agricultural Economics," September 1974, unprocessed material, RF, RG A81, Box R1736, Folder "311S, Universidad del Valle, Economics, 1972–74"; Jaime Mejía to Ralph K. Davidson, May 25, 1966, RF, RG 1.2, Series 311, Box 75, Folder 713.

60. CVC Acta 297, May 8, 1962; David Felix to Charles M. Hardin, July 9, 1962, RF, RG 1.2, Series 311, Box 73, Folder 698.

61. Charles M. Hardin, interview with Alberto Ruiz, August 28, 1963, unprocessed material, RF, RG A81, Box R1737, Folder "311S, Universidad del Valle, Economics, August–Dec 1963"; Luigi Laurenti to Reinaldo Scarpetta, March 26, 1965, UV Facultad Correspondencia, Box 2, Folder 4; CVC Acta 326, January 15, 1963; Charles M. Hardin, interview with Luigi Laurenti, October 15, 1962, RF, RG A81, Folder "311 S, Universidad del Valle, Economics, June–Dec 1962"; Ralph Kirby Davidson interview with Glenn L. Johnson, Gerald Trant, Lowell Hardin, Harry Wilhelm, March 18, 1966, unprocessed material, RF, RG A77, Box R1345, Folder "311S, Universidad del Valle, Agricultural Economics, January–June 1966"; Jesús Humberto Colmenares Vallejo, "Análisis de la producción agrícola en el Valle del Cauca, 1955–1962: Números índices de producción agrícola" (undergraduate thesis, Universidad del Valle, 1964); Luz Alba Weisz, "La demanda interna de azúcar en Colombia" (undergraduate thesis, Universidad del Valle, 1964); Jaime Buritica P., "Aspectos agroeconómicos de producción de tomate, cebolla de bulbo

y arveja en el departamento del Valle del Cauca" (undergraduate thesis, Universidad del Valle, 1964); Gerardo García Z. and Hernando Zuluaga E., "Costos de producción de caña de azúcar en la zona aledaña al Ingenio Castilla" (undergraduate thesis, Universidad del Valle, 1964); Neftaly Morales Abadía, "Números índices de precios recibidos por los agricultores: análisis de los precios agrícolas en el departamento del Valle del Cauca, 1955–1963" (undergraduate thesis, Universidad del Valle, 1964); Luis Alfonso Aragón Alvarez, "Estimación del consumo de algunos alimentos básicos en la ciudad de Cali" (undergraduate thesis, Universidad del Valle, 1964); Ceneydha Medina G., "Información sobre la situación actual en el país del ganado porcino" (undergraduate thesis, Universidad del Valle, 1964).

62. Cesar Tulio Ayora R. and Hernán Morales C., "Estudio sobre costos de producción de maíz en el Valle del Cauca" (undergraduate thesis, Universidad del Valle, 1964), 1, 110; Enrique Solorzano A., "Sistemas de mercadeo de los principales productos agrícolas del área Roldanillo-La Unión-Toro" (undergraduate thesis, Universidad del Valle, 1965), 1–2.

63. CVC Acta 303, July 10, 1962; Tomás López R., Oscar Mazuera G., and Guillermo Berón Ch., "La comercialización del ganado y de la carne en el departamento del Valle" (undergraduate thesis, Universidad del Valle, 1963); Juan Pablo Alvarez V. to Emilio Gómez Gaviria, February 8, 1966, CVC Correspondencia.

64. CVC Acta 343, June 11, 1963; CVC Acta 400, May 11, 1965; CVC Acta 406, July 26, 1965; CVC Acta 433, May 23, 1966.

65. CVC Acta 528, March 10, 1969; CVC Acta 546, August 4, 1969; CVC Acta 571, March 9, 1970; Juan G. Casas L. and Jorge Rodríguez N., "Análisis socio-económico del proyecto de adecuación de tierras, zona Obando-Cartago" (undergraduate thesis, Universidad del Valle, 1975); CVC Acta 846, September 28, 1976.

66. Juan Pablo Alvarez V. to Anacleto G. Apodaca, August 20, 1964, CVC Correspondencia; Juan Pablo Alvarez V. to Luis Arturo Fuenzalida, August 22, 1966, CVC Correspondencia; Vicente Aragón A. to Tomás López, October 14, 1966, CVC Correspondencia; CVC Acta 504, July 29, 1968; CVC Acta 600, November 2, 1970; CVC Acta 618, May 3, 1971.

67. INCORA Acta 12, April 23, 1962.

68. Bernardo Garcés Córdoba to Dr. Aragón, March 13, 1962, CVC Correspondencia; CVC Acta 328, January 29, 1963; CVC Acta 389, September 22, 1964; Juan Pablo Alvarez V. to Auditor Fiscal, December 7, 1964, CVC Correspondencia; CVC Acta 397, March 4, 1965; CVC Informe No. C-10877, *Proyecto La Victoria-Cartago: Estudio de Factabilidad*, August 1966, CVC Informes Técnicos.

69. US-born Jeanne Anderson Posada held a master's degree in political science from the University of Wisconsin and pursued doctoral studies in public administration at Berkeley during the 1960s on a Rockefeller Foundation scholarship. Jeanne Anderson Posada, "Public Housing in Milwaukee: A Case Study in Administration" (master's thesis, University of Wisconsin, 1947); CMH to RSM, VCS, JPH, LCD, March 5, 1962, RF, RG 1.2, Series 311, Box 73, Folder 698.

70. Antonio J. Posada and Jeanne Anderson Posada, *The CVC: Challenge to Underdevelopment and Traditionalism* (Bogotá: Ediciones Tercer Mundo, 1966); "A Memorandum of Agreement Relating to a Study of CVC's Impact on Land Resource Use in the Cauca Valley of Colombia," February 27, 1963, LTC Box "Research (by country), Colombia (1 of 2), '62–'75, Box 12 of 16," Folder "Colombia—CVC"; Land Tenure Center, Annual Report, AID/Repas-3, May 11, 1963, Land Tenure Center Annual Reports, Steenbock Library, University of Wisconsin.

71. Bernardo Garcés Córdoba to Antonio Posada F., August 23, 1965, CVC Correspondencia; and the following in LTC Box "Research & TA (by Country), Latin America (Cont), Colombia #2 of 2, Box 11 of 14," Folder "20.4-A (corresp) Posada, Antonio J., VIII": Antonio J. Posada to Raymond Penn, December 14, 1964; Raymond J. Penn to Tony Posada, May 20, 1966.

72. Juan Pablo Alvarez V. to Julio E. Basta, June 23, 1966, CVC Correspondencia; Juan Pablo Alvarez V. to Rodrigo Botero, August 18, 1966, CVC Correspondencia, Juan Pablo Alvarez V. to Norman Neil Brown, December 6, 1966, CVC Correspondencia.

73. Bernardo Garcés Córdoba to G. L. Johnson, March 7, 1957, CVC Correspondencia; Gerald Ion Trant, "Institutional Credit and the Efficiency of Selected Dairy Farms" (PhD thesis, Michigan State University, 1959).

74. Ralph Kirby Davidson, interview with Gerald Trant, May 27, 1966, unprocessed material, RF, RG A77, Box R1345, Folder "311S, Universidad del Valle, Agricultural Economics, January–June 1966"; and the contents of RF, RG 1.2, Series 311, Box 73, Folders 699–701; "Universidad del Valle, Visiting Faculty," unprocessed material, RF, RG A82, Box R1929, Folder 311S, Universidad del Valle, Program Review, 1974–75."

75. Grant GA HSS 6672, June 30, 1966, unprocessed material, RF, RG A77, Box R1345, Folder "311S, Universidad del Valle, Agricultural Economics, 1970–1973–75"; Luis Arturo Fuenzalida and Nora Peñaranda de Vargas, "La producción en el sector agropecuario: Problemas y oportunidades," April 1967, RF, RG 1.2, Series 311, Box 74, Folder 709A; GSH diary notes, February 23, 1967, RF, RG 1.2, Series 311, Box 75, Folder 716; José Humberto Ospina Velasco, "Análisis de costos de la maquinaria agrícola del Ingenio del Cauca S.A." (master's thesis, Universidad del Valle, 1970); Jaime Donado Baena and Sabas Pretelt de la Vega, "Estudio de inversiones en el Ingenio Meléndez S.A." (master's thesis, Universidad del Valle, 1971).

76. Juan Gabriel Valdés, *Pinochet's Economists: The Chicago School in Chile* (Cambridge: Cambridge University Press, 1995); International Bank for Reconstruction and Development, Report No. P-3906-CH, February 15, 1985, 12, documents.worldbank.org; Glen Biglaiser, "The Internationalization of Chicago's Economics in Latin America," *Economic Development and Cultural Change* 50, no. 2 (January 2002): 269–86.

77. "Universidad del Valle, Visiting Faculty," unprocessed material, RF, RG A82, Box R1929, Folder "311S, Universidad del Valle, Program Review, 1974–75"; excerpt from Charles M. Hardin diary with Arnold Harberger, March 6, 1964, and documents on de Castro in RF, RG 1.2, Series 311, Box 75, Folder 712; Ralph Kirby Davidson interview with Arnold Harberger, February 24, 1965, RF, RG 1.2, Series 311, Box 74, Folder 706; Luis Arturo Fuenzalida Asmussen, Curriculum Vitae and related documents, RF, RG 1.2, Series 311, Box 75, Folder 716.

78. GA HSS 6573, May 28, 1965, RF, RG 1.2, Series 311, Box 74, Folder 706; excerpt from GSH diary, February 14–March 6, 1966, RF, RG 1.2, Series 311, Box 74, Folder 708; Herbert W. Fraser to Ralph K. Davidson, February 8, 1965, unprocessed materials, RF, RG A81, Box R1737, Folder "311S, Universidad del Valle, Economics, January–June 1967."

79. Sergio de Castro to Charles M. Hardin, February 17, 1964, RF, RG 1.2, Series 311, Box 75, Folder 712; Salomón Levy T., "Colombia y la Asociación Latinoamericana de Libre Comercio" (undergraduate thesis, Universidad del Valle, 1964); Alberto Musalem, "Demand and Supply for Money, Inflation and Analysis of Short-Run Capital Movement," and Grant RF 66077, Allocation No. 116, August 28, 1967, RF, RG 1.2, Series 311, Box 76, Folder 720; "Universidad del

Valle, División de Ciencias Sociales y Económicas, 1968–1969," RF, RG 1.2, Series 311, Box 75, Folder 715; Valdés, *Pinochet's Economists*, 141–42.

80. Laurence deRycke to Kenneth W. Thompson, July 14, 1964, RF, RG 1.2, Series 311, Box 75, Folder 710; Reinaldo Scarpetta, "Progress Report to the Rockefeller Foundation," September 30, 1966, unprocessed material, RF, RG 1.2, Series A81, Box R1737, Folder "311S, Universidad del Valle, Economics, July–Dec 1966."

81. Ralph Kirby Davidson interview with Arnold C. Harberger, February 24, 1965, RF, RG 1.2, Series 311, Box 75, Folder 716.

82. Arnold C. Harberger, "Reflections on my Service with USAID," June 2010, 9–10, http://www.econ.ucla.edu/harberger/reflections2010.pdf.

83. Fabio Marulanda Cabrera, Luis Arturo Fuenzalida, and Nora Peñaranda de Vargas, *Empleo y desempleo de la mano de obra en la ciudad de Cali: Resultados de la encuesta efectuada entre el 1 y el 7 de marzo de 1965* (Cali: CEDE, Universidad de los Andes, 1965).

84. Luis Arturo Fuenzalida, *Rentabilidad de diversos cultivos agrícolas y explotaciones ganaderas en el Valle del Cauca* (Cali: CIDE, 1966).

85. Excerpt from GHS diary, September 20–October 5, 1965, RF, RG 1.2, Series 311, Box 74, Folder 707; Bernardo Garcés Córdoba to Luis A. Fuenzalida, April 6, 1966, CVC Correspondencia; James M. Daniel to Kirby Davidson, November 3, 1966, RF, RG 1.2, Series 311, Box 74, Folder 708A; Herbert W. Fraser, "Summary of Economics Faculty Seminars, 1st Semester 1965–66," n.d., unprocessed material, RF, RG A81, Box R1737, Folder "311S, Universidad del Valle, Economics (Jan–June 1966)"; James M. Daniel, Ernest A. Duff, Herbert W. Fraser, and Gerald I. Trant to Ralph Kirby Davidson, November 4, 1966, unprocessed material, RF, RG A81, Box R1737, Folder "311S, Universidad del Valle, Economics, July–December 1966."

86. Universidad del Valle, Divisón de Ciencias Sociales y Económicas, Facultad de Economía, March 1968, W. M. Myers Papers, Accession No. 30, Series 1, Box 6, Folder 51; *Bases para un plan de desarrollo del Valle del Cauca* (Cali: CIDE, 1966), RF, RG 1.2, Series 311, Box 75, Folder 713; Gerald I. Trant to Glenn L. Johnson, November 11, 1966, unprocessed material, RF, RG A77, Box R1345, Folder "311S, Universidad del Valle, Agricultural Economics, July–December, 1966"; Reinaldo Scarpetta to Kirby Davidson, July 18, 1966, RF, RG 1.2, Series 311, Box 74, Folder 708A.

87. Excerpt from James M. Daniel diary notes, August 31–September 5, 1966, RF, RG 1.2, Series 311, Box 75, Folder 746.

88. Antonio J. Posada F., *The Economics of Colombian Agriculture* (1952), 38–42, 90, 254–55.

89. Annotation on Carl Purcell and Carol Steele, "INCORA Fulfills Dreams in Colombia," *War on Hunger: A Report from the Agency for International Development* 4, no. 2 (February 1970), LTC Box "Research (by Country), Colombia (1 of 2), '62–'75, Box 12 of 16," Folder "INCORA—Colombia"; A. Eugene Havens to Peter Droner, July 17, 1969, LTC Box "Research (by Country), Colombia (1 of 2), '62–'75, Box 12 of 16," Folder "'69 Colombia Seminar"; "Memorial Resolution of the Faculty of the University of Wisconsin on the Death of Emeritus Professor Raymond J. Penn," Faculty Document 492, August 30, 1982, UW Bio Files, Folder "Penn, Raymond J."; "Memorial Resolution of the Faculty of the University of Wisconsin on the Death of Professor Emeritus William C. Thiesenhusen," Faculty Document 1875, November 7, 2005, UW Bio Files, Folder "Thiesenhusen, William C."

90. Posada and Posada, *CVC*, 123–30.

91. Bernardo Garcés Córdoba to Harold B. Dunkerley, November 9, 1963, CVC Correspondencia; Luigi Laurenti to Charles M. Hardin, December 26, 1963, unprocessed material, RF, RG A81, Box R1737, Folder "311S, Universidad del Valle, Economics, August–Dec 1963."

92. Joe Thome to Jake Beuscher, April 30, 1964, LTC Box "Research (by Country), Colombia (1 of 2), '62–'75, Box 12 of 16, Folder "INCORA—Colombia"; Juan Pablo Alvarez V. to Enrique Peñalosa Camargo, May 11, 1964, CVC Correspondencia; Bernardo Garcés Córdoba to Joseph Thome, May 20, 1964, CVC Correspondencia; A. Eugene Havens, Dale W. Adams, and Joseph R. Thome, "Summary of Colombian Research Activity of the Land Tenure Center," January 1966, Land Tenure Center, mimeograph provided to the author.

93. Luigi Laurenti to Bernardo Garcés Córdoba, August 26, 1964, CVC Correspondencia; Bernardo Garcés Córdoba to Thomas G. Cousins, September 4, 1964; Bernardo Garcés Córdoba to Luigi Laurenti, October 16, 1964, CVC Correspondencia; Bernardo Garcés Córdoba to Luigi Laurenti, June 9, 1965, CVC Correspondencia; *Guía para el inversionista en el área de Roldanillo-La Unión-Toro* (Cali: JUCODA, 1965), BLAA Colección General; *Censo agropecuario del área del proyecto Roldanillo-La Unión-Toro, área del proyecto CVC La Victoria-Cartago* (Cali: JUCODA, 1966).

94. Excerpt from L. Vince Padgett diary, February 1–28, 1966, RF, RG 1.2, Series 311, Box 74, Folder 708; Herbert W. Fraser, "Report on the Economics Faculty Seminars, 1965–1966," July 4, 1966, Herbert W. Fraser, "Report on Work with the Facultad de Economía," June 1965–October 1966, Herbert W. Fraser, "Report on the Research of the Division," September 7, 1966, all in unprocessed material, RF, RG A81, Box R1737, Folder "311S, Universidad del Valle, Economics, July–December 1966."

Chapter 5: Management as a Universal Technique

1. Reinaldo Scarpetta to David E. Lilienthal, June 17, 1968, DELP, Box 475, Folder "Fund for Multinational Management Education, 1968"; Reinaldo Scarpetta, "Jamaica: Towards a System of Management Education," May 10, 1969, UV, Correspondencia, Caja 2, Carpeta 5.

2. Johanna Bockman, *Markets in the Name of Socialism: The Left-Wing Origins of Neoliberalism* (Stanford, CA: Stanford University Press, 2011), 30–31, 66.

3. Kenneth W. Thompson interview with Arnold Harberger, July 9, 1962, and Robert Waugh to Charles Hardin, August 10, 1962, RF, RG A81, Box R1737, Folder "311S, Universidad del Valle, Economics, June–Dec 1962." The search is documented extensively in that folder, RF, RG A81, Box R1737, Folder "311S, Universidad del Valle, Economics, January–May 1962"; and RF, RG 1.2, Series 311, Box 76, Folder 721.

4. Reinaldo Scarpetta, interview by the author, June 6, 2010, New York, New York; CVC Acta 117, September 22, 1958; CVC Acta 148, April 7, 1959; Kenneth Thompson, interview with Antonio J. Posada, August 12, 1960, unprocessed material, RF, RG A81, Box R1738, Folder "311S, Universidad del Valle, Economics, 1958–1960"; Charles M. Hardin, interview with Joe D. Wray, May 25, 1963, RF, RG A81, Folder "311S, Universidad del Valle, Economics, June–Dec 1962"; Charles M. Hardin, interview, Universidad del Valle, October 30, 1963, unprocessed material, RF, RG A81, Box R1737, Folder "311S, Universidad del Valle, Economics, August–Dec 1963."

5. Charles M. Hardin, interview with Joe D. Wray, May 25, 1963, RF, RG A81, Folder "311S, Universidad del Valle, Economics, June–Dec 1962"; L. Vince Padgett and David W. Dent in

collaboration with Jorge Ernesto Holguin and Harold Rizo Otero, "Community Leadership and Social Change in Cali, Colombia," 1963, RF, RG 1.2, Series 311, Box 73, Folder 704.

6. Alfonso Ocampo to Charles Hardin, November 15, 1963, unprocessed material, RF, RG A81, Box R1737, Folder "311S, Universidad del Valle, Economics, August–Dec 1963"; Reinaldo Scarpetta, interview by the author.

7. Samir C. Daccach M. to Charles Hardin, May 29, 1963, and Charles M. Hardin, interview with Roderick F. O'Connor, June 17, 1963, RF, RG A81, Box R1737, Folder 311S, "Universidad del Valle, Economics, June–Dec 1962."

8. Elizabeth A. Fones-Wolf, *Selling Free Enterprise: The Business Assault on Labor and Liberalism, 1945–1960* (Urbana: University of Illinois Press, 1994); Kim Phillips-Fein, *Invisible Hands: The Making of the Conservative Movement from the New Deal to Reagan* (New York: W. W. Norton, 2009).

9. Laurence deRycke, "Two New Signposts of an Economic Trend," *Los Angeles Times*, June 21, 1948; Laurence deRycke, "The Significance of the Important Supplier Principle as Applied in the Negotiation of Reciprocal Trade Agreement Concessions," *Journal of Finance* 7 (September 1952): 481–82.

10. "Awards Won by Professors at Occidental," *Los Angeles Times*, February 24, 1953; Kevin M. Kruse, *One Nation under God: How Corporate America Invented Christian America* (New York: Basic Books, 2015), 69–77.

11. "Business Men's Responsibilities: Mr. L. de Rycke's Views," *Times of India*, February 25, 1959.

12. "NAM Invites Professor," *Los Angeles Times*, April 28, 1952; "School Heads to Discuss Economics at Oxy Sitting," *Los Angeles Times*, July 20, 1952; Robert E. Nichols, "Economics and Education: The 2 Must Go Together," *Los Angeles Times*, November 19, 1961.

13. George H. Fern to Kenneth R. Miller, September 4, 1957, Harry E. Buck to K. R. Miller, January 7, 1959, "NAM's Proposed Program for Improving Economic Understanding," November 26, 1958, "The NAM and Education," January 17, 1961, and related documents in NAM Series 1, Box 65, Folder "Economic Education Programs (Keep)"; G. Derwood Baker, "The Joint Council on Economic Education," *Journal of Educational Sociology* 23, no. 7 (March 1950): 389–96.

14. Laurence deRycke to Kenneth W. Thompson, July 14, 1964, RF, RG 1.2, Series 311, Box 75, Folder 710; Laurence deRycke, Curriculum Vitae, August 7, 1963 RF, RG A81, Box R1737, Folder "311S, Universidad del Valle, Economics, June–Dec 1962."

15. W. Walter Williams, "A Program to Increase Understanding of the American Economy," *Michigan Business Review* 2, no. 4 (July 1950): 24; Robert M. Collins, "American Corporatism: The Committee for Economic Development, 1942–1964," *The Historian* 44, no. 2 (February 1982): 155; Fones-Wolf, *Selling Free Enterprise*, 23–24, 33–34.

16. Charles M. Hardin, interview, Economics, August 28, 1963 unprocessed material, RF, RG A81, Box R1737, Folder "311S, Universidad del Valle, Economics, August–Dec 1963."

17. Charles M. Hardin, interview with Alfonso Ocampo Londoño, Laurence deRycke, Roderick O'Connor, August 28, 1963, unprocessed material, RF, RG A81, Box R1737, Folder "311S, Universidad del Valle, Economics, August–Dec 1963."

18. Laurence deRycke to Kenneth Thompson, April 30, 1964, unprocessed material, RF, RG A81, Box R1737, Folder "311S, Universidad del Valle, Economics, Jan–Apr 1964"; Laurence deRycke to Kenneth Thompson, July 25, 1964, RF, RG 1.2, Series 311, Box 75, Folder 710.

19. Rakesh Khurana, *From Higher Aims to Hired Hands: The Social Transformation of American Business Schools and the Unfulfilled Promise of Management as a Profession* (Princeton, NJ: Princeton University Press, 2007); Sanford M. Jacoby, *Employing Bureaucracy: Managers, Unions, and the Transformation of Work in American Industry, 1900–1945* (New York: Columbia University Press, 1985); David Montgomery, *The Fall of the House of Labor: The Workplace, the State, and American Labor Activism, 1865–1925* (Cambridge: Cambridge University Press, 1987); Alfred D. Chandler Jr., *The Visible Hand: The Managerial Revolution in American Business* (Cambridge, MA: Harvard University Press, 1977).

20. Charles M. Hardin, diary with Reinaldo Scarpetta, March 31, 1964, unprocessed material, RF, RG A71, Box R1737, Folder "311S, Universidad del Valle, Economics, Jan–Apr 1964"; excerpt from James M. Daniel diary, December 22, 1964, RF, RG 1.2, Series 311, Box 74, Folder 708A.

21. Khurana, *From Higher Aims*, 293–94.

22. "Rod O'Connor, Adviser to Presidents Here, Abroad," *Tech Topics* (Atlanta), Fall 2007, 38.

23. Charles M. Hardin, interview with Alfonso Ocampo Londoño, Laurence deRycke, Roderick O'Connor, August 28, 1963, unprocessed material, RF, RG A81, Box R1737, Folder "311S, Universidad del Valle, Economics, August–Dec 1963"; Álvaro García, "Graduate Program in Industrial Management," February 9, 1965, RF, RG A81, Box R1737, Folder "311S, Universidad del Valle, Economics, Jan–Apr 1965"; L. Vince Padgett diary notes, March 1–July 31, 1966, RF, RG 1.2, Series 311, Box 74, Folder 708A.

24. Roderick F. O'Connor to Alfonso Ocampo, October 2, 1963, UV Administración, Caja 1, Carpeta 1; Charles M. Hardin, interview with Reinaldo Scarpetta, Verne S. Atwater, Marshall Robinson, and William P. Gormbley Jr., January 6, 1964, and Reinaldo Scarpetta to Laurence deRycke, June 23, 1964, unprocessed material, RF, RG A81, Box R1737, Folder "311S, Universidad del Valle, Economics, Jan–Apr 1964"; Grant GA HSS 6401, Allocation No. 1, January 7, 1964, unprocessed material, RF, RG A81, Box R1736, Folder "311S, Universidad del Valle, Economics, 1975–77, 1979, 1981–82"; RLW, interview with Reinaldo Scarpetta, August 18–19, 1964, unprocessed material, RF, RG A81, Box R1737, Folder "311S, Universidad del Valle, Economics, Aug–Dec 1964"; Reinaldo Scarpetta to Ralph K. Davidson, September 17, 1965, unprocessed material, RF, RG A77, Box R1345, Folder "311S, Universidad del Valle, Agricultural Economics, 1964–1965"; Reinaldo Scarpetta to Stacey H. Widdicombe Jr., May 20, 1965, UV Facultad Correspondencia, Caja 2, Carpeta 4; Sarah Babb, *Managing Mexico: Economists from Nationalism to Neoliberalism* (Princeton, NJ: Princeton University Press, 2001), 70.

25. "Report to the Ford Foundation on the First Year of Operations of the Graduate Program of Industrial Management at the Universidad del Valle," October 5, 1965, RF, RG A81, Box R1737, Folder "311S, Universidad del Valle, Economics, Sept–Dec 1965"; "Progress Report to the Ford Foundation: Activities of the Graduate School of Business for the Year 1967," UV Rectoría Correspondencia Fundaciones Extranjeras, Caja 5, Carpeta 15; "Ezra Solomon, Former Business School Professor, Dies," *Stanford Report*, January 8, 2003; Juan Gabriel Valdés, *Pinochet's Economists: The Chicago School in Chile* (Cambridge: Cambridge University Press, 1995), 165; "The School of Management at the Universidad del Valle, Cali, Colombia: A Center for Training the Effective Executive of Private and Public Affairs," n.d., RF, RG A81, Box R1738, Folder "311S, Universidad del Valle, Economics, 1958–1960"; Álvaro García M., "Informe a la Fundación Ford sobre los adelantos del Programa Post-Graduado en Administración

Industrial," October 1964–March 1965, UV Administración, Caja 1, Carpeta 1; "Lista de Textos pedidos para la Facultad de Economía," April 30, 1965, UV Facultad Correspondencia, Caja 2, Carpeta 1.

26. Nils Gilman, "The Prophet of Post-Fordism: Peter Drucker and the Legitimation of the Corporation," in *American Capitalism: Social Thought and Political Economy in the Twentieth Century*, ed. Nelson Lichtenstein (Philadelphia: University of Pennsylvania Press, 2006), 109–31.

27. CVC Acta 420, January 24, 1966; CVC Acta 433, May 23, 1966; CVC Acta 565, January 12, 1970; "The School of Management at the Universidad del Valle, Cali, Colombia: A Center for Training the Effective Executive of Private and Public Affairs," n.d., unprocessed material, RF, RG A81, Box R1739, Folder "311S, Universidad del Valle, Economics, 1958–1960"; Universidad del Valle e INCOLDA, "Programa Nocturno de Administración de Empresas," n.d., W. M. Myers Papers, Accession No. 30, Series 1, Box 6, Folder 51.

28. Anacleto Apodaca to Charles M. Hardin, September 4, 1963, unprocessed material, RF, RG A81, Box R1737, Folder "311S, Universidad del Valle, Economics, August–Dec 1963"; Laurence deRycke to Robert West, September 18, 1964, unprocessed material, RF, RG A81, Box R1737, Folder "311S, Universidad del Valle, Economics, Aug–Dec 1964"; Henry J. Eder to Local Board #115, December 19, 1967, and Henry J. Eder to Jefes de Sección y Departamento, February 2, 1968, CVC Correspondencia; "Progress Report to the Ford Foundation: Activities of the Graduate School of Business for the Year 1967, Universidad del Valle, Cali, Colombia," UV Rectoría Correspondencia Fundaciones Extranjeras, Caja 5, Carpeta 15; Farnum W. Cole to David E. Lilienthal, January 16, 1968, and February 23, 1968, DELP, Box 474, Folder "Re Colombia 1968."

29. Bernardo Garcés Córdoba to Vicente Aragón et al., April 12, 1965; "Locations of MIT Fellows in Colombia," November 24, 1965; Henry J. Eder to Carroll L. Wilson, August 31, 1967, all in CVC Correspondencia.

30. "Intelectuales americanos preconizan entendimiento," *El Siglo* (Bogotá), February 17, 1967; John W. McPherrin to Philip D. Reed, April 26, 1967, IESC, "A Report to the President of the United States," May 25, 1967, Albrecht M. Lederer to David Rockefeller et al., November 30, 1967, all in PDR Series 3, Box 25, Folder "International Executive Service Corps, 1967"; Alden C. Smith, "The International Executive Service Corps Today," reprint from the *Price Waterhouse Review*, Summer 1970, PDR Series 3, Box 25, Folder "International Executive Service Corps, 1970."

31. "Guidelines: Commerce Committee for the Alliance for Progress (COMAP)," July 19, 1962, Joseph Carwell to Mr. Martin and Mr. May, August 22, 1962, and Peter Grace to J. Wilner Sundelson, November 29, 1962, all in NACP, RG 59, Entry A1 3178, Box 1, Folder "COMAP (Commerce Committee for Alliance for Progress)"; *CLA Report* 2, no. 2 (March 1966), NAM Series 1, Box 72, Folder "Council for Latin America, General, 1966"; David Rockefeller, "What Private Enterprise Means to Latin America," *Foreign Affairs* 44, no. 3 (April 1966): 403–16; Ruth Leacock, *Requiem for Revolution: The United States and Brazil, 1961–1969* (Kent, OH: Kent State University Press, 1990), 94–95, 133, 232–33; Walter LaFeber, "Thomas C. Mann and the Devolution of Latin American Policy: From the Good Neighbor to Military Intervention," in *Behind the Throne: Servants of Power to Imperial Presidents, 1898–1968*, ed. Thomas J. McCormick and Walter LaFeber (Madison: University of Wisconsin Press, 1993), 189.

32. Frank Pace Jr., "The World Management Crisis—Can It Be Solved?" University of Minnesota School of Business Administration, November 2, 1967, PDR Series 3, Box 25, Folder "International Executive Service Corps, 1968"; IESC, "A Report to the President of the United States," May 25, 1967, PDR Series 3, Box 25, Folder "International Executive Service Corps, 1967"; Frank B. Elliott to Frank Pace Jr., May 15, 1968, PDR Series 3, Box 25, Folder "International Executive Service Corps, 1968."

33. Mario A. Kaffury Silva and José Asbel López Arana, "Los costos y su utilidad en las Empresas Municipales de Cali" (undergraduate thesis, Universidad del Valle, 1964); José Humberto Ospina Velasco, "Análisis de costos de la maquinaria agrícola del Ingenio del Cauca S.A." (master's thesis, Universidad del Valle, 1970); Jaime Donado Baena and Sabas Pretelet de la Vega, "Estudio de inversiones en el Ingenio Meléndez S.A." (master's thesis, Universidad del Valle, 1971); Juan G. Casas L. and Jorge Rodríguez N., "Análisis socio-económico del proyecto de adecuación de tierras, zona Obando-Cartago" (master's thesis, Universidad del Valle, 1975).

34. Bernardo Garcés Córdoba to Señor Alvarez et al., March 16, 1966, CVC Correspondencia.

35. Reinaldo Scarpetta to Hans Simons, September 20, 1966, UV Rectoría Correspondencia Fundaciones Extranjeras, Caja 5, Carpeta 15; CIDE, "Universidad del Valle: Informe Financiero, 1961–1965 y proyecciones," UV Facultad Informes, Caja 3, Carpeta 1; Reinaldo Scarpetta to Matt Wiggington, February 5, 1969, RF, RG A81, Box R1736, Folder "311S, Universidad del Valle, Economics, 1969."

36. Fundación para la Educación Superior, Estatutos, January 1965, UV Decanatura Informes, Caja 14, Carpeta 6; Ralph Kirby Davidson interview with Reinaldo Scarpetta, July 9, 1968, RF, RG A81, Box R1737, Folder "311S, Universidad del Valle, Economics, July–December 1968"; Reinaldo Scarpetta to Matt Wigginton, February 5, 1969, unprocessed material, RF, RG A81, Box R1736, Folder "311S, Universidad del Valle, Economics, 1969"; Reinaldo Scarpetta to David E. Lilienthal, June 17, 1968, "Certificate of Incorporation of Fund for Multinational Management Education," 1968, DELP, Box 475, Folder "Fund for Multinational Management Education, 1968"; Reinaldo Scarpetta to David E. Lilienthal, February 26, 1969, David E. Lilienthal to Lazard Frères and Co., March 17, 1969, and March 28, 1969, Reinaldo Scarpetta to Martha Muse, August 3, 1969, all in DELP, Box 482, Folder "Fund for Multinational Management Education, 1969"; "Report to the Executive Committee of FMME," May 14, 1970, DELP, Box 489, Folder "Fund for Multinational Management Education, 1970."

37. Fund for Multinational Management Education (hereafter FMME), "International Management Project in Cooperation with Fundación para la Educación Superior and the Universidad del Valle, Cali, Colombia," DELP, Box 475, Folder "Fund for Multinational Management Education, 1968"; Reinaldo Scarpetta to David E. Lilienthal, February 26, 1969, DELP, Box 482, Folder "Fund for Multinational Management Education, 1969"; "Report to the Executive Committee of FMME," May 14, 1970, DELP, Box 489, Folder "Fund for Multinational Management Education, 1970"; JMW interview, May 17–22, 1968, unprocessed material, RF, RG A81, Box R1737, Folder "311S, Universidad del Valle, Economics, January–June 1968"; Henry J. Eder to Hugo Lora Camacho, December 4, 1968, CVC Correspondencia.

38. Alfonso Ocampo Londoño, "Informe del Rector, Universidad del Valle, 1968–69," MIUV; "Universidad del Valle, Grant Proposal to the Rockefeller Foundation, 1970–1972," September 1969, UV Rectoría Correspondencia, Caja 7, Carpeta 18; Alvaro García M., "Informe a

la Fundación Ford sobre los adelantos del Programa Post-Graduado en Administración Industrial," October 1964–March 1965, UV Administración, Caja 1, Carpeta 1.

39. As Daniel Immerwahr notes, US-backed community development programs generally empowered local elites. UniValle's history reveals the leading role of Colombians themselves in fashioning these arrangements, lining up US support, and articulating obscurantist defenses of class hierarchy. Peter F. Drucker to Roderick O'Connor, September 5, 1963, UV Administración, Caja 1, Carpeta 1; Laurence deRycke to R. K. Davidson, November 15, 1964, RF, RG 1.2, Series 311, Box 74, Folder 708A; Álvaro García M., "Informe a la Fundación Ford sobre los adelantos del Programa Post-Graduado en Administración Industrial," October 1964–March 1965, UV Administración, Caja 1, Carpeta 1; Reinaldo Scarpetta, "Some thoughts on management and management education for meeting of Fund for Multinational Management Education," December 9, 1968, DELP, Box 475, Folder "Fund for Multinational Management Education, 1968"; Daniel Immerwahr, *Thinking Small: The United States and the Lure of Community Development* (Cambridge, MA: Harvard University Press, 2015).

40. Roderick F. O'Connor, "This Revolution Starts at the Top," *Columbia Journal of World Business* (Fall 1966): 39–46; Enno Hobbing, "Modernizers of Latin America," *The Lamp* 51, no. 3 (1969): 12–15.

41. Peter F. Drucker, "A Warning to the Rich White World," *Harper's* (December 1968): 67–74; Reinaldo Scarpetta, "Management Education as a Key to Social Development," in *Preparing Tomorrow's Business Leaders Today*, ed. Peter F. Drucker (Englewood Cliffs, NJ: Prentice-Hall, 1969), 269–279; Peter F. Drucker, *Management: Tasks, Responsibilities, Practices* (New York: Harper and Row, 1974), 67; Matthew Connelly, "Taking Off the Cold War Lens: Visions of North–South Conflict during the Algerian War for Independence," *American Historical Review*, 105, no. 3 (June 2000): 739–69.

42. Ana Fernanda de Maiguashca, "Departamento de administración industrial: Bases para una evaluación," December 3, 1968, UV Administración, Caja 1, Carpeta 2.

43. Excerpt from Ralph Kirby Davidson Latin America Trip Diary, Discussion with R. K. Ready, Ford Foundation, April 8, 1967, unprocessed material, RF, RG A81, Box R1737, Folder "311S, Universidad del Valle, Economics, January–June 1967."

44. Herbert W. Fraser to Ralph Kirby Davidson, November 9, 1966, and Reinaldo Scarpetta to Guy Hayes, March 25, 1967, RF, RG 1.2, Series 311, Box 74, Folder 708A; Ralph K. Davidson to Reinaldo Scarpetta, November 19, 1965, RF, RG 1.2, Series 311, Box 74, Folder 707; Herbert W. Fraser, "Report on Work with the Facultad de Economía," June 1965–October 1966, unprocessed material, RF, RG A81, Box R1737, Folder "311S, Universidad del Valle, Economics, July–December 1966"; Herbert W. Fraser, "Report on the Present State of the Facultad de Economía," July 21, 1967, unprocessed material, RF, RG A81, Box R1737, Folder "311S, Universidad del Valle, Economics, July–December 1967"; Laurence deRycke to Ralph Kirby Davidson, July 9, 1965, unprocessed material, RF, RG A81, Box R1737, Folder "311S, Universidad del Valle, Economics, May–Aug 1965."

45. "Universidad del Valle, Visiting Faculty," RF, RG A82, Box R1929, Folder "311S, Universidad del Valle, Program Review, 1974–75"; excerpt from G. I. Trant Diary, November 18, 1967–January 18, 1968, unprocessed material, RF, RG A81, Box R1737, Folder "311S, Universidad del Valle, Economics, January–June 1968"; Guy S. Hayes to Ralph K. Davidson, September 26, 1967, RF, RG 2.1, Series 311, Box 75, Folder 715; Luis Arturo Fuenzalida to Ralph Kirby Davidson,

July 29, 1976, and "Notas preliminares para el proyecto de desarrollo de micro-empresas, de la Fundación Hernando Carvajal B.," July 1976, RF, RG 6.9, Series 4, Box 9, Folder 99; Reinaldo Scarpetta to David E. Lilienthal, October 17, 1968, DELP, Box 475, Folder "Fund for Multinational Management Education, 1968"; Patrick N. Owens to William C. Olson, January 7, 1969, and Reinaldo Scarpetta to Matt Wigginton, February 5, 1969, unprocessed material, RF, RG A81, Box R1736, Folder "311S, Universidad del Valle, Economics, 1969."

46. Reinaldo Scarpetta, interview by the author.

47. Grant RF 66077, Allocation No. 155, August 1, 1969, unprocessed material, RF, RG A81, Box R1736, Folder "311S, Universidad del Valle, Economics, 1975–77, 1979, 1981–92"; and the following in UV Facultad Actas/Proyectos, Caja 1, Carpeta 1: Consejo, División de Ciencias Sociales y Económicas, Acta 6, March 31, 1969; Acta 10, May 5, 1969; and Acta 20, August 4, 1969.

48. In 1971, students in a social science methods course asked three hundred of their classmates to explain the university's mission and the purpose of their education. Economics students identified most strongly with the mission of "preparing qualified personnel" (59.1 percent), and least with the mission of "maintaining social action programs" (16.2 percent). The economics program had the highest percentage of students reporting that they entered the university to "improve my position" (43.1 percent), and the lowest percentages saying they did so to "better understand the world" (14.7 percent) or "better serve the community" (42.2 percent). "Relaciones Universidad-Comunidad: Encuesta de Estudiantes de la Universidad del Valle," May 30, 1971, 8–14, 25, 30, UV Facultad, Informes, Caja 3, Carpeta 7.

49. Universidad del Valle División de Ciencias Sociales y Económicas, "Resúmen de los planteamientos de la Federación de Estudiantes," September 1968, UV Decanatura Informes, Caja 14, Carpeta 6; FEUV, "Bases para una discusión crítica a lo que ha sido la filosofía implícita o explícita de la Universidad del Valle," September 3, 1968, UV Movimientos, Caja 1, Carpeta 8; CEFEUV to Compañero estudiante, n.d., UV Movimientos, Caja 1, Carpeta 1.

50. "Acta de la entrevista realizada entre la Federación de Estudiantes de la Universidad del Valle y el Director del Departamento de Sociología, Luis H. Fajardo," UV Movimientos, Caja 1, Carpeta 1; Consejo Superior Estudiantil de la Universidad del Valle, "Denuncia del Consejo Superior Estudiantil sobre la Penetración Cultural en la Universidad del Valle," September 9, 1968, UV Movimientos, Caja 1, Carpeta 1; Comité Ejecutivo de la FEUV, "Resolución," September 10, 1968, UV Movimientos, Caja 1, Carpeta 1; FEUV Comité Ejecutivo y Consejo Superior, "Informe de actividades durante agosto, septiembre y principios de octubre," October 2, 1968, UV Movimientos, Caja 1, Carpeta 1.

51. Exerpt from Michael P. Todaro memo, October 8, 1970, excerpt from Michael P. Todaro Cali Trip Diary, November 30, 1970, excerpt from Michael P. Todaro Cali Trip Diary, December 2, 1970, and excerpt from G. I. Trant Diary, February 1–December 31, 1970, all in unprocessed material, RF, RG A81, Box R1736, Folder "311S, Universidad del Valle, Economics, 1970"; Alfredo Roa M., "La universidad y el movimiento estudiantil," March 19, 1971, UV Facultad, Correspondencia, Caja 2, Carpeta 6; Rolando Castañeda, "Macroeconomía Lectura No. 22" and "Macroeconomía II, Lectura No. 27," UV Facultad, Informes, Caja 1, Carpeta 1.

52. García had studied at the Nacional, Belgium's University of Louvain, and the University of Paris and had worked for the National Planning Department and DANE. "Curriculum Vitae, Bernardo García," unprocessed material, RF, RG A81, Box R1736, Folder "311S, Universidad del Valle, Economics, 1971; Comité de Huelga, "Polémica #1," and Comité Ejecutivo de la FEUV,

"Comunicado," 1971, UV Movimientos, Caja 1, Carpeta 8; Gustavo Adolfo Vivas, "Carta a los estudiantes de la Universidad del Valle," February 1, 1971, unprocessed material, RF, RG A81, Box R1736, Folder "311S, Universidad del Valle, Economics, 1971"; "Comunicado de la Asamblea de Estudiantes de Administración de Empresas," February 17, 1971, and Consejo Estudiantil de Economía, "Comunicado," May 25, 1971, both in UV Movimientos, Caja 1, Carpeta 2.

53. Guy S. Hayes, "1970–1975," "Total Rockefeller Foundation Scholarships and Fellowships to Universidad del Valle," unprocessed material, RF, RG A81, Box R1929, Folder "311S, Universidad del Valle, Program Review, 1974–75"; "El desalojo de la Universidad: la nueva situación," UV Movimientos, Caja 1, Carpeta 8; Ramón Delgado C. to Jaime López, June 15, 1972, UV Facultad, Planes, Caja 4, Carpeta 5; Ralph K. Davidson to Farzam Arbab, September 16, 1974, unprocessed material, RF, RG A81, Box R1736, Folder "311S, Universidad del Valle, Economics, 1972–74"; Susan W. Almy interview, visit to Cali and CIAT, June 28–July 3, 1974, unprocessed material, RF, RG A77, Box R1345, Folder "311S, Universidad del Valle, Agricultrual Economics, 1970–1973–75."

54. Patrick N. Owens to Virgil C. Scott, November 17, 1970, RF, RG 6.9, Series 2, Box 4, Folder 39; Guy S. Hayes, "Evaluation" and "1970–1975," unprocessed material, RF, RG A82, Box R1929, Folder "311S, Universidad del Valle, Program Review, 1974–75"; Ralph K. Davidson to Álvaro Escobar Navia, January 6, 1977, unprocessed material, RF, RG A81, Box R1736, Folder "311S, Universidad del Valle, Economics, 1975–77, 1979, 1981–82"; Luis A. Fuenzalida, "Trip Report to Visit Univalle in Cali," November 15, 1974, RF, RG 6.9, Series 4, Box 9, Folder 97; Alberto R. Musalem, "Trip Report to Visit the División de Ciencias Sociales y Económicas at Universidad del Valle," February 5, 1975, RF, RG 6.9, Series 4, Box 9, Folder 98.

55. "Análisis y planteamientos de los estudiantes del Departamento de Economía," n.d., UV Facultad, Informes, Caja 3, Carpeta 7; "Historia del movimiento estudiantil de economía, Universidad del Valle (1970 1971)," UV Movimientos, Caja 1, Carpeta 3; Edgar Vásquez, "Más allá del modelo," February 10, 1971, and "Notas sobre la distinción entre ciencias y técnica," March 1974, UV Facultad, Informes, Caja 3, Carpeta 8; Bernardo García, *AntiCurrie: Crítica a las teorías de desarrollo capitalista en Colombia* (Bogotá: Carreta, 1973); excerpt from G. I. Trant Diary, February 1–December 31, 1970, unprocessed material, RF, RG A81, Box R1736, Folder "311S, Universidad del Valle, Economics, 1970"; Consejo Estudiantil de Economía, "Comunicado No. 1," May 16, 1974, UV Movimientos, Caja 1, Carpeta 3.

56. Decanatura y Comité de Profesores to Consejo Estudiantil, January 4, 1972, UV Facultad, Planes, Caja 4, Carpeta 4; "Propuesta de Plan de Estudios que hace el profesorado de la División de Ciencias Sociales y Económicas," February 4, 1974, UV Facultad, Planes, Caja 4, Carpeta 6; Comité de Investigaciones, "Propuesta para la definición de una política de investigaciones en la División de Ciencias Sociales y Económicas," October 4, 1978, and Profesores, Departamento de Economía, "Elementos de discusión para el diseño de un nuevo plan de estudios de economía," September 1979, UV Facultad, Informes, Caja 3, Carpeta 9; "Propuesta de reforma al plan de estudios de economía," and related documents, UV Facultad, Planes, Caja 4, Carpeta 8; Edgar Vásquez B., "Las fuerzas de la crisis," UV Facultad, Informes, Caja 3, Carpeta 11; and the contents of UV Facultad, Proyectos, Caja 1, Carpeta 4.

57. Edgar Vásquez Benítez, *Ensayo sobre la historia urbana de Cali* (Cali: Universidad del Valle, 1980); Edgar Vásquez Benítez, *Historia del desarrollo urbano en Cali* (Cali: Universidad del Valle, 1980, 1982); Edgar Vásquez Benitez, *Panorama histórico del desenvolvimiento económico*

vallecaucano (Cali: Universidad del Valle, 1996); Edgar Vásquez Benítez, *Historia de Cali en el siglo 20: Sociedad, economía, cultura y espacio* (Cali: Universidad del Valle, Secretaria de Cultura y Turismo, Municipio de Cali, FIDUFES, Fondo Común Especial Arco Iris, FENALCO, ESAP-Valle, La Palabra, 2001); Arturo Escobar, *Encountering Development: The Making and Unmaking of the Third World* (Princeton, NJ: Princeton Univery Press, 1995), 238n13; Arturo Escobar, email to the author, January 18, 2018.

58. Alfonso Ocampo Londoño to Guy S. Hayes, May 22, 1965, UV Facultad Correspondencia, Caja 2, Carpeta 4; Reinaldo Scarpetta to Ralph Kirby Davidson, May 10, 1965, and "Ponencia de la Facultad de Economía de la Universidad del Valle al Tercer Seminario de Facultades de Economía," n.d., unprocessed material, RF, RG A81, Box R1737, Folder "311S, Universidad del Valle, Economics, May–Aug 1965"; Grant GA HSS 6579, June 9, 1965, unprocessed material, RF, RG A81, Box R1736, Folder "311S, Universidad del Valle, Economics, 1975–77, 1979, 1981–82."

59. Consejo Académico, Acta 144-67, May 2, 1967, Andes Archivo, Fondo Secretaria General, Serie Actas del Consejo Académico, Carpeta 1967; *Universidad del los Andes Boletín Informativo* No. 5, August 1969, and No. 12, March 1970, RFAM, RG 4, Series L, Box 254, Folder 2523.

60. The committee met with the dean of UniValle's management program, the Ford Foundation representative at UniValle, and a Harvard MBA who had taught at UniValle in 1964/65. The Nacional did not immediately accept the recommendation, but the report conveyed UniValle's emergence as a model. Lauchlin Currie et al., "A Report of a Committee on the Teaching of Business Administration in the National University of Colombia," May 1967, LBCP, Box 20, Folder "Teaching 1960–1993, Carpeta #8."

61. Manuel Rodríguez Becerra, Carlos Dávila Ladrón de Guevara, and Luis Ernesto Romero Ortiz, *Gerencia privada, generencia pública, educación en crisis: Una empresa docente* (Bogotá: Facultad de Administración, Universidad de los Andes, Bogotá, 1992), chap. 2; Ronald Stalin Pabón Suárez, "Los estudios de administración en Colombia: origen, expansión y diversificación," *Clio América* 1 (January 2007): 50–63.

62. By 1968, CLADEA included the Escola de Administração da Fundação Getulio Vargas in Brazil, the Instituto para el Desarrollo Empresarial de la Argentina, and the Instituto de Estudios Superiores de Administración in Venezuela. Reinaldo Scarpetta to Stacey H. Widdicombe Jr., May 20, 1965, UV Facultad Correspondencia, Caja 2, Carpeta 4; "Progress Report to the Ford Foundation: Activities of the Graduate School of Business for the Year 1967, Universidad del Valle, Cali, Colombia," UV Rectoría Correspondencia Fundaciones Extranjeras, Caja 5, Carpeta 15; George Cabot Lodge, "The Birth of INCAE (1963–1965)," *ReVista/DRCLAS News* (Cambridge, MA) (Fall 2009): 36–38; CLADEA brochure, "The Purpose of the Council for Latin America," n.d., DELP, Box 475, Folder "Fund for Multinational Management Education, 1968."

63. Harvard Graduate School of Business Administration, *Preliminary Report: Central American Survey*, October 1963, IV-2, FJA Box 12, Folder "Central America Survey: Prelim Report, October 1963"; Reinaldo Scarpetta, "Jamaica: Towards a System of Management Education," May 10, 1969," UV Facultad Correspondencia, Caja 2, Carpeta 5; Reinaldo Scarpetta, "Sample Invitation Letter for Conference of Deans of Schools of Business Administration," January 3, 1966, RF, RG 1.2, Series 311, Box 74, Folder 708.

64. CLADEA brochure, "The purpose of the Council for Latin America," n.d., DELP, Box 475, Folder "Fund for Multinational Management Education, 1968."

65. R. K. Ready, "Can Business Schools in Latin America Lead a Revolution?" *Columbia Journal of World Business* 3 (November–December 1968): 75–80; "Robert Knowles 'RK' Ready," *Herald Tribune* (Sarasota, FL), August 7, 2014.

66. Gilman, "Prophet of Post-Fordism," 110; Bockman, *Markets in the Name of Socialism.*

67. CLA Report vol. 5, no. 5 (May 1969), RF, RG A81, Box R1736, Folder "311S, Universidad del Valle, Economics, 1969"; "Again, the Investment Climate in Colombia," n.d., DELP, Box 475, Folder "Fund for Multinational Management Education, 1968"; "The School of Management at the Universidad del Valle, Cali, Colombia," DELP, Box 489, Folder "Fund for Multinational Management Education, 1970."

68. CLADEA brochure, "The Purpose of the Council for Latin America," n.d., DELP, Box 475, Folder "Fund for Multinational Management Education, 1968"; Edgard Moncayo, Philippe De Lombaerde, and Oscar Guinea Ibáñez, "Latin American Regionalism and the Role of UN-ECLAC, 1948–2000," in Claude Auroi and Aline Helg, eds., *Latin America, 1810–2010: Dreams and Legacies* (London: Imperial College Press, 2012), 359–86.

69. The inclusion of the Peruvian dictatorship was curious, given its left orientation. "International Management and Development Institute—Worldwide Network of Management Centers: A Multi-National Joint Venture in Management," October 20, 1970, and FMME, President's Report, 1970, DELP, Box 489, Folder "Fund for Multinational Management Education, 1970"; Reinaldo Scarpetta to William Lurie, July 16, 1971, FMME President's Report, December 1971, FMME Board of Directors, Minutes, December 6, 1971, DELP, Box 495, Folder "Fund for Mutinational Management Education, 1971"; Margold, Ersken, and Wang to FMME, May 10, 1973, DELP, Box 507, Folder "Fund for Multinational Management Education, 1973"; FMME President's Report, November 1971–October 1973, DELP, Box 512, Folder "Fund for Multinational Mgmt Ed, 1974."

70. Nils Gilman, "The New International Economic Order: A Reintroduction," *Humanity* 6, no. 1 (Spring 2015): 1–16; Christy Thornton, "A Mexican International Economic Order? Tracing the Hidden Roots of the Charter of Economic Rights and Duties of States," *Humanity* 9, no. 3 (Winter 2018): 389–421; Jack N. Behrman, "A Career in the Early Limbo of International Business: Policy, Research and Education," *Journal of International Business Studies* 37, no. 3 (May 2006): 437; FMME Annual Report, 1976 and "Fund for Multinational Management Education: A Critical Resource in International Public Policy Debates," both in Kenneth Holland Papers, Box 58, Folder "Fund for Multinational Management Education"; FMME Annual Report, 1975, DELP, Box 523, Folder "Fund for Multinational Management Education, 1976."

71. Mexican Oil and Technology Transfer: Hearings before the Subcommittee on Investigations and Oversight of the Committee on Science and Technology, US House of Representatives, 96th Congress, First Session, July 31–August 1, 1979, 230; Muhammad Baghal to Taher Amin, August 13, 1974, and FMME Annual Report, 1976, Kenneth Holland Papers, Box 58, Folder "Fund for Multinational Management Education"; Jean Wilkowski, "The US and UNC-STD," *Technology in Society* 1 (1979): 153–58.

72. Henry R. Geyelin, FMME President's Report, November 1971–October 1973, DELP, Box 512, Folder "Fund for Multinational Management Education, 1974"; FMME Annual Report, 1975, DELP, Box 523, Folder "Fund for Multinational Management Education, 1976"; Behrman, "A Career"; Henry R. Geyelin to FMME Board of Directors, October 13, 1975, and FMME Annual Report, 1976, Kenneth Holland Papers, Box 58, Folder "Fund for Multinational Management Education."

Chapter 6: The Great Society as Good Business

1. David E. Lilienthal to Jacob K. Javits, April 11, 1960, DELP, Box 19, Folder "Javits, Jacob K. 1960."

2. David E. Lilienthal, "The Changing Role of the Businessman in Public Affairs," *Civil Service Journal* (October–December 1967): 20, emphasis in original.

3. David E. Lilienthal, "Urbanism: The New International Frontier," April 5, 1962, DELP, Box 428, Folder "Re Speech [Lecture]: Rutgers University Urban Studies Center, New Brunswick, New Jersey, 'Urbanism: The New International Frontier.'"

4. "The Goal of Management Is to 'Get Things Done': An Interview with David Lilienthal," *Columbia Journal of World Business* (November–December 1968): 56. Nearly the same sentence appears in David E. Lilienthal, *Management: A Humanist Art* (New York: Columbia University Press, 1967), 17; David E. Lilienthal to Manuel Carvajal, June 28, 1971, DELP, Box 494, Folder "Carvajal, Manuel, 1971."

5. Lilienthal, *Management*, 12–13, 17, 28–29, 56, 61, 59–63.

6. David E. Lilienthal to Frank B. Jewett Jr., May 20, 1969, DELP, Box 481, Folder "Development and Resources Corporation 1969."

7. Lilienthal made the same case to New York Mayor John Lindsay in 1968: "What D&R is trying to do in urban America—as it has done with not a little success overseas—is to promote *public* objectives through the medium of a *private* corporation, owned by its staff, and subject to the discipline of having to support itself, make a profit, and pay taxes." David E. Lilienthal to John V. Lindsay, April 23, 1968, DELP, Box 477, Folder "Lindsay, John V., 1968."

8. "Management Is the Key to Making Deserts Bloom," *International Management* (April 1961): 16.

9. Development & Resources Corporation (hereafter D&R), *Agriculture*, n.d., 13, DELP, Box 452, Folder "Development and Resources Corporation 1965"; David Ekbladh, *The Great American Mission: Modernization and the Construction of an American World Order* (Princeton, NJ: Princeton University Press, 2010), 190–225.

10. "Selling Self-Help—At a Profit," *Business Abroad*, August 12, 1967; Katherine C. Epstein, *Torpedo: Inventing the Military-Industrial Complex in the United States and Great Britain* (Cambridge, MA: Harvard University Press, 2014); Julie Greene, *The Canal Builders: Making America's Empire at the Panama Canal* (New York: Penguin, 2009), 55–56; Jana K. Lipman, *Guantánamo: A Working-Class History between Empire and Revolution* (Berkeley: University of California Press, 2009), 37; Bruce J. Schulman, *From Cotton Belt to Sun Belt: Federal Policy, Economic Development, and the Transformation of the South, 1938-1980* (New York: Oxford University Press, 1991), 91, 141; Elizabeth Tandy Shermer, *Sunbelt Capitalism: Phoenix and the Transformation of American Politics* (Philadelphia: University of Pennsylvania Press, 2013), 73, 77; Jason Scott Smith, *Building New Deal Liberalism: The Political Economy of Public Works, 1933–1956* (Cambridge: Cambridge University Press, 2006), 19–20, 111.

11. "The Goal of Management Is to 'Get Things Done,'" 57; Lilienthal, *Management*, 13.

12. Daniel Amsterdam, *Roaring Metropolis: Businessmen's Campaign for a Civic Welfare State* (Philadelphia: University of Pennsylvania Press, 2016); Julia F. Irwin, *Making the World Safe: The American Red Cross and a Nation's Humanitarian Awakening* (Oxford: Oxford University Press, 2013); Michael B. Katz, *In the Shadow of the Poorhouse: A Social History of Welfare in*

America (New York: Basic Books, 1996); Michael B. Katz, *The Irony of Early School Reform: Educational Innovation in Mid-Nineteenth Century Massachusetts* (New York: Teachers College Press, 2001), 164–66; Larry Cuban, *The Blackboard and the Bottom Line: Why Schools Can't Be Businesses* (Cambridge: Cambridge University Press, 2007), 39–50; Roy Rosenzweig and Elizabeth Blackmar, *The Park and the People: A History of Central Park* (Ithaca, NY: Cornell University Press, 1998); Ian Tyrrell, *Reforming the World: The Creation of America's Moral Empire* (Princeton, NJ: Princeton University Press, 2010).

13. "The Goal of Management Is to 'Get Things Done,'" 57; Lilienthal, *Management*, 17, 38; David E. Lilienthal to Theodore V. Houser, August 28, 1962, DELP, Box 431, Folder "Committee for Economic Development 1962."

14. Lilienthal, *Management*, 38; Mary Jean Bennett, "The Bookshelf: Businessman as Humanist," *Wall Street Journal*, December 18, 1967. Mary Jean Bennett was later and better known as Mary Bennett Peterson. Lawrence Glickman, *Buying Power: A History of Consumer Activism in America* (Chicago: University of Chicago Press, 2012), 295. Lilienthal's 1966 lecture, published as *Management* in 1967, contains the first use of "social entrepreneurship" to refer to the capitalist strategy of providing at a profit social goods previously delivered through public or nonprofit means. The phrase "social entrepreneurship" appeared in a few earlier publications bearing fundamentally different meanings. Studying nationalization in 1955, Martin Bronfenbrenner used the term to describe the entrepreneurial activity of nationalized or socialized firms working in ordinary areas of industrial production. He distinguished the "social entrepreneurship" of the state or the owners of social property from the "private entrepreneurship" of an individual owner or private-sector firm. In 1960, Neil J. Smelser used "social entrepreneurship" figuratively to describe the work of popularizing an idea, generating public support for it, and transforming it into law. In contrast, Richard S. Rosenbloom in 1969 used "social entrepreneurship" as Lilienthal had in 1966, suggesting that the phrase began to acquire a new, stable meaning during the late 1960s. M. Bronfenbrenner, "The Appeal of Confiscation in Economic Development," *Economic Development and Cultural Change* 3, no. 3 (April 1955): 201–18; Richard S. Rosenbloom, "Comments on Social Entrepreneurship," *Harvard Business School Bulletin* 45 (June 1969): 22–26; Neil J. Smelser, *Social Change in the Industrial Revolution: An Application of Theory to the British Cotton Industry* (London: Routledge, 1959), 294.

15. John Oliver to D&R Staff, July 18, 1968, D&R, Box 80, Folder 9; "The Goal of Management Is to 'Get Things Done': An Interview with David Lilienthal," *Columbia Journal of World Business* (November–December 1968): 57.

16. D&R's US contracts are detailed in hundreds of documents in D&R and DELP. Key sources on the New York metropolitan region include D&R, *Report to Commerce, Labor, Industry Corporation of Kings on the Estimated Costs to Rehabilitate Buildings 3, 5, 77, 200 & 275 in the Brooklyn Navy Yard*, March 20, 1969, D&R, Box 68, Folder 11; D&R, "Model Cities Program and Its Relevance to South Jamaica: Report Prepared for JCC," September 6, 1968, D&R, Box 69, Folder 5; Charles Morris, "Airport Employment Programs in South Jamaica," n.d., D&R, Box 69, Folder 4; D&R, *Welfare Island Yesterday and Today: A Report Prepared for the Welfare Island Planning and Development Corporation*, April 9, 1968, D&R, Box 381, Folder 1; *Report of the Welfare Island Planning and Development Committee*, February 1969, D&R, Box 71, Folder 2; D&R, *Detailed Project Report: Flood Protection on Pequest River for Belvidere, New Jersey*, D&R, Box 379, Folder 1; D&R, *Feasibility Report: Great Falls Hydroelectric Project, Prepared for the City*

of Paterson, New Jersey, October 1978, D&R, Box 379, Folder 2; D&R, *New York City's Power Supply,* October 1969, D&R, Box 381, Folder 4; *State of New York Investigation of the New York City Blackout, July 13, 1977: Report by Norman M. Clapp, Special Consultant in Charge of Investigation,* January 1978, D&R, Box 380, Folder 10; and the contents of D&R, Box 371, Folder 3 (Meadowlands); D&R, Box 138, Folder 5 (New Jersey water management); D&R, Box 82, Folder 3 (Jamaica Community Corporation); DELP, Box 491, Folder "New York City's Power Supply 1971"; DELP, Box 530, Folder "Clapp, Norman M., 1977."

17. By the early 1970s, D&R's US clients, in addition to those already mentioned, included the Army Corps of Engineers; HUD; the EPA's Office of Water Programs; the Department of the Interior's Bureau of Land Management; the State of California; East Montana State College; the Montana Power Co.; the Hackensack Meadowlands Development Commission in New Jersey; the City of New York; the Oakland County Planning Commission in Pontiac, Michigan; the Aqueduct and Sewer Authority and the Water Resources Authority in Puerto Rico; and the State of Washington's Department of Water Resources and Department of Ecology. US corporate clients included energy giants Mobil Oil Corp., Pennzoil United, and Peabody Coal. "Development and Resources Corporation," brochure, 1970s (undated), DELP, Box 500, Folder "Development and Resources Corporation 1972."

18. Thomas C. Field, *From Development to Dictatorship: Bolivia and the Alliance for Progress in the Kennedy Era* (Ithaca, NY: Cornell University Press, 2014); Ruth Leacock, *Requiem for Revolution: The United States and Brazil, 1961–1969* (Kent, OH: Kent State University Press, 1990), 94–95, 133, 232–33.

19. CLA, "Report to the Members, 1967–1968," NAM Series 1, Box 72, Folder "Council for Latin America, General, 1966"; Enno Hobbing, "Doing Business in Latin America," reprinted in *NACLA* 1, no. 6 (August 1967): 6–7; Matthew David Edel, "The Colombian Community Action Program: An Economic Evaluation" (PhD diss., Yale University, 1968), 442; Norman A. Bailey, "The Colombian 'Black Hand': A Case Study of Neoliberalism in Latin America," *Review of Politics* 27, no. 4 (1965): 461.

20. James N. Green, *We Cannot Remain Silent: Opposition to the Brazilian Military Dictatorship in the United States* (Durham, NC: Duke University Press, 2010), 42, 57, 206; Barbara Weinstein, *For Social Peace in Brazil: Industrialists and the Remaking of the Working Class in São Paulo, 1920–1964* (Chapel Hill: University of North Carolina Press, 1996), 280–344.

21. Hobbing, "Doing Business in Latin America," 6–7; Bryce Woods, *The Dismantling of the Good Neighbor Policy* (Austin: University of Texas Press, 1985), 169–70; Seymour M. Hersh, *The Price of Power: Kissinger in the Nixon White House* (New York: Summit Books, 1983), 260; Ekbladh, *Great American Mission,* 231–33.

22. *Foreign Assistance Act of 1964: Hearings before the Committee on Foreign Affairs, House of Representatives, Eighty-Eighth Congress, Second Session, May 5–6, 1964* (Washington, DC: USGPO, 1964), 1113–15; David Rockefeller, "Council For Latin America Membership List," *NACLA* 1, no. 7 (1967); "Invitation List—dinner for businessmen, Thursday, March 12, 1964," "President's Task Force for the War against Poverty, Businessmen's Meeting, 3 June 1964," both in JFK Shriver, Box 62, Folder "Business Leadership Advisory Council."

23. "Invitation List—dinner for businessmen, Thursday, March 12, 1964" and "President's Task Force for the War against Poverty, Businessmen's Meeting, 3 June 1964," both in JFK Shriver, Box 62, Folder "Business Leadership Advisory Council"; David Rockefeller, "Council for Latin America Membership List," *NACLA* 1, no. 7 (1967).

24. John H. Rubel to Vern Alden and Sargent Shriver, April 14, 1964, NACP, RG 381, Entry A1 1038, Box 5, Folder "Miscellaneous Correspondence"; "Four Business Chiefs Enlist in Federal War on Poverty," *Washington Post*, March 29, 1964; "Shriver Program Put into High Gear," *Christian Science Monitor*, April 23, 1964; "Litton Memo Provides Poverty War Strategy," *Los Angeles Times*, July 23, 1964; Judith Sealander, *The Failed Century of the Child: Governing America's Young in the Twentieth Century* (Cambridge: Cambridge University Press, 2003), 167; Scott Stossel, *Sarge: The Life and Times of Sargent Shriver* (New York: Other Press, 2011), 374–75; Paul William Combs, "Job Corps to 1973" (PhD diss., Virginia Polytechnic Institute, 1985), 90–91.

25. Shriver to Adam Clayton Powell, March 22, 1965, JFK Shriver, Box 66, Folder "Statement before the House Committee on Education and Labor, 4/12/65 2"; Amy C. Offner, "Classroom Management," forthcoming; Alexandra Rutherford, *Beyond the Box: B. F. Skinner's Technology of Behavior from Laboratory to Life, 1950s–1970s* (Toronto: University of Toronto Press, 2009); Bill Ferster, *Teaching Machines: Learning from the Intersection of Education and Technology* (Baltimore: Johns Hopkins University Press, 2014), 50–92; John H. Rubel to Vern Alden and Sargent Shriver, April 14, 1964, NACP, RG 381, Entry A1 1038, Box 5, Folder "Miscellaneous Correspondence."

26. John H. Rubel to Vern Alden and Sargent Shriver, April 14, 1964, NACP, RG 381, Entry A1 1038, Box 5, Folder "Miscellaneous Correspondence."

27. Peter Malof to John H. Rubel, April 9, 1964, Press Release, April 15, 1964, "Task Force Business Incentives Conference," June 10–11, 1964, "Meeting of Ad Hoc Steering Committee," June 16, 1964, all in NACP, RG 381, Entry A1 1038, Box 5, Folder "Miscellaneous Historical"; Sargent Shriver to Charles E. Scripps, April 23, 1964, John Rubel to Theron J. Rice, May 8, 1964, and John H. Rubel to Vern Alden, Sargent Shriver, May 11, 1964, all in NACP, RG 381, Entry A1 1038, Box 5, Folder "Miscellaneous Correspondence"; John Rubel to Adam Yarmolinsky, May 26, 1964, NACP, RG 381, Entry A1 1038, Box 5, Folder "Reading File"; Thomas S. Nichols to Ferd Nadherny, September 13, 1965, NACP, RG 381, Entry A1 1010, Box 1, Folder "BLAC Meeting Sept. 10, 1965"; Vernon R. Alden to Sargent Shriver, May 4, 1964, Marie O'Donahoe to Mr. Larry Willey, May 4, 1964, Marie O'Donahoe to Willey, Robinson, and Young, May 15, 1964, NACP, RG 381, Entry A1 1038, Box 6, Folder "Planning Book"; Offner, "Classroom Management."

28. Universities, the YWCA, and other nonprofit organizations operated the remaining urban centers. In rural areas, the Departments of Agriculture and Interior directed roughly one hundred small conservation camps. From the 1960s to the 1990s, Job Corps operated an average of one hundred centers enrolling 45,000 young people per year. Sargent Shriver, Keynote Speech at Sales and Marketing Executives International Convention, New Orleans, June 5, 1967, JFK Shriver, Box 54; *Economic Opportunity Act Amendments of 1967: Hearings before the Committee on Education and Labor, House of Representatives, Nineteenth Congress, First Session, June 12 and 16, 1967* (Washington, DC: USGPO, 1967), 782-784; William S. Clayson, *Freedom Is Not Enough: The War on Poverty and the Civil Rights Movement in Texas* (Austin: University of Texas Press, 2010), 59; Sealander, *Failed Century of the Child*, 167–68.

29. *Roswell Residential Training Center and Related Indian Vocational Education Policy: Hearings before the Subcommittee on the Department of the Interior and Related Agencies of the Committee on Appropriations, United States Senate, Ninety-Second Congress, Second Session* (Washington, DC: USGPO, 1972), 4, 10; *Departments of Labor and Health, Education, and Welfare Appropriations for 1969: Hearings before a Subcommittee of the Committee on Appropriations, House of Representatives, Ninetieth Congress, Second Session, Part 6, Office of Economic Opportunity*

(Washington, DC: USGPO, 1968), 340; Sar A. Levitan, Garth L. Magnum, and Robert Taggart III, *Economic Opportunity in the Ghetto: The Partnership of Government and Business* (Baltimore: Johns Hopkins University Press, 1970), 18–45; Arthur I. Blaustein and Geoffrey Faux, *The Star-Spangled Hustle* (Garden City, NY: Doubleday, 1972), 94–95.

30. S. M. Amadae, *Rationalizing Capitalist Democracy* (Chicago: University of Chicago Press, 2003), 27–73; David Tyack and Larry Cuban, *Tinkering toward Utopia: A Century of Public School Reform* (Cambridge, MA: Harvard University Press, 1995), 115–17.

31. Larry W. Burt, "Factories on Reservations: The Industrial Development Programs of Commissioner Glenn Emmons, 1953–1960," *Arizona and the West* 19, no. 4 (Winter 1977): 317–32; Larry W. Burt, *Tribalism in Crisis: Federal Indian Policy, 1953–1961* (Albuquerque: University of New Mexico Press, 1982); Cathleen D. Cahill, *Federal Fathers and Mothers: A Social History of the United States Indian Service, 1869–1933* (Chapel Hill: University of North Carolina Press, 2013); Andrew Needham, *Power Lines: Phoenix and the Making of the Modern Southwest* (Princeton, NJ: Princeton University Press, 2014), 150–52; Azusa Ono, "The Relocation and Employment Assistance Programs, 1948–1970: Federal Indian Policy and the Early Development of the Denver Indian Community," *Indigenous Nations Studies Journal* 5, no. 1 (Spring 2004): 27–50; Kenneth R. Philp, *Termination Revisited: American Indians on the Trail to Self-Determination, 1933–1953* (Lincoln: University of Nebraska Press, 1999).

32. Needham, *Power Lines*, 123–25, 148–56.

33. "Report to the Secretary of the Interior by the Task Force on Indian Affairs," July 10, 1961, 38–39, LBJ WHCF IN, Box 4, Folder "IN/S"; Philleo Nash, Speech in Cleveland, April 11, 1964, LBJ Department of the Interior, Box 33, Folder "Indian Affairs 2/64–12/65"; Larry Burt, "Western Tribes and Balance Sheets: Business Development Programs in the 1960s and 1970s," *Western Historical Quarterly* 23, no. 4 (November 1992): 479–481; "Cites Success of Job Training Aid to Indians," *Chicago Tribune*, July 10, 1964.

34. *Roswell Residential Training Center and Related Indian Vocational Education Policy: Hearings before the Subcommittee on the Department of the Interior and Related Agencies of the Committee on Appropriations, United States Senate, Ninety-Second Congress, Second Session* (Washington, DC: USGPO, 1972), 4, 10; Burt, "Western Tribes and Balance Sheets," *Western Historical Quarterly* 23, no. 4 (November 1992): 475–95; Keith LaVerne Fay, *Developing Indian Employment Opportunities* (Washington, DC: BIA, 1976), 1, 5–7, 46.

35. RCA Government Services, "Proposal to Establish a Training Center for American Indians," September 29, 1966, 7/2–7/4, 7/6–7/8, 7/15–7/18, NAW, RG 75, Entry 1410-B, Box 1, Folder "Proposal—Training Program for American Indians—28 September 1966, RCA, 2 of 2"; "Report of the Interagency Task Force on American Indians," October 23, 1967, 21, LBJ Task Force Reports, Box 20, Folder "1968 American Indians."

36. "ITT is teaching Mike Fontenot how to bake a cake," *Foreign Affairs* 44, no. 4 (July 1966): A-13, and *Financial Analysts Journal* 22, no. 3 (May–June 1966): front matter; "The World of ITT," *Wall Street Journal*, October 28, 1965; Combs, "Job Corps to 1973," 95–96.

37. Robert L. Marquardt, "Encouraging Home Ownership," *IEEE Transactions on Aerospace and Electronic Systems*, vol. AES-6, no. 3 (May 1970): 382–86; Thiokol Chemical Corporation, *Annual Report*, 1970, 22–23; Robert L. Marquardt to Nicholas Philip, April 5, 1968, D&R Box 69, Folder 2; Thiokol Chemical Corporation, "Advanced Corpsman Institute," Thiokol Chemical Corporation, "Peace Corps Training, Iran," "Clearfield Job Corps Urban Center," all in NAW,

RG 75, Entry 1410-B, Box 2, Folder "Thiokol Chemical Corp. Career Development Program, Walker Air Force Base, Roswell."

38. Roscoe Drummond, "Job Corps Is Harnessing Profit Motive to Gain Social Progress," *Los Angeles Times*, March 22, 1965.

39. RCA Government Services, "Cost Proposal," Prepared for Bureau of Indian Affairs, 5/4/67, NAW, RG 75, Entry 1410-B, Box 1, Folder "Cost Proposal—4 May 1967"; *Hearings before the Senate Subcommittee on Employment, Manpower, and Poverty of the Committee on Labor and Public Welfare, United States Senate, Ninetieth Congress, First Session on Examining the War on Poverty, Sparta, Wisconsin, May 26, 1967, Part 14* (Washington, DC: USGO, 1967), 4327, 4333, 4344–47.

40. Jefferson Cowie, *Capital Moves: RCA's Seventy-Year Quest for Cheap Labor* (Ithaca, NY: Cornell University Press, 1999), 115 and all.

41. The Roswell contract ultimately went to Thiokol. RCA Government Services, "Proposal to Establish a Training Center for American Indians," Prepared for Bureau of Indian Affairs, September 29, 1966, RG 75, Entry 1410-B, Box 1, Folder "Proposal—Training Program for American Indians—28 September 1966, RCA, 1 of 2"; Burt, "Western Tribes and Balance Sheets," 484; Prentice Mooney, "Indian Country Is a Frontier Again," *Nation's Business* (September 1969): 77; Fay, *Developing Indian Employment Opportunities*.

42. Alyosha Goldstein, *Poverty in Common: The Politics of Community Action during the American Century* (Durham, NC: Duke University Press, 2012), 185–98; Daniel M. Cobb, *Native Activism in Cold War America: The Struggle for Sovereignty* (Lawrence: University Press of Kansas, 2008).

43. Fairchild Camera and Instrument Corporation moved into Indian country during the same period that it began manufacturing in the Third World; in 1965, it was already building integrated circuits and transistors in Hong Kong, and by 1973, it was operating factories in Korea and Mexico. *Fairchild Camera and Instrument Corporation Annual Report*, 1965, 15–16; *Fairchild Camera and Instrument Corporation Annual Report*, 1972, 6; Cowie, *Capital Moves*, 115.

44. David Kamper, *The Work of Sovereignty: Tribal Labor Relations and Self-Determination at the Navajo Nation* (Santa Fe: School for Advanced Research Press, 2010), 28.

45. Fay, *Developing Indian Employment Opportunities*, 74, 174–75; Lorraine Turner Ruffing, "The Navajo Nation: A History of Dependence and Underdevelopment," *Review of Radical Political Economics* 11, no. 2 (July 1979): 34.

46. *Fairchild Camera and Instrument Corporation Annual Report*, 1965, 15; Fairchild Semiconductor, Invitation for Ground Breaking Ceremonies at the Shiprock, NM Facility, 1969, Computer History Museum, Lot X5184.2009; "Indians Heard Loud and Clear," *Christian Science Monitor*, April 16, 1969.

47. Vinita V. Lewis, an African American BIA official, agreed that Navajo workers possessed distinctive talents. As the reservation attracted capital investment during the 1960s—the Fairchild factory flourished alongside a new electrical plant at Four Corners and expanding uranium and coal mines—Lewis wrote that Navajos' "manual dexterity and competence in eye and hand coordination has been a hidden resource just as the uranium deposits were a hidden resource beneath the Navajo lands." Paul Stuart, *Nations within a Nation: Historical Statistics of American Indians* (New York: Greenwood Press, 1987), 200; Fairchild Semiconductor, Invitation for Ground Breaking Ceremonies at the Shiprock, NM Facility, 1969, Computer History Museum, Lot X5184.2009; *Fairchild Camera and Instrument Corporation Annual Report*, 1972, 13; Lisa

Nakamura, "Indigenous Circuits: Navajo Women and the Racialization of Early Electronic Manufacture," *American Quarterly* 4 (December 2014): 925–26; Vinita V. Lewis to Commissioner, October 25, 1966, and Vinita V. Lewis to George Schmidt, June 8, 1966, both in NAW, RG 75, Entry 784A, Box 22, Folder "Shiprock-Navajo Development Committee, 1 of 3."

48. Marsha L. Weisiger, *Dreaming of Sheep in Navajo Country* (Seattle: University of Washington Press, 2009); Alexandra Harmon, Colleen O'Neill, and Paul C. Rosier, "Interwoven Economic Histories: American Indians in a Capitalist America," *Journal of American History* 98, no. 3 (December 2011): 698–722; Needham, *Power Lines*, 42–51; Colleen O'Neill, *Working the Navajo Way. Labor and Culture in the Twentieth Century* (Lawrence: University Press of Kansas, 2005); Area Director, BIA Navajo Area Office, Window Rock, to Commissioner of Indian Affairs, December 9, 1966, NAW, RG 75, Entry 784A, Box 22, Folder "Shiprock-Navajo Development Committee, 1 of 3."

49. Vinita V. Lewis to Commissioner, October 25, 1966; Commissioner Bennett to Graham Holmes, September 9, 1966; "Summary of Meeting with New Mexico Department of Public Welfare Representative, Navajo Agency and Area Welfare Staff, April 20, 1965 and Summary of Meeting at Navajo Agency with Tribal Judges, Tribal Public Service & Agency and Area Welfare Staff, April 21, 1965"; William C. Howard Jr. to Vinita Lewis, May 18, 1967; Walter J. Knoedel to Chief, Branch of Welfare, December 14, 1966; "Social and Economic Goals BIA—Fiscal Year 1965 to Fiscal Year 1975"; all in NAW, RG 75, Entry 784A, Box 22, Folder "Shiprock-Navajo Development Committee, 1 of 3"; Margaret D. Jacobs, *A Generation Removed: The Fostering and Adoption of Indigenous Children in the Postwar World* (Lincoln: University of Nebraska Press, 2014); Margaret D. Jacobs, *White Mother to a Dark Race: Settler Colonialism, Maternalism, and the Removal of Indigenous Children in the American West and Australia, 1880–1940* (Lincoln: University of Nebraska Press, 2009); David Wallace Adams, *Education for Extinction: American Indians and the Boarding School Experience, 1875–1928* (Lawrence: University Press of Kansas, 1995); "Navajos Build Homes, Learn at Same Time," *Los Angeles Times*, August 29, 1971.

50. Vinita V. Lewis to Commissioner, October 25, 1966, NAW, RG 75, Entry 784A, Box 22, Folder "Shiprock-Navajo Development Committee, 1 of 3."

51. As Andrew Needham notes, the AIM occupation also critiqued ecological destruction wrought by industrial development on the reservation and occurred just four months after AIM occupied the Black Mesa Mine No. 1. "Accord Ends Factory Siege by Indians," *Washington Post*, March 4, 1975; "Armed Indians Seize Navajo Firm," *Chicago Tribune*, February 25, 1975; "Indian Protesters Occupy Electronics Plant in NM," *Los Angeles Times*, February 25, 1975; "20 Armed Indians Seize a Building on Navajo Land," *New York Times*, February 25, 1975; "Fairchild Takeover Aftereffects Lasted Decades," *Navajo Times*, February 24, 2005; "Chairman Trudell Says AIM Group Can Prove Charges," *New Mexico Daily Lobo*, March 5, 1975; Needham, *Power Lines*, 216–17, 242–43.

52. Burt, "Western Tribes and Balance Sheets," 484; Stuart, *Nations within a Nation*, 196–97, 200.

53. Cowie, *Capital Moves*; "RCA Aids Reform of Camden Schools," *New York Times*, June 21, 1970; "RCA Applies Industrial Know-How to Staff Training," *Christian Science Monitor*, May 8, 1971; LeRoy B. Allen, "Replications of the Educational Park Concept for the Disadvantaged," *Journal of Negro Education* 40, no. 3 (Summer 1971): 229.

54. Offner, "Classroom Management"; Tyack and Cuban, *Tinkering toward Utopia*, 114–20; Carol Ascher, "Performance Contracting: A Forgotten Experiment in School Privatization," *Phi*

Delta Kappan 77, no. 9 (1996): 615–21; Harvey J. Brudner, "Will Business Training Ideas Work in School?" *Educational Leadership* (April 1975): 448–51.

55. Charles Blaschke, "Ventures in Performance Contracting," in *Performance Contracting: A Balanced View*, ed. Richard R. Anderson (Madison: Wisconsin Department of Public Instruction), 116, ERIC ED083709; James A. Mecklenburger, *Performance Contracting* (Worthington, OH: C. A. Jones Pub. Co., 1972), 26, 48–49; Polly Carpenter and George R. Hall, *Case Studies in Educational Performance Contracting: Conclusions and Implications* (Washington, DC: RAND Corporation, 1971); Thiokol Chemical Corporation, 1970 Annual Report, 12–13; Thiokol Chemical Corporation, 1971 Annual Report, 10.

56. Fred Lazarus to David E. Lilienthal, April 23, 1962, Robert F. Lenhart to David E. Lilienthal, May 18, 1962, and David E. Lilienthal to Theodore V. Houser, August 28, 1962, all in DELP, Box 431, Folder "Committee for Economic Development 1962."

57. R. H. Mulford, "The Basic Role of Industry," June 5, 1965, Mulford to David E. Lilienthal, January 12, 1966, and Robert C. Sprague, "The Profit Motive," June 12, 1965, all in DELP, Box 458, Folder "Committee for Economic Development 1966 (1 of 2)."

58. Emphasis in original. Robert F. Lenhart to David E. Lilienthal, August 3, 1965, and David E. Lilienthal to Subcommittee on Business Structure and Performance, November 24, 1965, both in DELP, Box 452, Folder "Committee for Economic Development 1965"; David E. Lilienthal to Alfred C. Neal, March 25, 1966, DELP, Box 458, Folder "Committee for Economic Development 1966 (1 of 2)"; David E. Lilienthal to Alfred C. Neal, December 14, 1966, DELP, Box 458, Folder "Committee for Economic Development 1966 (2 of 2)"; Neal to David E. Lilienthal, May 26, 1967, all in DELP, Box 466, Folder "Committee for Economic Development 1967."

59. Richard M. Cyert and James G. March, *A Behavioral Theory of the Firm* (Englewood Cliffs, NJ: Prentice-Hall, 1963); Richard M. Cyert, "Memorandum on Antitrust Research," DELP, Box 458, "Committee for Economic Development 1966 (1 of 2)"; Richard M. Cyert and Oliver E. Williamson, "Proposal for Research on Anti-Trust Policy for the CED," in DELP, Box 458, "Committee for Economic Development 1966 (2 of 2)"; Alfred D. Chandler, "The Large Industrial Corporation and the Making of the Modern American Economy," March 1967, and Richard M. Cyert and Oliver E. Williamson, "Information as an Economic Control," both in DELP, Box 466, Folder "Committee for Economic Development 1967."

60. S. Abbot Smith to David E. Lilienthal, January 17, 1966, and E. W. Carter to David E. Lilienthal, January 17, 1966, both in DELP, Box 458, Folder "Committee for Economic Development 1966 (1 of 2)"; David E. Lilienthal to Alfred C. Neal, December 14, 1966, and Alfred C. Neal to David E. Lilienthal, DELP, Box 458, Folder "Committee for Economic Development 1966 (2 of 2)."

61. Winfield Best to David E. Lilienthal, February 22, 1971, and Mildred Baron to Winfield Best, March 3, 1971, DELP, Box 493, Folder "Businessmen's Educational Fund."

62. Emphasis in original. George Champion, "Private Enterprise and Public Responsibility in a Free Society," March 24, 1966, 3, 4, 13, DELP, Box 458, Folder "Committee for Economic Development 1966 (1 of 2)"; W. H. Wheeler Jr. to David E. Lilienthal, November 2, 1966, DELP, Box 458, Folder "Committee for Economic Development 1966 (2 of 2)"; "A Conscience in the Boardroom," *Management Review* 55, no. 5 (May 1966): 52–56; "Statement by Gerald L. Philippe," May 10, 1967," and "Members of the Business Leadership Advisory Council, May 1967," both in JFK Shriver, Box 62, Folder "Business Leadership Advisory Council."

63. "A Conscience in the Boardroom," 54; "The Big Business Do-Gooders: Private War on Poverty," *Look*, August 9, 1966, 15–19.

64. Champion, "Private Enterprise and Public Responsibility in a Free Economy," March 24, 1966, DELP, Box 458, Folder "Committee for Economic Development 1966 (1 of 2)"; William C. Stolk, "Beyond Profitability—Defining Corporate Goals," September 26, 1968, DELP, Box 474, Folder "Committee for Economic Development, 1968."

65. John J. Corson to David E. Lilienthal, November 11, 1966, DELP, Box 458, Folder "Committee for Economic Development 1966 (2 of 2)"; John J. Corson, "Social Security: A Recollection," *Social Security Bulletin* 48, no. 8 (August 1985): 23–24; "John Corson 3d Dies; Business Consultant and a US Aide, 84," *New York Times*, September 12, 1990; John J. Corson, *Executives for the Federal Service* (New York: Columbia University Press, 1952); John J. Corson to Bernard L. Gladieux, October 24, 1952, JFK Corson, Box 7, Folder "Improving Executive Talent in the Federal Government, 1952"; T. P. Pike to Harold Boeschenstein, January 7, 1954, and Corson to John Cowles et al., JFK Corson, Box 3, Folder "Business Advisory Council, 1954–1955"; Corson to John Cowles et al., April 14, 1955, JFK Corson, Box 3, Folder "Business Advisory Council, 1954–1955"; Walter White to John J. Corson, January 1, 1955, JFK Corson, Box 4, Folder "Business Advisory Council, 1954–1955."

66. Henry Wallich to Alfred C. Neal, October 15, 1966, W. H. Wheeler Jr. to David E. Lilienthal, November 2, 1966, both in DELP, Box 458, Folder "Committee for Economic Development 1966 (2 of 2)"; Jennifer A. Delton, *Racial Integration in Corporate America, 1940–1990* (Cambridge: Cambridge University Press, 2009), 130, 153–62.

67. Committee for Economic Development (CED), *Social Responsibilities of Business Corporations* (New York: CED, June 1971), foreword.

68. CED, *Social Responsibilities*, 22–23; Richard M. Cyert and James G. March, *A Behavioral Theory of the Firm* (Englewood Cliffs, NJ: Prentice-Hall, 1963); and Alfred C. Neal to David E. Lilienthal, December 9, 1966, Richard M. Cyert and Oliver E. Williamson, "Proposal for Research on Anti-Trust Policy for the CED," and Hans B. Thorelli, "The Political Economy of the Firm: Basis for a New Theory of Competition?" all in DELP, Box 458, Folder "Committee for Economic Development 1966 (2 of 2)."

69. CED, *Social Responsibilities* 31–33, 51–52, 55–57.

70. In a review of the final report, *Time* applauded CED's search for "profitable 'social market' activities" that would benefit the corporation's public "constituency." "Responsibility Beyond Profit," *Time*, July 12, 1971, 69; John J. Corson to David E. Lilienthal, November 11, 1966, DELP, Box 458, Folder "Committee for Economic Development 1966 (2 of 2)"; William C. Stolk, "Beyond Profitability—Defining Corporate Goals," September 26, 1968, DELP, Box 474, Folder "Committee for Economic Development, 1968"; CED, *Social Responsibilities*, 54.

71. Edward M. Gramlich and Patricia P. Koshel, *Educational Performance Contracting: An Evaluation of an Experiment* (Washington, DC: Brookings Institution, 1975), 26–31; Mecklenburger, *Performance Contracting*, 3; "Taxpayers and Parents Want Tangible Results Not Negative Reasons," *Christian Science Monitor*, June 7, 1971; AFT cartoon reprinted in *Newsday*, January 18, 1971; "Bronx to Take Study-for-Pay Gamble," *The News* (New York, NY), August 2, 1970; David Selden, "The State of Our Union: The President's Report to the 54th Annual Convention of the American Federation of Teachers," August 17, 1970, 4–5, ERIC ED043592.

Chapter 7: The American Dream Comes Home

1. Ian Donald Terner, "Obstacles to Owner-Building: A Quest for Responsive Housebuilding Technologies," in *The Responsive House*, ed. Edward Allen (Cambridge, MA: MIT Press, 1974), 89.

2. "Tenant Leader Questionnaire, Section 2," Folder "UHAB, Don Turner [sic] #117," Box 8, Ronald Lawson: *Tenant Movement in New York City* Research Files, Tamiment Library.

3. Ian Donald Terner and Robert Herz, "Squatter-Inspired," *Architectural Digest* 38 (August 1968): 367–68; UHAB Annual Report, 1974, Ronald Lawson: *Tenant Movement in New York City* Research Files, Box 8, Folder "UHAB, Don Turner [sic] #117."

4. At times, these circuits intersected. Greek architect Constantinos A. Doxiadis helped design his country's self-help housing program after World War II, collaborated with veterans of the Puerto Rican experiment in 1947, won support from the Ford Foundation and US government, and became a legendary international consultant designing self-help projects across the Middle East, Africa, South Asia, and the Americas. Richard Harris, "The Silence of the Experts: 'Aided Self-Help Housing,' 1939–1954," *Habitat International* 22 (1998): 165–89; Richard Harris and Ceinwen Giles, "A Mixed Message: The Agents and Forms of International Housing Policy, 1945–1973," *Habitat International* 27 (2003): 167–91; Statement of A. Fernós-Isern, *Establishment of the Caribbean Organization: Hearing before the Subcommittee on International Organizations and Movements of the Committee on Foreign Affairs, House of Representatives, April 20, 1961*, 17; John G. Papaioannou, "C. A. Doxiadis' Early Career and the Birth of Ekistics," *Ekistics* 41 no. 247 (June 1976): 313–19; "Constantinos A. Doxiadis," *Ekistics* 72 no. 430/435 (January–December 2005): 10–12; Nathan J. Citino, *Envisioning the Arab Future: Modernization in US-Arab Relations, 1945–1967* (Cambridge: Cambridge University Press, 2017), 135–41.

5. ICT, *Informe al Señor Ministro de Desarrollo Económico* (Bogotá: ICT, 1963), 89; Tricia Schulist and Richard Harris, "'Build Your Own Home': State-Assisted Self-Help Housing in Canada, 1942–75," *Planning Perspectives* 17, no. 4 (2002): 346.

6. Richard Harris, "Slipping through the Cracks: The Origins of Aided Self-Help Housing, 1918–53," *Housing Studies* 14, no. 3 (1999): 287–88.

7. Russell Lord and Paul H. Johnstone, eds., *A Place on Earth: A Critical Appraisal of Subsistence Homesteads* (Washington, DC: US Department of Agriculture, 1942), 12, 44–47, 83–86. The Iona Self-Help Cooperative in Idaho, founded in 1934, did manage to finance self-help housing with a federal grant from the Federal Emergency Relief Administration. See Florence E. Parker, "Cooperation in the Building of Homes," *Monthly Labor Review* 52, no. 2 (February 1941): 295.

8. Frederick L. W. Richardson, "Community Resettlement in a Coal Region," *Applied Anthropology* 1 (October–December 1941): 24–53; Historical American Buildings Survey, "Town of Penn-Craft," HABS No. PA-5920, Library of Congress Prints and Photographs Division; "Self-Help Cooperative Housing," *Monthly Labor Review* 49, no. 3 (September 1939): 566–77.

9. Richard J. Margolis, *Something to Build On: The Future of Self-Help Housing in the Struggle against Poverty* (Washington, DC: International Self-Help Housing Associates, AFSC, 1967), 20–22; "An Antibiotic for the Slum," *New York Times*, October 25, 1953.

10. "Brief Resume of the Experience of Bard McAllister in Self-Help Housing," George Loft Papers, Hoover Institution, Box 8, Folder 8.4; Richard Harris, "Flattered but Not Imitated:

Co-operative Self-Help and the Nova Scotia Housing Commission, 1936–1973," *Acadiensis* 31, no. 1 (Fall 2001): 103–28.

11. Harris, *Building a Market*, 309–10.

12. Before 1960, the most publicized self-help initiative under FmHA aupices was organized not by federal officials but by the Tuskegee Institute in Alabama. Researchers there developed a concrete block construction system during the 1940s, and they convinced FmHA officials to allow its use among loan recipients. Ernest E. Neal, *Low Cash Cost Housing: Rural Life Information Series, Bulletin Number 2* (Tuskegee, AL: Tuskegee Institute, 1950), 25.

13. Nancy H. Kwak, *A World of Homeowners: American Power and the Politics of Housing Aid* (Chicago: University of Chicago Press, 2015), 180–95.

14. Gordon Macgregor, "Anthropology in Government: United States," *Yearbook of Anthropology* (1955): 421–33; BIA news releases, October 24, 1964, and December 30, 1964, LBJ Department of the Interior, Box 34, Folder "Indian Affairs 12/63-6/65."

15. Alyosha Goldstein, *Poverty in Common: The Politics of Community Action during the American Century* (Durham, NC: Duke University Press, 2012), 83–88; Daniel M. Cobb, *Native Activism in Cold War America: The Struggle for Sovereignty* (Lawrence: University Press of Kansas, 2008), 8–29.

16. Roger Biles, "Public Housing on the Reservation," *American Indian Culture and Research Journal* 24, no. 2 (2000): 50–57; "Report to the Secretary of the Interior by the Task Force on Indian Affairs," July 10, 1961, 38–39, LBJ WHCF IN, Box 4, Folder "IN/S"; Milton Semer to Lee White, January 17, 1964, and "Background of Indian Program," January 20, 1964, LBJ WHCF IN, Box 1, Folder "IN 11/22/63-2/29/64"; Urban Institute, *Assessment of American Indian Housing Needs and Programs: Final Report* (Washington, DC: Urban Institute, 1996), 122–23.

17. During the Indian New Deal, BIA commissioner John Collier had secured $1.3 million from the Resettlement Administration to finance self-help programs that included home building and repair. But there was no public housing policy, and that infusion of funds gave rise to no extended program. "Indian Housing in South Dakota: 1946–1975," prepared for the South Dakota State Historic Preservation Office, April 15, 2000, history.sd.gov, 3–4.

18. Milton Semer to Lee White, January 17, 1964, LBJ WHCF IN, Box 1, Folder "IN 11/22/63-2/29/64."

19. As of 1962, Arizona had only eight housing authorities administering PHA low-rent housing projects, compared with 189 authorities with active programs in Georgia. Housing and Home Finance Agency, *Sixteenth Annual Report* (Washington, DC: HFFA, 1962), 219.

20. Bruce J. Schulman, *From Cotton Belt to Sun Belt: Federal Policy, Economic Development, and the Transformation of the South, 1938–1980* (New York: Oxford University Press, 1991), chap. 6; Jason Scott Smith, *Building New Deal Liberalism: The Political Economy of Public Works, 1933–1956* (Cambridge: Cambridge University Press, 2009), 2.

21. Cybelle Fox, *Three Worlds of Relief: Race, Immigration, and the Welfare State from the Progressive Era to the New Deal* (Princeton, NJ: Princeton University Press, 2012); Linda Gordon, *Pitied but Not Entitled: Single Mothers and the History of Welfare, 1890–1935* (New York: Free Press, 1994).

22. The states were South Dakota, Iowa, Oklahoma, Utah, Vermont, and Wyoming. Housing and Home Finance Agency, *Fourteenth Annual Report* (Washington, DC: HFFA, 1960–61), 231. As of 1949, local housing authorities had built only seven hundred rural units in five southern states. By 1976, per-capita federal outlays for housing programs were still nearly twice as large

in metropolitan as nonmetropolitan counties. Norman Williams Jr., "Discrimination and Segregation in Minority Housing," *American Journal of Economics and Sociology* 9, no. 1 (October 1949): 87; J. Norman Reid, W. Maureen Godsey, and Fred K. Hines, *Federal Outlays in Fiscal 1976* (Washington, DC: USDA, 1978), 13.

23. Philleo Nash, speech in Cleveland, April 11, 1964, 8, and Philleo Nash, "The Indian Bureau and the War on Poverty," June 18, 1964, both in LBJ Department of the Interior, Box 33, Folder "Indian Affairs 2/64-12/65."

24. The agencies were the BIA, OEO, FmHA, and HUD. Under HUD, the FHA, PHA, Low Income Demonstration Housing Program, and Housing Assistance Administration participated. Margolis, *Something to Build On*, 2, 22–23.

25. Reeve H. Barceloux to Irvine Finch, June 29, 1966, California State Archives, F3751:142; "Wirtz Scores Condition of Farm Labor Camp," *Los Angeles Times*, March 26, 1965; "Wirtz Cites 'Shame' at Farm Labor Camps," *Washington Post*, March 26, 1965.

26. A. S. Coe, "Special Meeting on Farm Worker Housing," December 8, 1965, California State Archives F3751:142.

27. Cindy Hahamovitch, *No Man's Land: Jamaican Guestworkers in America and the Global History of Deportable Labor* (Princeton, NJ: Princeton University Press, 2011), 97–100; Paul S. Taylor, "Perspective on Housing Migratory Agricultural Laborers," *Land Economics* 27, no. 3 (August 1951): 198–200; Matt Garcia, *From the Jaws of Victory: The Triumph and Tragedy of Cesar Chavez and the Farm Worker Movement* (Berkeley: University of California Press, 2012), 17–18; John Thompson, "The Settlement Geography of the Sacramento–San Joaquin Delta, California" (PhD diss., Stanford University, 1957), 433–35.

28. Frank Bardacke, *Trampling Out the Vintage: Cesar Chavez and the Two Souls of the United Farm Workers* (London: Verso, 2011), 95–96; Oliver McMillan, "Housing Deficiencies of Agricultural Workers and Other Low Income Groups in Rural and Urban Fringe Communities," Governor's Advisory Commission on Housing Problems, *Appendix to Report on Housing in California* (San Francisco: The Commission, 1963), 654–58, 676, 699.

29. "Modernization of Tachi Indian Buildings Begins," *Los Angeles Times*, January 29, 1961; "Interview with Jim Stein and Bard McAllister," September 1993, 5–8, Self-Help Enterprises Inc. office files (hereafter SHE); AFSC, "Self-Help Housing for the Seasonal Farm Labor," November 1, 1959, SHE; Julius (Jim) Stein, "The Beginning of Self-Help Housing in the San Joaquin Valley: The Story of Self-Help Enterprises, Inc., 1965–1970," April 26, 1970, Bancroft Library; "Brief Resume of the Experience of Bard McAllister in Self-Help Housing," Hoover Institution, George Loft Papers, Box 8, Folder 8.4.

30. Richard J. Margolis, "Self-Help Enterprises, Inc.: A General Evaluation," October 24, 1966, 12, California State Archives F3751:260; Richard J. Margolis, *All Their Days, All Their Nights: Notes on Rural America* (Washington, DC: Rural Housing Alliance, 1969), 21.

31. *Report of the Administrator of the Farmers Home Administration, 1952* (Washington, DC: United States Department of Agriculture, 1952), 18–19.

32. *Housing for Domestic Farm Labor: Hearing before a Subcommittee of the Committee on Banking and Currency,* Senate, 88th Congress (1963), 23–24 (Statement of Howard Bertsch); " 'Pilot' Town Attacks Farm Labor's Problem," *Los Angeles Times*, October 24, 1963.

33. Farmers Home Administration, *Do-It-Yourself Home Construction by Farm Workers May Be One Answer to Knotty Rural Housing Problem*, October 1963, SHE.

34. Bernard L. Boutin, "Remarks to the Conference on Antipoverty Programs for Migrant Farm Workers," January 18, 1966, and "Fact Sheet: Migrant and Seasonal Farm Workers, Community Action Program," both in LBJ Papers of Bernard L. Boutin, Box 22, Folder "Migrant Farm Workers Conference on Antipoverty Programs—1/18/66"; "A Summary of Anti-Poverty Programs for Migrant and Seasonal Farm Workers," LBJ OEO, Box 14, Folder "Correspondence and Memoranda pertaining to US Mexican Commission on Economic and Social Development of the Border Area, 1966–1967."

35. Immerwahr, *Thinking Small*; Goldstein, *Poverty in Common*; Sheyda Jahanbani, "One Global War on Poverty: The Johnson Administration Fights Poverty at Home and Abroad, 1964–1968," in *Beyond the Cold War: Lyndon Johnson and the New Global Challenges of the 1960s*, ed. Francis J. Gavin and Mark Atwood Lawrence (Oxford: Oxford University Press, 2014), 97–117.

36. Ervan Bueneman to Mason Barr, August 26, 1965, NAW, RG 75, Entry 999-C, Box 22, Folder 392 "Mutual Help Housing Gen. 2"; Ervan R. Bueneman and George R. Jordan, *The Development of Low-Cost Housing through Cooperatives: With Special Reference to the Area Served by the Caribbean Commission* (Port of Spain, Trinidad and Tobago: Caribbean Commission, 1957); Ervan R. Bueneman, "Aided Self-Help Housing: Puerto Rico," *Caribbean* 11 (August 1957): 7–11; E. R. Bueneman, "The Tobago Story: Example of Cooperation at All Levels," *Caribbean* 12 (August 1958): 6–10.

37. *Report of the First National Conference on Self-Help Housing: Airlie House, Warrenton, Virginia, December 6–9, 1965* (Philadelphia: Community Relations Division, American Friends Service Committee, 1965), 23, 61, 68.

38. AFSC, "Tulare Co. Self-Help Housing Booklet, Rough Draft," California State Archives F3751:261; Walter J. Monasch to Paul O'Rourke, November 23, 1966, California State Archives F3751:260.

39. Goldstein, *Poverty in Common*, 60–62.

40. Bernardo Garcés Córdoba to Orvis Schmidt, February 24, 1962, CVC Correspondencia.

41. Harold Robinson, *Aided Self-Help Housing: Its History and Potential* (Washington, DC: US Department of Housing and Urban Development, Office of International Affairs, 1976), 38.

42. *Migratory Labor: Hearings before the Subcommittee on Migratory Labor of the Committee on Labor and the Public Welfare*, Senate, 86th Congress (1960), 1169–73 (Statement of Bard McAllister); "Memorial Minute for Bard McAllister," visaliaquakers.org.

43. Franz Dolp, "Stabilizing Employment of Farm Labor through Cooperative Organization: A Study of Sequoia Farm Labor Association, Tulare County, California" (PhD diss., University of California, Berkeley, 1964), 12–42; Bard McAllister to Phil Buskirk, July 16, 1965, California State Archives F3751:261.

44. Graciela Martinez, interview by the author, Visalia, California, May 28, 2013; Eleanor A. Eaton to National Community Relations Committee, December 18, 1970, and Thelma Segal to Files, October 1, 1970, both in AFSC Folder "CRD Housing/Urban Affairs: Comms & Orgs, UFWOC 1970"; Robert Marshall, interview by the author, Visalia, California, May 29, 2013.

45. Ralph Rosedale, interview by the author, Visalia, California, May 29, 2013; "Help for India Will Be Topic," *Los Angeles Times*, July 7, 1956.

46. Ralph Rosedale, interviews by the author, Visalia, California, May 29–30, 2013; "President Richard Nixon's Daily Diary, September 22, 1972, Appendix I, www.nixonlibrary.gov;

Problems of Agricultural Land: Testimony Taken before a Joint Meeting of the Assembly Interim Committees on Revenue and Taxation and Agriculture of the California State Legislature, 1964, 68.

47. Ralph Rosedale, interview by the author, May 29, 2013.

48. Another supportive farmer, Calvin Helty, had worked with the AFSC in Puerto Rico. "Interview with Jim Stein and Bard McAllister," 23–24, SHE; "Self-Help Enterprises (A Non-Profit Corporation)," California State Archives F3751:259; David S. Bovée, *The Church and the Land: The National Catholic Rural Life Conference and American Society, 1923–2007* (Washington, DC: Catholic University of America Press, 2010); Edward S. Shapiro, "Catholic Agrarian Thought and the New Deal," *Catholic Historical Review* 65 (1979): 583–99; and the following at stanislausconnections.org: Samuel R. Tyson, "Tuolumne Co-Op Farm," *Roots and Fruit* 7; Samuel R. Tyson, "Self-Help Enterprises," *Roots and Fruit*, n.d.; Sandy Sample, "Sam Tyson: A Remembrance," *Stanislaus Connections*, February 2009.

49. "Negro Farm Town Sinks to Poverty," *Los Angeles Times*, October 3, 1962; McMillan, "Housing Deficiencies," 699.

50. Tom Collinshaw, *Teviston: No Time to Look Back* (Visalia, CA: Self-Help Enterprises, 1981, SHE).

51. Mark Newman, *Divine Agitators: The Delta Ministry and Civil Rights in Mississippi* (Athens: University of Georgia Press, 2004), 127–48; "Dispossessed Farm Workers to Get Housing," *Economic Opportunity Report*, April 3, 1967, California State Archives, F3751:260; Delta Ministry, Freedom City brochure, February 1967, University of Southern Mississippi Digital Collections, Goodman (Jill Wakeman) Civil Rights Collection, Box 1, Folder 4.

52. *Report of the First National Conference on Self-Help Housing*, 3–5, 24–29; *"People Have a Right . . ." The Report of the First National Conference on Rural Housing, Airlie House, Warrenton, Virginia, June 9–12, 1969* (Washington, DC: 1969), 9–11, 15, 20, 22–26, 33, AFSC, Folder "CRD Housing/Urban Affairs, National Rural Housing Conference, 1969"; *Migrant and Seasonal Farmworker Powerlessness: Hearings before the Subcommittee on Migratory Labor of the Committee on Labor and the Public Welfare*, Senate, 91st Congress (1970), 5521–37 (Statement of Clay L. Cochran).

53. ISHA was founded in 1965; RHA and NRHC in 1969; and Rural America in 1976. On the creation, see Housing Assistance Council, *A Brief History of Rural Mutual Self-Help Housing in the United States* (Washington, DC: HAC, 2012), 4–5.

54. "Slum Today; Own Housing Tomorrow," *Fresno Bee*, March 27, 1966; Rural Housing Alliance, *OEO and Rural Housing* (Washington, DC: Rural Housing Alliance, 1972), 40–41, 44–47, 51, 81, 106, 119; Stephen Butler and Susan Peck, *Alternative Low-Income Housing Delivery Systems for Rural America* (Washington, DC: Housing Assistance Council, 1974); Richard J. Margolis, *Self-Help Housing in Urban Areas* (Washington, DC: International Self-Help Housing Association, 1968), 30–31; California Farm Worker Housing Conference, April 19–20, 1976, Wyckoff Santa Cruz Box 16, Folder "California Farmworker Housing Conference, 1976"; Herb Foster, "Cooperative Farm Labor Housing Project," November 4, 1966, California State Archives F3751:259; "Recommendations from Midwest Conference on Housing, Sponsored by the Division for the Spanish Speaking, Midwest Region," May 28, 1969, Nixon Library WHCF Subject Files, Box 3, Folder "[Gen] HS 7/1/69-9/30/69 [1 of 2]."

55. Margolis, *Something to Build On*, 25; Margolis, *All Their Days*; "Interview with Jim Stein and Bard McAllister," September 1993, 16, SHE; "Richard J. Margolis, Writer for Children and

Columnist, 61," *New York Times*, April 23, 1991; Housing Assistance Council, *A Brief History of Rural Mutual Self-Help Housing in the United States*, 4.

56. *Report of the First National Conference on Self-Help Housing*, 66.

57. Ronald G. Lewis, "Challenges to Self-Help Housing," in *Report of the First National Conference on Self-Help Housing*, 45; Terner and Herz, "Squatter-Inspired," 367; Margolis, *Something to Build On*, 72; "People Have a Right . . . ," 27.

58. Orren Beaty to Paul M. Popple, April 23, 1965, LBJ Department of the Interior, Box 6, Folder "Subject File 125"; Donald Hanson, "Some International Dimensions of Self-Help Housing," in *Report of the First National Conference on Self-Help Housing: Airlie House, Warrenton, Virginia, December 6-9, 1965*, 60; BIA news release, "New 'House Plan' Service to Spur Indian Home Building," November 5, 1965, LBJ Department of the Interior, Box 34, Folder "Indian Affairs 12/63-6/65"; Margolis, *Something to Build On*, 58.

59. On job training claims, see "American Indians, Migrant and Farm Workers," 388-94, LBJ Administrative Histories, Office of Economic Opportunity, Box 1, Folder "Volume I, Part II, Narrative History (2 of 3)"; Judith Russell, *Economics, Bureaucracy, and Race: How Keynesians Misguided the War on Poverty* (New York: Columbia University Press, 2004); Margaret Weir, *Politics and Jobs: The Boundaries of Employment Policy in the United States* (Princeton, NJ: Princeton University Press, 1992).

60. Margolis, *All Their Days*, 26.

61. Jonathan Levy, *Freaks of Fortune: The Emerging World of Capitalism and Risk in America* (Cambridge, MA: Harvard University Press, 2012), 106; Amy Dru Stanley, *From Bondage to Contract: Wage Labor, Marriage, and the Market in the Age of Slave Emancipation* (Cambridge: Cambridge University Press, 1998).

62. George Elfie Ballis, *New Housing by Poor Farm Workers* (Visalia, CA: Self-Help Enterprises, 1968).

63. Young used the word "property" in place of "ownership." Margolis, *Something to Build On*, frontispiece and 48.

64. Margolis, *Something to Build On*, 65-67.

65. Clay L. Cochran to Board and Staff, Rural Housing Alliance, February 24, 1970, and Herbert M. Franklin, "A New Generation of Lower-Income Housing: A Proposal for Consolidation and Reform," December 22, 1969, both in AFSC Folder "CRD Housing/Urban Affairs: Comms & Orgs, Rural Housing Alliance 1970."

66. On debates over the nature of federalism, see Karen M. Tani, *States of Dependency: Welfare, Rights, and American Governance, 1935-1972* (Cambridge: Cambridge University Press, 2016); Brent Cebul, *Illusions of Progress: Business, Poverty, and Liberalism in the American Century*, forthcoming, University of Pennsylvania Press.

67. Emphasis in the original. James E. Upchurch Jr. "Testimony Prepared for the Civil Rights Oversight Subcommittee of the House Committee on the Judiciary Regarding Federal Government's Role in the Achievement of Equal Opportunity in Housing," November 11, 1971, AFSC Folder "CRD Housing/Urban Affairs: Regional Office, High Point—East Coast Migrant Housing Program, 1971"; AFSC, *Abuse of Power: Studies of Bad Housing in America* (Washington, DC: Rural Housing Alliance, 1971), 3-7, 15, AFSC Folder "CRD Housing/Urban Affairs, San Francisco–Tulare County Tenant Union 1971"; "Criticized FmHA Supervisor Was First in State

Helping the Poor Get Housing," *Miami Herald*, October 24, 1971; "Government Housing Denounced as a 'Myth' for Low Incomes," *Sun-Sentinel* (Boca Raton), August 11, 1971.

68. National Center for Appropriate Technology brochure, Carter Presidential Library, Records of the National Commission on Neighborhoods, Box 31, Folder "New York City (2)."

69. "Jim Upchurch," *Rural Voices* 6, no. 3 (Fall 2001): 14; statement of James E. Upchurch Jr., in James H. Harvey et al., "Testimony Prepared for the Select Committee on Nutrition and Human Needs of the United States Senate Regarding Housing in Rural Areas and Smaller Cities and Towns," October 6, 1970, AFSC Folder "CRD Housing/Urban Affairs: General, Statements and Testimonies 1970."

70. "Homes Constructed of Interchangeable Parts to Be Tested," *Chicago Tribune*, June 3, 1967; " 'Floating' Concrete Can Save 30 Percent," *Boston Globe*, July 7, 1968; "Building Blocks for the Slums," *Washington Post*, July 14, 1968.

71. Welfare Housing Conference, BIA Portland Area Office, October 24, 1963, NAW, RG 75, Entry 999-C, Box 17, Folder 394-P-00, "Portland HI, 2 of 2"; Layton L. Littlejohn to Compton I. White, June 3, 1965, and Henry A. Bushman to Fred M. Haverland, December 20, 1966, NAW, RG 75, Entry 999-C, Box 17, Folder 394-P-00 "Portland HI."

72. Wayne Phillips to Bill D. Moyers, June 30, 1966, LBJ WHCF IN, Box 3, Folder "IN/A–Z."

73. Charles Blomfield to T. E. Elliott, October 30, 1963, NAW, RG 75, Entry 999-C, Box 6, Folder 392-E, "Metlakatla Mutual Help"; *Housing Legislation of 1966: Hearings before a Subcommittee of the Committee on Banking and Currency, United States Senate, Eighty-Ninth Congress, Second Session, Part 2, April 27–29, 1966* (Washington, DC: USGPO, 1966), 590.

74. Enrique Peñalosa, "Why Housing Needs Must be a World Concern," November 10, 1975, and Department of State Briefing Paper, October 15, 1975, Ford Library, Orlebeke Papers, Box 5, Folder "HABITAT (1)."

75. Victoria de Grazia, *Irresistible Empire: America's Advance through Twentieth-Century Europe* (Cambridge, MA: Harvard University Press, 2005); Nick Cullather, *The Hungry World: America's Cold War Battle against Poverty in Asia* (Cambridge, MA: Harvard University Press, 2010).

76. Doris E. Mersdorf, "How the Turnkey Method Works," address to CEO/Appalachian Housing Conference, June 15–16, 1967, Ohio University, in LBJ OEO, Box 16, Folder "Institute for Regional Development, Ohio University (3)."

77. "Feedback on Operation Breakthrough, 1972," Box 2, Rudard A. Jones Papers, University of Illinois Archives.

78. A. T. Maasberg to Nicholas Phillip, April 10, 1968, and Robert L. Marquardt to Nicholas Philip, April 5, 1968, both in D&R Box 69, Folder 2; Robert L. Marquardt, "Encouraging Homeownership," *IEEE Transactions on Aerospace and Electronic Systems* 6, no. 3 (May 1970): 382–86; Thiokol Chemical Corporation, *Forest Heights Low-Income Homeownership Program* (Ogden, UT: Thiokol Chemical Corporation, Economic Development Operations, 1970).

79. Rural Housing Alliance, *OEO and Rural Housing* (Washington, DC: Rural Housing Alliance, 1972), 202–7.

80. *Housing Assistance Council Information*, March 19, 1973, Wyckoff Santa Cruz, Box 17, Folder "Housing Assistance Council Information"; *Housing Assistance Council News*, July 31, 1973, Wyckoff Santa Cruz, Box 17, Folder "Housing Assistance Council News"; *RHA Reporter*,

October 1973, and *Self-Help Reporter*, March 1973, Wyckoff Santa Cruz, Box 24, Folder "The RHA Reporter (The Self-Help Reporter)."

81. *RHA Reporter*, February 1978 and March 1978, 3, Wyckoff Santa Cruz, Box 24, Folder "The RHA Reporter (The Self-Help Reporter)."

82. HAC, "In the Interim: Survival Strategies for Rural Nonprofits," November 1981, Wyckoff Berkeley Carton 17, Folder 17:8; "Rural Units Seek New Funds as US Housing Effort Slows," *New York Times*, September 9, 1985; TECHO, untitled document beginning "TECHO is a nonprofit corporation . . . ," 1985, Wyckoff Berkeley Carton 17, Folder 17:32.

83. Statements of Dana Jones, Jim Upchurch, and Peter Carey, *Rural Voices* 6, no. 3 (Fall 2001): 9, 12, 14–15.

84. Ian Donald Terner, *Self-Help Infrastructure: Applications of Irregular, Small-Scale, Incremental Systems for Residential Utilities*, unpublished manuscript, April–May 1974, 31, UC Berkeley Libraries.

85. "For Executives, Search for Business Turns to Tragedy," *Washington Post*, April 4, 1996; "Bridge Housing Corp. comments on President Don Terner's role in Ron Brown's business delegation to Bosnia," *Business Wire*, April 4, 1996; Department of Housing and Community Development, *California Statewide Housing Plan, 1979 Update*, December 1979, 5, 65, California State Archives, Accession 93-03-18, Box 5; "Housing Ingenuity," *Orange County Register*, May 28, 1992; "Chevron Breaks New Ground," PR Newswire, June 24, 1988; Jayne Elizabeth Zangelin, "High Performance Investing: Harnessing the Power of Pension Funds to Promote Economic Growth and Workplace Integrity," *Labor Lawyer* 11, no. 1 (1995): 78–79.

86. Beginning in 1971, self-help housing also relied on technical assistance grants from Section 523 of the 1968 Housing and Urban Development Act. Section 502 financed housing starts, and 523 facilitated improvements. By the turn of the twenty-first century, total new 523 grants averaged $25 million annually. Housing Assistance Council, *A Brief and Selective Historical Outline of Rural Mutual Self-Help Housing in the United States* (Washington, DC: HAC, 2004), 7–8, 53–54.

87. *The National Homeownership Strategy: Partners in the American Dream* (Washington, DC: Department of Housing and Urban Development, 1995), 6–11.

88. AFSC, *Chawama Self-Help Housing Project: Kafue, Zambia, 1968–1973* (Philadelphia: AFSC in cooperation with Kafue Township Council and the Republic of Zambia, 1975), George Loft Papers, Box 9, Folder 9.5.

Chapter 8: Decentralization Reborn

1. Eduardo Wiesner Durán, "Decentralized Public Establishments," unpublished manuscript, 1963, BRZ; CVC Acta 934, September 6, 1978; Montague Yudelman interview, "University of the Andes," December 1–6, 1958, RF, RG 1.2, Series 311, Box 78, Folder 740.

2. Eduardo Wiesner Durán, "Barreras artificiales a la inversión doméstica en la industria nacional," *Revista del Banco de la República*, no. 383 (September 1959): 1065–73; John M. Hunter and Eduardo Wiesner, "International Communications between Scholars in the Social Sciences: Colombia, Venezuela, Ecuador, Peru, and Bolivia," unpublished manuscript, December 1959, BSE; Eduardo Wiesner Durán, *Control personal de la economía colombiana* (Bogotá: CEDE Monografía No. 6, 1960); Ramón de Zubiria to Charles M. Hardin, February 21, 1964, RF, RG 1.2, Series 311, Box 79, Folder 745; Eduardo Wiesner Durán to Ralph K. Davidson, February 16, 1966,

RF, RG 1.2, Series 311, Box 79, Folder 746; Eduardo Dargent, *Technocracy and Democracy in Latin America: The Experts Running Government* (Cambridge: Cambridge University Press, 2015), 82.

3. Bernardo Garcés Córdoba to Dr. Palacín, May 29, 1962, CVC Correspondencia; Grant-in-Aid GA HSS 6387, July 18, 1963, and Gene E. Martin to Charles Hardin, October 17, 1962, RF, RG 1.2, Series 311, Box 79, Folder 747; interview by Charles M. Hardin with Dean Oscar Gómez, October 19, 1961, RF, RG 1.2, Series 311, Box 79, Folder 744.

4. Jorge Franco Holguín to David E. Lilienthal, April 21, 1960, DELP, Box 417, Folder "Re Colombia CVC 1960."

5. Wiesner Durán, "Decentralized Public Establishments," 1–5; Charles David Collins, "The Rise and Fall of the National 'Decentralized Agencies' in Colombia," *Public Administration and Development* 9, no. 2 (April/May 1989): 129–46; Richard M. Bird, *Intergovernmental Finance in Colombia: Final Report of the Mission on Intergovernmental Finance* (Cambridge, MA: International Tax Program, Harvard Law School, 1984), 311, 328, 344; Tulia G. Falleti, *Decentralization and Subnational Politics in Latin America* (Cambridge: Cambridge University Press, 2010), 132.

6. Wiesner Durán, "Decentralized Public Establishments," 22–28; CVC Acta 287, February 27, 1962; CVC Acta 289, March 13, 1962; CVC Acta 489, March 25, 1968.

7. "IMF Aide's Hard Latin Role," *New York Times*, June 25, 1984.

8. Eduardo Wiesner, "Perspectivas de la planificación y de la programación presupuestaria," in *Informe final del Tercer Seminario Interamericano de Presupuesto, Santiago, Chile, 7–11 de mayo de 1973* (Washington, DC: OAS, 1974), 36, 40.

9. Olga Lucia Acosta and Richard M. Bird, "The Dilemma of Decentralization in Colombia," in *Fiscal Reform in Colombia: Problems and Prospects*, ed. Richard M. Bird, James M. Poterba, and Joel Slemrod (Cambridge, MA: MIT Press, 2005), 247–86; Gabriel Rosas Vega, *El pensamiento económico de Carlos Lleras Restrepo* (Bogotá: Taurus, 2008), 119–43.

10. CVC Acta 481, January 8, 1968; CVC Acta 524, February 3, 1969; CVC Acta 921, May 23, 1978.

11. José Castro Borrero to David E. Lilienthal, DELP, Box 494, Folder "Re Colombia 1971."

12. This conflict appears throughout the CVC board minutes beginning with CVC Acta 481, January 8, 1968. For key episodes before 1980, see Henry J. Eder to Elba Ortiz, March 17, 1969, CVC Correspondencia; CVC Acta 524, February 3, 1969; CVC Acta 753, August 12, 1974; CVC Acta 842, August 31, 1976; CVC Acta 921, May 23, 1978; CVC Acta 927, July 11, 1978; CVC Acta 964, April 25, 1979; *Génesis y desarrollo de una visión de progreso, CVC: Cincuenta años* (Cali: CVC, 2004), 85–90.

13. Ernesto Sánchez Triana, "How Rent Seeking, Learning and Path Dependence Shape Environmental Institutions: The Case of the Cauca Valley Corporation in Colombia" (PhD diss., Stanford University, 1998), 124–29.

14. Mauricio Archila Neira, *Idas y venidas, vueltas y revueltas: Protestas sociales en Colombia, 1958–1990* (Bogotá: ICANH and CINEP, 2003), 148, 386; Christopher Abel and Marco Palacios, "Colombia since 1958," in *Cambridge History of Latin America*, vol. 8, ed. Leslie Bethell (Cambridge: Cambridge University Press, 1991), 633–34, 662–64; Miguel Urrutia Montoya, "Democracia y derecho de huelga en un servicio público esencial," *Coyuntura económica* 14, no. 2 (1984): 168–83; Ricardo Sánchez Ángel, *Huelga! Luchas de la clase trabajadora en Colombia, 1975–1981* (Bogotá: UNIJUS, 2009).

15. CVC Acta 760, September 30, 1974; CVC Acta 762, October 14, 1974; CVC Acta 934, September 9, 1978; CVC Acta 961, March 28, 1979; CVC Acta 970, June 20, 1979; CVC Acta No. 975, August 1, 1979.

16. Miguel Urrutia, *Cincuenta años de desarrollo económico colombiano* (Bogotá: Carreta, 1979), 365–71; Kim Phillips-Fein, *Fear City: New York City's Fiscal Crisis and the Rise of Austerity Politics* (New York: Metropolitan Books, 2017); Tony Judt, *Postwar: A History of Europe since 1945* (New York: Penguin, 2005), 390–421; Donna Jean Murch, *Living for the City: Migration, Education, and the Rise of the Black Panther Party in Oakland, California* (Chapel Hill: University of North Carolina Press, 2010); Jeremi Suri, *Power and Protest: Global Revolution and the Rise of Détente* (Cambridge, MA: Harvard University Press, 2003).

17. Eduardo Wiesner Durán, "El origen político del desequilibrio fiscal," in *Déficit fiscal en Colombia: Recopilación de las ponencias, comentarios y resúmenes referentes a los dos foros realizados en Medellín y Bogotá en septiembre 7 y 21 respectivamente* (Bogotá: Contraloría General de la República and FESCOL, 1982), 125–44.

18. Wiesner Durán, "El origen político del desequilibrio fiscal," 134–37.

19. Bird, *Intergovernmental Finance in Colombia*, 333, 344.

20. Bird, *Intergovernmental Finance in Colombia*, 8–9, 11.

21. Boughton, *Silent Revolution*, 359–414; "IMF Aide's Hard Latin Role," *New York Times*, June 25, 1984; Klaus Veigel, *Dictatorship, Democracy, and Globalization: Argentina and the Cost of Paralysis, 1973–2001* (University Park: Pennsylvania State University Press, 2009); "IMF Seen as Unlikely to Accept Plan," *New York Times*, June 12, 1984.

22. Paul Gootenberg, *Andean Cocaine: The Making of a Global Drug* (Chapel Hill: University of North Carolina Press, 2008), 273–316; Marco Palacios, *Between Legitimacy and Violence: A History of Colombia, 1975–2002* (Durham, NC: Duke University Press, 2006), 197–213.

23. Roberto Junguito and Hernán Rincón, "La política fiscal en el siglo XX en Colombia," *Borradores de economía*, no. 318 (Bogotá: Banco de la República, December 2004): 82–87; Falleti, *Decentralization*, 125–42; Alan Angell, Pamela Lowden, and Rosemary Thorp, *Decentralizing Development: The Political Economy of Institutional Change in Colombia and Chile* (New York: Oxford University Press, 2001), 24–26; Jorge Iván González, "Los aportes de Eduardo Wiesner al pensamiento económico colombiano," *Revista de Economía Institucional* 8, no. 14 (2006): 28.

24. CVC Acta, January 14, 1987; CVC Acta 1,211, March 4, 1987; CVC Acta 1,212, March 18, 1987; CVC Acta 1,218, July 1, 1987; CVC Acta 1,230, March 9, 1988.

25. Brett Troyan, *Cauca's Indigenous Movement in Southwestern Colombia: Land, Violence, and Ethnic Identity* (London: Lexington Books, 2015); Myriam Jimeno, *Juan Gregorio Palechor: The Story of My Life* (Durham, NC: Duke University Press, 2014); Joanne Rappaport, *The Politics of Memory: Native Historical Interpretation in the Colombian Andes* (Cambridge: Cambridge University Press, 1998); Christian Gros, *Colombia indígena: Identidad cultural y cambio social* (Bogotá: CEREC, 1991).

26. Bettina Ng'weno, *Turf Wars: Territory and Citizenship in the Contemporary State* (Palo Alto, CA: Stanford University Press, 2007); Peter Wade, *Blackness and Race Mixture: The Dynamics of Racial Identity in Colombia* (Baltimore: Johns Hopkins University Press, 1993); Kiran Asher, *Black and Green: Afro-Colombians, Development, and Nature in the Pacific Lowlands* (Durham, NC: Duke University Press, 2009); Nina S. de Friedemann and Jaime Arocha, *De sol a sol: Génesis, transformación y presencia de los negros en Colombia* (Bogotá: Planeta Colombia

Editorial, 1986); Arturo Escobar, *Territories of Difference: Place, Movements, Life, Redes* (Durham, NC: Duke University Press, 2008).

27. Movimiento de Autoridades Inígenas del Suroccidente, "Pueblos indígenas y reforma municipal," 139, Jorge Flórez Flórez, "Nuestra experiencia con la descentralización en el municipio de Puerto Gaitán (Meta)," 98–100, Lorenzo Muelas Hurtado, "Reflexiones en torno al reordenamiento territorial," 179–81, in *Colombia multiétnica y pluricultural: Memorias, Seminario Taller Reforma Descentralista y Minorías Étnicas en Colombia, Santa Fe de Bogotá, 14, 15 y 16 de febrero de 1991* (Bogotá: ESAP, 1991).

28. Alberto Mendoza Morales, "Resguardo, modelo de descentralización y autogobierno," 118, and Roque Arévalo and Joaquín Herrera, "Los cabildos como entes públicos," 127–29, in *Colombia multiétnica y pluricultural.*

29. Angell, Lowden, and Thorp, *Decentralizing Development*, 27–28; Falleti, *Decentralization*, 135–37; Gustavo Gallón G., ed., *Guerra y Constituyente* (Bogotá: Comisión Andina de Juristas Seccional Colombiana, 1991).

30. Donna Lee Van Cott, *The Friendly Liquidation of the Past: The Politics of Diversity in Latin America* (Pittsburgh: University of Pittsburgh Press, 2000), 67–69, 76; Hernando Andrés Pulido Londoño, "Violencia y asimitrías étnicas: Multiculturalismo, debate antropológico y etnicidad de los afrocolombianos (1980–1990)," *Antípoda* 11 (July December 2010): 270–72; and the following in *Colombia multiétnica y pluricultural*: Orlando Fals Borda, "Reflexiones sobre reordenamiento territorial," 59–62; Trismila Rentería, "Reseña histórica de la etnia negra en el Pacífico colombiano y la descentralización," 93; Francisco Rojas Birry, "La autonomía de los grupos étnicos o la descentralización étnica," 170; Nina S. de Friedemann, "Negros en Colombia: invisibilidad y legitimdad de su identidad," 347–60; Juan de Dios Mosquera Mosquera, "Racismo y discriminación racial en Colombia," 361–70; Amir Smith Córdoba, "Exclusión y pluralismo racial en Colombia," 371–82; Adelmo Carabalí, "Estrategia para conserver la cultura y los derechos de la comunidad negra," 399–402; Jaime Arocha Rodríguez, "Mestizaje en Colombia: ¿Igualdad, fraternidad y libertad?" 407–16.

31. Falleti, *Decentralization*, 141; CVC Acta 1,289, March 20, 1991; CVC Acta 1,293, July 17, 1991.

32. Sebastian Edwards, *The Economics and Politics of Transition to an Open Market Economy: Colombia* (Paris: OECD Development Centre, 2001), 60; Bird, *Intergovernmental Finance in Colombia*, 3; Eduardo Wiesner Durán, *Colombia, descentralización y federalismo: Informe final de la Misión para la Descentralización* (Bogotá: Presidencia and DNP, 1992), 28–29.

33. Falleti, *Decentralization*, 138–42, 144–46; Angell, Lowden, and Thorp, *Decentralizing Development*, 31; Wiesner Durán, *Colombia*, 321–44.

34. Asher, *Black and Green*, 1–5; Bettina Ng'weno, "Can Ethnicity Replace Race? Afro-Colombians, Indigineity and the Colombian Multicultural State," *Journal of Latin American and Caribbean Anthropology* 12, no. 2 (November 2007): 414–40; Van Cott, *Friendly Liquidation*, 85–87, 97–98; Wade, *Blackness and Race Mixture*, 351–58.

35. Sánchez Triana, "How Rent Seeking," vi, 16; Irene Vélez-Torres, "Water Grabbing in the Cauca Basin: The Capitalist Exploitation of Water and Dispossession of Afro-Descendant Communities," *Water Alternatives* 5, no. 2 (2012): 440–42; CVC Acta 1,293, July 17, 1991; CVC Acta 1,294, September 18, 1991.

36. Asher, *Black and Green*, 103–8.

37. David D. Gow, *Countering Development: Indigenous Modernity and the Moral Imagination* (Durham, NC: Duke University Press, 2008); Asher, *Black and Green*; Escobar, *Territories of Difference*.

38. Richard M. Bird, "Fiscal Decentralization in Colombia: A Work (Still) in Progress," International Center for Public Policy, Working Paper 12-23, April 2012, 3–6, 21–23; Eduardo Wiesner Durán, "La evaluación de resultados en la modernización del Estado en América Latina," *Revista de Economía Institucional* 4, no. 6 (2002): 135.

39. Eduardo Wiesner, *From Macroeconomic Correction to Public Sector Reform* (Washington, DC: International Bank for Reconstruction and Development, 1993); Eduardo Wiesner and Robert Picciotto, eds., *Evaluation and Development: The Institutional Dimension* (New Brunswick, NJ: Transaction Publishers, 1998).

40. Eduardo Wiesner, "Latin American Debt: Lessons and Pending Issues," *American Economic Review* 75, no. 2 (May 1985): 191–95.

41. Eduardo Wiesner, "Transaction Cost Economics and Public Sector Rent-Seeking in Developing Countries: Toward a Theory of Governance Failure," in Wiesner and Picciotto, *Evaluation and Development*, 108–23; Eduardo Wiesner Durán, "Las implicaciones fiscales del marco de política de la descentralización en Colombia," in *El reto de la descentralización*, ed. Jaime Jaramillo Vallejo (Bogotá: Pontificia Universidad Javeriana, 1996), 111–31.

42. Shahid Javed Burki and Guillermo E. Perry, *Beyond the Washington Consensus: Institutions Matter* (Washington, DC: World Bank, 1998), 36, 101, 125; Shahid Javed Burki, Guillermo E. Perry, and William R. Dillinger, *Beyond the Center: Decentralizing the State* (Washington, DC: World Bank, 1999), 4, 44–46.

43. Eduardo Wiesner, "Latin America's Policy Response to the Debt Crisis: Learning from Adversity," in *International Economic Cooperation*, ed. Martin Feldstein (Chicago: University of Chicago Press, 1988), 290–305; Wiesner Durán, *Colombia*, 30, 89–99.

44. Yves Dezalay and Bryant G. Garth, *The Internationalization of Palace Wars: Lawyers, Economists, and the Contest to Transform Latin American States* (Chicago: University of Chicago Press, 2002), 171–73; Howard Stein, *Beyond the World Bank Agenda: An Institutional Approach to Development* (Chicago: University of Chicago Press, 2008), 101–3; Interview with Robert Picciotto, November 1, 2000, 1, 4, 12, 14, 37, World Bank/IFC Oral History Program; Robert Picciotto to Ismail Serageldin, September 2, 1997, IEG Folder 1791129; Robert Picciotto to George Siebeck, April 28, 1997, and Robert Picciotto to Eduardo Wiesner, March 6, 1997, IEG Folder 1791128; Robert Picciotto to Ishrat Husain, March 17, 1997, World Bank Archives, Item 1458380, Folder "Conference on Evaluation and Development—Operations Evaluation Department [OED]—April 1 and 2, 1997—Correspondence."

45. Eduardo Wiesner, "Introduction," in Wiesner and Picciotto, *Evaluation and Development*, xi; Eduardo Wiesner, *Función de evaluación de planes, programas, estrategias y proyectos* (Santiago de Chile: Naciones Unidas, May 2000); Eduardo Wiesner, *Fiscal Federalism in Latin America: From Entitlements to Markets* (Washington, DC: Inter-American Development Bank, 2003); Eduardo Wiesner D., "Descentralización y equidad en América Latina: enlaces institucionales y de política," *Coyuntura social* 29 (December 2003): 125–52; Wiesner, *From Macroeconomic Correction to Public Sector Reform*, 6–9, 13, 31; Eduardo Wiesner, "La economía política de la justicia distributiva en Colombia," *Desarrollo y sociedad* (primer semestre, 2008), 117–60.

46. Quoted in González, "Los aportes de Eduardo Wiesner al pensamiento económico colombiano," 45.

Epilogue: Sorting Out the Mixed Economy

1. "Management and Training Corporation," *International Directory of Company Histories*, vol. 28 (Detroit: St. James Press, 1999), 253–56; "Dr. Robert L. Marquardt," *Salt Lake Tribune*, January 15, 2012; Gary Hunter, "Management & Training Corp. Struggles to Maintain Market Share," *Prison Legal News*, September 15, 2007.

2. Amy C. Offner, "Classroom Management," forthcoming.

3. Lauchlin Currie, "Residential Building as a Leading Sector," *Housing Finance International* 6, no. 3 (March 1992): 11–19; "NAR Receives International Shelter Recognition Award," *PR Newswire*, November 20, 1990; "Draft Materials from the Third International Shelter Conference," LBCP, Box 18, Folder "Housing—Urban, 1959–1993, carpeta #12."

4. For a similar view, see Béatrice Hibou, ed., *Privatizing the State* (New York: Columbia University Press, 2004).

5. John F. C. Turner and Robert Fichter, eds., *Freedom to Build: Dweller Control of the Housing Process* (New York: Macmillan, 1972); Helen Elizabeth Gyger, "The Informal as a Project: Self-Help Housing in Peru, 1954–1986" (PhD diss., Columbia University, 2013).

6. Richard Harris, "A Double Irony: The Originality and Influence of John F. C. Turner," *Habitat International* 27 (2003): 245–69; Ian Donald Terner, "Sites and Services Programs," 1972, unpublished draft of a paper for the World Bank, Loeb Library, Harvard University.

7. Susan E. Brown, "Housing in Bogotá: A Synthesis of Recent Research and Notes on Anthropological Contributions to the Study of Housing," *Urban Anthropology* 6, no. 3 (Fall 1997): 249–67.

8. Timothy Mitchell, "How Neoliberalism Makes Its World: The Urban Property Rights Project in Peru," in *The Road from Mont Pèlerin: The Making of the Neoliberal Thought Collective*, ed. Philip Mirowski and Dieter Plehwe (Cambridge, MA: Harvard University Press, 2009), 386–416.

9. Gyger, "The Informal as a Project"; Hernando de Soto, *The Other Path: The Invisible Revolution in the Third World* (New York: Harper and Row, 1989), 13–55.

10. https://www.pearsonassessments.com/meet_us/History.html, accessed April 17, 2018; Offner, "Classroom Management."

11. Susan George, "How to Win the War of Ideas: Lessons from the Gramscian Right," *Dissent* (Summer 1997): 47–53; Juan Gabriel Valdés, *Pinochet's Economists: The Chicago School in Chile* (Cambridge: Cambridge University Press, 1995).

12. Johanna Bockman, *Markets in the Name of Socialism: The Left-Wing Origins of Neoliberalism* (Stanford, CA: Stanford University Press, 2011); Arturo Escobar, *Territories of Difference: Place, Movements, Life, Redes* (Durham, NC: Duke University Press, 2008); James Ferguson, "The Uses of Neoliberalism," *Antipode* 41 (2009): 166–84; James Ferguson, *Give a Man a Fish: Reflections on the New Politics of Distribution* (Durham, NC: Duke University Press, 2015).

ARCHIVES AND REPOSITORIES, WITH ABBREVIATIONS

American Friends Service Committee Archive, Philadelphia (AFSC)
Archivo de Bogotá
    Archivo Jorge Enrique Rivera Farfán
    Colección General
Archivo General de la Nación, Bogotá (AGN)
    Fondo Departamento Nacional de Planeación
    Fondo Presidencia
    Instituto Nacional de Adecuación de Tierras (INAT)
    Ministerio de Gobierno/Interior, Despacho Ministro (Min Gobierno)
Baker Library, Harvard Business School
    Francis J. Aguilar Papers (FJA)
Bancroft Library, University of California at Berkeley
    Florence Richardson Wyckoff Papers (Wyckoff Berkeley)
Biblioteca Luis Ángel Arango, Bogotá
    Archivo Carlos Lleras Restrepo (ACLR)
    Colección General (BLAA Colección General)
California State Archives, Sacramento
    Office of Economic Opportunity Records
Columbia University, Rare Book and Manuscript Library
    George Kalmanoff Papers (Kalmanoff)
    World Bank Oral History Project
Corporación Autónoma Regional del Valle del Cauca, Cali
    Archivo Central, Actas (CVC Actas)
    Archivo Central, Correspondencia (CVC Correspondencia)
    Biblioteca, Informes Técnicos (CVC Informes Técnicos)
Duke University
    Lauchlin Bernard Currie Papers (LBCP)
Dwight Eisenhower Presidential Library
    Abbott Washburn Papers (AWP)
    Dennis A. Fitzgerald Papers (Fitzgerald)
Gerald Ford Presidential Library
    Charles J. Orlebeke Papers
Hagley Library
    National Association of Manufacturers Papers (NAM)
    Philip D. Reed Papers (PDR)

Hoover Institution, Stanford University
  George Loft Papers
  John S. Applegarth Papers
  Kenneth Holland Papers
Instituto Colombiano de la Reforma Agraria, Bogotá
  Actas de la Junta Directiva (INCORA Actas)
  As of 2012, the papers of INCORA were kept in a Bogotá warehouse administered by the Instituto Colombiano de Desarrollo Rural (INCODER).
Jimmy Carter Presidential Library
  Records of the National Commission on Neighborhoods
Lyndon Baines Johnson Presidential Library
  Administrative Histories
  Department of the Interior
  Office of Economic Opportunity (LBJ OEO)
  Papers of Bernard L. Boutin (LBJ Boutin)
  Task Force Reports
  White House Central Files (LBJ WHCF)
John F. Kennedy Presidential Library
  John Corson Personal Papers (JFK Corson)
  National Security Files (JFK NSF)
  Papers of Thomas M. C. Johnston (TMCJ)
  President's Office Files (JFK POF)
  Sargent Shriver Papers (JFK Shriver)
  White House Central Files (JFK WHCF)
McHenry Library Special Collections and Archives, University of California, Santa Cruz
  Florence Richardson Wyckoff Papers (Wyckoff Santa Cruz)
National Archives, College Park, Maryland (NACP)
  Records of the Community Services Administration (RG 381)
  Records of the Department of State (RG 59)
  Records of US Foreign Assistance Agencies, 1948–51 (RG 469)
National Archives, Washington, DC (NAW)
  Bureau of Indian Affairs (RG 75)
Princeton University, Seeley G. Mudd Manuscript Library
  Albert O. Hirschman Papers (AOHP)
  David E. Lilienthal Papers (DELP)
  Development & Resources Corporation Records (D&R)
Rockefeller Archive Center, Sleepy Hollow, New York
  Biography Files (BF)
  Rockefeller Family Archive (RFAM)
  Rockefeller Foundation Archives (RF)
  W. M. Myers Papers
Self-Help Enterprises, Office Records, Visalia, California (SHE)
    Tamiment Library, New York University
        Ronald Lawson Research Files

Tufts University
    University Archives
Universidad de los Andes, Bogotá
    Archivo Institucional (Andes Archivo)
    Biblioteca Ramón de Zubiria (BRZ)
    Colección General, Biblioteca Satélite de Economía (BSE)
Universidad del Valle, Cali
    Biblioteca Mario Carvajal, Colección General (BMC)
    Colección Memorial Institucional Universidad del Valle, Colecciones Especiales, Biblioteca
        Mario Carvajal (MIUV)
Universidad del Valle, Archivo Central, Cali
    Decanatura de Estudios, Oficina de Decano, Informes (UV Decanatura Informes)
    División/Facultad de Ciencias Sociales y Económicas, Decanatura, Actas/Proyectos
        (UV Facultad Actas/Proyectos)
    División/Facultad de Ciencias Sociales y Económicas, Decanatura, Correspondencia (UV
        Facultad Correspondencia)
    División/Facultad de Ciencias Sociales y Económicas, Decanatura, Informes (UV Facultad
        Informes)
    División/Facultad de Ciencias Sociales y Económicas, Decanatura, Planes (UV Facultad
        Planes)
    División/Facultad de Ciencias Sociales y Económicas, Decanatura, Proyectos (UV Facultad
        Proyectos)
    División de Ciencias Sociales, Departamento de Administración Industrial (UV
        Administración)
    Documentos de movimientos y organizaciones estudiantiles, Comunicados Corresponden-
        cia (UV Movimientos)
    Rectoría, Oficina del Rector, Correspondencia (UV Rectoría Correspondencia)
    Rectoría, Oficina del Rector, Correspondencia, Correspondencia Fundaciones Extranjeras
        (UV Rectoría Correspondencia Fundaciones Extranjeras)
Universidad Nacional de Colombia, División de Archivos y Correspondencia (Bogotá)
    Fondo CINVA
    Fondo Instituto de Ciencias Económicas, Correspondencia (ICE)
University of Virginia Library, Special Collections
    Alice Jackson Stuart Papers
University of Wisconsin
    Agricultural Economics Library, Taylor Hall (AEL)
    Biographical Files, University Archives, Steenbock Library (UW Bio Files)
    Land Tenure Center Records, University Archives, Steenbock Library (LTC)
    Steenbock Library
World Bank Group, Washington, DC
    Independent Evaluation Group Records (IEG)
    World Bank Archives
    World Bank/IFC Oral History Program

ORAL HISTORY INTERVIEWS

Graciela García de Avendaño. Interview by the author. Bogotá, Colombia. February 11, 2011.

Ana Teresa Huertas de Díaz. Interview by the author. Bogotá, Colombia. February 10, 2011.

Robert Marshall. Interview by the author. Visalia, California. May 29, 2013.

Graciela Martinez. Interview by the author. Visalia, California. May 28, 2013.

Aura Morena de Fajardo. Interview by the author. Bogotá, Colombia. January 28, 2011.

Aura Morena de Fajardo and Alcira Peñuela de Guerrero. Interview by the author. Bogotá, Colombia. January 31, 2011.

Clímaco Patiño Sepúlveda and María del Carmen Samboni de Patiño. Interview by the author. Bogotá, Colombia. February 21, 2011.

María Ester Ramírez. Interview by the author. Bogotá, Colombia. February 3, 2011.

Ralph Rosedale. Interview by the author. Visalia, California. May 28 and May 30, 2013.

Reinaldo Scarpetta. Interview by the author. New York, New York. June 6, 2010.

Elizabeth Torres. Interview by the author. Bogotá, Colombia. February 3, 2011.

A NOTE ON THE TYPE

This book has been composed in Arno, an Old-style serif typeface in the classic Venetian tradition, designed by Robert Slimbach at Adobe.